AMOS

A COMMENTARY

Library of Biblical Interpretation

AMOS

A COMMENTARY

GARY V. SMITH

Regency
Reference Library
Zondervan Publishing House
Grand Rapids, Michigan

AMOS: A COMMENTARY
Copyright © 1989 by Gary V. Smith

Regency Reference Library is an imprint of Zondervan Publishing House,
1415 Lake Drive, S.E., Grand Rapids, Michigan 49506.

Library of Congress Cataloging in Publication Data

Smith, Gary V., 1943-
    Amos : a commentary / Gary V. Smith.
      p.   cm.   – (Library of Biblical interpretation)
    Bibliography: p.
    Includes index.
    ISBN 0-310-41210-2 : $17.95
    1. Bible.   O.T.   Amos–Commentaries.   I. Bible.   O.T.   Amos.
English.   1989.   II. Title.   III. Series.
BS1585.3.S63   1989
224'.807–dc19   88-15660
                                                    CIP

Printed in the United States of America

89   90   91   92   93   94   95 / EE / 10 9 8 7 6 5 4 3 2 1

In honor of my parents

Verlan R. Smith
Twylah L. Smith

CONTENTS

PREFACE

The development of the prophetic movement is among the most significant acts of God in the history of Israel. Amos, one of the earliest writing prophets, was the voice of God confronting and challenging the accepted patterns of belief and behavior in Israel. Although the settings are sometimes foreign to our modern day, his message has a theological significance that removes the chaff of pleasure, pride, and religious traditon with amazing skill. His message and rhetorical methods prod the reader to allow the word of God to speak in a fresh way.

The commentary is by no means exhaustive, but it does attempt to deal seriously with (1) the important textual and philological questions, (2) background studies on the literary traditions and forms employed, (3) rhetorical markers of structure that unite paragraphs or larger units, (4) exegetical issues of interpretation, and (5) the main theological themes within each unit. Those who are familiar with the commentaries of H. W. Wolff, W. Rudolph, and a host of others, will recognize the great debt I owe to these incisive studies. My prayer and hope is that this work will in some way further the task of understanding the word of God delivered by Amos.

I wish to thank the Board of Directors of Winnipeg Theological Seminary for graciously providing funds for a nine-month sabbatical in Cambridge, England where this project began. I must also acknowledge the generosity of Bethel Theological Seminary for the help of two excellent typists, Ruth Anderson and Gloria Metz. My wife, Susan, also typed several chapters of the first draft.

Soli Deo Gloria
July 1986

Gary V. Smith
Bethel Theological Seminary
St. Paul, Minnesota 55112

——Abbreviations——

A. Periodicals, Series, and Standard Reference Works:

AB   Anchor Bible
ABR   Australian Biblical Review
AJSL   American Journal of Semitic Languages and Literature
ALUOS   Annual of Leeds University Oriental Society
AnBib   Analecta Biblica
ANEP   J. B. Pritchard (ed), *Ancient Near East in Pictures*
        Relating to the Old Testament. Princeton:
        Princeton Univ., 1954.
ANET   J. B. Pritchard (ed), *Ancient Near Eastern*
        Texts. Princeton: Princeton Univ., 1969.
AnOr   Analecta Orientalia
Aq.   Aquila
ATD   Das Alte Testament Deutsch
ATR   Anglican Theological Review
AUSS   Andrews University Seminary Studies
BA   Biblical Archaeologist
BAR   Biblical Archaeologist Reader
BASOR   Bulletin of the American School of Oriental Research
BBB   Bonner Biblische Beiträge
BETS   Bulletin of the Evangelical Theological Society
BHK   Biblia Hebraica (Kittel)
BHS   Biblia Hebraica Stuttgartensia
Bib   Biblica
BibOr   Biblica et Orientalia
BibRev Biblical Review
BibTh   Biblical Theology
BJRL   Bulletin of the John Rylands University Library of Manchester
BK   Bibel und Kirche
BKAT   Biblischer Kommentar Altes Testament
BR   Biblical Research
BSac   Bibliotheca Sacra
BSt   Biblische Studien
BT   The Bible Translator
BTB   Biblical Theology Bulletin
BWANT Beiträge zur Wissenschaft vom Alten and Neuen Testament
BZ   Biblische Zeitschrift

BZAW	Beihefte zur ZAW
CAD	A. L. Oppenheim (ed), *The Assyrian Dictionary of the Institute of the University of Chicago.* Chicago: Univ. of Chicago, 1956ff.
CBQ	Catholic Biblical Quarterly
CJT	Canadian Journal of Theology
CTJ	Calvin Theological Journal
CTM	Concordia Theological Monthly
CurTM	Currents in Theology and Missions
DJD	*Discoveries in the Judean Desert.* Oxford: Clarendon, 1961ff.
Enc	Encounter
EvQ	Evangelical Quarterly
EvT	Evangelische Theologie
Exp	Expositor
ExpT	Expository Times
FRLANT	Forschungen zur Religion und Literatur des Alten und Neuen Testaments
GKC	Gesenius, Kautzsch, Cowley, *Gesenius' Hebrew Grammar.* Oxford: Clarendon, 1910.
HAT	Handbuch zum Alten Testament
HTR	Harvard Theological Review
HUCA	Hebrew Union College Annual
IB	Interpreter's Bible
IBS	Irish Biblical Studies
ICC	International Critical Commentary
IDB	G. A. Buttrick (ed.), *Interpreter's Dictionary of the Bible.* Nashville: Abingdon, 1962.
IEJ	Israel Exploration Journal
Int	Interpretation
ITQ	Irish Theological Quarterly
JAOS	Journal of the American Oriental Society
JBL	Journal of Biblical Literature
JCS	Journal of Cuneiform Studies
JETS	Journal of the Evangelical Theological Society
JNES	Journal of Near Eastern Studies
JNSL	Journal of Northwest Semitic Languages
JPOS	Journal of the Palestine Oriental Society
JQR	Jewish Quarterly Review
JSOT	Journal for the Study of the Old Testament
JSS	Journal of Semitic Studies
JTS	Journal of Theological Studies
KAI	H. Donner and W. Röllig (eds.) *Kanaanäische und Aramäische Inschriften.* Wiesbaden: Harrassowitz, 1962.
KAT	Kommentar zum Alten Testament
LCL	Loeb Classical Library

LXX	Septuagint
MAARAV	Journal for the Study of Northwest Semitic Languages and Literature
MS(S)	Manuscript(s)
MT	Massoretic
NASB	New American Standard Bible
NEB	New English Bible
NICOT	New International Commentary on Old Testament
NKZ	Neue Kirchliche Zeitschrift
NT	New Testament
OG	Old Greek Version
OL	Old Latin Version
Or An	Oriens Antiquus
OT	Old Testament
OTL	Old Testament Library
OTS	Oudtestamentische Studiën
OTWSA	Die Ou Testamentiese Werkgemeenskap in Suid-Afrika
PEQ	Palestine Exploration Quarterly
PTR	Princeton Theological Review
RB	Revue biblique
RestQ	Restoration Quarterly
RevExp	Review and Expositor
RevQ	Revue de Qumran
RSR	Recherches de science religieuse
RSV	Revised Standard Version
RTR	Reformed Theological Review
SBT	Studies in Biblical Theology
SEÄ	Svensk Exegetisk Årsbok
Sem	Semitica
SJT	Scottish Journal of Theology
ST	Studia Theologica
Sym	Symmachus
SVT	Supplements to Vetus Testamentum
SWJT	Southwest Journal of Theology
TANE	J. B. Pritchard (ed), *The Ancient Near East*. Princeton: Princeton Univ., 1958.
TB	Tyndale Bulletin
TBT	The Bible Today
TDNT	G. Kittel and G. Friedrich (eds.), *Theological Dictionary of the New Testament*. Grand Rapids: Eerdmans, 1964–74.
TDOT	G. Bromiley, H. Ringgren (eds), *Theological Dictionary of the Old Testament*. Grand Rapids: Eerdmans, 1974–85.
TF	Theologische Forschung
THAT	*Theologische Handwörterbuch zum Alten Testament*

Theod	Theodotion
TLZ	Theologische Literaturzeitung
TRev	Theologische Revue
TS	Theological Studies
TToday	Theology Today
TZ	Theologische Zeitschrift
UF	Ugarit-Forschungen
Vg	Vulgate
VT	Vetus Testamentum
WTJ	Westminster Theological Journal
WMANT	Wissenschaftliche Monographien zum Alten und Neuen Testament
ZAW	Zeitschrift für die alttestamentliche Wissenschaft
ZDPV	Zeitschrift des deutschen Palästina-Vereins
ZTK	Zeitschrift für Theologie und Kirke

B. Commentaries Frequently Abbreviated:

Cripps, *Amos*

Cripps, R. S., *A Critical and Exegetical Commentary on the Book of Amos*. London: SPCK, 1955.

Driver, *Amos*

Driver, S. F., *The Book of Joel and Amos*, Cambridge Bible for Schools and Colleges. Cambridge: Cambridge Univ. 1926.

Edghill, *Amos*

Edghill, E. A., *The Book of Amos*, Westminister Commentaries. London: Methuen, 1914.

Fosbroke, *Amos*

Fosbroke, H. E. W., "The Book of Amos: Introduction and Exegesis," *Interpreter's Bible* 6. Nashville: Abingdon, 1956.

Hammershaimb, *Amos*

Hammershaimb, E. H., *The Book of Amos: A Commentary*. Oxford: Blackwell, 1970.

Harper, *Amos*

Harper, W. R., *A Critical and Exegetical Commentary on Amos and Hosea*, International Critical Commentary. Edinburgh: T & T Clark, 1905.

Kapelrud, *Amos*

Kapelrud, A. S., *Central Ideas in Amos*. Oslo: Aschehoug, 1956.

Koch, *Amos*

Koch, K., et al., *Amos, untersucht mit den Methoden einer strukturalen Formgeschlichte* 1-2. Neukirchen-Vluyn: Neukirchener Verlag, 1967.

Maag, *Amos*

Maag, V., *Text, Wortschatz und Begriffswelt des Buches Amos*. Leiden: Brill, 1951.

Marti, *Amos*

Marti, K., *Das Dodekapropheten erklärt*, Kurzer Hand-Kommentar zum Alten Testament 13. Tübingen: J. C. Mohr, 1904.

Mays, *Amos*
Mays, J. L., *Amos: A Commentary*, Old Testament Library. Philadelphia: Westminster, 1969.

Morgenstern, *Amos Studies*
Morgenstern, J., *Amos Studies*. Cincinnati: Hebrew Union College, 1941.

Reventlow, *Amos*
Reventlow, H. G., *Das Amt des Propheten bei Amos*, FRLANT 80. Göttingen: Vandenhoeck und Ruprecht, 1962.

Rudolph, *Amos*
Rudolph, W., *Joel-Amos-Obadja-Jona*, Kommentar zum Alten Testament 13/2. Gütersloh: G. Mohn, 1971.

Snaith, *Amos*
Snaith, N. H., *The Book of Amos* 1-2. London: Epworth, 1945-46.

Watts, *Amos*
Watts, J. D. W., *Vision and Prophecy in Amos*. Grand Rapids: Eerdmans, 1958.

Weiser, *Amos*
Weiser, A. and Elliger, K., *Das Buch der zwölf Kleinen Propheten*, Das Alte Testament Deutsch 24/1. Göttingen: Vandenhoeck und Ruprecht, 1964.

Weiser, *Profetie*
Weiser, A., *Die Profetie des Amos*, BZAW 53. Giessen: Töpelmann, 1929.

Wolff, *Amos*
Wolff, H. W., *Joel and Amos*, Hermeneia. Philadelphia: Fortress, 1977.

Introduction

Historical Setting

In the superscription to the book (1:1) and in a dispute between Amos and Amaziah (7:10-17), the historical period of Amos is synchronized with the reign of Jeroboam II in Israel. At that time Uzziah was king of Judah (1:1), and both Israel and Judah were militarily strong. Since the reign of these two kings overlapped from about 785-750 B.C., the phrase "two years before the earthquake" (1:1) is the only guide to an exact date during this thirty-five year period. Yadin's excavation of Hazor associated severe earthquake damage in stratum VI with Amos 1:1 and assigned it a date between 765-760 B.C.[1] The prosperity of Israel, its sense of security (6:1-6), and its military victories (6:13) also point to a period in the reign of Jeroboam II, when the monarchy was well established.

The history of the ancient Near East during this period was filled with many political changes. Egypt was fragmented by Libyan and Sudanese kings and was no longer a strong influence in Palestine. Further, Syrian and Assyrian involvement with Israel was more complicated, for well before the time of Amos, Jehu paid tribute to the Assyrians (ca. 841 B.C.).[2] Soon after this payment the Assyrians were distracted by their northern neighbors in Urartu, and this opened the door for the Syrians to gain power and attack Israel. The Syrian kings, Hazael and Benhadad, treated Israel mercilessly (2 Kings 10:32; 12:17-18; 13:7) but around 805 B.C. a new Assyrian king came to power and defeated Syria. Amos remembered these Syrian atrocities and predicted a further defeat of the Syrian forces (1:3-5). Since the next three Assyrian kings were weak, and Syria had just been defeated, Jeroboam II of Israel and Uzziah of Judah became strong monarchs during the period of Amos. Territory taken from Israel was reconquered (2 Kings 13:25) and eventually Jeroboam II extended the border of Israel as far north as Hamath (2 Kings 14:25; Amos 6:14). There is little information on Jeroboam's strength, but his forces were certainly as strong as Uzziah's army of 307,500 troops (2 Chron. 26:1-15). Israel's relationships with some of her close neighbors are described in the oracles against the foreign nations in 1:3-2:3.

---

[1] Y. Yadin, et al., *Hazor II: An Account of the Second Season of Excavation, 1956* (Jerusalem: Magnes Press, 1960) 24-26, 36-37.
[2] *ANET*, 280-81.

The military success of Jeroboam II made the ministry of Amos very difficult, for few took his warnings of impending doom seriously. The people
were proud and at ease (6:1), thus Amos' warnings of death, exile, and the
end of Israel seemed out of touch with the political realities they saw around
them. Because of his negative political message, Amos faced considerable
official opposition (7:10-17).

Political power had a major effect on social conditions in Israel. The control over trade routes brought new wealth and access to expensive ivories and
furniture (3:15; 6:4). With new wealth came cultural influences, new patterns
of morality, and business ethics which were not consistent with Israel's traditions (2:6-8; 6:4-6; 8:4-6). Gradually a new class of wealthy landlords, government officials and merchants began to emerge in Israel. They built
beautiful palaces (5:11) that looked more like fortresses (6:8). These were
great houses (3:15; 6:11) and some owned both summer and winter homes
(3:15). Oppression, violence, and a seeming ignorance of the difference between right and wrong characterized life in the nation's palace-fortresses
(3:9-10). Luxurious living with the best wine, oil, music, and meat were a
regular part of life for the rich (6:4-7). These people felt very secure, very
proud, and thoroughly unconcerned with the misery allotted to the rest of
the population (6:1, 6, 8).

These material goods were attained through various legal and illegal
means. Amos condemned the wealthy women of Samaria for crushing the
needy (4:1), the merchants for shady business practices (8:4-6), the landlords
for exacting exorbitant taxes or rents (5:11), and others for bribery in the
court (5:10, 12). The poor, the weak, the debtor and the servant were mistreated, and some were sold into slavery (2:6-8; 8:4, 6). Social conditions
were soured by sin and greed. Amos, the shepherd, opposed this evil and predicted the humiliation and captivity of those who ignored God's standards of
justice in social relationships.

The religious situation is only partially described in Amos. Amos says very
little about the Baalism that confronted Hosea. Amos recognized the evil of
worshiping other gods (5:26; 8:14) and perceived this as a real part of Israel's
problem, but he did not focus on this aspect. Instead, Amos concentrated on
showing the nation how Israelite religious institutions and theology were
being perverted, misunderstood, and rejected. Temple worship, songs, sacrifices, and tithes are not described as non-Israelite but as transgressions
and proud demonstrations of piety (4:4-5). They are unrelated to justice and
righteousness (5:21-24) or to a real seeking after God (5:4-6). The temples at
Bethel, Gilgal, and Beersheba (4:4; 5:5) were full of activity that was religious in nature, but those worshiping did not turn from their sin and return to
God (4:6-13).

Some people outwardly opposed prophets and Nazarites, who were called
by God to warn the nation of their sins (2:11-12; 7:10-17). This repression of

prophetic criticism did not cause the people to reject Israel's past theological traditions. The nation still remembered God's election of them out of all the families of the earth (3:1-2), God's grace in delivering the nation from Egypt (2:10; 3:1; 9:7), his destruction of the Amorites (2:9) and the giving of the land of Palestine as a possession for Israel (2:10; 9:15). They knew God's promise was that he would be with them (5:14), protect them from all dangers (9:10), and save them on the great Day of Yahweh (5:18-20). These theological beliefs and religious practices only gave the people the impression that they were doing all the right things and believing all the right doctrines. Religion had become the opiate of the people. The promises of God were proclaimed, but the personal presence of God was unknown.

Amos was sent by God to share the roar of the lion (3:8). God had spoken out against his people and Amos was the messenger God chose to deliver his words of challenge and rebuke. Amos was not sent to pagans who had never heard God's word, he was sent to God's own people who failed to recognize sin in their lives.

The Prophet Amos

Amos is not mentioned elsewhere in the Hebrew canon. The only information about him comes from this book. His date of birth and death are not given, and his age at the time when these prophecies were given is unknown. Verse 1:1 connects Amos with the small city of Tekoa, a village about six miles south of Bethlehem and twelve miles south of Jerusalem. Amos lived in the Tekoa area when he was called by God to be a prophet (7:15). The city is on the borderline between the barren desert, leading down to the Dead Sea on the east, and the hilly pastureland to the west. The area was used for raising sheep and goats, and Amos made his living by supervising a group of shepherds (1:1; 7:14-15). He was not a lowly shepherd but a man of some responsibility. He also worked with sycamore trees, probably in the area of the Dead Sea, but it is not clear what his responsibilities were. Imagery within the book reflects the life of a shepherd who had heard lions roar (3:4, 7), used traps (3:5), knew the legal requirement of a shepherd (3:12), and had used a grain sieve (9:9).

The date of his calling (7:14-15) was between 765-760 B.C. The length of his ministry is unknown, but certainly it did not last over a year. The speeches that have been recorded suggest a ministry in the capital city of Samaria (3:9; 4:1; 6:1) and at the Bethel temple (7:10-17). The oracles and visions seem to have a chronological order, with the later ones assuming the earlier. The written production of the book of Amos came approximately two years after his ministry in the northern nation (1:1). He was a foreigner from Judah speaking to people who had a similar background but separate political and theological identities.

Amos was an educated person who had a wide understanding of the political affairs of his day (1:3—2:3). He had a grasp of international relationships which included details about foreign kings (1:4), major cities in different countries (1:5, 8, 12, 14; 2:2), previous battles (1:3, 13; 2:1), and some ancient history (1:5; 9:7). He also understood the situation in Israel (6:2, 13-14). He had observed the way the poor were being treated by the wealthy (2:6-8; 3:9-10; 4:1), how the merchant managed to dishonestly conduct business (8:4-6), how the courts operated on the basis of bribery instead of integrity (5:10, 12, 15), and how the landlords drove people into slavery through heavy rents (5:11). In his eyes the beautiful palace-fortresses of the rich stood out as landmarks of greed and luxury (3:15). Their opulant banquets were but another evidence of the degenerate state of Israel (6:1-7). With these insights into the thinking and social behavior of his audience, Amos was able to deliver a message which addressed their areas of need. Through the voice of God speaking to the prophet, Amos was given a word that challenged the accepted social norms of Israelite society.

Amos also had a keen spiritual sensitivity to the religious practices in the nation. He repeatedly delivered God's words of condemnation against worship at Bethel (3:14; 4:4-5; 5:4-5, 21-26; 7:9) and the other temples (8:14). God regarded their worship as an unacceptable activity; he hated it because there was no true meeting with God (5:6, 21-24). Amos knew the religious traditions of Israel. He refers to the creation of the mountains, winds, stars and the heavens (4:13; 5:7; 9:5), the story of the flood (5:9; 9:6), the destruction of Sodom and Gomorrah (4:11), the exodus from Egypt (2:10; 3:1; 9:7), the wilderness journey and the defeat of the Amorites in Palestine (2:9-10), numerous legal and religious norms from the law (2:4, 6-8; 4:4-5; 5:10, 12, 15, 21-24; 8:5, 11-12), and the nation's great hope in the Day of Yahweh (5:18-20). He quotes a hymn of praise to God used in the worship of the nation (4:13; 5:8-9; 9:5-6), is versed in the covenant curses (4:6-11), and knows about the nation's Davidic promise (9:11-14). Although Amos was deeply steeped in the religious traditions of Israel, of equal if not greater importance was the voice of God which revealed to him a word for the needs of his audience in each new situation.

The ministry of Amos is not what one would normally expect from a Judean shepherd. His regular activities of life were interrupted by an irresistible compulsion from God (3:8). God moved him from tending sheep to declaring a message against Israel (7:10-17). Amos was neither a stubborn Judean nationalist, a religious zealot, nor a cultic prophet; rather he was a man who had received the word and several visions from God (7:1—9:10).

The Book of Amos

Text

The Hebrew text of Amos is fairly well preserved.[3] Several difficulties with the Hebrew text do exist. Amos 2:7 and 8:4 have a form of *ša'ap* "desire," but the context seems to demand *šūp* "crush." The problem may be scribal or a variant spelling. Confusion between aleph and ayin caused a form of *t'b* "abhor" to be written *t'b* "desire" in 6:8. A *s* probably should be replaced by a *ś* in *mśrp* "corpse-burner" in 6:10, while *rib bā'ēš* "contend by fire" might be better rendered *rᵉ bîb 'ēš* "rain of fire" in 7:4. Amos 3:12 and 6:12 make better sense if the word division is adjusted slightly and 8:8 has "as light" for "as the Nile."

The Old Greek translation and the versions of Aquila, Symmachus, and Theodotian differ from the Hebrew at many places.[4] In being unfamiliar with the names of some cities, the Hebrew text is sometimes translated instead of transliterated (1:5, 12; 6:2; 9:7), but in 3:11 "adversary" *ṣar* was read *ṣōr* "Tyre," in 7:1 *gizzê* "mowing" became *gôg* "Gog," and in 1:56 and 9 *šᵉlēmāh* "complete" was read "Solomon." In 1:1, 4, 5; 4:5 and 7:1 a Hebrew *r* and *d* are confused by the Greek translators. A difference in vocalization is evident in the translation of 3:11; 4:10, and 8:3. "All" *kol* and *kalnēh* "Calnah" are confused in 6:2 and *kol* "all" and *klh* "destroy" are mixed up in 8:8 and 9:5. Ashdod in 3:9 must have been deliberately reinterpreted to refer to Assyria in light of Assyria's defeat of Israel. The reference to the "Messiah" in 4:13 was caused by making two Hebrew words one. Explanatory additions are found in 1:3; 2:8, 16; 3:4, 11 and double readings in 5:8 and 6:3. In 4:4-5 the Old Greek translators missed the ironic tone and removed the imperative; in 4:6 they turned the metaphor of "cleanness of teeth" into a "toothache." Some renditions show freedom and good insight into the meaning. The rather bland reference to the "destruction" of the tree in 2:9 is changed to "drying up" of the fruit and the root. The calves in the stall in 6:4 are properly described as "sucking calves" in the Old Greek and the snake in 9:3 is identified as the "sea serpent."

Although the Old Greek is often a good translation, its readings are superior to the Hebrew MT in very few cases. Frequently the versions of Aquila, Symmachus, or Theodotian will be closer to the Hebrew. The number of variations and the kinds of misunderstandings present in the Old Greek do not

---

[3]Harper, *Amos* clxxiii-clxxviii, gives his impression of the text and versions.
[4]J. A. Arieti, "The Vocabulary of Septuagint Amos," *JBL* 93 (1974) 338-47, J. de Waard, "Translation Techniques Used by the Greek Translators of Amos," *Bib* 59 (1978) 339-50 and S. E. Johnson, *The Septuagint of Amos* (Chicago: Univ. of Chicago, 1936) give further details on the Old Greek of Amos. T. Muraoka, "Is the Septuagint Amos VIII:12—IX:10 a Separate Unit?" *VT* 20 (1970) 496-98 rejects the evidence of G. Howard, "Some Notes on the Septuagint of Amos," *VT* 20 (1970) 108-12.

inspire great confidence in its interpretation, particularly in some of the more difficult passages (cf. 3:12; 4:2; 5:26; 6:3, 10). Because of the importance of having the best text possible, the details of the variations within the various texts of Amos will be noted after the translation of each section within the commentary below.

Style

Most of the book of Amos should be displayed in poetic form. No attempt has been made to use any predetermined method of stress or syllable counting to identify what is or is not poetry, and the poetic length of a line is not used as a tool of textual criticism. A considerable amount of flexibility in poetic construction is demonstrated throughout the book, thus any straightjacket on the prophet's literary freedom seems unwarranted. Introductory and concluding formulas like "declares Yahweh" may seem unnecessary (cf. 6:5 "like David"), but the authenticity of an oracle cannot be based on a rigid conformity to a predetermined poetic style (cf. 1:9-10, 11-12).

Participles are frequent in the hymnic sections (4:13; 5:8-9; 9:5-6) but also throughout the rest of the book.[5] Rhetorical questions are used in 3:3-6, 8; 5:18, 20, 25; 6:2, 12; 7:8; 8:2, 8; 9:7 and assonance is found in 5:5 using the "gl" sounds, 6:7 using "sr" sounds and 9:1 using "hr" sounds. Many rare words are also used.[6] Amos uses a number of phrases more than once. In 1:3—2:16, "for three transgressions and for four, I will not vacillate, because...So I will send fire upon" is repeated eight times. "Go into exile" is found in 1:5; 5:5, 27; 6:7; 7:11, 17. Righteousness and justice occur in 5:7, 24; 6:12 and the poor and needy in 2:6; 4:1; 5:11-12; 8:4, 6.

Evidence of distinctive style is present in the pairing of oracles against the nations (1:3-2:16), the pairing of questions (3:4-8), and the pairing of visions (7:1-8:14). There are five chastenings and five repetitions of "You did not return to me" in 4:6-11, five visions in 7:1-9:10, and five parallel, conditional clauses in 9:2-4. The habit of quoting what others say is evident in 2:12; 4:1; 5:14; 6:13; 7:10, 11, 16; 8:5-6, 14; 9:10. The prophet quotes Israelite traditions in 2:9-10; 3:1; 5:6, 14; 9:7; traditional hymns in 1:2; 4:13; 5:8-9; 9:5-6; borrows wisdom sayings in 3:3-6; 6:12; and refers to legal and cultic regulations in 2:6-8; 3:12; 4:4-5; 5:10, 12, 21-24; 8:5-6, 14; 9:7. Each plays an important part in Amos' rhetorical style of persuading his audience.

Amos also borrows and transforms well-known forms of speech. The ora-

---

[5] 1:1, 5, 8; 2:3, 7, 13, 15; 3:10, 12; 4:1, 2, 11; 5:3, 7, 10, 12, 16, 18; 6:1, 3, 4, 5, 6, 7, 11, 13, 14; 7:1, 4, 7, 8, 14; 8:1, 4, 8, 11, 14; 9:1, 9, 10, 11, 12, 13, 14.

[6] 2:13 *m'îq*; 3:12 *mšq*; 4:2 *ṣinnôt* and *sîrôt*; 4:3 *harmônāh*; 5:8 *kîmāh* and *kesîl*; 5:9 *mablîg*; 5:16 *'ikkār*; 5:26 *kiyyûn*; 6:5 *pôrṭîm*; 6:6, 7 *mizraq*; 6:10 *mĕsārpô*; 6:11 *resîsîm*; 7:1 *gizzê*; 7:7 *'ănāk* and *bôls*; 7:9, 16 *yiśḥāq*; 8:14 *derek*; 9:9 *serôr* and *kĕbārāh*.

cles against the nations have many of the characteristics of a war oracle that predicts the fall of Israel's enemies and salvation for Israel. Amos takes this way of speaking and transforms the conclusion into a surprising oracle of judgment on Israel. He also reverses into judgment the exodus tradition (3:1-2; 9:7) and the promises of the Day of Yahweh (5:18-20). With great sarcasm Amos encourages the people to continue their sinful worship (4:4-5), using words that a priest might use to call the people to worship. The lamentation of a funeral stands behind his woe oracles (5:18-27; 6:1-14) and his dirge (5:1-17), and the funeral banquet may well be imitated in 6:1-7. A disputation style of confrontation is evident in the structure and content of 3:1-8; 7:10-17, and 9:7-10. In the vision reports Amos uses elements common to the framework of other later visions (7:1-3, 4-6, 7-9; 8:1-3; 9:1-4). A form-critical investigation into the background and use of each of these borrowed and culturally bound ways of speaking unlocks a great deal of the background for understanding each message.

By far the most basic type of speech in Amos is the messenger speech. The messenger formula introduces and closes many oracles. "Declares Yahweh" or "thus says Yahweh" comes from the context of exchanging information (politically, socially, or intimately) by means of a carrier or messenger. The messenger formula gives the source of the information and the authority behind the message. The pervasiveness of these formulas in all the different types of literature in Amos is an overwhelming witness to the divine authority of the message which the prophet delivers. It is used at the beginning and at the end of most of the short oracles against the nations, in judgment speeches either with the reproach or the threat, in the visions and in the salvation oracle in 9:11-15. The oath formula (4:2; 6:8; 8:7) and the vision formula are two other emphatic means of stressing the announcement of God's revelation.

Each of these methods of communicating the word of God is influenced by the style of Amos. His rich background of imagery from life in the country, his sarcastic use of tradition, his quotations, his puns and word plays, and his use of culturally significant speech patterns enabled him to effectively address his audience in meaningful ways. His use of rhetorical devices to introduce, develop, and persuade his listeners are significant indicators of the emphasis he builds into the messages. The repetition of introductory formulas, the use of a new form of speech, and many other characteristics of the prophet's style are valuable guides for determining the structure of each oracle.

Structure

The book of Amos can be divided into three major sections: (1) the oracles against the nations (1:3—2:16) which are preceded by a brief introduction (1:1-2); (2) the verification of God's warnings of punishment on Samaria

(3:1—6:14); and (3) the visions and exhortations concerning the end (7:1—9:10) which are followed by a brief epilogue (9:11-15).

The first secton (1:3—2:16) is structurally defined by the regular repetition of (a) the messenger formula, "thus says Yahweh;" (b) an indictment; "for three transgressions and for four, I will not vacillate...because you have...;" (c) a punishment clause; "therefore I will send fire upon...;" and (d) a concluding divine confirmation formula; "says Yahweh." These structural markers are repeated eight times with enough variation to create a pairing of the oracles. Lexical interconnections between the oracles strengthen the pairing and connect one group to the next. The final oracle against Israel is expanded both in its accusation and its punishment, thus a rhetorical emphasis is achieved by the surprising use of the established pattern against Israel.

The second section (3:1—6:14) is marked by the introductory summons to "hear" (3:1, 9, 13; 4:1; 5:1) and the introductory "woe" (5:18; 6:1). Thematic continuity is a stronger force than a regular pattern for each oracle. The prophet repeatedly charges the nation with the perversion of justice (3:9-11, 15; 4:1; 5:10, 12; 6:4—6); with excessive luxury in their palace-fortresses (3:9—11, 15; 4:1; 5:9; 6:1, 8, 11), and predicts defeat and exile (3:12; 4:2-3; 5:5, 27; 6:7, 14). In spite of these consistent emphases, 5:1—6:14 is set apart from 3:1—4:13 by its emphasis on death and the use of funeral woes and dirges to convince the nation that Israel will die and not rise again.

The third section (7:1—9:10) is marked by the introductory "thus the Lord Yahweh showed me" before the visions. The structure of the visions and their conclusions shows a pairing of the visions. The last three visions (7:7-9; 8:1-3; 9:1-4) have expanded statements derived from key thoughts within the visions; 7:10-17 and 9:7-10 are disputes which arose because the message of the visions was rejected.

The structure of the larger and smaller segments, the frequent thematic connections, and the rhetorical bridges between points draw the book together as a reasonably unified whole. In spite of these characteristics, some believe that words, phrases, verses, and paragraphs have been added by later redactors during the process of the formation of the book. The superscription (1:1), the oracles against Tyre (1:9-10), Edom (1:11-12) and Judah (2:4-5), the description of prophecy (3:7), the hymns (4:13; 5:8-9; 9:5-6), and the final salvation oracle (9:11-15) are among the most common sections attributed to a later hand. Individual commentators vary from accepting everything as the work of Amos to those who see the book going through four or five revisions stretching over two hundred years into the post-exilic era. The conclusion one takes on these issues must be based on a full consideration of the evidence within the text.

Although the individual who wrote out the words of Amos is unknown and relatively unimportant, it is very significant to determine whether the oracles in the book have their source in the words received from God by the prophet

Amos. Most paragraphs in the book contain stylistic, rhetorical, structural, and thematic signs that point to an intial compilation of the oracles by a careful and faithful preserver of the inspired words of the prophet. This balance suggests that a conservative attitude toward the unity of the book should predominate the study of the text. This approach dare not prevent the consideration of evidence to the contrary, for the fair weighing of critical observations can only help to reveal the truth. Nevertheless, one should not be quick to invent hypothetical redactors to make easy escapes from theological traditions that accurately portray the conflicting tensions within a belief system. Too many have stripped the heart of the message from the prophet's grasp by: (1) limiting his use of traditional material (2:9-10; 3:1-2, 7; 4:13; 5:14-15; 9:11-15); (2) demanding of the prophet literary and theological criteria more consistent with a narrowly focused research book than an oral debate on some new and rather contradictory implications of God's word; and (3) ignoring stylistic and structural factors that point toward the unity of the text.

Throughout the book there is a creative dynamic that challenges Israel's accepted way of understanding God and his work. The old forms and traditions are repeatedly reversed and reinterpreted in fresh and startling ways. The secular aspects of doing business (8:5) or having a party (6:4-7) are intimately connected to the sacred, while the sacred traditions of election (3:1-2; 9:7) are seen as insignificant in determining the future of the nation. The inspired prophet used style and structure to stamp God's theological challenge with his own creative spirit. These structural factors will be carefully examined to evaluate the unity within each section.

Theological Themes

The theology of Amos is only partially revealed in the short series of sermons recorded in his book. Although incomplete and slanted toward the needs of his audience in Israel, these messages could be integrated with the theology of Hosea, Isaiah, and Micah to give a broader perspective on theological thinking in the eighth century B.C. This larger picture will not be attempted, but some contrasts between Amos and his contemporaries will be noted. The form of this summary will be determined by a synthesis of the theological themes and topics covered in the book.

The method used will not attempt to support a predetermined center for Old Testament theology but will let the text describe the structural relationships within the book. These structures are based on the language of the text, which can be found by studying: (1) the meaning of words, names and titles; (2) the use of metaphors; (3) the relationships implied by the placement of pronouns; (4) the verbal terms which describe relationships; (5) the placement of relative, causal, purpose, result, and circumstantial clauses which explain structural connections; and (6) the repetition of words and themes.

It is assumed that the theology of the book is rooted in syntactical and semantic indicators in the language of the book.

Names, titles, and nouns within Amos can be divided into two broad groups: (a) references to deities and (b) references to nature, people, places, or things other than deities. The references to deities include: Yahweh (forty-seven times); Lord Yahweh (nineteen times); Lord Yahweh God of hosts (3:13); Lord Yahweh of hosts (9:5); Yahweh, God of hosts, Lord (5:16); Yahweh God of hosts (4:13; 5:14, 15, 27; 6:8, 14); Yahweh your God (9:15); God (4:11, 12); and gods/god (2:8; 5:26; 8:14); and Sikkût and Kîyyûn (5:26). In five instances Amos indicates that a title is a name of God (4:13; 5:8, 27; 6:10; 9:6), while "name" is used as a substitute for a title twice (2:7; 9:12). In addition, eighty-four first-person singular verbs describe Yahweh as the "I" behind some action, five third-person singular verbs are used, and ten first-singular object pronouns refer to Yahweh. The metaphor of the lion (1:1; 3:8) is used of Yahweh while the false gods are described as images, a star, a king (5:26), the "guilt of Samaria" and the "power of Beersheba" (8:14). Anthropomorphisms of "his hand, power" (1:8; 7:7; 9:2) and "my eyes" (9:3, 4, 8) graphically refer to characteristics of God. The possessive pronouns "his, my" connect God to "statutes" (2:4), "secrets" (3:7), "holiness" (2:7; 4:2), the "upper chambers," the vault of heaven" (9:6) and "the people of Israel" (7:8, 15; 8:2; 9:10, 14). Construct relations connect "word," "law," "name," and "day" to Yahweh (2:4; 5:18, 20; 6:10; 8:11-12). The false gods are connected to a "house" or temple (2:8) and to the cities of Samaria and Beersheba (8:14).

Before looking at the verbs used to define the activity of God and the gods, the significance of the above data must be noted. Yahweh and its various forms predominate the theology of Amos. Astral, man-made images, and other gods were reverenced particularly at several of the significant temples, but these gods receive very little attention from Amos. They are not the main evil that Amos attacks. They are sworn to by the people but recognized by Amos as sinful (8:14). They are called kings, a typical ancient Near Eastern concept of a god.[7] Instead of making a negative case against the other gods, Amos develops the concept of Yahweh. The emphasis (seven times) on the name must be something of a polemic against the names of other gods. The name Yahweh is not connected to the covenant but to "God of hosts" (eight times). This appellation is similar to Yahweh of hosts (9:5) which is used 267 times in the Old Testament. It portrays Yahweh as the commander-in-chief of military forces, a God of great power and might. In light of this meaning, it is surprising that this title is never used in chapters 1-2 or any of the visions (7-9). It is used in positive (5:14-15) as well as negative contexts (5:27). Yahweh

---

[7] G. V. Smith, "The Concept of God/the gods as King in the Ancient Near East and the Bible," *Trinity Journal* 3 (1982) 18-38.

is the Lord, the sovereign master (nineteen times) particularly in the visions in 7:1—9:10 (eleven times), but Yahweh is the most common name throughout the book. He possesses "holiness" (2:7; 4:2), "power" (1:8, 7:7; 9:2), "eyes, sovereign knowledge" (9:3, 4, 8), "secrets" (3:7), "words, law" (2:4; 8:11-12), has a "day" (5:18-20), an "upper chamber" (9:6), and his own people Israel (7:8, 15; 8:2; 9:12, 14). This limited list stands in contrast to the many verbal activities related to Yahweh which are the main method of expressing Amos' theology about God.

God's activity is related to places and people. Places like the mountains, stars, upper chambers, and the vaulted dome over the earth were "built, created, and established" by Yahweh (4:13; 5:8; 9:6). The sun and moon can be darkened by God (4:13; 5:8; 8:9) and heaven and Sheol are within his sovereign power (9:2). All parts of nature are subservient to his rule. The earth quakes when he touches it (1:1; 8:8; 9:1, 5), the rain is given or withheld by God (4:7-8), and God can pour out the waters of the sea on the face of the earth to destroy the land (5:8; 9:6). He prevents the plants of a nation from being productive (1:2; 4:9; 5:11; 7:4) and at other times causes them to grow and produce abundantly (9:13-14). He sends the caterpillar (4:9), the snake and the bear (5:19), the locusts (7:1), fire (1:3—2:5; 7:4), and the sea serpent (9:3) to perform his acts of judgment. God is not just a God of history; he is totally in charge of all parts of nature to bring about his praise, his judgments, or his blessings.

God's activities and relationships with people are described by verbs of communication, destruction, and blessing. The concluding or introductory formulas attached to many of the oracles in the book of Amos indicate that God's revelation of himself through words is of major importance. He "says," or "declares" (forty-nine times), swears (4:2; 6:8; 8:7), commands (6:11; 9:3, 4, 9), roars (1:2; 3:8), reveals secrets (3:7), declares human thoughts (4:13), gives his words and statutes (2:4; 3:1; 7:16; 8:11-12), and demonstrates his word through visions (7:1, 4, 7; 8:1; 9:1). The messenger formula is the sign of authority for the prophet. Since God always reveals his secrets of the prophets before he does them, the priority of communication before destruction or blessing is established.

God's acts of destruction and blessing are not determined by the place, person, or object but by its moral character and the grace of God. God worked in grace with Syria (9:7) but in the future he will judge them (1:3-5). The Philistines were led from Caphtor to Philistia (9:7), but later they will be destroyed (1:6-8). The Edomites are ripe for God's judgement (1:11-12), but a remnant of Edom will enjoy great blessings in the future (9:12). The future of Tyre, Ammon, and Moab (1:9-11, 13-15; 2:1-3) and all the nations (9:9) are known and under God's control (9:9). Those who submit to God, and are called by his name from Israel and the nations will be blessed. Judah (2:4-5) and especially Israel will be destroyed by God (9:8a), but there is also hope for the remnant of Jacob (5:14-15). God's future control of the nations is not in doubt, for in the past he destroyed the Amorites (2:9-10), Sodom and Gomorrah (4:11), and chastened Israel with five curses (4:6-11). God is in control of all history.

God's acts of judgment are purposeful acts: "I will do it" (4:12), "I will set my eyes against them for calamity and not for good" (9:4). When he decides to judge he declares: "I will not vacillate" (1:3, 6, 9, 11, 13; 2:1, 4, 6), yet at other times there seems to be hope of life for those who seek God (5:6, 14-15). Representative of his acts of judgment are: "I will send fire" (1:4, 7, 10, 12, 14; 2:2, 5); "I will punish you" (3:2); "I will smite" (3:15; 4:9); "I overthrew you" (4:11); "I will pass through your midst" (5:17); "I will make you go into exile" (5:26); "I will spare you no longer" (7:8; 8:2); and "I will destroy you from the face of the land" (9:8).

The reason for these judgments is found in reproaches like: "I know your many transgressions" (5:12); "I will punish you for all your sins" (3:2); or "I will punish Israel for their transgressions" (3:14). The judgment in 5:18-20, 27 is directly related to God's evaluation of the nation's worship. God says, "I hate, I despise your feast" (5:21-23). He also "abhors the arrogance of Jacob, hates their palace-fortress" (6:8), and "will never forget their deeds" (8:7). Causal clauses like "on account of three transgressions and four" (1:3, 6, 9, 11, 13; 2:1, 4, 6), "because they threshed Gilead" (1:3), "because he pursued his brother with the sword" (1:11), "because they despised the law of Yahweh" (2:4), "because they sell the righteous for silver" (2:6), and many independent clauses describe the sinful activity of the people (see below). Sin is the cause of judgment and death.

When God acts in destruction it is often simply Yahweh who is mentioned. Sometimes he sends fire to destroy the cities (1:3—2:6), an earthquake (8:8; 9:1, 6), the sword (7:9, 17; 9:4, 10) or an unnamed army is pictured (3:11; 4:2-3; 5:3, 27; 6:7, 8-14; 7:11, 17; 9:4, 9). When God judges a nation he destroys the king and other rulers (1:5, 8, 15; 2:3; 7:9, 11), the inhabitants of the land (1:5, 8; 6:9-10; 8:2-3; 9:1-4, 8), the cities with their walls, gates and palace-fortresses (1:4-5, 7, 10, 12, 14; 2:2, 5; 3:11, 15; 5:9, 11; 6:8, 11), their armies (2:14-16; 4:10; 5:2-3), their land (1:2; 7:1, 4, 17), their temples (3:14; 5:5-6; 7:9; 8:3; 9:1), and sends the remainder into exile (1:5; 4:2-3; 5:27; 6:7; 7:17; 9:4). This will take place in that day, the Day of Yahweh, a day that marks the end of Israel (5:18-20).

God's acts of blessing and grace are equally important to the theology of the book of Amos. God brought Israel up out of Egypt (2:10; 3:1; 9:7), the Philistines from Caphtor and Syria from Kir (9:7). He chose Israel out of all the families of the earth (3:2), led them through the wilderness (2:10), and gave them the land of Palestine after defeating the Amorites (2:9-10). His grace is seen in sending prophets (2:11; 3:8; 7:15-16) who announce God's acts before they take place (3:7). He offers life to those who seek God, strive to do good, and establish justice in the gate (5:6, 14-15). He acts in compassion when the prophet intercedes on behalf of the nation Israel (7:1-3, 4-6). Finally, God promises to kill only the sinners, not the whole house of Israel (9:8). These and the remnant of the nations who submit to the rule of God and are committed to his name will receive the blessings of the renewed Davidic kingdom (9:10). The land will produce abundant crops, the people will return to the land and rebuild its ruined cities and farms, and the people will live there forever (9:11-15). The popular theology of the Israelites concerning God's presence with them (5:14), God's protection of them (9:10) and the blessings of the Day of Yahweh (5:18-20) carry on true traditions about the grace of God, but Amos points out that these acts of grace no longer apply to the sinful nation of Israel. Amos attributes no activity to the false gods mentioned in the book, but if the people were swearing by them (8:14) this implies that the people believed that these gods might be able to save them from destruction by Yahweh.

The theology of the book is heavily centered around the acts of God. He acts as creator, a revealer of these acts, a lawgiver, judge, divine warrior, gracious deliverer, and protector of his own people. No one can escape from his presence, all nations are within his realm of power, and the destiny of all peoples is determined by their relationship to him. Life and death are his to decree and these are granted according to a people's sin or their seeking after God.

Through the prophet's description of God's acts there emerges a theology of nature, people, places, and things other than God. The mountains, stars, the upper chambers of the heavens, and the wind (4:13; 5:8; 9:6) are objects created by God. They have no moral character and are evidence of the power of God. The rain from the heavens, the water from the sea, the productivity of the land, and the animals of nature are instruments God uses to determine the future of the people on the earth. Thus nature and places like Damascus, Gaza, Moab, Calnah, Hamath, and Samaria are an integral part of the triangular relationship between God, nature and the peoples of the earth.

The inhabitants of various places are defined by (1) country or city, (2) the basis of their acts toward God and other people, or (3) some moral, social, political, or occupational characteristic. Some are simply called "the inhabitants of Ashdod" (1:8) or "the sons of Israel dwelling in Samaria" (3:12). *Social* distinctions exist between the needy, helpless (2:6-8; 4:1; 5:11-12; 8:4-6) and those who impose heavy rents, who turn aside the poor in the gate (5:11-12) and who are compared to the "cows of Bashan" (4:1). Political and occupational nouns include: king (1:1, 15; 7:10); priest (7:10); prophet (2:11; 3:7-8; 7:12-16); professional mourner and farmer (5:16); and warrior (1:16). *Moral* characteristics are encapsulated by verbs, pronouns, subordinate clauses, quotations, and accusations by God. They "thresh Gilead, deport people, reject the law of God, sell the poor, hoard up violence, oppress the poor, multiply transgressions, do not return to God, abhor him who speaks with integrity, long for the Day of Yahweh, do not grieve over the ruin of Joseph, have turned justice into bitterness, cheat with fraudulent scales, and swear by the guilt of Samaria." The *possessive pronouns* "his," "their," "your" referring to these people show that they have "anger and fury" (1:11), "lies" (2:4), "strength and palace-fortresses" (3:11; 6:8, 13), "sacrifices and tithes" (4:4), "transgressions" (5:12), "burnt offerings and songs" (5:21-23; 8:10), and "images and gods" (5:26; 8:14). *Subordinate clauses* reveal that the Ammonites ripped open pregnant women "in order to enlarge their borders" (1:13), while the Israelites sin "in order to profane my holy name" (2:7). Israel is the family "which I brought up from the land of Egypt" (3:1) but their motivation for worship is increased "because they love to make known" what they have done for God (4:5). *Quotations* reveal something of the popular theology of the nation Israel (2:12; 4:1; 5:14; 6:13; 7:16; 8:4-6, 14; 9:10). The subject pronoun "they," or "you" of the verb applies to the people (seventy-five times). The book pictures the people among the nations as well as the Israelites as guilty of immoral sins against the weak among humanity.

Violence is characteristic of the palace-fortresses where the rich and powerful live (1:3—2:3; 3:9-11; 4:1) in Israel and the other nations (1:3—2:3). Theological traditions are known, and worship patterns are observed, but justice, righteousness, and seeking after God are absent. By their action they hope to control their future, their status and their wealth, but these are under God's rather than human control. What the sinful kingdoms want can only be given by God (9:11-15). The eternal kingdom and its blessings will be established by God who will give it to Israel and the remnant of the nations who are called by his name (9:11-15).

PART ONE

JUDGMENTS ON THE NATIONS

Amos 1:1—2:16

This initial section is made up of a series of highly structured prophecies which begin with, "Thus says Yahweh, for three transgressions and for four, I will not vacillate, because they have..." (1:3, 6, 9, 11, 13; 2:1, 4, 6). The title of the book in 1:1-2 does not follow this structure but gives information about the author, date, and audience, plus a short poetic verse that sets the tone for the revelation of judgment in the rest of the book.

The oracles against the nations are carefully constructed in pairs by the repetition of phrases and words, by the inclusion or exclusion of the final confirmation formula, and by changing the length of the accusation or punishment statements. The charges build to a grand climax in the last oracle against Israel (2:6-16), which has a greatly expanded accusation and a lengthy punishment. By using a regular structure Amos causes the audience to accept the theological position that each nation should be judged for its sins against humanity. When Amos reaches the climax, he does not give the expected salvation oracle for Israel but uses the logic of the preceding oracles to convict Israel of its guilt.

The oracles against the nations not only prove God's sovereign control over all nations but demonstrate the moral accountability of all nations to God. The theological basis for this judgment is not covenant law, or some ideal Davidic kingdom against which the nations have rebelled, but each nation's (including Israel's) inhuman treatment of other people. These crimes are based on their rejection of the laws of conscience, are contrary to every society's sense of right and wrong, and break legal codes and international treaties. If the Syrians, Edomites, and Ammonites deserve God's judgment, surely God's people Israel will feel the heavy hand of divine wrath.

The Title of The Book of Amos

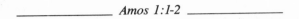

Introduction

An initial heading which reveals basic information about the author, audience, date, and message, precedes the actual spoken prophecies of Amos. It includes a superscription (1:1) and a statement that seems to encapsulate the warnings of the prophet (1:2). This material is not part of the highly structured oracles against the nations (1:3—2:16). Instead, it stands apart from the immediate context and functions as an introduction to the whole book, because the title was placed at the beginning of the book during the editing stage when the spoken messages of the prophet were established in writing. The length of time between the original proclamations by Amos and their first appearance in some written form is unknown, but the prophecies included in the book are full of a vigor and aggressiveness that carries the stamp of prophetic originality and divine authority. "Two years before the earthquake" may indicate that the oral messages were spoken approximately two years before they were put into their present written form.

Background

The literary practice of introducing a written document with information concerning its author, date, and addressee was known elsewhere in the ancient Near East. This kind of data appears in historical documents,[1] wisdom and prophetic texts, and letters.[2] These examples are not strictly parallel to the type of literature found in Amos, but they illustrate the general pattern that was used. Some biblical examples are similar (Prov. 30:1, "the words of

---

[1] Egyptian examples: "Year 21, 1st day of the second season, day 21 under the majesty of the King of Upper and Lower Egypt: User-maat-Re: son of Re:Rameses," in *ANET* 199; "The prince, count...royal secretary, Nebneteru, son of the mayor, visier, mouth of Nekhen, Nesaramun, born of Muthetepi, says," in M. Lichtheim, *Ancient Egyptian Literature*, Vol. 3 (Berkeley: Univ. of California, 1980) 19; Assyrian examples: "I, Ashur-nasir-apli, strong king...in my accession year," in A. K. Grayson, *Assyrian Royal Inscriptions*, II (Wiesbaden: Harrassowitz, 1976) 119; Palestinian examples in the Samaria Ostracon: "In the tenth year. The Gaddiyau from Azzo," in *ANET* 321. W. G. Lambert, "Ancestors, Authors, and Canonicity," *JCS* 11 (1957) 1 connects the superscriptions at the beginning of prophetic books to Akkadian colophons at the end of a literary piece, but the colophons refer more to the scribe or owner, not to the author, date, or title of the document.

[2] An Egyptian wisdom text: "The beginning of the instructions and teachings which the scribe Ani of the Temple of the King Nefer...Re Teri made" *ANET* 420). Letters from Egypt (*ANET* 475), Mari (*ANET* 482), and Sumer (*ANET* 480) give the author and addressee but often do not have a reference to a date.

Agur"; 1 Kings 11:41, "The words of Solomon"; Jer. 1:1, "The words of Jeremiah"), but other prophetic superscriptions are the clearest parallels.

Amos 1:2 does not give biographical or chronological data, and its style is distinct from 1:1. The style of poetry employed is sometimes associated with hymnic material,[3] and the content is related to theophany accounts or cultic ceremonies.[4] Wolff demonstrates that 1:2 differs in many ways from the formal characteristics of theophanies,[5] and Rudolph finds the announcement of judgment on God's own land to be contrary to the purpose of earlier theophanies that picture God's presence as a guarantee of his protection over the land.[6] These contrasts indicate a radical transformation of a theophany account and an altered setting. This transformation is in line with the new reconstruction of the Day of the Lord in Amos (5:18-20) when God "will pass through your midst" (5:17) in judgment.

Structure and Unity

Structure

The outline below illustrates the syntactical relationships and parallelisms between the words in 1:1-2. The exegesis of the text will follow the English outline.

The Title of the Book of Amos
Amos 1:1—2

The words of Amos,
      ªwho was among the herdsmenᵇ from Tekoa,
 which he saw concerning Israelᶜ
    in the days of Uzziah, king of Judah,
   and in the days of Jeroboam,
     son of Joash, king of Israel,
   two years before the earthquake.
	1:1 A. Superscription
	           1. The author
	           2. Recipients of the
	              message
	           3. Date

---

[3]Mays, *Amos* 21; Wolff, *Amos* 118.

[4]J. Jeremias, *Theophanie: Die Geschichte einer alttestamentlichen Gattung*, WMANT 10 (Neukirchen-Vluyn: Neukirchener, 1965) 142-57; J. L. Crenshaw, "Amos and the Theophany Tradition," *ZAW* 80 (1968) 203-15; A. Bentzen, "The Ritual Background of Amos 1:2-2:16," *OTS* 8 (1950) 95-97; Mays, *Amos* 21 and Wolff, *Amos* 118-22 see theophany motifs in a cultic hymn.

[5]Amos 1:2 has imperfect verbs instead of the more usual infinitive, participle, or perfect; uses unusual vocabulary to describe the revelation of a theophany; places the theophany in Zion instead of Sinai or in the heavens; and looks for a negative instead of a positive result for the land. See Wolff, *Amos* 116-18.

[6]Wolff, *Amos* 118-19; Rudolph, *Amos* 117.

And he said,
    Yahweh roars[d] from Zion
      and utters[d] his voice from Jerusalem.
    So the pastures of the shepherds wilt,[d]
      and the top of Carmel withers.[d]
	1:2 B. The message
	      1. The source of
	          judgment
	      2. Content of judg-
	          ment

1:1a. The Hebrew relative clause modifies "Amos" rather than the plural "words of" as in the Greek translation, "The words of Amos that were among the Nakkarim from Tekoa." C. D. Isbell proposed a translation of the Hebrew according to the Greek because: (1) the Hebrew relative pronoun may be either singular or plural; (2) the phraseology of 1:1 is very different from the other prophetic superscriptions that use these same terms; and (3) the number (singular) of the verb may be determined by the closest Hebrew noun, "Amos" (GKC 146a and note 1), instead of the principal idea, "words," which it could modify.[7] This analysis may help explain how the Greek translators understood the Hebrew text, but it is not the normal way one would understand this Hebrew clause. The peculiar syntax of 1:1 points to its early formulation before a standard way of introducing prophetic books was developed.

1:1b. *nōqdîm* "herdsmen" is orthographically close to *bōqēr* "shepherd" in Amos 7:14 and could be based on a confusion between *r* and *d*, *b* and *n*. The Greek *nakkarim* illustrates this possibility since the *d* has become an *r*. The Syriac agrees with the Hebrew consonants, and Theod. *nōkedeim* presupposes the Masoretic Text.

1:1c. For "Israel" the Old Greek translation has "Jerusalem," which Harper (*Amos*, 2) attributes to a misunderstanding of an abbreviation in the Masoretic Text. The contents of the book are about Israel not Jerusalem.[8]

1:2d. The Old Greek translation uses aorist verbs in 1:2, but the versions, Syriac, and Targum have imperfect verbs. The Hebrew imperfect verbs in the first couplet express continual action (GKC 107a). A fragment of Amos 1:2 from Qumran essentially agrees with the Massoretic Text.[9]

Verses 1 and 2 are structurally independent of one another but lumped together because they both function in an introductory role. Although the verses are held together by references to the "words of Amos" (1:1) and what "he said" (1:2), they can be divided by their theme, style, and structure into two fairly independent units. The syntactical outline of the first verse reveals a narrative text with two relative clauses ("who, which") and two prepositional phrases ("in the days of"), but neither is found in v. 2. The outline of 1:2 is made up of two sets of parallel verbal causes which are poetic in style. The symbolism and judgment motifs within v. 2 are foreign to the rather biographical details of 1:1. Because these verses are structurally unrelated to one another and the next unit (1:3—2:16), the relationship of these verses with the rest of the book is more tenuous.

Unity

Both the superscription and the "message statement" fit the general context and content of the prophecies within the book. Several commentators be-

[7]C. D. Isbell, "A Note on Amos 1:1," *JNES* 36 (1977) 213-14.

[8]Wolff, *Amos* 116.

[9]M. Baillet, et al. "Les 'Petites Grottes' de Qumran," *DJD* III (Oxford: Clarendon, 1962) 173.

lieve "who was among the shepherds" is a later addition to 1:1 because the two relative clauses in the verse do not flow together smoothly.[10] A few believe that "in the days of Uzziah, king of Judah and in the days of Jeroboam, son of Joash, king of Israel" is a conventional dating formula introduced by redactors from a much later period.[11] Both conclusions are based on comparisons with later prophetic superscriptions; yet none is completely parallel to Amos 1:1. Rudolph rejects any dependence on a deuteronomistic redaction based on the chronology of Kings, for the relationship between Amos and Jeroboam is found elsewhere at 7:10-14.[12] The reference to the prophet's previous occupation, the absence of an initial allusion to the word of the Lord, and the clumsy syntax of 1:1 are unique when compared to later prophetic superscriptions. These peculiarities suggest that the introduction must have been written before any standard style was established. A later redaction of the verse would have smoothed out the rough syntax and reconstructed the introduction on the basis of more traditional patterns.

Bentzen makes Amos 1:2 the introduction for the long unit 1:2—2:16, but most treat it as an independent unit.[13] Because of its independence, its hymnic style, its similarity to Joel 3:16 (Heb. 4:16), and its reference to Jerusalem, a number of scholars attribute all of 1:2 to a later editor and not Amos.[14] Wolff dates the addition to the time of Josiah's reform (621 B.C.), but Morgenstern

---

[10]Harper, *Amos* 2; Wolff, *Amos* 117; and Mays, *Amos* 18 object to the authenticity of parts of 1:1 because of the awkward syntax which the first relative clause creates; Fosbroke, *Amos* 777 and Hammershaimb, *Amos* 19 suggest that the first clause is a redactional addition based on information from Amos 7:10-14, and H. F. Fuhs, "Amos 1:1. Erwägungen zur Tradition und Redaktion des Amosbuches," *Bausteine biblischer Theologie: Festschrift G. J. Botterweck*, BBB 50 (1977) 271-89, sees the vocational data as "deuteronomistic" and no earlier than Jeremiah's superscription which includes vocational information.

[11]May, *Amos* 18; Wolff, *Amos* 117-18; W. H. Schmidt, "Die deuteronomistische Redaktion des Amosbuches," *ZAW* 77 (1965) 170 and G. M. Tucker, "Prophetic Superscriptions and the Growth of a Canon," *Canon and Authority*, ed. G. W. Coats and B. O. Long (Philadelphia: Fortress Press, 1977) 56-70, considers the synchronistic dating by means of the kings of Israel and Judah to be the work of later deuteronomistic editors who follow dating formulas used in the book of Kings. F. E. Peiser, "*Šenātayim lipnē hārā'aš*. Eine philologische Studie," *ZAW* 36 (1916) 218-24, believes that "two years before the earthquake" is a later addition. He suggests that 1:2b was drawn from Joel 1:18-19, while 1:2a was from Joel 2:10-11 and 3:16 (4:16) (both contain references to earthquakes, thus the addition at the end of 1:1). "Two years" is a corruption of "heavens" in Joel 2:11.

[12]Rudolph, *Amos* 112, 115. Kings and Chronicles never mention Amos, so it is difficult to see how that editor could have added the chronological notes here. Rudolph would date the superscription before 722 B.C. and the fall of Israel.

[13]Bentzen, "Ritual Background," 95-96 notes the continuity between the concept of God as a judge in 1:2 and 1:3—2:16 as well as the similarity between 1:2, Joel 3:16[Heb 4:16] and Jer. 25:30 which are part of oracles against foreign nations. Most do not connect Amos 1:2 to the following oracle because the structure of 1:2 does not fit the pattern of 1:3—2:16 and because the content of 1:2 ("God speaks from Zion; the pastures will wilt") is foreign to the content of 1:3—2:16. Kapelrud, *Amos* 19 identifies the shepherds as foreign kings to make the connection with 1:3—2:16. The Targum also refers to kings and their castles in 1:2.

[14]Harper, *Amos* 9-10; Wolff, *Amos* 121; and Mays, *Amos* 21.

prefers a post-exilic date.[15] This date cannot be supported by the position that Amos 1:2 is an editorial recasting of Joel 3:16, for Wolff and Rudolph have persuasively shown that Joel is dependent on Amos.[16] Mays denies any literary connection and hypothesizes only a knowledge of some Jerusalem temple tradition. If the views of Wolff, Rudolph, and Mays are accepted, the dating of 1:2 revolves primarily around the positive reference to Zion and Jerusalem (the poetic or hymnic style of 1:2 cannot be dated).

Gottlieb's study of the relationship of Amos to Jerusalem points to the antiquity of Jerusalem traditions well before the time of Amos.[17] The traditions concerning David's bringing of the ark to Jerusalem (2 Samuel 6-7) and Solomon's construction and dedication of the temple in Jerusalem (1 Kings 8) affected the prophet's understanding of the dwelling place of God in Zion. Other early prophets like Isaiah used traditions concerning God dwelling in Jerusalem. The existence of temple literature and the prophet's participation in temple worship in Jerusalem influenced his understanding of God's presence at Jerusalem. The early Davidic and Zion traditions in various Psalms (46, 47, 48, 50, 74, 99) and in Isaiah (6:1-13; 8:18; 31:9) demonstrate the existence of early theological traditions about Zion before and at the time of Amos.

The availability of Jerusalem tradition does not fully answer doubts about the unique view of Jerusalem in Amos 1:2. References to Jerusalem within Amos condemn its present sinfulness (2:4-5; 6:1) and tell of its future restoration (9:11-15), as did Isaiah. But during the prophet's ministry in Israel, Amos never refers to God dwelling in Jerusalem. Therefore the reference to Zion in 1:2 likely reveals the prophet's Judean theological background. Amos 1:2 does not pretend to be part of his oral message in the north but was added to his oral message when he left Israel and went home to Judah. This setting is unique from the rest of the book, thus Amos adds a fresh perspective based on his Judean setting when editing the book. Neither verse contains material which must be dated to a period later than Amos.[18]

---

[15]Wolff, *Amos* 12; Morgenstern, *Amos Studies* 118-21.

[16]Cripps, *Amos* 115; Harper, *Amos* 9-10; and Marti, *Amos* 157 partially base their dating of Amos 1:2 on the position that it is borrowed from Joel, but Wolff, *Amos* 81 and Rudolph, *Amos* 117 demonstrate the opposite source of dependence.

[17]H. Gottlieb, "Amos und Jerusalem," *VT* 17 (1967) 430-63 investigates the validity of I. Engnell's claim that the early classical prophets were "pre-deuteronomic propagandists" who located God at Jerusalem. Evidence based on the syncretism between El and Yahweh at Jerusalem and the involvement of the prophets in the New Year's Festival at the sanctuary in Jerusalem are so hypothetical that they do not lend support to the overall case he reconstructs. S. Wagner, "Überlegunger zur Frage nach der Beziehungen des Prophet en Amos zum Südreich," *TLZ* 96 (1971) 653-70 studies all the references to Judah and concludes: (1) Amos did write 1:2 and (2) it is a testimony to his theological traditions which are rooted in the Southern Kingdom.

[18]R. Clements, *Prophecy and Covenant* (London: SCM, 1965) 43, n 1, maintains "that no absolute ground for denying it [1:2] to Amos exists."

Interpretation

The Superscription (1:1)

1. The author: Amos (1:1*a*)

"The words of Amos" identifies the human author of the oracles included within this collection of prophecies. Although later prophetic books
have similar superscriptions, they frequently place the prophet in a more subordinate position and begin: "the words of Yahweh..." (Zeph. 1:1; Hag.
1:1; Zech. 1:1). This lack of theological refinement is a sign that the superscription preceded the development of any standard formula for literary introductions to prophetic books. On the other hand, the prophet does not claim to
be the sole author, for the later subordinate relative clause, "which he saw,"
indicates that Amos received these words from another source. The verb
hāzāh "he saw, viewed" could refer specifically to his reception of the visionary material in Amos 7-9, but it is more likely that it has a general sense
like "a divine revelation."[19] By the inclusion of the dependent clause, divine
authority and origin are claimed (note the frequency of phrases like "thus
says Yahweh" 1:3, 5, 6, 8, 9, etc.) and a divine calling is presupposed (7:14-
15). Amos proclaimed what he heard; he reported what he saw.

Biographical information concerning Amos is limited to the portrait revealed within this book. His name is not mentioned elsewhere (he is not the
Amoz of Isa. 1:1 or the Amasiah of 2 Chron. 17:16),[20] and the attempts to
identify him with the "man of God" from Judah who condemned Jeroboam I
and the altar at Bethel in 1 Kings 13 are historically impossible.[21] Like Oba-

---

[19]*hāzāh* "he saw" is not used in 7:1, 4, 8; 8:1; and 9:1 to describe what Amos saw in his visions. In these passages the parallel root *rā'āh* "he saw" is employed, and thus the direct connection between 1:1 and the visions is weakened. Amaziah does call Amos a *hōzeh* "seer" in
7:12. This terminology was used to describe divine revelations even when they were not visionary. Micah 1:1 and Isa. 1:1, "The words of...which he saw," appear in a nonvisionary context of
receiving "words." The addition of this clause distinguishes the prophetic titles from the wisdom
introductions that Wolff (*Amos* 119-20) compares. The "intellectual affinity" that Wolff derives
from the similarity between the titles ignores the difference between the prophets and the wise
men. Since similar introductions are found throughout the ancient Near East (see the section on
Background); a connection with wisdom introductions is at best indirect. A full study of the Hebrew root can be found in H. R. Fuhs, *Sehen und Schauen: Die Wurzel hzh im Alten Orient und
im Alten Testament* (Würzburg: Echter, 1978).

[20]The meaning of the name Amos "to carry, bear" is investigated by J. J. Stamm, "Der Name
des Propheten Amos und sein sprachlicher Hintergrund," *Prophecy: Essays Presented to G.
Fohrer on His Sixty-Fifth Birthday*, ed. J. A. Emerton (Berlin: W. de Gruyter, 1980) 137-42.

[21]O. Eissfeldt, "Amos und Jona in volkstümlicher Überlieferung," *Kleine Schriften* 4 (1968)
137-42 and J. Morgenstern, *Amos Studies* I (Cincinnati: Hebrew Union, 1941) 164-79, have re-
vived this hypothesis which was first suggested by J. Wellhausen, *Die Kleinen Propheten* (Berlin:
G. Reimer, 1898) 244. Most reject this suggestion and ignore it altogether, but it does seem that
1 Kings 13 provides some valuable background for understanding worship at Bethel. See J. L.

diah, Habakkuk, Nahum, and Haggai, the age of the prophet and his family tree are omitted.

The superscription states that Amos was one of the "herdsmen" from Tekoa, while 7:14 describes him as a shepherd and one who worked with sycamore figs. These details provide a geographical and occupational background for the prophet. The village of Tekoa may have been the birth place of the prophet, but it is more probable to conclude that Tekoa was the place where Amos lived when he was called to announce God's message to Israel. This would place the prophet in the southern Judean hill country about twelve miles south of Jerusalem, with Bethlehem to the north, Hebron to the south, and the Dead Sea to the east. The village is on the line between the desolate wilderness area to the east and the agricultural lands to the west. Pottery from the site dates back to the Early and Middle Bronze Age, and recent excavations have found Iron II pottery from around 750 B.C., the time of Amos.[22]

Tekoa is perhaps best known because of the wise woman employed by Joab to convince David to be merciful to Absalom (2 Sam. 14:2-9). Tekoa also had a military fortress associated with it during the period of Rehoboam (*ca.* 920; 2 Chron. 11:5-7), Jehoshaphat (*ca.* 860; 2 Chron. 17:2; 20:20), and Uzziah (*ca.* 760; 2 Chron. 26:10). These factors made Amos more aware of military matters within and outside of Judah.

Amos was employed as a "herdsman, sheep breeder" in Tekoa. This term is used one other time in the Old Testament (2 Kings 3:4) to describe the king of Moab, who was required to pay Ahab, the king of Israel, 100,000 lambs and wool from 100,000 rams. Some connect the root for herdsman with the Arabic *naqad* (used of a sheep); thus one who cares for this type of sheep would be called a *nōqēd* "a herdsman."[23] Others have used the reference to a *rb nqd* "chief herdsmen," which occurs parallel to "chief priest" in the Ugaritic "Poem of Baal and Anath" (*ANET* 141), to conclude that Amos was

---

Crenshaw, *Prophetic Conflict* (Berlin: W. de Gruyter, 1971) 41-46. It is argued by F. Crüsemann, "Kritik an Amos im deuteronomistischen Geschichtswerk," ed. H. H. Wolff *Probleme biblisher Theologie* (München: Chr. Kaiser, 1971) 57-63, that 2 Kings 14:27 "Yahweh had not said that he would blot out the name of Israel from under heaven" is a direct attack against the message of Amos.

[22]P. M. Lapp, "Palestine: Known But Mostly Unknown," *BA* 26 (1963) 124; M. H. Heicksen, "Tekoa; Historical and Cultural Profile," *JETS* 13 (1970) 81-89, bases his information on excavations completed in 1968. See also V. R. Gold, "Tekoa," *IDB* IV (1962) 527-28, for the early references by Eusebius and Jerome to the tomb of Amos in Tekoa and passages from the Mishnah and Babylonian Talmud concerning Tekoa's reputation for olive oil. S. Speier, "Bemerkungen zu Amos," *VT* 3 (1953) 305-06, located Tekoa in Israel instead of Judah, but this conclusion is not based on acceptable evidence.

[23]Fosbroke, *Amos* 777; Harper, *Amos* 8; Hammershaimb, *Amos* 17; and J. J. Glück, "Nagid-Shepherd," *VT* 13 (1963) 146 refer to a similar view in the Mishnah and in Kimchi's commentaries.

connected to a cultic establishment.[24] Bič even proposes, from the Akkadian *naqadu* "to probe," to make Amos into an hepatoscoper who practices augury by the examination of livers. This view cannot be accepted.[25] A fuller investigation of *nqd* in Ugaritic, Akkadian, Hurrian, and Moabite shows that these managers of sheep had a higher status than the ordinary shepherds, were employed by the royal court (which controlled both political and religious institutions) but had no sacred role in the services at the temple.[26] The extent of parallelism between the role of the *nōqēd* in Israelite and Ugaritic social structure is an additional unknown factor which must be taken into consideration.

A "herdsman" indicates a nonprophetic background (7:14-15) for the prophet. A shepherd would naturally choose metaphors concerning the roar of the lions (1:2; 3:4), traps (3:5), rescuing the remains of an animal attacked by a lion (3:12), and might well be astonished at the riches of the upper class (6:1-6). But being a shepherd is not identical to being a simple uneducated peasant. The literary style, method of argument, and knowledge of international politics clearly demonstrates that Amos is an educated and knowledgeable person.

2. The recipients of the message: Israel (1:1*b*)

The words of Amos, the herdsman from the Judean village of Tekoa, are addressed to the northern nation of Israel which was ruled by Jeroboam II. The references to Samaria (3:9, 12; 4:1; 6:1; 8:14), Bethel (3:14; 4:4; 5:5, 6; 7:13), the house of Israel (5:1, 3, 25; 6:1, 14), Jacob (7:2, 5; 9:8) and many other direct and indirect references confirm that these oracles were given in Israel. No specific group within Israel is identified in 1:1, but internal evidence suggests several different audiences in Israel. Most conceive of a fairly short ministry in Israel centered around the capital city of Samaria and the national temple of Bethel. The political, social, and religious behavior of the audience is described by Amos in great detail within each prophecy. The audience response is often unknown, with the exception of the strong negative response in 7:10-13.

---

[24]J. Gray, *The Legacy of Canaan*, 2nd ed., SVT 5 (Leiden: Brill, 1957) 156; Kapelrud, *Amos* 5-7; J. Gray, *I and II Kings* (Philadelphia: Westminster, 1964) 434; and the summary by H. H. Rowley, *From Moses to Qumran* (New York: Association Pr., 1963) 122-23, and J. D. W. Watts, *Vision and Prophecy in Amos* (Grand Rapids: Eerdmans, 1958) 6-7.

[25]M. Bič, "Der Prophet Amos-ein Heapatoskopos," *VT* 1 (1951) 293-96, builds on the cultic interpretations of Engnell and A. Haldar, *Associations of Cult Prophets* (Uppsala: Almqvist and Wiksell, 1945) 79, but A. Murtonen, "The Prophet Amos—A Hepatoscoper," *VT* 2 (1952) 170-71 and S. Segart, "Zur Bedeutung des Wortes *nōqēd*," *Hebräische Wortforschung: Festchrift zum 80. Geburtstag von W. Baumgartner*, SVT 16 (Leiden: Brill, 1967) 279-83, have pointed out the weakness of this interpretation.

[26]P. C. Craige, "Amos the *NŌQĒD* in Light of Ugaritic," *Studies in Religion* II (1982) 29-33.

3. The date (1:1c)

The historical time period is defined in three ways. The first two relate to the kings who ruled in Judah and Israel. Uzziah was the king of Judah, the homeland of Amos, for approximately fifty years (2 Kings 15:1-2; 2 Chron. 26:1-3). Uzziah's reign has been alternatively dated from 791-40, 787-36, and 783-42 B.C.[27] Uzziah was a strong king who repaired the walls and towers of Jerusalem (2 Chron. 26:9), built defensive towers in the wilderness (2 Chron. 26:10),[28] reorganized and re-equipped a massive army of 307,500 men (2 Chron. 26:11-15), and gained control over Philistine, Arab, and Ammonite areas, and Elath (2 Chron. 26:2, 6-8). His powerful rule brought security and great prosperity to Judah, but his rule was cut short because he contracted leprosy, a direct result of his pride (2 Chron. 26:16-21). Since there is no reference to his son Jotham in Amos 1:1, the ministry of Amos probably ended before 750 B.C. and began after 767 B.C., the date when Uzziah's co-regency with his father Amaziah ended and he became the sole ruler.

Jeroboam's reign is dated around 787/6-47/6 or 793-53 B.C.[29] Jeroboam II was also a powerful military leader. He restored the northern Solomonic border of Israel (1 Kings 8:65) to the entrance of Hamath (2 Kings 14:25; Amos 6:14). The prosperity of Israel is evident in Amos 6:1-7, the nation's worship of Baal is fully described by Hosea, and the social disintegration of the nation is evident throughout Amos.[30] The rest of the book of Amos is a commentary on life in Israel under Jeroboam II.

The date of the editing and publication of the book of Amos could be as early as two years after his oral delivery of the prophecies within the book. "Two years before the earthquake" is an exact date, and many associate this event with the signs of a severe earthquake found during the excavation of Hazor, in area A, stratum VI (a date of 760 B.C. is proposed by Yadin).[31] There is still some disagreement concerning the association of this level with stra-

---

[27]J. Bright, *A History of Israel* (Philadelphia: Westminster, 1972) 245 and Mays, *Amos* 20 use 783/6—42 B.C.; Wolff, *Amos* 87, 124 and Rudolph, *Amos* 114 give the dates 787-36, while E. Thiele, *The Mysterious Numbers of the Hebrew Kings* (Grand Rapids: Eerdmans, 1965) 75-81 and W. Hallo, *The Ancient Near East: A History* (New York: Harcourt, Brace, Javonovich, 1971) 132 have 791-40, which is adopted here.

[28]The fortress of Tekoa was build earlier by Rehoboam and it was probably still an important outpost during the time of Uzziah. Y. Aharoni, "Forerunners of the Lines: Iron Age Fortresses in the Negev," *IEJ* 17 (1967) 1-17, lists nineteen of the fortresses which Uzziah may have built. Most are between Kadesh Barnea and Beersheba. It is likely that the whole southern border was secured with fortresses at this time, including Tekoa.

[29]Bright, *History of Israel* 245; Mays, *Amos* 20; Wolff, *Amos* 89; and Rudolph, *Amos* 114, give the dates 787-47 B.C. while Thiele, *Mysterious Numbers of the Hebrew Kings* 75-81 and Hallo, *Ancient Near East* 132, have 793-53, which is adopted here.

[30]See the Introduction for more details on life in Israel during this period.

[31]Y. Yadin, *et al.*, *Hazor II 24-26, 36-37; Y. Yadin "Excavation at Hazor (1955-58)," BAR*, ed. E. F. Campbell and D. N. Freedman, 2 (Garden City: Doubleday Anchor Books, 1964) 197.

tum IV or V in Samaria,[32] but a date for the earthquake between 765 and 760 is probable regardless of the problems of synchronization with Samaria. Although Morgenstern and Watts prefer a date for Amos around 750, and Cripps and Snaith place Amos around 745, most modern discussions of the issue date Amos 1:1 on the basis of the earthquake which struck Hazor between 765-60.[33] The reference to this earthquake at a later time (Zech. 14:5) is a testimony to the significance of this earthquake, but the connection of it in Josephus (*Antiquities* IX, 10.4) with the transgression of Uzziah in the temple is unlikely.[34]

B. The Message is Confirmed (1:2)

1. The source of judgment: God roars from Zion (1:2a).

The first couplet announces God's action of judgment; it reveals that the awesome power of God is active in Zion. Although 9:6 isolates God's dwelling place in the heavens, it was also natural for Amos to locate God's dwelling place in Jerusalem. The Judean understanding of God's presence in Jerusalem was initiated when David brought the ark to Jerusalem (2 Samuel 6-7) and solidified when Solomon built a temple to contain the ark (1 Kings 8). Amos was aware of these theological traditions in Judah, for he lived in Judah before he was sent to preach to the northern kingdom and returned to Judah after his ministry in Israel.

The action of God involves his "voice," so a literal interpretation might envisage a new revelation of God's word.[35] The utterances of God's voice and his roaring are also parallel in Amos 3:7-8, but the full significance of 3:7-8 is understood only if it is read in conjunction with 3:4 and 6. The roar of God is not just a reference to his "secret words" to the prophets, it is a warning of

---

[32]Y. Yadin, "Ancient Judaean Weights and the Date of the Samaria Ostraca," *Scripta Hierosolymitana* 3 (1960) 24, connects Hazor VI with Samaria IV while Y. Aharoni and R. Amiran, "New Sub-divisions of the Iron Age," *IEJ* 8 (1958) 183, connect Hazor VI with Samaria V. See also G. E. Wright, "Samaria," *BAR* 2 (1964) 248-57.

[33]Morgenstern, *Amos Studies* 172; Watts, *Amos* 35; Cripps, *Amos* 36; Snaith, *Amos* 8.

[34]J. A. Soggin, "Das Erdbeben von Amos 1, 1 und die Chronologie der Könige Ussia and Jotham von Juda," *ZAW* 82 (1970) 117-21, might accept Josephus's information if the beginning of Jotham's reign, or "Uzziah's sin," is placed around 756 or 759 B.C. with the chronology of Begrich and Jepsen, instead of 750. Morgenstern, *Amos Studies* 108, 121-24, 131-43, 172, accepts Josephus's account, and Watts, *Amos* 34-35, seems to follow Morgenstern. A comprehensive list of earthquakes in Palestine is given in D. H. Kallner-Amiran, "A Revised Earthquake-Catalogue of Palestine," *IEJ* 1 (1950/51) 226.

[35]J. Lindblom, *Prophecy in Ancient Israel* (Philadelphia: Fortress, 1962) 116, takes the word literally and gives examples of similar usages in Babylonian hymns: "His (Nergal) word when it goes below destroys the land."

judgment, a symbol of the beginning of an attack.[36] The roar is not a theophany using the imagery of a thunderstorm (cf. Ps. 18:7-15 [Heb. 18:8-16]).[37] Instead, Amos now looks back at his earlier spoken words (3:7-8; 4:13; 5:17-20; 9:1) as a warning of God's attack. The earthquake in 1:1 is part of the fulfillment of the earlier warning and another proof that the roaring attack by God has already begun.[38] This would make Amos 1:1-2 a confirmation of the earlier oracles and a further warning that the Day of Yahweh is drawing near.

2. Content of judgment: A drought will come (1:2b)

No matter how one interprets 1:2a, the following half of the verse seems somewhat unrelated to 1:2a as well as to the rest of the book of Amos. Lack of rain is not a central theme in Amos. God withheld the rain as a chastisement in 4:7-8, and the idea appears as a metaphor of a future spiritual thirst for the word of God in 8:11-12, but neither seem to be related to 1:2b. In other prophets, drought is a symbol of God's wrath (Isa. 5:6, 19:7, 42:15), and it appears here as one of many symbols for judgment in Amos (locust 7:1; fire 7:4). Amos 5:16-17 refers to the wailing of farmers and those who work in the vineyard in a similar manner. When God passes through the midst of the nation, he will roar and destroy the land.

For a herdsman like Amos, two of the best illustrations of devastation would be the withering of the shepherd's pasture land and the lush Carmel ridge. When all the grass is gone, and the vineyards and trees of Carmel fade, the observant Israelite recognizes the hand of God at work.[39]

The introduction not only summarizes the prophet's prediction that God will judge the nation, it also confirms the validity of the words of judgment spoken by Amos while in Israel. The land already withers under the powerful hand of God. The earthquake has happened (1:1); the judgment has begun. The warning concerning God's roar (3:4, 7-8) has now resulted in an attack. The Day of the Lord is here—a day of darkness. It is impossible to escape (5:18-20).

Theological Developments

Amos 1:1 does not reveal all the details of the theological background of the prophet, but it does provide a general theological setting. Many significant theological events preceded Amos, and his proclamations reflect a knowledge of these traditions. His understanding of his task was influenced

---

[36]M. Weiss "Methodologisches über die Behandlung der Metaphor dargelegt an Amos 1, 2," *TZ* 23 (1967) 1-25, examines the literal interpretations of the roar but opts for a metaphorical understanding which produces the psychological effect of fear.

[37]Mays, *Amos* 22; Wolff, *Amos* 118-19.

[38]Rudolph, *Amos* 115-16.

[39]Kapelrud, *Amos* 19, identifies the shepherds with kings and the head of Carmel with Israel's king, but this view cannot be accepted.

by a knowledge of earlier prophets, an acquaintance with the worship of the people, and his view of responsibility to God and fellow human beings. His expression of theological ideas was shaped by experience and circumstances.

Despite these limitations which are determined by time, setting, and background, the "words of Amos" carry a significance because they were derived from "what he saw" by divine revelation. The result of the divine experience was expressed in his words, but the authority and inspiration came from a power outside the prophet himself. The fulfillment of his prophecy of an earthquake profoundly affected the prophet's view of God's word through him. This confirmation had a great deal to do with the decision to put these oracles into writing and certainly affected the communities' recognition of their canonical status.

Verse 2 sets the tone for much of the book. God is in the process of judging his land. He warns and he acts. His power controls the course of history and nature. The nature of this judgment is developed throughout the book, but Yahweh's connection with Zion is a distinctive declaration which is not common in the rest of the book. This phrase reveals that the prophet's background has much in common with traditions more fully developed in Isaiah.[40] Zion was important because the temple of God was in Jerusalem and its significance was based on the real presence of God in the temple. The paucity of references to Zion is an evidence of the prophet's ability to fit the oral message in the rest of the book to the level where the Israelite audience lived.[41] It is not an indication of a later insertion of Zion theology but an integral part of his overall theological perspective. The concept of God's judgment on Israel is central to the message of Amos, but the expression of the theme is unique in 1:2.

---

[40]Th. Vriezen, "Essentials of the Theology of Isaiah," *Israel's Prophetic Heritage*, ed. B. W. Anderson and W. Harrelson (New York: Harper and Row, 1962) 129-31. The Zion ideology of Isaiah, which tends to relate to the inviolability of Zion, discussed by J. Hayes, "The Tradition of Zion's Inviolability," *JBL* 82 (1963) 419-25, does not appear in Amos until chapter 9 and is not a key concept in his thinking. See also R. de Vaux, "Jerusalem and the Prophets," *Interpreting the Prophetic Traditions* (Cincinnati: Hebrew Union College, 1969) 275-300; R. E. Clements, *God and Temple* (Philadelphia: Fortress, 1965) 55, especially his chapter on "The Presence of God in Israel's Worship," 63-75.

[41]Many believe Isaiah derived this tradition from Psalms like 46, 48, and 47 (Ps. 132:11-14; 102:12-17; 53:7; 128:5 carry on a similar tradition) and other Davidic traditions. S. Erlandsson, *The Burden of Babylon* (Lund: Gleerup, 1970) 103-05; Clements *Prophecy and Covenant* 19-21, and especially 49-53. Clements reverses his view in his later book *Isaiah and the Deliverance of Jerusalem* (Sheffield: JSOT, 1980) 72-89.

The Oracles Against the Nations

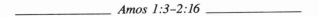

_____ *Amos 1:3–2:16* _____

Introduction

Judgments against foreign nations are found in many of the prophetic books after Amos (Isa. 13-23; Jer. 46-51; Ezek. 25-32; Nahum, Obadiah). These later prophetic oracles are related to the prophecies against the nations in Amos, but because Amos was the first to include this type of message and because his prophecies have a distinctive structure, they are used by Amos in a unique way. When comparing other oracles against the nations with Amos 1:3—2:16 a distinction must be made between (1) the common use of the same words and themes and (2) the many different ways in which the same basic theme is used.[1]

The oracles against the nations in Amos are distinct from earlier examples in biblical and non-biblical documents. Some early curses against other nations were set in a cultic context, while others were connected with preparations for battle against an enemy. The exact setting for Amos' oracles against the nations is not clearly defined, but the distinctive structuring of the prophecies does provide insight into the prophet's intentions. Because the nations are full of violence and inhumanity to people in other nations, God will destroy these violent nations. Because Israel has oppressed its own people, it will also suffer defeat. The uniformity of structure within each oracle is very consistent, thus the final expanded and irregular prophecy against Israel stands out from the rest.

The surprising transformation of the normally positive climax into a negative statement demonstrates the prophet's rhetorical abilities and his deep passion to communicate God's work to his own people. He presents his message in a form which captures the mind of the listener and demands their acceptance. He pricks the nation's conscience because he requires them to evaluate their nationalistic expectations and to recognize their failures.

---

[1]G. Fohrer, "Remarks on Modern Interpretations of the Prophets," *JBL* 80 (1961) 309-19, gives many examples of the misuse of form criticism and identifies two misconceptions which pervade most form-critical works. Some believe that when a prophet uses a specific form of speech that he also takes with him the setting, and he functions in the role of an individual in the original setting (priest, judge, singer, king). Fohrer calls this uncritical romanticism. His second criticism is that form and content are not always distinguished. The utilization of a form is not determined by its content, for one motif can be used in many different speeches and for quite diverse purposes.

Background

Three areas of background need to be investigated: (1) the literary background of the oracles in Amos 1:3—2:16, (2) the setting and use of similar oracles, and (3) the theological perspective which provided the basis for the accusations within these oracles.

(1) Literary texts predicting the defeat of an enemy are common before the time of Amos. Christensen divides the pre-Amos war oracles into four types.[2] Oracular divinations (by means of the ephod, a fleece, or urim and thummim) were obtained before going into battle to determine if or when an attack should begin (Judg. 1:1-2; 7:9-14; 20:23-28; 1 Sam. 14:18-19; Hos. 4:12). These deal with the theme of war; but the means by which the message was obtained, the literary structure, and the setting are foreign to the prophecies against the nations in Amos. The second group, the summons to battle (Numb. 14:41-43; 21:34; 31:1-4; Josh. 6:1-5; 8:1-8; Judges 19-20), is closer to later prophetic oracles, but these and the third category, the summons to flight, provide only a general theological and lexical background for Amos and the later prophets.[3] All of these prophecies picture God as a warrior who controls the history of the nations and fights for his people. The final type, the prophecy of victory or defeat, found in the Balaam oracle in Numbers 24:15-24, has the most similarities with Amos. It contains a long series of prophecies against several nations and is not a call to war. His oracle served as a discouragement to Balak and as a message of assurance to Israel. In spite of some similarities, the purpose and the formal structure of Balaam's prophecies is different from Amos 1:3—2:16. These comparisons show that holy war ideology influenced the theology of Amos and provided ideas and phrases, but the overall structure and function of the oracles against the nations in Amos were not taken directly from earlier known war oracles.[4] The

---

[2] D. Christensen, *Transformations of the War Oracle in Old Testament Prophecy* (Missoula: Scholars Press, 1975) 1-15.

[3] Many examples given by Christensen, *Transformations of the War Oracle* 38-48, N. Gottwald, *All the Kingdoms of the Earth* 47-85; J. H. Hayes, "The Usage of Oracles against Foreign Nations in Ancient Israel," *JBL* 87 (1968) 81-84, are of general interest for comparison (they contain condemnations of the enemies, a promise of victory, provide encouragement, demonstrate God's sovereignty and use similar vocabulary); Y. Hoffman, "From Oracle to Prophecy: The Growth, Crystalization and Disintegration of a Biblical Gattung," *JNSL* 10 (1982) 75-81, contends that Amos transformed the "Oracle Before Battle" by filling it with new content. These early non-moralistic nationalistic salvation oracles were refocused by basing the judgment on sin and by highlighting the universal power and justice of God rather than the national salvation of Israel. Various Psalms (20, 21, 60, 91) also provide a general theological setting. See G. von Rad's discussion of the holy war in Isaiah's oracles against the nations in his *Old Testament Theology*, II (New York: Harper and Row, 1965) 156-65.

[4] J. Barton, *Amos's Oracles Against the Nations* (Cambridge: Cambridge University, 1980) 9, and R. E. Clements, *Prophecy and Tradition* (Atlanta: John Knox, 1975) 70-71, deny the holy war setting because Amos was not trying to give assurance to Israel; Israel was not at war with all the nations; some of the nations have not offended Israel; and because it is never said that Israel will defeat these nations (it also will suffer defeat).

terminology and rhetoric of the first six oracles may include political war propaganda in order to gain audience acceptance, but the climax is a clear break from expected tradition.

Calls to battle and promises of victory over an enemy are found in the literature of other nations in the ancient Near East. Assyrian and Babylonian prophets predict the military defeat of the king's enemy with assurances like, "I am Ishtar of Arbela, O Esarhaddon, King of Assyria...your gracious leader am I...I have given you confidence...your foes I shall crush" (*ANET* 449-51, 604-06). The prophets from Mari predict, through the god Dagon, that Zimrilim would be successful in his military conquest of Babylon.[5] The Hittites also pronounced curses on their enemies before a battle (*ANET* 354-55). These include an indictment, "The Kashkean people also began war. From the Hittites ye took away their cities" and a punishment clause which calls for revenge. The Egyptian execration texts contained curses on the nation's enemies (*ANET* 328-29). These examples are somewhat similar to Old Testament prophecies before battles.

(2) Some suggest that the ritual setting of the Mari, Hittite, and Egyptian prophecies, and the presence of similar themes at the end of the laments in Psalms 20, 21, 60 and 2 Kings 19:14-28, provide a hypothetical setting for the oracles against the nations in the prophets. Within this reconstruction, the oracles against other nations function as "salvation oracles."[6] The prophet is one of the cultic personnel, and he announces the Lord's response of salvation to Israel's lament concerning her enemies. In order to account for the negative message against Israel in Amos, Würthwein advocates a transformation of Amos into a prophet of doom at a later date. At this time the final section of 2:6-16 was added at the end of the salvation oracle.[7] The ritual ceremonies where these prophecies were used may have been the feast of tabernacles (Würthwein), a covenant renewal festival (Reventlow), or a royal court ceremony at the king's coronation at the beginning of each new year.[8] Bentzen's reconstruction of the background of Amos 1 and 2 from the Egyptian execration texts was accepted by N. Gottwald and further developed along

---

[5]Hayes, "Oracles against Foreign Nations," 84-86; A. Malamat, "Prophetic Revelations in New Documents from Mari and Bible," *Volume du congrès Genève 1965* SVT 15 (Leiden: Brill, 1966) 214-19.

[6]Hayes, "Oracles against Foreign Nations," 87-89.

[7]E. Würthwein, "Amos-Studien," *ZAW* 62 (1950) 10-52. This view has not gained acceptance. It destroys the unity of Amos 1:3—2:16, and it is based on Amos' change from being only a prophet of salvation to one who only gives messages of doom, by making a strong division between the first two visions in 7:1-6 and the later ones. The cultic association and the context of lament are not found in Amos 1-2.

[8]For these views see E. Würthwein, "Der Ursprung der prophetischen Gerichtsrede," *ZTK* 59 (1962) 1-16; H. G. Reventlow, *Das Amt des Propheten bei Amos* FRLANT (Göttingen: Vandenhoeck and Ruprecht, 1962) 56-75; S. Mowinckel, *The Psalms in Israel's Worship*, I (Nashville: Abingdon, 1962) 154; H. J. Kraus, *Worship in Israel* (Richmond: John Knox, 1965) 222-24; Bentzen, "Ritual Background," 91-94.

royal lines by Hayes, but Wolff, Rudolph, and Weiss have shown how weak and untenable this view is.[9] The language and form of the execration texts, the order of the nations, the basis for the condemnation, and the role of the divine power are distinct in Amos. Although common themes are developed, the positive evidence for a cultic setting is very weak. One must agree with Clements' judgment that Amos has been influenced by many areas of Israelite life, that no one setting can explain the oracles against the foreign nations in Amos, and that Amos is probably developing a somewhat new form of prophetic speech.[10]

Some of the later prophetic oracles against the nations (Isa. 14:1-4; 17:13-14; Jer. 46:27-28; 50:4-5, 19-20; 51:8-10, 45-46; Ezek. 28:25-26; 29:21) were employed to give assurance to God's people.[11] Other oracles were intended to discourage Israel's dependence on foreign allies (Isa. 19:1-15; Jeremiah 46; Ezekiel 29-32). The inclusion of prophecies against Israel in Isaiah 22:1-14, the positive conclusions at the end of some prophecies against the nations (Isa. 19:19-25; Jer. 48:47; 49:6, 39), and the primary concern for condemnation of sins against God and humanity (not specifically Israel), indicate that the establishment of right conduct and God's rule is more important than nationalistic goals. Amos 1:3—2:16 does not condemn the nations for sins against "Israel" or "my people," although this could be the general intent in some cases. The focus is not on the ones sinned against; the emphasis is on each nation's responsibility for its own inhumanity. In the structure of each oracle Amos contrasts the nation's guilt ("for three rebellious acts ...because they have") with God's rule and judgment ("I will not vacillate...I will send fire"). A sense of false assurance is initially provided for the militant nationalist, but the final pair of oracles dash all such hopes. This false sense of assurance is derived from the purpose and general conceptual framework of the war oracles against other nations. By removing the content and structure of the oracles from the setting of a military campaign, Amos was able to awaken the nation to its own responsibility for inhumanity.

(3) This emphasis on national responsibility raises a question concerning the theological perspective of the accusations in Amos 1:3—2:16. Those who find the background of these prophecies in earlier war oracles or the cult believe that a strong nationalistic theology is behind the prophet's thinking.[12] The nations have injured God's people; therefore they will be punished. The

---

[9]Gottwald, *Kingdoms* 112; Hayes, "Oracles against Foreign Nations," 90-91; Wolff, *Amos* 145-47; Rudolph, *Amos* 131 and M. Weiss, "The Pattern of the 'Execration Text' in the Prophetic Literature," *IEJ* 19 (1969) 150-57.

[10]Clements, *Prophecy and Tradition* 66-67, 72.

[11]Erlandsson, *Burden of Babylon* 65-66.

[12]Y. Hoffman, "From Oracle to Prophecy: The Growth, Crystalization and Disintegration of a Biblical Gattung," *JNSL* (1982) 75-78, rejects the nationalistic view of the oracles against foreign nations in the prophets.

phrase "brotherly obligations" (1:9) could refer to a notice of the earlier covenant relationship (under Yahweh) which united these nations during the period of David under the *imperium* of God. By logical extension, the covenant
norms are applied to the nations, and the curses are based on their breach of
these covenant laws.[13]

This attractive hypothesis, which integrates the final Davidic oracle of salvation in Amos with the first oracle of doom, reconstructs a dubious theological base for Amos 1:3—2:16. The imposition of covenant theology over all
of Amos 1-2 is unjustified, for the "covenant of brothers" in 1:9 refers specifically to a political treaty between Israel and Tyre, a country which never
was part of the Davidic empire. The judgment of Israel in Amos 2 and on the
Day of the Lord in Amos 5-6, as well as God's negative attitude to Israel's
present acquisition of control over much of Solomon's empire (6:12-13), are
not based on Israel's rejection, or any other nation's rejection, of the unified
national ideal under David. The universalism of Amos is clear, but the nations were not always seen through the Judean theological perspective of the
covenant. Each was responsible for its actions before Yahweh, the ruler of all
nations; both those within and those outside the covenant.[14]

The basis for the accusations against the nations is a more universal law of
right and wrong which is based on conscience, national legal codes, international treaty rights, and a common sense of morality.[15] Responsibility for ignoring such conventional principles cannot be avoided. The guilt of those
accused is beyond the question of debate (even Ashdod and Egypt know what
is right, 3:9-10) and is not dependent on the offending nation's acceptance of
a foreign theological covenant. Each nation is responsible before God for its
inhuman treatment of others. Israel's rejection of God's grace (2:9-10) and
the inhuman treatment of her own people (2:6-8) are even greater acts of rebellion. The even-handed judgment of God will fall on each nation. The logic
of the prophet's case is unavoidable; Israel and its neighbors are responsible
for their rebellion and will be judged. The prophet constructs his oracles in
such a convincing way that Israel's assent to the first oracles against other na

---

[13]G. E. Wright, "The Nations in Hebrew Prophecy," *Enc* 26 (1965) 236; J. Mauchline, "Implicit Signs of a Persistent Belief in the Davidic Empire," *VT* 20 (1970) 288-90; Christensen,
Transformations of the War Oracle 55-75.

[14]See the discussion of this issue in Barton, *Oracles Against the Nations* 39-45. The strong
trend to relate all curses to a covenant relationship shows a similarity of ideology and morality
but often that is all. F. C. Fensham, "Common Trends in Curses of the Near Eastern Treaties
and *Kudurru* Inscriptions Compared with the Maledictions of Amos and Isaiah," *ZAW* 75 (1963)
155-76.

[15]G. H. Jones, "An Examination of Some Leading Motifs in the Prophetic Oracles against
the Nations," an unpublished Ph.D. dissertation at University College of North Wales, Bangor, 1970 and Barton, *Oracles Against the Nations* 42-61 survey the commonly accepted
norms of international behavior in Hittite, Egyptian, and Babylonian literature. This should
not be understood as binding international law but as a common morality which is often
expressed in treaties, law codes, and international correspondence.

tions requires them to accept the inevitability of their own judgment.

The life-setting of Amos 1-2 cannot be located in a ritual ceremony, a new year's, or a covenant festival. The location is unknown, but Samaria, the center of the military power, is likely. This oracle logically precedes chapters 3-6 and was probably delivered at the beginning of the prophet's career. There is nothing inconsistent about hypothesizing a national day of significance as the occasion for the prophet to deliver his message, but if his prophecies were delivered at such an event, the influence of the setting has not penetrated the fiber of the text enough to make it a prime criterion for understanding the message of the prophet. Such an hypothesis adds realism to the message, but the danger of contriving a false reality forces one to give less attention to the unknown physical setting and more attention to the historical, theological, and rhetorical function of these oracles.

Jeroboam II was ascending to the height of his power around 765 B.C. He had won back control over a few tracts of land which formerly belonged to Solomon's empire. Israel was a nation obsessed with the defeat and exploitation of its neighbors through war. Political predictions of further conquests in neighboring lands were part of the nation's propaganda campaign (6:1-2, 13); thus the first seven oracles against the foreign nations would have gained an immediate positive response. By the inclusion of a negative oracle against Israel instead of a final salvation oracle, Amos transforms the total package into a devastating critique.

Structure and Unity

Structure

The paragraphs within the larger unit of 1:3—2:16 are divided by the introductory words "thus says Yahweh, for three rebellious acts of..." A careful analysis of the paragraphs reveals several common elements: (1) the source of the message: "thus says Yahweh"; (2) an indictment: "for three rebellious acts and because of four, I will not revoke...because they have..."; (3) the punishment: "therefore I will send fire upon..."; and (4) a concluding divine confirmation formula: "says Yahweh." These structural markers define the eight paragraphs within 1:3—2:16. The paragraphs can be further grouped into pairs by means of various rhetorical, structural, and lexical criteria. Because of the length of this long unit, it is convenient to discuss the material in two segments. The first will include the first six oracles (the first three pairs) in 1:3—2:3, and the second part will include the last two oracles in 2:4-16. This division of the text does not imply disunity within 1:3—2:16,[16] it merely facilitates the discussion of the material into more manageable blocks.

---

[16]Würthwein, "Amos-Studien," 10-52 denies the unity of 1:3—2:16 and supposes that Amos gave 1:3—2:3 as a salvation oracle for Israel. Later he became a prophet of doom and added the rest of Chapter 2.

Oracles Against the Nations
Amos 1:3—2:3

1:3

Thus says Yahweh,
    because of 3 rebellious acts of Damascus
  and because of 4,
I will not vacillate about it,[a]
    [b]because they have threshed Gilead
      with iron threshing sledges.[b]

A. God's judgment against Syria
1. Source of the message
2. Indictment concerning Damascus
   a. Because of great sinfulness
   b. Accountability is demanded
   c. Specific sin described

1:4

So I will send fire on the house of Hazael,
    and it will devour the palace-fortresses[c] of Benhadad.[d]
I will break the gate bar of Damascus.
I will cut off the inhabitants[e] from the Valley of Aven;[f]
    the one who holds the sceptre from Beth Eden[g] **1:5**
    and the people of Syria will go into exile in Kir,[h]
says Yahweh.

3. Punishment of destruction
   a. On the secure palace-fortresses
   b. On the people in the chief cities
   c. Those left will be exiled
4. Divine confirmation formula

1:6

Thus says Yahweh,
    because of 3 rebellious acts of Gaza
  and because of 4,
I will not vacillate about it,
    because they took captive whole[i] masses of captives
      in order to deliver them to Edom.[j]

B. God's judgment against Philistia
1. Source of the message
2. Indictment concerning Gaza
   a. Because of great sinfulness
   b. Accountability is demanded
   c. Specific sin described

1:7

So I will send fire on the wall of Gaza,
    and it will devour her palace-fortresses.

3. Punishment of destruction
   a. On their secure palace-fortresses

I will cut off the inhabitants from Ashdod,   **1:8**   b. On the people
    the one who holds the sceptre from Ashkelon.   in the chief
I will turn my hand against Ekron,   cities
    and the rest of the Philistines will perish,   c. Those left will
says the Lord Yahweh.   perish
                                       4. Divine
                                         confirmation for-
                                       mula

                                 1:9   C. God's judgment
                                     against Tyre
Thus says Yahweh,   1. Source of the
    because of 3 rebellious acts of Tyre   message
and because of 4,   2. Indictment con-
I will not vacillate about it,   cerning Tyre
    because they delivered a whole mass[j] of captives to Edom,[j]   a. Because of
        and they did not remember their covenant of   great sin-
        brotherhood.   fulness
                                         b. Accountability
                                       is demanded
                                       c. Specific sin
                                       described

                             1:10   3. Punishment of
So I will send fire on the wall of Tyre,   destruction
    and it shall devour her palace-fortresses.   a. On their se-
                                         cure palace-
                                         fortresses

                             1:11 D. God's judgment
                                     against Edom
Thus says Yahweh,   1. Source of the
    because of 3 rebellious acts of Edom   message
and because of 4,   2. Indictment
I will not vacillate about it,   against Edom
    because he pursued his brother with the sword   a. Because of
        and destroyed his kinship affection;[k]   great sin-
        his anger tore[l] relentlessly,[m]   fulness
        his wrath kept going[n] forever.   b. Accountability
                                       is demanded
                                       c. Specific sin
                                       described

                             1:12   3. Punishment of
So I will send fire on Teman,   destruction
    and it shall devour the palace-fortresses of Bozrah.   a. On their se-
                                         cure palace-
                                         fortresses

1:13 E. God's judgment against Ammon
    1. Source of the message

Thus says Yahweh,
    because of 3 rebellious acts of Ammon
and because of 4,
I will not vacillate about it,
    because they have ripped open the pregnant women[o]
      of Gilead
      in order to enlarge their borders.

    2. Indictment against Ammon
      a. Because of great sinfulness
      b. Accountability is demanded
      c. Specific sin described

1:14 3. Punishment of destruction

So I will kindle[p] a fire on the walls of Rabbah,
    and it will devour her palace-fortresses,
    amid a war cry on the day of battle,
    amid a whirlwind[q] on the day of storm.[r]
So their king[s] will go into captivity,
    he[t] and his officials together,
says Yahweh.

      a. On the secure palace-fortresses
      b. In the day of battle
1:15   c. Leaders will be exiled
    4. Divine confirmation formula

2:1 F. God's judgment against Moab
    1. Source of the message

Thus says Yahweh,
    because of 3 rebellious acts of Moab
and because of 4,
I will not vacillate about it,
    because he burned[u] to lime the bones of the
      king of Edom.[u]

    2. Indictment concerning Moab
      a. Because of great sinfulness
      b. Accountability is demanded
      c. Specific sin described

2:2 3. Punishment of destruction

So I will send fire on Moab,
    and it will devour the palace-fortresses of Kerioth;[v]
    amid a battle-roar[w] Moab will die,
    amid a war-cry and the blast of the trumpet,
    thus I will cut off the judge from her[x] midst
    and I will slay all her[x] officials with him,
says Yahweh.

      3. On the secure palace-fortresses
      b. In the day of battle
      c. Leaders will perish
    4. Divine confirmation formula

1:3a. The Syriac Peshitta and Targum have a plural suffix "them," but the textual evidence for the singular "it" is very strong. The verb is "forgive" in the Targum, and Sym. has "I will not accept him."

1:3b-b. A Qumran fragment of Amos 1:3 [M. Baillet, et al. *DJD* 3 (1962) 173] has what appears to be "the pregnant ones of Gilead," which is identical to the Old Greek translation. This is parallel to Amos 1:13 and may be based on the events described in 2 Kings 8:12.

1:4c. The "palace-fortresses" is translated "foundations" in the Old Greek in 1:4, 7, 10, 12, 14; 2:2, 5 but "country" in 3:9, 10 and 6:8.[17] Aq. and Sym. have "large house" and Theod. uses "court, palace."

1:4d. The Hebrew "*h*ᵃ*dād*" is written *hader* in the Old Greek. This indicates either a confusion between *r* and *d,* a purposeful change to remove the reference to the god Hadad (Rudolph, *Amos* 126), or a dialectical reproduction of the Assyrian *Adad-idri* which also ends with an "r" sound (see 1 Chron. 18:3 where some MSS have "Hadar" instead of "Hadad").

1:5e. *yôšēb* may be translated "one who sits, rules" parallel to "the one who holds the sceptre" in the next line,[18] or it may be a collective (GKC 145 b-d; BDB 442) and translated "those who dwell, inhabitants"[19] as in the Old Greek "inhabitants." Both solutions make sense, but neither is required by the context.

1:5f. The Old Greek translators render the Hebrew *'āwen* with the transliteration *ōn* (reflecting a different vocalization than the Masoretic tradition) and connect the city with Baalbek. As a center for sun worship, it may have had the same name as the Egyptian city, On (Gen. 41:45; Ezek. 30:17) or Heliopolis, the "sun city." The Greek versions translate the word but represent a text closer to the Masoretic vocalization: Aq. "uselessness," Sym. "wickedness."

1:5g. Eden is "Haran" in the Greek, which may be a scribal error of *d* for *r* (Harper, *Amos* 129) or a clarification of where Eden is (Wolff, *Amos* 129). Sym. transliterates the word as "Eden" while Theod. translates it with "luxury."

1:5h. Kir is translated "chosen" in the Old Greek, but it is transliterated in the versions. The Vulgate connects the site with Cyrene.

1:6, 9i. The Hebrew "whole, complete, peaceful" is transliterated "of Solomon" in the Old Greek translation (also in 1:9) to show that the captives were Israelites, but Sym., Theod. and Aq. have "complete, whole."

1:6j, 9. M. Haran, "Observations on the Historical Background of Amos 1:2—2:6" *IEJ* 18 (1968) 206 changes Edom to Aram (*d* to *r*) in this verse and in 1:9. The Old Greek has "Idumea," a term which refers to the land of Edom.

1:11k. The Old Greek translation has "he destroyed [his] mother/womb upon the earth" which understands the Hebrew *rhm* to mean "womb, maiden" instead of "compassion, pity." D. L. Christensen, "The Prosodic Structure of Amos 1-2," *HTR* 67 (1974) 431 believes "upon the earth" is a Greek attempt to translate "Edom," which they confused with "land" *'ādām*.

1:11l. The Hebrew "and he tore" is sometimes emended to a similar root "he kept" to agree with the Syriac and Vulgate.[20] This change improves the parallelism between these two poetic lines and is encouraged by the parallel use of these terms in Jer. 3:5 and Ps. 103:9. Wolff, *Amos* 130 rejects this change because: (1) the Old Greek supports the Hebrew text; (2) the present text has a parallel in Job 16:9; (3) "he kept his anger" is not used elsewhere; and (4) the syntax supports the unemended text.

1:11m. *lā'ad* "continually, relentlessly" is a good parallel to "forever" in the last line, but the Old Greek used a different vocalization and translated the word "witness" from *lā'ēd* (with a sere). The other Greek versions have "forever."

1:11n. The vocalization of the verb "kept going" is unusual, so many commentators

[17]P. Heawood, "*'rmnôt* and *'rm*," *JTS* 13 (1912) 66-73.

[18]Hammershaimb, *Amos* 27; Rudolph, *Amos* 126; Wolff, *Amos* 129.

[19]Fosbroke, *Amos* 779; Harper, *Amos* 19; Mays, *Amos* 29.

[20]Cripps, *Amos* 131; Harper, *Amos* 33; M. Fishbane, "The Treaty Background of Amos 1:11 and Related Matters," *JBL* 89 (1970) 317 n 21; M. Haran, "Observations on the Historical Background of Amos 1:2-2:6," *IEJ* 18 (1968) 207 n 17.

revocalize it to read "he kept (it) forever." The final *h* has no mappik in it to indicate that it is the pronominal suffix "it." GKC 58 g explains the final *h* as a pronominal suffix which does not have the mappik because of the retraction of the tone, while Wolff, *Amos* 131 revocalizes the form to a regular third, feminine, singular verb. "Forever" is translated "victory" in the Old Greek text.

1:13o. Harper, *Amos* 36 changes *hārôt* "pregnant women" to *harîm* "mountains."

1:14p. "I will kindle" replaces the usual "I will send" and Wolff, *Amos* 131, 161 suggests that this reading is derived from the Ammon oracle in Jer. 49:2 and inserted here by a later scribe. If this were the case, one would expect the Damascus oracle in Jer. 49:27 to have influenced Amos 1:4-5, but this is not the case. The Old Greek recognized the change in the verb and gives "I will kindle" instead of the usual "I will send."

1:14q. The Hebrew noun "whirlwind" is translated in the Old Greek text "he shall be stirred up" as if the noun were a verb.

1:14r. Hebrew *sûpāh* "storm" is translated "her end" in the Greek. This interpretation is derived from the root *sōp* "end" plus the *h* pronominal suffix instead of *sûpāh*.

1:15s. Hebrew *malkām* "their king" was understood to be a reference to the Ammonite god "Milkom" in Aq. and Sym. and Jer. 49:1, 3 (in the Old Greek this is Jer. 30:1, 3). Some commentators accept Milkom as the proper reading,[21] but "officials" forms a much better parallel with "king" than the name of a god. Amos does not oppose religious beliefs but inhumanity in these oracles.

1:15t. The Old Greek, Sym., Aq. and Theod. have "their priests" which is conflated from Jer. 49:3 (Old Greek, 30:3).

2:1u-u. W. F. Albright has revocalized the line to read "because he burns bones...of a human sacrifice to a demon." A second approach to the line is Harper's translation, "In order to desecrate the dead because of violence done to Moab," which is modeled after the purpose clause in 1:13. J. Morgenstern believes the final word "to line" is a corruption of the name of an Edomite king, which most philologists properly reject.[22]

2:2v. "Kerioth" is translated "of its cities" in the Old Greek because it was not recognized as the name of a city. Some suggest that the definite article on Kerioth should be connected to the preceding word and serve as its suffix, similar to 1:7, 10, 14. Some proper nouns do take an article (GKC 125e).

2:2w. The Hebrew "amid a battle roar" is translated in the Old Greek as "without power," but the Hebrew text gives a much better parallel with the next line.

2:3x. The feminine pronominal suffix is sometimes changed to a masculine because in 2:2b Moab (the people) is connected to a masculine verb "he will die." The land of Moab is feminine (GKC 122h) and therefore the suffix is properly feminine. "With him" refers to the judge in the preceding line.

The relationships between the paragraphs is based on three structural characteristics: (1) the length of the indictment clause which describes the specific sins; (2) the length of the punishment clause; and (3) the inclusion or omission of the final divine confirmation formula. The structural outline contains the following characteristics:[23]

---

[21]E. Puech, "Milkom, Le Dieu Ammonite, en Amos 1:15," *VT* 17 (1967) 117-23; D. L. Christensen, "The Prosodic Structure of Amos 1-2," *HTR* 67 (1974) 432-34; Driver, *Amos* 146.

[22]W. F. Albright, *Yahweh and the Gods of Canaan* (Garden City: Doubleday, 1968) 209; Harper, *Amos* 38, 41; J. Morgenstern, "Amos-Studies," *HUCA* 32 (1961) 314-15.

[23]Christensen, "Prosodic Structure," 428-29, 434-36 comes to somewhat similar conclusions about the first six paragraphs. His identification of conflated material applies some unrealistic restrictions on prophetic style.

PATTERN A	PATTERN B
Paragraph 1 and 2	*Paragraph 3 and 4*
Specific sins: 1 or 2 clauses	2 or 4 clauses
Punishment: 6 clauses	2 clauses
Divine confirmation: included	omitted

Paragraph 5 and 6	*Paragraph 7*	*Paragraph 8*
Specific sins: 1 or 2 clauses	4 clauses	4 clauses lengthy and unique
Punishment: 6 clauses	2 clauses	2 clauses lengthy and unique
Divine confirmation: included	omitted	included twice

Lexical similarities provide a second criterion for dividing the paragraphs into pairs. The first two paragraphs refer to "cutting off the inhabitants" and "the one who holds the scepter" (1:5, 8), paragraphs 3 and 4 condemn offenses against one's "brother" (1:9, 11), and paragraphs 5 and 6 described "shouting" in the time of war and the removal of princes and rulers (1:14-15; 2:2-3).

A lexical interconnection also explains the order of the paragraphs. Paragraphs 3 and 4 follow 1 and 2, because 2 and 3 contain the common phrase "delivered a whole mass of captives to Edom" (1:6, 9). Paragraphs 3 and 4 are not connected to 5 and 6 by any lexical repetition, but 1:11 and 1:13 contain conceptual connections.[24] Judah and Israel are last for rhetorical reasons.

The internal structure of each paragraph is varied only by the lengthening of the prophet's description of that nation's specific sins or a more detailed account of their punishment. When several clauses are used to describe a nation's sins, the normal "because of " plus an infinitive construct begins the series, but this is followed by a number of different grammatical structures. The punishment clauses consistently begin with a conjunction plus a first person singular, perfect verb, "therefore I will send" plus a perfect third feminine singular "it shall consume." When this clause is lengthened (1:5, 8, 14-15; 2:2-3) a variety of parallel and complementary grammatical constructions are employed. Although these variations seem to be purposely designed within the oracles to give a paired structure, some exegetes understand these variations very differently.

Unity

Historical references, which reflect a date later than Amos, and literary inconsistencies are used as criteria to deny the authenticity of short sections in 1:3—2:16. The oracles which receive the severest questions are the prophe-

---

[24]S. M. Paul, "Amos 1:2—2:3; A Concatenous Literary Pattern," *JBL* 90 (1971) 401-03 defines the lexical connections between the paragraphs and proposes the dubious translation of "compassion" as "woman" in 1:11 to parallel 1:13.

cies against Tyre in 1:9-10, Edom in 1:11-12, Judah in 2:4-5, and the short segment against Israel in 2:9-10. The authenticity of the Philistine oracle in 1:6-8 was rejected by Marti, but his view has not gained acceptance.[25]

The oracle against Edom (1:11-12) is considered secondary because it reflects a later historical period and because it does not follow the structure of the other oracles in 1:3-216.[26] :If the "pursuing of his brother with the sword" is connected with the activities of Edom at the fall of Jerusalem in 587/6 B.C., the verse must be a later addition. This dating holds that Jeremiah 49:7-22; Obadiah 11-14; Ezekiel 25:12-14; 35:1-15 and Lamentations contain descriptions of Edom's exploitation of Judah in 587/6 B.C. which are parallel to Amos 1:11. Three objections to this interpretation are: (1) the history of Judah's relationship with Edom is full of incidents before the time of Amos which could be the source of the condemnation in 1:11 (see the exegesis of 1:11); (2) specific reference to Edom's behavior at Jerusalem, which is found in the later prophets, is not present in Amos; instead, Amos refers to a long-term policy of revenge and hatred toward his brother; (3) the intense condemnation of Edom in later prophets is absent in Amos' account. These differences imply that the prophecy in Amos came before 587/86 B.C.[27]

More recent studies focus on the form-critical irregularities in the Edom prophecy.[28] The expanded indictment clauses, the shortened punishment clause, and the omission of the final divine confirmation formula break the formal pattern and are seen as evidence of disunity. Amos 1:11 is considered a "pale generalization" of 1:3b and 1:13b, thus a later redactor's work. Re-

---

[25]K. Marti, *Amos* (Tübingen: Mohr, 1904) 160-61 argues that 1:6-8 reflects historical circumstances after Sargon's defeat of Gath in 711 B.C. (Gath is omitted in 1:6-8); is based on Joel 3:4-8; lacks originality and interrupts the natural geographic progression. The defeat of Gath by Hazael (2 Kings 12:17) and Uzziah (2 Chron. 26:6) before the time of Amos, instead of Sargon's defeat, may explain the decline of Gath and its absence in 1:6-8.

[26]Fosbroke, *Amos* 782; Mays, *Amos* 25, 36; Wolff, *Amos* 140, 160; Barton, *Oracles Against the Nations* 22-24 and W. H. Schmidt, "Die deuteronomistische Redaktion des Amosbuches," *ZAW* 77 (1965) 174-28, reject the oracle. G. Pfeifer, "Denkformenanalyse als exegetische Methode, erläutert an Amos 1, 2-2, 16," *ZAW* 88 (1976) 56-71, finds a "movement of thought" characterized by repetition, concreteness, and consistency in the oracles against Damascus, Ammon, Moab, and Israel. The Philistine oracle lacks concreteness, the Tyre and Edom oracles reflect attitudes, and the Judah oracle denounces disobedience to the law. These follow a different flow of thought, so Pfeifer concludes that they were not written by Amos. On the other hand W. Rudolph, "Die angefochtenen Völkersprüche in Amos 1 and 2," *Schalom. Studien zu Glaube und Geschichte Israels*, ed. K. H. Bernhardt (Stuttgart: Calwer, 1971) 45-49, defends the genuineness of all the sayings against the nations except the last line of 1:11 and the last line of 2:4. He properly rejects objections based on exaggerated expectations of schematic uniformity which deny creative freedom of expression to the author.

[27]Bentzen, "Ritual Background," 91 n 14; Hammershaimb, *Amos* 38; Christensen, *Transformation of the War Oracle* 67; Paul, "A Concatenous Literary Pattern," 400; K. N. Schoville, "A Note on the Oracles against Gaza, Tyre and Edom," *SVT* 26 (1974) 55-63; Haran, "Historical Background of Amos 1:2-2:6," 207-212, who also cites Kaufmann's positive view on the Edom oracle.

[28]Wolff, *Amos* 140 and Barton, *Oracles against the Nations* 22.

ventlow solves the uniformity problem by emending all the oracles down to a basic one-line accusation and a one-line punishment clause; thus, most of the Edom oracle is kept.[29] Both of these approaches err because they demand absolute uniformity.[30] Total uniformity is not found in other prophetic literary genre and should not be expected here.[31] Variations within formal structures enable the prophet to create emphasis, to build structure into a pattern, to make comparisons, and to break monotony. The irregular pattern in the Edom oracle fits the paired structure of these oracles and is a positive sign of the purposeful design of these oracles. The Edom oracle is not a later addition; indeed, it would be peculiar if this close neighbor was omitted.

The case against the authenticity of the Tyre oracle in 1:9-10 is similar yet weaker than the evidence against the Edom oracle, for there is no historical problem in accepting the words against Tyre. Its unity with the other oracles is questioned because: (1) it also has a long indictment, a short punishment statement, and no confirmation formula; (2) it seems to be dependent on the accusation against the Philistines in 1:6b; and (3) it contains various deuteronomistic signs.[32] The first two objections relate to the purposeful design and structure of the oracles. Wolff's rejection of the interpretation which connects "remembering the covenant of brothers" with the treaty relationship between Tyre and David (2 Sam. 5:11), Solomon (1 Kings 5:1-12) and Ahab (1 Kings 16:31), and his preference for a deuteronomistic explanation, has not gained acceptance, for it runs counter to biblical and lexical evidence (see the exegesis of 1:9). The Tyre oracle matches the structural variations in the Edom oracle and is a necessary complement to it, if the prophet's pairing of the oracles is to be uniform and complete.

Interpretation

A. God's Judgment Against Syria (1:3-5)

1. The source of the message (1:3a)

The prophet's speech begins with a statement that identifies the original

---

[29]Reventlow, *Amos* 52-62, omits parts of the long punishment (1:5, 8, 14-15; 2:2-3) and indictment clauses (1:9, 11; 2:4) in order to maintain a consistent pattern. Christensen, *Transformation of the War Oracles*, 59-72 also finds secondary additions. J. Priest, "The Covenant of Brothers," *JBL* 84 (1965) 405-06, takes the position that all the oracles were originally long (just the opposite of Reventlow).

[30]Rudolph, *Amos* 119 argues for allowing the prophets creative freedom.

[31]C. Westermann, *Basic Forms of Prophetic Speech* (Philadelphia: Westminster, 1967) 169-89, gives examples of the modification and amplification of judgment speeches. Variations in Amos 1-2 include: The usual "I will send" is "I will kindle" in 1:14; "says the Lord" in 1:5, 15; 2:3 is "says the Lord Yahweh" in 1:8; "declares Yahweh" in 2:11, 16 is omitted in 1:10, 12:2:5.

[32]Wolff, *Amos* 158-59 identifies the references to exile, remember, and brother as deuteronomic.

author of the message. "Thus says Yahweh" introduces a statement by God thirteen times in Amos (1:3, 6, 9, 11; 2:1, 4, 6; 3:11, 12; 5:3, 4, 16; 7:17), and all of the examples in chapters 1 and 2 come at the beginning of a new oracle. This introductory phrase is called a "messenger speech formula."[33] When a messenger delivers a message, it is normal to introduce the one sending the message. An example of this is found in the narrative of Genesis 32:3-4. Jacob sends messengers to Esau with the instructions, "Thus you shall say to Esau: 'Thus says your servant Jacob, I have sojourned with Laban.' " In Amos 7:11 Amaziah reports to Jeroboam saying, "Thus Amos has said, 'Jeroboam shall die by the sword.'" This messenger formula is found in the Mari correspondence (*ANET* 624-25) where Zimrilim says, "To my lord say: 'Thus says your servant.' " This method of introducing the word of God is commonplace in the prophets (especially Jeremiah and Ezekiel) and indicates that God is the author of the words of the prophets.

2. The indictment concerning Damascus (1:3*a-b*)

a. Because of great sinfulness (1:3*a*). The message begins with a graded numerical saying, "Because of three rebellious acts of Damascus and because of four." Such sayings occur in the Old Testament, the Ugaritic epic of Baal and Anat, the Aramaic story of Aḥiqar from Elephantine, and in other Jewish literature.[34] The significance of this type of saying is still debated. Some hold that numerical sequences refer to a large indefinite number of sins.[35] It is an idiomatic or rhetorical device which should not be taken literally. Although this view fits many examples, the actual listing of the items after some sequences has led others to conclude that the highest number should be understood literally.[36] These nations have committed three sins, which is bad enough; but when the fourth is added, it creates an excessive number of sins which cannot be forgiven or ignored by God's hand of judgment.[37] A third view takes three and four to be components of the number seven, the number which symbolizes completeness. This conclusion is supported by the

---

[33]Westermann, *Basic Forms of Prophetic Speech* 98-128.

[34]Biblical examples include Deut. 32:30; Ps. 62:11[Heb 62:12]; Job 33:14; 40:5 (one and two), Hos. 6:2 (two and three), Job 5:19; Prov. 6:16 (six and seven), Micah 5:5 (Heb. 5:4) (seven and eight). Three and four are used in Amos 1-2; Prov. 30:15, 18, 21, 29. The words of Aḥiqar (*ANET* 428) "Two things (which) are meet, and the third pleasing to Shamesh"; the poem of Baal and Anath (*ANET* 132) "For two (kinds of) banquets Baal hates, three the Rider of the clouds"; W. M. W. Roth, *Numerical Sayings in the Old Testament*, SVT 13 (Leiden: Brill, 1965) and his "The Numerical Sequence x/x + 1 in the Old Testament," *VT* 12 (1962) 300-11, discuss these and many other examples in biblical and non-biblical texts.

[35]Harper, *Amos* 14; Cripps, *Amos* 118; GKC 134s.

[36]Hammershaimb, *Amos* 22; Mays, *Amos* 24; H. W. Wolff *Amos' geistege Heimat* WMANT (Neukirchen: Neukirchener, 1964) 24-30; B. K. Soper, "For Three Transgressions and for Four," *ExpT* 71 (1959) 86-87.

[37]The Babylonian Talmud says, "If a man commits a trangression the first, second and third time, he is forgiven; the fourth time he is not forgiven" and then it quotes Amos 2:6 (Yoma 86*b*). Roth, "Numerical Sequence," 304, concludes that the definite and the indefinite interpretations are both possible. Context must determine which is best.

distinctive syntax of the numerical clause in Amos, the listing of seven sins against Israel (2:6-8), and Amos' use of the number seven elsewhere (2:14-16 lists seven defeats; 4:6-12 has seven disasters; 9:1-4 contains seven acts of destruction).[38]

In spite of diverse approaches there is a similar conclusion;[39] the nation has committed many sins (four which is more than what God will forgive; seven or its complete sins; or an indefinite number), and because of these rebellious acts God will judge them. Certainly the use of numbers indicates more than just an indefinite number; they stress the magnitude and extent of their sin in a symbolic way.[40]

The Hebrew root *pš'* shows that the nations were in "rebellion." Elsewhere this word is used to describe the rebellion of Israel against the rule of Rehoboam (1 Kings 12:19) and the rebellion of Edom against Judah (2 Kings 8:20). It is a willful breach of trust; a flaunting of authority on the domestic (Exod. 22:9 [Heb. 22:8]), political (2 Kings 1:1; 3:5, 7; 2 Chron. 21:8, 10) or religious level (Isa. 1:2, 28; Jer. 2:8, 29; Ezek. 2:3).[41] The rebellious acts of Damascus are specified later in the verse. The emphasis of the first clause is centered on the nation's willful and purposeful rebellion. This kind of action is not a mistake but an arrogant denial of another's authority by asserting one's own power. Such actions carry full responsibility.

b. Accountability is demanded (1:3a). The phrase *lō' ʾăšîbenû* may be translated literally as "I will not cause it to return." The verbal clause is difficult because the final pronominal suffix "it" is not clearly defined.[42] Many

---

[38]M. Weiss, "The Pattern of Numerical Sequence in Amos 1-2: A Reexamination," *JBL* 86 (1967) 416-23, notes that all other sequences have a verb in the first line, but this is not the case in Amos 1-2. Aside from the two numbers there is not even any parallelism. Luther and Calvin held this view and the symbolic significance of seven is known throughout the ancient Near East, A. R. Kapelrud, "The Number Seven in Ugaritic Texts," *VT* 18 (1968) 494-99; H. A. Brongers, "Die Zehnzahl in der Bibel und in ihrer Umwelt," *Studia Biblica et Semitica* (1966) 40-45.

[39]Rudolph, *Amos* 129.

[40]Although many of the biblical parallels are in wisdom literature, and Wolff, *Amos* 138 holds that Amos derived the saying from his contact with popular clan wisdom instruction, broader research into the use of number sayings (see footnote 37-39) indicates that the numerical sayings were used in many types of literature. The distinctive syntax of Amos' phrase also argues against a direct wisdom connection.

[41]The root *pšᵉ* "to rebel" is used as a verb (forty-one times) and as a noun (ninety-three times) in the Old Testament. It is not a cultic word but a political word which can be applied to many situations. For the twenty uses of the root in Isaiah see B. D. Napier, "Isaiah and the Isaiah," *SVT* 13 (1965) 248-51 or for a more general survey, G. Quell, "*hamartanō*," *TDNT* I (1964) 273-79. Wolff's derivation of the term from wisdom literature (it is used twelve times in Proverbs) misses the main thrust of the word. It is not just an "infraction" of rights but also a willful rebellion against authority (*Amos* 152-53).

[42]J. Morgenstern, "Amos Studies IV," *HUCA* 32 (1961) 314, does not solve the problem of the text by changing the text to "I will not make them return to me." Christensen, *Transformations of the War Oracle*, 62 removes the final pronoun. H. W. Hogg, "The Starting Point of the Religious Message of Amos," *Transactions of the Third International Congress for the History of Religions*, 1 (1908) 325-27, thinks "it" refers to the Assyrians, but they are never mentioned elsewhere in Amos.

commentators suggest that "it" refers to the punishment announced in verses 4 and 5.[43] Others have identified "it" with the word or decree of Yahweh which cannot be changed.[44] From parallel passages where "I will not turn back" appears, "it" possibly refers to the "anger of Yahweh."[45] The use of this formula in the war oracle against Ephraim in Isaiah 9:8-10:4 (a setting similar to Amos 1-2), and the expansion of it in Jeremiah 23:20 and 30:24 to, "the anger of Yahweh will not turn back until he has executed and accomplished the intents of his mind," indicates that the phrase expresses the purpose of God and his recognition of human responsibility on man. God's anger will not return; thus his word will not change and the punishment will be unavoidable. The implication is, the nation will now be held responsible for its many sins. It is not a punishment statement but a way of stating God's determination to hold the nation accountable because of its guilt.[46]

c. Specific sin described (1:3b). Special mention is made of the crimes committed against the people of Gilead. The Aramean state of Syria, whose capital was Damascus, was located east of Gilead, and many of the battles between the kings of Israel and the kings of Syria took place in Gilead. It was something of a buffer zone for the hundred years before the time of Amos (760 B.C.) as well as much earlier.

The territory on the east side of the Jordon occupied by Reuben, Gad and half of Manasseh corresponds to the general area of Gilead (Numbers 32; Deuteronomy 3; Joshua 13; Judges 10-12).[47] During the reign of David, an Aramean confederation gained a considerable degree of power, for the Egyptians, Hittites, and Assyrian-Babylonian kingdoms were in a state of general decline. Hadadezer, king of Zobah, consolidated his rule over a larger area;

---

[43]Hammershaimb, Amos 25; Rudolph, Amos 129-30; W. L. Holladay, The Root ŠUBH in the Old Testament (Leiden: Brill, 1959) 101-02.

[44]Wolff, Amos 128, 153-54 compares this idea with the experience of Amos in Amos 7. God changed his decree in the first two visions, but there was no change during the last ones. The phrase, "I will never pass by him again" (7:8; 8:2; 9:4) is a similar irrevocable statement. Numb. 23:20; Isa. 45:23; 55:11 also describe God's intention not to revoke a word he has spoken. Weiss, "Numerical Sequence," 416 refers to a similar view by I. L. Seeligmann: "The group of visions (chaps. 7-8), left the incisive impression upon Amos' mind that God forgives once or twice–but that he can no longer disregard the sin of the people the third or fourth time." The fact that Amos 7-8 are probably later than Amos 1-2 makes this background for the phrase weak. Mays, Amos 24 refers "it" to the voice of Yahweh in 1:2.

[45]R. P. Knierim, "I will not cause it to return in Amos 1 and 2," Canon and Authority, ed. G. W. Coats, B. O. Long (Philadelphia: Fortress, 1977) 163-75, notes the dissimilarities between the phrases Wolff compares in Amos 1 and 7 and points out that "it" in Numbers and Isaiah is determined by context and is not totally parallel to Amos. Knierim finds twenty-five examples of "turning away the anger of Yahweh" and eight are negative like Amos 1:3 (Isa. 5:25; 9:11 [12]; 16 [17], 20 [21]; 10:4; Jer. 23:20; 30:24; 2 Kings 23:26). Harper, Amos 16 also believes that "it" refers to God's anger.

[46]Knierim's analysis of the structure of 1:3 is based on the idea that the phrase "I will not cause it to return" is a statement of punishment parallel to "I will send fire," but the punishment clause begins in 1:4. This clause emphasizes God's determination, not his punishment.

[47]M. Ottosson, Gilead: Tradition and History (Lund: Gleerup, 1969) 53-176, surveys the modern literary and historical investigations concerning Gilead in biblical and extra-biblical sources.

and when his interests came into conflict with the expansion that David was conducting in that area, the Syrians fought beside Zobah and were defeated by David (2 Sam. 8:3-8; 10:16-19; 1 Chron. 19:16). With the removal of the Damascus-Zobah league, David took control of the whole area and established a garrison in Damascus.[48] Part of this territory was lost during the reign of Solomon when Rezon recaptured Damascus (1 Kings 11:23-25). There is no reference to the persecution of Gilead in this early period, but Benhadad I did ravage many cities in Israel and Gilead during the reign of Baasha (1 Kings 15:18-22).

The two main periods of struggle for control of Gilead were during the days of Ahab of Israel and Benhadad II of Syria (1 Kings 20-22) and during the reign of the Israelite kings Joram and Jehu and the Syrian kings Hazael and Benhadad III (2 Kings 8-13). There is still a great deal of discussion concerning the historical reconstruction of both of these periods, but the text seems to indicate that Ahab defeated the Syrian King Benhadad II (1 Kings 20), then Ahab was defeated and killed in an attempt to regain the town of Ramoth-Gilead (1 Kings 22).[49]

The next period of Syrian oppression of Gilead began with Hazael's defeat of Joram at Ramoth-Gilead (2 Kings 8:28-29) and major losses during the reign of Jehu (2 Kings 10:32-33) when Hazael spread his influence as far as Gath and Jerusalem (2 Kings 12:17-18). This oppression continued during the reign of Jehoahaz (2 Kings 13:1-7) under the leadership of Benhadad III until the Assyrian king Adadnirari III defeated Benhadad III around 805/2 B.C. Joash defeated Benhadad III three times (2 Kings 13:22-25), and Jeroboam his son returned the rest of Gilead to Israelite control (2 Kings 14:23-27). Haran places Amos 1:3-5 before Jeroboam's conquest of Gilead and defeat of Damascus.[50] Certainly this was not accomplished until after the Assyrian defeat of Damascus in 773 B.C. It most likely took place around 765 (after Assur-dan III campaigned in the west) rather than after 755 (after Assur-nirari V campaigned in the west) as Haran supposes.

---

[48]A detailed survey of these events is found in A. Malamat, "The Kingdom of David and Solomon in its Contact with Egypt and Aram Naharaim," *BAR* 2 (1957) 94-98; A. Malamat, "The Arameans," *Peoples of Old Testament Times*, ed. D. J. Wiseman (Oxford: Clarendon, 1973) 141-43; B. Mazar, "The Aramean Empire and its Relations with Israel," *BAR* 2 (1957) 131-33.

[49]J. M. Miller "The Elisha Cycle and the Accounts of the Omride Wars," *JBL* 85 (1966) 441-54, believes these three battles are those prophesied by Elisha in 2 Kings 13:19. This theory enables him to eliminate one Benhadad, alleviate the tension of having Benhadad and Ahab as allies at Qarqar and enemies immediately before that, and explain various historical peculiarities. (2 Kings 10:32-33 seems to imply that Israel did not loose Gilead until the reign of Hazael.) Many of these points are in accord with the earlier study of C. F. Whitley, "The Deuteronomic Presentation of the House of Omri," *VT* 2 (1952) 137-52 and Barton, *Oracles against the Nations* 26-27. Although this reconstruction eases several tensions in the text, Bright, *A History of Israel* 239-55, has shown that these reinterpretations are not necessary to make sense out of the history of this period.

[50]M. Haran, "The Rise and Decline of the Empire of Jeroboam ben Joash," *VT* 17 (1967) 226-81.

The historical setting for this oracle against Damascus includes several factors. Israel suffered severely under Syrian military might for the previous hundred years with only brief periods of relief. The area of Gilead, being closer to Syria, was the battleground for much of the fighting between the nations. Joash had recently won three battles against Damascus and Jeroboam was in the process of gaining even greater control of the area. Because of the defeat of Damascus by the Assyrians in 773 B.C. the Israelites who hear Amos are convinced of their ability to solidify their control of the area. The present Assyrian king, Assur-dan III (773-755), is a weak king, so Israel will not be prevented from avenging their earlier humiliation. Because of this setting the audience strongly supported the condemnation of Damascus which Amos proclaimed.

The crime of "threshing Gilead with iron threshing sledges" could be related to the events in 2 Kings 13:7, but this text primarily describes the destruction of the army of Jehoahaz. Some maintain that this threshing refers to events which took place during the life of Jeroboam II rather than events thirty to one hundred years earlier.[51] A contemporary date for these war crimes is not as likely as the earlier events, for even if one hypothesizes a resurgence of Syrian power during the reign of Jeroboam II, there is no record of any major defeat of Israel after the victories of Joash (2 Kings 13:22-25).[52]

The "threshing" may be a metaphor of the inhuman treatment of those conquered in war, or the phrase could be taken quite literally.[53] The threshing sledge was usually made of wooden planks with stones or iron knives attached to the bottom. Tiglath-pileser I used similar language to describe his treatment of the people he conquered: "the land Bit-Amukkani I threshed as with a threshing instrument." Another Assyrian king, Ashur-nasir-apli II, describes similar inhumanity.

> I burnt many captives from them. I captured many troops alive; I cut off of some their arms [and] hands; I cut off of others their noses, ears, and extremeties. I gouged out the eyes of many troops. I made a pile of the living [and] one of the heads. I hung their heads on trees around the city. I burnt their adolescent boys [and] girls.[54]

Finally, it should be noted that it is Gilead, not the people of Samaria who suffered. Covenantal language is absent. God does not indict Syria for taking

---

[51]Wolff, Amos 150; S. Cohen, "The Political Background of the Words of Amos," HUCA 36 (1965) 155; Barton, Oracles against the Nations 30-31.

[52]The understanding of Jeroboam's situation in Amos 1-2 seems to be different from Amos 6. Mays, Amos 30 assumes Jeroboam is already at the height of his power, that Gilead was now in Israelite hands and Damascus was in ruins. The events pictured throughout chapter 1 do not agree with this position—"the nations will be destroyed by fire." This does not mean that all of the sins of Damascus refer to events during Jeroboam's reign.

[53]Hammershaimb, Amos 26; Mays, Amos 30; Wolff, Amos 154.

[54]A. K. Grayson, Royal Assyrian Inscriptions, II (Wiesbaden: Harrosowitz, 1976) 126.

land but for senseless brutal inhumanity to people. God will hold Damascus responsible for its uncivilized and immoral treatment of helpless people.

3. Punishment of destruction (1:4-5b)

a. On the secure palace-fortresses (1:4). The punishment formula "I will..." occurs in each of the following oracles (1:7, 10, 12, 14; 2:2, 5). It is self-evident that those who commit such atrocities deserve punishment. Common sense and human instinct would judge them guilty. The focus of the punishment clauses is on God's defeat of the nation. Yahweh will accomplish this deed; the nation he will use is unknown.

The defeat of Syria centers around the elimination of pivotal centers of political and military importance. The political and military leaders were responsible for the military exploits carried out in Gilead. These strategists devised the nation's policies concerning the treatment of the population of defeated lands; therefore they receive first attention.

The "house of Hazael" and the "palace-fortresses of Benhadad" will be destroyed. The word "house" can mean "family, dynasty" as in 2 Samuel 7:11 or 1 Kings 13:34, but the parallelism with palace-fortress indicates that buildings are being described (by implication the inhabitants are meant). The reference to the kings, Hazael and Benhadad, may imply that the crimes against Gilead were committed during their reigns. The reference to buildings rather than people draws attention to the destruction of the most expensive and securest fortification in the nation. If the elaborate royal fortresses cannot withstand Yahweh's attack, the rest of the nation does not stand a chance. The towers, massive walls, and the king's elite army will not be able to keep the stronghold of the nation, the nation's treasury, or its king from the fire of God's judgment.

The only instrument identified in 1:4 is fire, but the "breaking of the gate-bar of Damascus" in 1:5 indicates defeat by a military force. The use of "fire" in 1:14 or 2:2 is in a military context and indicates that fire may be a metaphor for war rather than something like lightning or the great fire seen in the vision in Amos 7:4. The association of fire with God's burning anger is common elsewhere (Deut. 32:22; Isa. 5:24-25; 9:17-18; 66:15; Jer. 15:14; 17:4; Zeph. 1:18; 3:8), and the frequent practice of burning conquered cities is known from biblical and ancient Near Eastern texts.[55] These inpregnable and secure strongholds will be "eaten up" by the fire. It will destroy their beauty and their strength and reduce them to ruins and rubble.

b. On the people in the chief cities (1:5a-b). The second proclamation of judgment extends from Damascus, the capital, to the other centers of power

---

[55]Josh. 6:24; 11:11; Judg. 9:52; 1 Sam. 30:14; 1 Kings 16:18; 2 Kings 25:9; Isa. 1:7; Jer. 37:10; 39:8; Grayson, *Royal Assyrian Inscriptions*, II, 112-26, 129-32 records examples of the burning of cities which are in rebellion against the king. "I razed, destroyed and burnt the city/ their cities."

within the Syrian empire. Aven may refer to Baalbek, a city not far north of Damascus, which was later famous for its sun worship (see textual note *f*); thus some commentators believe that *'āwen* "evil, idolatry" may be a pun.

Hosea later refers to Bethel, "the house of God," as Beth-aven "House of idolatry" (Hos. 4:15; 10:5) but Amos 5:5 does not use the same pun. A reference to idolatry would seem out of place in the military context of 1:4-5. If the following reference to Beth-Eden is geographic, a parallel geographic location (similar to the geographic places in the other oracles) would be expected. The valley is likely the valley between Lebanon and Anti-Lebanon, the area that is sometimes called the Valley of Lebanon (Josh. 11:17).

The second location is the province Bit-adini, an Aramean region between the Euphrates and Balikh rivers. This area is mentioned in Assyrian documents[56] and in 2 Kings 19:12, Isaiah 37:12, and Ezekiel 27:23. The capital of this district was at Til-Barsip (now *Tell 'Aḥmer*) which is about fifteen miles south of Carchemish.[57] Malamat believes that the "sceptre holder" in 1:5 is Shamshi-ilu, a powerful and somewhat independent ruler of Beth-Eden from around 780-752 B.C. Others reject this suggestion since Shalmaneser III turned Beth-Eden into an Assyrian province in 855.[58] They suggest that Amos is predicting the fall of a geographic area and the "people of Eden." Because Beth-Eden was not under the control of Damascus, Mays concludes that Amos expects this destruction to fall on another Aramean state in the same general area as Beth-Eden.[59] But if Shamshi-ilu maintained his rule through the years of the weak kings, Assur-dan III and Assur-nirari V, there is no reason why he could not have been in league with Damascus at the time of Amos after 773 B.C.[60]

The military defeat of the whole region is announced. The strong gates of Damascus which were secured in the closed position by iron or bronze bars (1 Kings 4:13) will no longer protect the capital of Syria. A tremendous force would be required to break these bars, but once the gates were opened, the people of the city were at the mercy of the invading forces. God's power will not only render Damascus defenseless, but he will "cut off the inhabitants" and the "sceptre holder" from surrounding areas. Both small and great will suffer defeat as Yahweh judges and establishes his rule over the Aramean nation. Those who brutally defeated others will be defeated.

c. Those left will be exiled (1:5c). The final clause may suggest the direction from which the future military force will come and where the survivors will be deported. Kir is the country from which the Arameans originally

---

[56]Grayson, *Assyrian Royal Inscriptions* II, 40, 41, 47, 60; *ANET* 277.

[57]A. Malamat, "Amos 1:5 in the Light of the Til-Barsip Inscriptions," *BASOR* 129 (1953) 25-26.

[58]Haran, "Empire of Jeroboam ben Joash," 276-77; Rudolph, *Amos* 131.

[59]Mays, *Amos* 31.

[60]Wolff, *Amos* 156; Rudolph, *Amos* 132.

came (Amos 9:7). Its association with Elam in Isaiah 22:6 points toward a site in southern Mesopotamia near Elam, but others prefer an area near the Caspian Sea by the river Kur.[61] The exact identity of the Kir of Amos is still unknown. According to 2 Kings 16:9, the Assyrians defeated Damascus and deported them to Kir. This was accomplished in 732 B.C. (*ANET* 283) approximately thirty years after Amos gave this prophecy. The practice of deportation, which some believe Tiglath-pileser III introduced, was employed by earlier kings on a more limited scale.[62] The extent of the deportation will affect all who survive the military defeat of the nation.

4. Divine confirmation formula (1:5c)

The oracle ends with an echo of the opening messenger formula (1:8, 15; 2:3). This and similar phrases mark the end of several oracles (2:16; 3:15; 4:3, 5; 5:17, 27; 7:3, 6). The repetition functions as an emphasis; it verifies the message and seals it with a divine stamp.

B. God's Judgment Against Philistia (1:6-8)

1. The source of the message (1:6a)

Like the first oracle (1:3), this prophecy is introduced with a divine messenger formula which identifies the source of the message. Yahweh has revealed the second of a series of messages to Amos. Divine authority stands behind the second proclamation also.

2. The indictment concerning Gaza (1:6a-c)

a. Because of great sinfulness (1:6a). The indictment within the second oracle follows the pattern used in the first oracle. By the repetition of the same phraseology the prophet begins to create a rhetorical pattern which is predictable. The use of an identical style establishes a link with the audience because they know what comes next. The acceptance of the logical relationship between the parts of the pattern in the early oracles enables the prophet to cash in on the momentum of the structure at the end of his speech. Because the listener has no problem with accepting this as God's word concerning other nations, and is quite willing to approve of God's harsh judgment of the sins of other people, the prophet is able to persuasively prepare his audience for God's word concerning Israel in his climactic oracle.

The oracle against the Philistines focuses on Gaza. Gaza is a representative of the Philistine nation because it was one of the largest and most important Philistine cities at this time. It was situated in the southern coastal plain of the Mediterranean Sea. The city was founded on two main trade routes; one went from Egypt to Damascus, and the other ran east to Beersheba and on to

---

[61]Mays, *Amos* 31.

[62]Harper, *Amos* 20; Gottwald, *Kingdoms of the Earth* 97-100. B. Odad, *Mass Deportations and Deportees in the Neo-Assyrian Empire* (Wiesbaden: Reichart, 1979).

Edom, Elath, and southern Arabia.[63] Gaza's central location on the trade route to Edom suggests that it may have played a key role in the slave trade to Edom.

b. Accountability is demanded (1:6b). Because of the nation's great sinfulness, God holds the Philistines responsible. He is determined to deal seriously with their willful rebellious acts against his authority. Yahweh's anger will not be turned back; he will not alter his decree or change their judgment. Yahweh will hold Philistia accountable for its deeds.

c. Specific sin described (1:6c). The sin identified may refer to the deportation of "peaceful captives" or "a whole [complete] mass of captives." The oracles could pertain to an isolated border raid, the taking of captives from a nation which had a peace treaty with Gaza, the taking of large numbers of captives during a time of war with some enemy, or the taking of captives by means other than military conflict. The text is silent about how these slaves were obtained, and it does not identify them as Israelites or Judeans, although the latter may legitimately be conjectured since Judah was a close neighbor. There is no indication that Israelites from the northern tribes were deported.

Since the rebellious acts in the first oracle and the oracles which follow have a military setting, it is natural to place the crimes in 1:6 within a similar context. The use of a similar phrase in 1:9 "they delivered over a whole mass of captives to Edom" suggests the possibility that Gaza and Tyre were involved in a cooperative effort.[64] The geographical location of Gaza would allow it to serve as a middleman between Tyre and Edom.

If military conflict is presumed, the nature of the crime is not particularly obvious, for the taking of prisoners of war was a common practice throughout the ancient Near Eastern world. Examples of this practice are available from Sumerian, Assyrian, Babylonian, Egyptian, and Canaanite literature.[65] Biblical laws did not condemn slavery but allowed prisoners of war to be put into forced labor gangs (Deut. 20:10-11; 21:10; Judg. 5:30; 1 Sam. 30:3; 2 Chron. 28:8), and regulated the buying and selling of slaves (Exod. 21:2-11; Lev. 25:39-54; Deut. 15:12-18). Gaza cannot be condemned for acts which were not considered wrong. The rebellious act may be hinted at in the words "peaceful, complete."

[63]*The Westminster Historical Atlas to the Bible*, rev. ed. G. E. Wright and F. V. Filson (Philadelphia: Westminster, 1958) 32, 42, for maps with these roads. W. F. Stinespring, "Gaza" *IDB* II (1962) 357, refers to a Minean inscription (S. Arabian) which tells of an important female slave sent from Gaza. Pliny and Strabo refer to Gaza when describing the established trade routes of their day. See G. W. van Beek, "Frankincense and Myrr," *BA* 23 (1960) 76.

[64]Paul, "Concatenous Literary Pattern," 400, agrees with M. Haran that the repetition of the same formula against Tyre expresses complicity in a similar crime. In Joel 3:4-8 (Heb. 4:4-8) Philistia and Tyre are condemned for their selling of Jews. The grammatical use of the infinitive construct with a suffix as its subject is discussed in GKC 115h.

[65]I. Mendelsohn, "Slavery in the Ancient Near East," *BAR* 3 (1970) 127-43 or his book *Slavery in the Ancient Near East* (New York: Oxford, 1949).

Although many allow for the translation "peaceful populace," one view suggests that Philistia ignored its peace treaty with its allies and took captives from one of them.[66] "Peace, friendship" can be used in Akkadian and biblical texts like 1 Kings 5:12 (Heb. 5:26) in a treaty context.[67] The difficulty with this view is that the treaty context of the Philistine oracle must be implied from the later oracle against Tyre, which explicitly mentions the "covenant of brotherhood" in 1:9. A covenant relationship may have existed between David or Solomon, and the Philistine city of Gath (1 Sam. 29; 2 Sam. 15:19; 1 Kings 2:39-40; 1 Chron. 18:1), but there is no reference to Gath in Amos 1:6-8.[68] Therefore, the covenant hypothesis is most unlikely.

The guilt of Gaza must be related to its forcible dislocation of "complete masses of captives" for the purpose of economic gain. Their kidnapping of entire villages was probably not the result of war. They made slave raids to satisfy their desire for wealth. Amos attacks Gaza's hardened cruelty in "taking captives," and then the underlying motive is condemned "to deliver them to Edom." The taking of slaves from those who are defeated in war would be understandable, but it is immoral to treat the innocent people of another nation like cattle to be sold to the highest bidder. The size of the operation condemns them—"whole masses of captives." Removal by kidnapping for the sole purpose of resale is contrary to even the lowest sense of morality.[69] People are not things; rather they are creations of God.[70]

There is very little evidence to suggest when these crimes were committed. If they refer to slave raids against Judean villages, one might point to the conflict during the time of Jehoram, king of Judah, in 2 Chronicles 21:16. Schoville prefers a date during the reign of Jehu, after his surrender to the Assyrian King Shalmaneser III in 841 B.C. (*ANET* 280).[71] The exact date is beyond accurate historical recovery, but these Philistine raids likely took place during a period of Judean weakness. The condemnation of slave trading again in Joel 3:4-8 (Heb. 4:4-8) implies that such practices were carried on by the Philistines for many years.

3. The punishment of destruction (1:7-8)

a. On their secure palace-fortresses (1:7). The punishment clause employed in 1:4 appears again in this oracle against Gaza. It emphasized God's

---

[66]Schoville, "Oracles of Amos against Gaza, Tyre, and Edom," 57-61 reads the treaty relationship reflected in the word "brother" in the Tyre oracle back into the Gaza oracle since they both committed similar crimes. Christensen, "Prosodic Structure of Amos 1-2," 431, builds on the idea that the Hittite word "peace" also means treaty and Biblical references to peace in Ps. 7:4 [Heb 7:5]; 41:9 [Heb 41:10]; Isa. 54:10; Jer. 20:10 and Obad. 7. He revocalizes *salem* in Gen. 14:18 to *selomoh* "peace, ally" following W. F. Albright, "Abraham and the Caravan Trade," *BASOR* 44 (1961) 52 n 75. Only Obad. 7 supports his case.

[67]F. C. Fensham, "The Treaty between the Israelites and the Tyrians," *SVT* 17 (1968) 77.

[68]H. E. Kassis, "Gath and the Structure of the 'Philistine' Society," *JBL* 84 (1965) 268-69.

[69]The use of the infinitive construct to express purpose; GKC 114fg.

[70]Rudolph, *Amos* 133.

[71]Schoville, "Oracles of Amos against Gath, Tyre, and Edom," 61-63.

action ("I will") against the city. He will destroy all forms of security which protect those who have been involved with slave raiding and the inhuman selling of great masses of innocent people for economic gain. The thick walls of the city and the strongly fortified palaces which have been built and richly furnished through slave trading will be destroyed.[72] The flames of war (see 1:4) will "eat up" these secure places of refuge.

Gaza was defeated by Hezekiah (2 Kings 18:8) and the Assyrian kings Tiglath-pileser III (*ANET* 282-83), Sargon II (*ANET* 284), and Sennacherib (*ANET* 288).

b. On the people of the chief cities (1:8*a-b*). The use of the phrase "I will cut off the inhabitants of...and the one who holds the sceptre from..." in 1:5 and 1:8 links these two oracles together and sets them apart as a pair (see the section on structure and unity). Syria and Philistia will suffer similar defeats. God will destroy the main source of military power (people and the rulers) from the chief cities in both nations. The very important as well as the insignificant will feel the terror of God's judgment.

Three additional cities are pinpointed for destruction. Ashdod, which is about twenty-five miles north of Gaza, was built a few miles from the Mediterranean Sea on the main highway going north to Damascus. It, along with Gaza and Ashkelon, dates back to pre-Philistine days according to written documents from Ugarit as well as the excavation reports.[73] The religious importance of the city is indicated by the presence of the great temple to Dagon here (1 Sam. 5:1-8), and its military strength is confirmed by walls which measure up to 8.7 meters thick. The city of Ashdod was attacked and partially destroyed by Uzziah during the lifetime of Amos (2 Kings 18:8), and several Assyrian kings attacked it in the years which followed.[74] Ashkelon, which lies halfway between Gaza and Ashdod, was an important seaport for the Philistines. The city is mentioned in the Amarna letters (*ANET* 489-90, no 289, 320) but is seldom referred to in the biblical text. Only minimal excavation has been completed on the city, but Assyrian literary sources indi-

---

[72]Gaza was occupied by 1468 B.C. according to the annals of the Egyptian king Thutmose III (*ANET* 235). It is mentioned one hundred years later in the Amarna letters (*ANET* 489 no 289) and was a key Philistine city which the Israelites found hard to control (Josh. 10:41; Judg. 1:18 and the Old Greek reading; 1 Sam. 6:17; 1 Kings 4:24). Excavation accounts of Gaza (Tell Harube) were prepared by W. J. Phythian-Adams, "Reports on Soundings at Gaza," *PEQ* 55 (1923) 11-36 and A. Ovadish, "Gaza," *Encyclopedia of Archeological Excavations in the Holy Land,* II (New York: Prentice-Hall, 1975) 408-17.

[73]A summary of the archeological reports is given in M. Dothan, "Ashdod," *Encyclopedia of Archeological Excavations in the Holy Land,* I (New York: Prentice-Hall, 1975) 103-19. See also G. E. Wright, "Fresh Evidence for the Philistine Story," *BA* 29 (1966) 74 and D. H. Freedman, "The Second Season at Ancient Ashdod," *BA* 26 (1963) 134-39.

[74]Sargon II (*ANET* 284, 286 and Isa. 20:1), Sennacherib (*ANET* 287-88), Esarhaddon (*ANET* 291), Ashurbanipal (*ANET* 294), and Nebuchadnezzar II (*ANET* 308). See the surveys by K. A. Kitchen, "The Philistines," *Peoples of Old Testament Times,* ed. D. J. Wiseman (Oxford: Clarendon, 1973) 65-67 and the extensive study by H. Tadmor, "Philistia under Assyrian Rule," *BA* 29 (1966) 86-102.

cate that Ashkelon was defeated by the same Assyrian kings which destroyed the other Philistine towns.[75] The third town, Ekron, is not securely identified (possibly Qatra or Khirbet el-Muqanna'), but it is famous for its god, Baalzebub, whom Ahaziah consulted (2 Kings 1:2-16). Sennacherib took the city around 702 B.C. (*ANET* 283).

Gath is the only major Philistine city that is not mentioned. One could conclude that its absence proves that this oracle was written after 711 B.C., the date when Sargon II destroyed Gath; but Gath was also defeated by Hazael (2 Kings 12:17) before the time of Amos and by Uzziah (2 Chron. 26:6) during the time of Amos. Gath may have been ruled by Ashdod at this time or it may be included in the last phrase "the rest of the Philistines."[76]

c. Those left will perish (1:8b). The final clause is all inclusive and either summarizes what precedes or condemns the few Philistines that will remain after the nation is devastated. The picture of total destruction is employed to illustrate the severity of God's judgment. The audience surely agreed wholeheartedly with God's judgment of the Philistines.

4. Divine confirmation formula (1:8c). This concluding messenger formula verifies that the preceding message is God's word. Its inclusion confirms divine authority on the message which Amos has delivered and brings the oracle to a close.

C. God's Judgment Against Tyre (1:9-10)

1. The source of the message (1:9a).

"Thus says Yahweh" identifies the authority who sent Amos to deliver this message.

a. Because of great sinfulness (1:9a). "Because of three rebellious acts and because of four" stresses the magnitude of the crimes and removes any doubt about their guilt. The Ugaritic epic of Keret (*ANET* 145) and an Amarna letter from Abi-milki, king of Tyre, to Amenophis III, king of Egypt (*ANET* 484) are early witnesses to the importance of Tyre long before the time of Amos. Although the city lies on the border of the territory of Asher (Josh. 19:29), there seems to be little contact between the Israelites and the city of Tyre until the time of David and Solomon. Hiram, the king of Tyre, supplied wood, carpenters, and stoneworkers for David and Solomon to build the temple in Jerusalem (2 Sam. 5:11; 1 Kings 5:1-12[Heb 5:15-27]); and the two countries established a treaty of peace between them. Hiram also helped

---

[75]W. J. Phythian-Adams, "Excavations at Ascalon," *PEQ* 33 (1921) 163-69 and *New International Dictionary of Biblical Archaeology,* ed. E. M. Blaiklock and R. K. Harrison (Grand Rapids: Zondervan, 1973) 75-76.

[76]Kassis, "Gath and the Structure of the 'Philistine' Society," 259-71 discusses the location of Gath and its relationship to the biblical references to Gittaim, as does B. Mazar, "Gath and Gittaim," *IEJ* 4 (1954) 227-35.

Solomon develop a seaport at Ezion-geber (1 Kings 9:27). Almost two hundred years later Omri, the king of Israel, negotiated an alliance with the Phonecians and had his son Ahab marry Jezebel, the daughter of the king of the Sidonians. This brought a renewed surge of Baalism to Israel (1 Kings 16:29-33) but had the advantage of producing positive economic conditions with Tyre, which was famous for its merchants and international trade (Ezek. 27-28).[77] The many sins of Tyre are recounted by Ezekiel, but Amos and Joel focus on their immoral trading of people.

b. Accountability is demanded (1:9b). "I will not vacillate about it" expresses God's determination to hold the people of Tyre responsible for their rebellious acts. Yahweh's anger will not turn back; he will carry out his decree of judgment.

c. Specific sin described (1:9c). The sin of Tyre is described in two clauses, the first one being very similar to the crime committed by Gaza (1:6). This repetition is not a sign of a secondary addition to the text based on the Philistine oracle but a natural way of expressing the mutual involvement and cooperation of the two nations in the trading of slaves.[78]

The rebellious acts of Tyre are not totally identical to those charged against Gaza. Tyre is only charged with selling its captives. Tyre functioned as a broker who received slaves and passed them on to Greece (Joel 3:4-8 [Heb. 4:4-8]) or to Gaza so that they could be sent on to Edom. Tyre was unconcerned about who was being traded; morality, humanity and treaty agreements were subordinate factors in their business ethics.

A more precise setting is alluded to in the phrase "and they did not remember their covenant of brotherhood." Although these crimes may be against other Phoenician cities (their own brothers), most refer to the breaking of a treaty with some unknown country, the breaking of the brotherly bond between Israel and Edom by selling Jewish slaves to Edom, or the breaking of a political treaty relationship between Israel and Tyre which was first established in the reign of Solomon and Hiram (1 Kings 5:1, 12 [Heb. 5:15, 25]; 9:11-14).[79] This conclusion is supported by the use of "brotherhood" termi-

---

[77]General studies on Phoenician history and culture include: H. J. Katzenstein, *The History of Tyre* (Jerusalem: Schocken Institute of Jewish Research, 1973) 259-86; S. Mascoti, *The World of the Phoenicians* (London: Weidenfeld and Nicolson, 1968) and W. A. Ward (ed), *The Role of the Phoenicians in the Interaction of Mediterranean Civilizations* (Beirut: American Univ. of Beirut, 1968).

[78]Paul, "Concatenous Literary Pattern," 400, agrees with Haran on this point. Paul also shows how this repetition explains the ordering of the pairs of oracles (three and four are after one and two because of the repetition of a similar clause "to deliver over a whole mass of captives in Edom" in oracles two and three). The cooperation between these countries in slave trade is also noted in Joel 3:4-8 (Heb. 4:4-8).

[79]Driver, *Amos* 141 opts for some unknown country while Fosbroke, *Amos* 781 takes the second point of view. Hammershaimb, *Amos* 34-35; Harper, *Amos* 29-30, Mays, *Amos* 34: Rudolph, *Amos* 133 and most others believe that Amos is describing the disintegration of a political treaty between Israel and Tyre.

nology in covenant treaties between other nations.[80] These include Hittite (*ANET* 200-01), Egyptian (*ANET* 199) and other examples. Recent studies support this position and deny the late "deuteronomistic" origin of Amos 1:9 (see the section on structure and unity).[81] Although the political treaty context of "brotherhood" is firmly established, the text does not specify the treaty partner of Tyre. Since Amos was speaking to an Israelite audience, he was probably referring to breaking a treaty with Israel.

The violent purge of the family of Ahab by Jehu (2 Kings 9:1-10, 30-37; 10:1-11, 18-28) would have provided a significant reason for Tyre to retaliate and break her part of the treaty with Israel. This plus Jehu's submission to the Assyrian king Shalmaneser III (*ANET* 280) in 841 B.C. may have led to the abuse Amos describes.[82] The identity of the nations and the time of the breaking of the covenant is not given by Amos. He emphasizes only the offensive action which Tyre has perpetrated on another people who trusted her to be loyal to her covenant agreements. If one sells his brother's people, he deserves to be punished severely. A traitor is the worst of all friends.

3. The Punishment of Destruction (1:10)

a. On their secure palace-fortresses (1:10). The punishment clause used in 1:4 appears again in this oracle against Tyre. It emphasizes God's active ("I will") participation in bringing destruction on all forms of security which protect those who have been selling great masses of people. Tyre's ally believed that Tyre did not return the property of citizens of its treaty partner to their homeland. The thick walls of the city and the strongly fortified palace-fortresses will go up in flames of war (see 1:4). The audience certainly would have supported God's judgment of Tyre.

The city of Tyre was besieged for five years by Shalmaneser according to Josephus (*Jewish Antiquities* IX. 14. 2) but not defeated. Josephus (*Jewish Antiquities* X. 11. 2 and *Against Apion* I. 21) also describes the thirteen-year siege of Tyre by Nebuchadnezzar in 585-73 B.C. (see the prophecy of Ezekiel 26 and 29:17-18)[83] and Alexander the Great's conquest of the city in 332 B.C.

D. God's Judgment Against Edom (1:11-12)

1. The source of the message (1:11a). "Thus says Yahweh" identifies the authority and the source of the message concerning Edom.

---

[80]J. M. Munn-Rankin, "Diplomacy in Western Asia in the Early Second Millennium B.C.," *Iraq* 18 (1956) 68-69 and E. Gerstenberger, "Covenant and Commandment," *JBL* 84 (1965) 39-42.

[81]J. Priest, "The Covenant of Brothers," *JBL* 84 (1965) 400-06; Fensham, "The Treaty between the Israelites and the Tyrians," 71-87; Schoville, "Oracles of Amos Against Gaza, Tyre and Edom," 55-63.

[82]Schoville, "Oracles of Amos Against Gaza, Tyre and Edom," 61-63, develops this interpretation, but Rudolph, *Amos* 134 conjectures that this covenant was broken during the reign of Jeroboam II.

[83]Katzenstein, *The History of Tyre* 220-29, weights the evidence for the historicity of

2. The indictment concerning Edom (1:11b-c)

a. Because of great sinfulness (1:11b). "Because of three rebellious acts and because of four" repeats the indictment formula used in each of the earlier accusations. There is no doubt about the magnitude of Edom's sinfulness. This accusation names the nation Edom rather than a city within it. The Edomites were the seed of Esau, the twin brother of Jacob (Gen. 25:21-6); they settled in the land of Seir or Edom (Gen. 32:3; 36:8-9; Deut. 2:1-8, 12). David subdued the Edomites (2 Sam. 8:11-14; 1 Kings 11:15-16) and killed thousands of them. They threw off Judean control during the time of Joram (2 Kings 8:20-22), but their freedom did not last for Amaziah slaughtered ten thousand Edomites (2 Kings 14:7), and shortly after that Uzziah re-established Judean authority over the port of Elath during the lifetime of Amos (2 Kings 14:22). The port did not remain under Judean control for long though, for during the reign of Ahaz (743 B.C.) Edom took control of Elath and regained her freedom (2 Kings 16:6).[84] This struggle for control of Edom, the Arabah down to Elath, and the copper mines within the Arabah provide the background for the accusations brought against Edom.

b. Accountability is demanded (1:11b). "I will not vacillate about it" expresses God's determination to hold the people of Edom accountable for their rebellious acts. Yahweh's anger will not turn back; he will carry out his decree and punish Edom for its great sinfulness.

c. Specific sin described (1:11c). Four clauses describe the rebellious acts of Edom. The first, "he pursued his brother with the sword," reflects the nature of the hostility between the nations. Edom is using military action to solve a dispute which brothers should be able to solve by some other means. This designation of "brother" may contain treaty connotations, similar to 1:9, or it may refer to the physical kinship between Jacob and Esau, and the two nations they founded. Fishbane assumes that the relationship between the two nations was normalized by a treaty, but no treaty between Judah and Edom is described elsewhere.[85] The use of the term "brothers" in other pas-

---

Shalmaneser's attack which Josephus derived from Menander (the translator of Tyre's history into Greek)as well as Nebuchadnezzar's partial victory over Tyre.

[84]For a more complete survey and bibliography on Edom see J. R. Bartlett, "The Moabites and Edomites," The Peoples of Old Testament Times, ed. D. J. Wiseman (Oxford: Clarendon, 1973) 229-58.

[85]M. Fishbane, "The Treaty Background of Amos 1:11 and Related Matters," JBL 89 (1970) 313-18, also translates "his compassion" as "his ally." Schoville, "Oracles of Amos Against Gaza, Tyre and Edom," 60-61, also accepts the treaty interpretation. R. B. Coote, "Amos 1:11: RHMYW," JBL 90 (1971) 206-08, rejects Fishbane's translation "his ally" and prefers "covenant mercy." Fishbane's response is found in "Additional Remarks on RHMYW (Amos 1:11)," JBL 91 (1972) 391-93. M. L. Barré, "Amos 1:11 Reconsidered," CBQ 47 (1985) 420-27, follows Fishbane. G. Schmuttermayer, "RHM-Eine lexikalische Studie," Bib 51 (1970) 509-12, supports Fishbane's etymological studies, but Paul, "Concatenous Literary Patterns," 402-03 translates the term, "girl, maiden."

sages does not prove a covenant relationship,[86] for cooperation on the basis of brotherhood (physical or political) was rejected by the Edomites when the nations first came into contact with one another. The use of this term could describe the bond of friendship, mercy, and affection which exists between parties who are related by birth, adoption into a family (servants), or inclusion by treaty into a common community. Evidence of a treaty relationship between the nations is necessary before Fishbane's translation "his friend, ally" can be accepted. The destruction of trust and "kinship affection" by "pursuing with the sword" is a rejection of the deep emotional ties which bind two parties together. Edom and Judah were brothers, but neither wasted any love or compassion on the other.

Edom's guilt revealed itself in the wrathful attitude it had toward Judah. The natural instincts to cherish a relative were replaced by the raging hatred of a wild beast. In anger Edom lost control of her emotions and nurtured a bitter grudge against her neighbor. Relentlessly Edom attacked and attacked for the sake of spite. "Keeping his wrath forever" identifies the nation's preoccupation with inhuman and senseless behavior which characterizes a maniac. Because of these rebellious acts, God will judge Edom.

The whole prophecy against Edom is sometimes rejected as secondary because it reflects the hatred of Edom toward Jerusalem in 587/6 B.C. when the Babylonians destroyed Jerusalem. It is better to date this outpouring of Edom's inhumanity in the reign of Jehu (841 B.C.; 2 Kings 10:32-33) or during the reign of Uzziah, because just before Uzziah came to power Amaziah defeated Edom in the Valley of Salt (2 Kings 14:7, 22).[87] This horrible and merciless defeat of Sela (ten thousand were killed) just before the time of Amos was certainly one of the reasons for Edom's terrible anger.

The existence of several battles between Judah and Edom before the time of Amos, weakens the argument that Amos 1:11 is a secondary addition referring to the activity of Edom at the fall of Jerusalem in 587/6 B.C. The use of terms like "relentless, continual" and "forever" in this verse point to a long-term attitude and many acts of hostility, not just one act. Specific terminology in passages which condemn Edom for its activity at the fall of Jerusalem are absent from 1:11.[88] Therefore, the sin of Edom should be connected not to the fall of Jerusalem but with the hostility which took place over many years before the time of Amos. Although Edom's sin was probably against Judah rather than Israel, the people of Israel would have completely agreed with his condemnation of Edom.

---

[86]Numb. 20:14; Deut. 2:4; 8; 23:7; Obad. 10, 12.

[87]Schoville, "Oracles of Amos Against Gaza, Tyre and Edom," 61-63 and Haran, "Historical Background of Amos 1:2—2:6," 207-12.

[88]Obadiah 11-14 refer to Edom "standing aloof on the day strangers carried off its wealth," to Edom's "gloating, rejoicing, boasting, entering the gates, looting his goods, delivering up the survivors on the day of distress and calamity," but these ideas are not in Amos 1:11. Amos refers to Edom's "wrath, tearing anger and pursuing with the sword," but these ideas are not used in Obad. 11-14. Only Ezekiel 35-36 mentions Edom's use of the sword.

3. Punishment of destruction (1:12)

a. On their secure palace-fortresses (1:12). The punishment clause used in 1:4 appears again in this oracle against Edom with only minor alterations. There is no mention of the walls of a city; thus Teman may refer to a district. Most place Teman in the north of Edom, but its location and history are largely unknown.[89] The frequent references to Teman in passages about Edom confirm its importance, and Borzah's palace-fortresses imply that it was the capital city of Edom at this time. The strong fortifications which protect the leaders of Edom will be destroyed by the fire of war.

Since the cities or districts are difficult to define, the date of their destruction is hard to pinpoint. Nebuchadnezzar conquered the area (Jeremiah 27) around 590 B.C., and some years later the Edomites appeared in Idumaea, the southern part of Judah. The Nabateans later moved into the area of Edom around 300 B.C.

E. God's Judgment Against Ammon (1:13-15)

1. The source of the message (1:13a)

"Thus says Yahweh" identifies the source of the message and the authority behind the words of Amos.

2. The indictment concerning Ammon (1:13b-c)

a. Because of great sinfulness (1:13b). "Because of three rebellious acts and because of four" repeats the indictment formula in the earlier accusations. This indictment names the nation of Ammon, the descendents of one of Lot's daughters (Gen. 19:30-38). This tribe settled in transjordan between the river Arnon and Jabbok after driving out the Zamzummin (Deut. 2:9-21). The tribe of Gad was given part of their land (Josh. 13:25), and conflict between the Ammonites and Israel (Judg. 3:13; 10:7-8; 11:4-6, 32-33) included brutality. In 1 Samuel 11:1-2 they demanded that the right eye be gouged out of the people of Jabesh-gilead. Later David defeated the Ammonites (2 Sam. 10; 12:26-31; 1 Chron. 19—20:3) and enslaved some of them. The Ammonites were defeated in the time of Jehoshaphat (2 Chronicles 20) and paid tribute to Uzziah (2 Chron. 26:8), but there is no record of their inhuman treatment of the people of Gilead similar to that found later in verse 13.

b. Accountability is demanded (1:13b). "I will not vacillate about it" expresses God's determination to hold the Ammonites responsible for their rebellious acts. Yahweh's anger will not change, he will act and punish Ammon for its unhuman acts.

c. Specific sin described (1:13c). The rebellious acts of Ammon are related to its military activity in Gilead. The act of "ripping open pregnant women" is attributed to the Syrians in 2 Kings 8:12. The Israelite king Mena-

---

[89]Teman seems to be a synonym for Edom in Hab. 3:3; Jer. 49:20; Obad. 8-9. It may be an area or district in Gen. 36:42 and Job 2:11 (Eliphaz was a Temanite). Mays, *Amos* 35 puts Teman in the southern part of Edom.

hem (2 Kings 15:16) is accused of similar atrocities after the time of Amos. The Greeks and Assyrians infrequently used similar methods to terrorize their enemies.[90] Amos and his audience would consider such cruelty to be against every sense of human dignity. A helpless and defenseless pregnant woman was of no military significance, and the heartless murder of unborn children had no purpose. Ammon may have carried out these senseless acts of barbarity when Hazael oppressed Israel (2 Kings 8:12; 10:32), but a date immediately before the time of Amos is preferred, when Urartu weakened Assyria's control over the western nations around Palestine.[91]

The purpose clause which concludes the accusation gives the reason for these atrocities. These acts were committed to enable the Ammonites to extend their borders. The Ammonites did not act in self defense, but in cold blood terrorized the people of Gilead into submission. In their aggressive search for greater power and territory, the Ammonites showed no mercy to anyone. Such crimes are outrageous and the audience would have wholeheartedly agreed that Ammon deserved to be judged, even though these acts were not committed against the people of Samaria themselves.

3. Punishment of destruction

a. On the secure palace-fortresses (1:14a). With only a slight variation, the punishment clause employed in the earlier oracles is used again. It emphasizes God's decisive action ("I will") against the Ammonites and particularly its capital Rabbah-Ammon (2 Sam. 11:1; 12:26). God will "kindle a fire"[92] in it and bring the secure and strongly fortified palaces and walls to the ground. Ezekiel 25:1-7; 21:20 predict that Rabbah will be destroyed by the king of Babylon and later the "people from the East." Remains from the occupation of the site during the 7th and 8th century B.C. were found during the excavation of the city.[93]

b. On the day of battle (1:14b). The "shout, cry" on the day of battle can describe the cry of those being attacked (Isa. 15:4; Mic. 4:9) or the sounding of the alarm that an enemy is approaching (Joel 2:1; Hos. 5:8), but most instances refer to the war cry of troops on the attack (Josh. 6:5; 1 Sam. 4:5-6; Zeph. 1; 16; Amos 2:2). This ferocious primeval yell is a psychological boost to the troops and a demoralizing warning for anyone standing in front of the charging forces. The whirlwind and storm imagery are used figuratively to describe assaults on a city (Isa. 27:8; 28:2), although recent explanations of

---

[90] Homer, *The Iliad* (LCL) I (1924) 266-67 and Wolff, *Amos* 161.

[91] Wolff, *Amos* 150; Barton, *Oracles against the Nations* 32.

[92] The *y* of the root *yṣt* is assimilated into the *ṣ* (thus the dagesh) and the final *t* is doubled because of the first person, singular ending *tî* (GKC 71).

[93] M. Avi-Yonah and E. Stern, *Encyclopedia of Archeological Excavations in the Holy Land*, IV (New Jersey: Prentice-Hall, 1968) 987-93, gives a survey of the history and excavation of Rabbah as well as a short bibliography of the most significant studies which relate to the city and the inscription which were discovered there.

this figure interpret it to be a theophany of Yahweh.[94] God's appearance in conjunction with a whirlwind is not infrequent (Job 38:1; 40:6; Ezek. 1:4) and the wrath of God is sometimes metaphorically described as a tempest or storm (Isa. 29:6; 66:15; Jer. 23:19; Ezek. 13:13; and Nah. 1:3). The combination of theophany and judgment is consistent with the transformation of the "Day of Yahweh" elsewhere in Amos. The "day of battle" comes from human war traditions, but the "day of the storm" tradition indicates that the battle is a confrontation with the power of God. There is no theophany per se, but the infiltration of God into history broadens the sphere of God's presence to the point where history becomes a revelation of himself (Amos 1:2). The full implications of the prophet's teaching are not formulated in this verse (see Amos 5:18-20), for the imagery was primarily understood in military terms without the insight of the overall perspective of the book of Amos. Nevertheless, the configuration of these motifs together lays a foundation for the transformation of the people's theology in later addresses.

c. Leaders will be exiled (1:15a). The punishment against Ammon concludes with a direct statement against the leaders who are responsible for the inhumanity of Ammon, not its false religion (see the textual notes). The capital cities where they dwell will be destroyed (1:14a) and the people will be captured and deported. The king and his officials are accountable for their military policies; therefore God's judgment will fall on them in a special way. They will have no power; they will suffer the humiliation of being exiled to a foreign land. The destruction of Ammon's strongholds and the removal of its royal and military leaders will leave Ammon helpless before God. The audience would have wholeheartedly approved of this judgment on Ammon.

4. Divine Confirmation formula (1:15b)

The concluding formula verifies that the preceding message is the word of Yahweh. It confirms divine authority on the message of Amos and marks the end of the words of God concerning Ammon.

F. God's Judgment Against Moab (2:1-3)

1. The source of the message (2:1a)

"Thus says Yahweh" identifies the source of the message and the authority behind the words of Amos.

2. The indictment concerning Moab (2:1b-c)

a. Because of great sinfulness (2:1b). "Because of three rebellious acts and because of four" repeats the indictment formula used in the earlier accusations. The nation which Amos condemns is Moab, the descendents of Lot's

---

[94] Mays, *Amos* 38; Wolff, *Amos* 161; S. G. Farr, "The Language of Amos, Prophetic or Cultic?" *VT* 16 (1966) 316-17; J. L. Crenshaw, "Amos and the Theophanic Tradition," *ZAW* 80 (1968) 213.

younger daugher (Gen. 19:37-38). The Moabites settled in Transjordan east of the Dead Sea and north of the Edomites. When the Israelites came to this region, the tribe of Reuben (Numb. 21:24-26; 32:37-38) took control of the territory north of the river Arnon. The most notorious contact between Israel and Moab was the incident at Baal-Peor (Numbers 25). The Moabites were subdued by David (2 Sam. 8:1-2), but the Moabite Stone (*ANET* 320-21) and 2 Kings 1:1; 3:4-27 describe one of the many military encounters involving Israel, Moab, and Edom.[95] The extent of Jeroboam's control in this area is unknown.

b. Accountability is demanded (2:1*b*). "I will not vacillate about it" expresses God's determination to hold the Moabites responsible for their rebellious acts. Yahweh's anger will not change; he will act according to his word and punish Moab for its inhuman acts.

c. Specific sin described (2:1*c*). The crime of the Moabites appears to be an act of vindictiveness which disregarded the rights of the dead. Although bones can represent the "body" (Ps. 6:2[Heb. 6:3]; 31:10[Heb. 31:11]; Prov. 3:8; 14:30), it is more likely to suppose that the Moabites burned the remains of a dead Edomite king. The desecration of a tomb or a dead body was a means by which a nation could show its total disrespect for its enemies (2 Kings 23:16) or for criminals (Lev. 20:14; 21:9; Josh. 7:15, 25). This event is sometimes connected with the war between Israel, Edom, and Moab recorded in 2 Kings 3. The Moabite king attacked the Edomite army (2 Kings 3:26) but failed to escape; therefore he sacrificed his son, and the flow of the battle was reversed. This verse cannot refer to the burning of the son, the next king of Moab.[96] Jewish tradition contains the view that the Moabites burned the bones of the king of Edom who did not let them escape in 2 Kings 3:26-27. These interpretations as well as attempts to emend the text to improve the sense are of minimal value.[97] The when and the why of this rebellious act against the king of Edom are unknown.

The burning of the bones "to lime" represents the totality of the destruction of the king. The Targum interprets the reference to "lime" to be an indication that the Moabites used the ashes from the royal bones to whitewash their houses, and Wolff accepts this interpretation.[98] This goes well beyond what the text says, for the primary crime relates to the vile act of disturbing

---

[95]A survey of Moabite history is available in J. R. Bartlett, "The Moabites and Edomites," *Peoples of Old Testament Times*, ed. D. J. Wiseman (Oxford: Clarendon, 1977) 229-58 and A. H. van Zyl, *The Moabites* (Leiden: Brill, 1960).

[96]Bartlett, "Moabites and Edomites," 254.

[97]The historicity, date, and understanding of the relationship between Israel and Moab outlined in 2 Kings 3 and the Moabite Stone still contain several problems. Compare K. H. Bernhardt, "Der Feldzug der drei Könige," *Schalom, Studien zu Glaube und Geschichte Israels:* (Stuttgart: Calwer, 1971) 11-22, which is summarized by Barton, *Oracles against the Nations*, 33-35 and R. E. Murphy, "Israel and Moab in the Ninth Century B.C.," *CBQ* (1953) 409-17.

[98]Wolff, *Amos* 132, 162-3.

and desecrating the king's bones. As in several of the other oracles, the crime is not a sin against Israel or the people of Samaria.

3. Punishment of destruction

a. On the secure palace-fortresses (2:2a). The punishment clause of 1:4 is used to construct the first part of the announcement of judgment against Moab. God is the power which will accomplish this deed; he will send the fire of war on the nation and remove its secure and strongly fortified buildings. Kerioth is singled out as a place of significance here and in Jeremiah 48:24, 41. The reference on the Moabite Stone (line 13[99]) to dragging the lion figure of David to Kerioth and placing it before Chemosh, the god of the Moabites (Numb. 21:29), suggests that an important temple was located there.[100]

b. On the day of battle (2:2b). Using terminology similar to that found in the Ammon oracle (1:14 "war cry"), Amos describes the great battle which will bring about the annihilation of Moab and her cities. The prophet pictures a tumultuous battle scene with sound effects. The uproar of troops being signaled forward, their screaming yell as they charge the enemy and the various sounds of the clashing armies reproduce the judgment scene for Moab.[101] Moab will lose this battle because Yahweh controls the welfare of Moab as well as her enemies.

c. Their leaders will be cut off (2:3a-b). The expanded punishment section and the repetition of vocabulary ("her officials") further define the close relationship between the Ammon and Moab pair of oracles. The punishment will specifically be borne by the leaders of Moab who carry ultimate responsibility for the inhumanity against the dead Edomite king. It is likely that "judge" is synonymous with the term "king" (2 Sam. 8:15; 1 Kings 7:7; Jer. 21:12; Mic. 5:1 [Heb. 4:14]), for one of the important duties of the king was to administer justice among his people. The use of "judge" probably does not indicate anything about the political status of Moab or its political makeup, for the Moabite Stone as well as 2 Kings 3:4, 5, 7, 26 refer to the leader of Moab as the king. The chief ruler and his princes receive the brunt of God's indignation. The audience would have heartily agreed with God's plans to judge the Moabites.

Moab paid tribute to Tiglath-pileser (*ANET* 282), Sennacherib (*ANET* 287), Esarhaddon (*ANET* 291), and Ashurbanipal (*ANET* 294, 298, 301).

---

[99]*ANET* 320; J. C. L. Gibson, *Textbook of Syrian Semitic Inscriptions* (Oxford: Clarendon, 1971) 75-80.

[100]Kerioth has been associated with 'Ar by Hammershaimb, *Amos* 42; other suggestions are given in van Zyl, *The Moabites* 83.

[101]*šā'ôn* refers to the roar of waters (Isa. 17:12; Ps. 65:7 [Heb 65:8]), which is similar to the noise of waves of troops surging forward (Isa. 13:4; Jer. 25:31; 51:55; Hos. 10:14; Ps. 74:23). The trumpet "horn" signaled the troop for battle (Judg. 3:27; Jer. 4:19; Zeph. 1:16) and warned the city of the approach of an enemy (Amos 3:6; Hos. 5:8; 8:1; Jer. 6:17).

Josephus (*Jewish Antiquities*, x. 9. 7) records that Nebuchadnezzar defeated the Moabites and the Ammonites in 582 B.C.[102]

4. Divine Confirmation formula (2:3c)

The concluding formula verifies that the preceding message is the word of Yahweh. It confirms divine authority on the oracle of Amos and marks the end of the words of God concerning Moab.

Theological Developments

The theological message of this long section is determined by the content, common structure, and the overall relationship of the first six oracles with the final two oracles against Judah and Israel in 2:4-16. Because the repetition of various phrases is such an overt part of the structuring of the oracles, these phrases create a cumulative theological emphasis in themselves. Therefore, the material in this section will be considered under the major structural headings which appear in each paragraph.

"Thus says Yahweh"

This short and seemingly insignificant clause is repeated at the beginning and at the end of each oracle (except 1:10, 12). The introductory messenger formula and concluding divine confirmation formula specify the source and authority behind the prophet's words. He is announcing the will of God which was revealed to him. This communication process requires a divine-human relationship to clarify the reality of God's thoughts. Through this experience Amos received knowledge concerning God's desires and plans. When Amos says, "Thus says Yahweh," he is not giving the word of God from the page of a sacred book which was written hundreds of years earlier; he himself perceives the living and powerful word of God about a present reality. God's self-communication in this case is the decisive power which determines the course of history. The formulas themselves assure the listener that the messenger is a spokesman of God and that the message between the initial and final "thus says Yahweh" is the word of God. The audience acceptance of the word of God as authoritative for others enabled the prophet to gain maximum persuasive advantage for a similar message against Israel in 2:6-16.

"Because of three rebellious acts and because of four"

This clause begins the indictment section of each oracle. It emphasizes the magnitude of each nation's rebellious acts. Their rebellion is never defined as

---

[102]van Zyl, *Moabites* 148-59.

rebellion against a covenant or a divine law, although all religions believed that the gods did expect people to observe various norms which give order to life. All human actions are either in agreement with societal or divine patterns for behavior or in rebellion against such principles. Whether these stipulations are written or simply part of cultural tradition, the human conscience is an inner sixth sense which urges one to follow accepted patterns which will insure personal well-being. Such factors encourage responsibility and produce guilt when the accepted attitude or behavior is ignored or purposefully refuted. Human ability to choose and to change allows one the freedom to wilfully reject any norm.

The oracles against the nations show the pervasive extent of human rebellion through the widespread misuse of popular will (in every nation). This opposition to approved behavior became a perverted pattern (note the frequency of their rebellion), and it is the cause for God's revelation of himself to Amos. God is aware of human rebellion; no nation can hide from his eyes and no nation is exempt from responsibility for its action.

"I will not vacillate about it"

This clause announces God's determination to take each nation's rebellion seriously and to demand that each be accountable for its great sinfulness. By its sinfulness, each nation declares itself liable to punishment. Yet many acts of rebellion go unnoticed and unpunished in most societies. This may be due to the fact that the offended party is unable to force the guilty party to stand accountable for its rebellious violation of an accepted norm. Sometimes the offended party considers the deed a single act which it is willing to forgive. Persistent violations of accepted patterns of behavior either force a change in accepted patterns of behavior or require punishments of some sort. When a person's will is asserted above all other considerations and norms of behavior, reactions to this behavior become strongly solidified, and that attitude will not vacillate until the offender has been made accountable.

The fact that God holds each nation accountable indicates either (1) that the rebellious acts have been committed against Yahweh himself or (2) that Yahweh functions in the role of the protector of what is right and is the judge of those who are rebellious. The great sinfulness which God sees within the nations causes him to decide on a course of action which will make the rebellious accountable. God will not overlook this evil; he will not change his mind about their guilt; he will not cool his anger until the consequence of such deeds are accepted.

"The specific sin described"

Each oracle delineates a particular rebellious act which each nation has committed. These rebellious acts are crimes by cities or nations against peo-

ple from other nations. None of these acts was committed against the city of
Samaria, the audience which Amos addressed, although Israelites may well
have suffered during the attack of Damascus and Ammon on Gilead (1:3,
13). The protection of Samaria, Judah, or the unified Davidic empire never
formally enters the picture. The rebellious act of Damascus (1:3), Edom
(1:11), and Ammon (1:13) appear to be acts committed in the heat of battle,
while the rebellious deed of Moab was carried out on the bones of a dead man
(2:1). Gaza (1:6) and Edom (1:9) enslaved innocent people in a time of
peace. The common denominator in each oracle is that a stronger nation or
city committed inhuman acts against a weaker and often defenseless people
within society.

The rebellious acts include: gross acts of cruelty upon people defeated in
war (1:3), the thoughtless enslavement of large numbers of innocent people
for the sake of economic gain (1:6), the selling of a large number of people
who were protected under a treaty agreement (1:9), the rejection of all feelings of affection toward relatives for an attitude of fierce hatred and continual
bitterness (1:11), the terrorization of the defenseless for political gain (1:13),
and the desecration of the dead (2:1). Each act betrays a disrespect for humanity, a callous treatment of people as objects which can be manipulated,
used, and mistreated according to the desires of the mighty. People were considered things, not humans made in the image of God. God regards these
deeds as willful acts of rebellion.

The basis for each nation's responsibility is not their acknowledgement of
the covenant stipulation in the Jewish law but a much broader concept of human rights, popular morality, common sense, and a general belief that the
gods/God establishes justice in the world. All communities have or develop a
sense of order which regulates social relationships. This complex set of rules
governs how one treats an elder, who can marry, how to join the community,
what are the male and female roles, how religious rituals are to be carried
out, what punishments are given for those who break communal cultural
rules, and how one treats one's enemies. These norms of conduct are the
foundation of the society and provide a sense of solidarity and stability for its
members.[103] This cohesive bond results in a feeling of right (conduct according to societal laws) and wrong (breaking these written or unwritten laws).

These cultural regulations carefully determine and protect family or kinship life. If an act of violence is done against a kinship group or if a member
of the family is dishonored, revenge will result. Conversely, the norms of
conduct set up a framework for what is right, proper, and moral within the
group. Honor is to be given to one's parents, hospitality is to be provided,
conduct according to the standard is rewarded, life is to be preserved, and
friendship is enjoyed. When these norms of conduct are combined with

---

[103]W. Eichrodt, *Theology of the Old Testament* II (1967) 316-22.

religious sanctions and the blessing of the divine, a very strong popular morality is developed in even the most primitive society. The nobility of man becomes a theological belief. Care for the clan or kinship group becomes a divine imperative. Stealing, murder, and rape will bring a demonic curse on the guilty party.

Although the culture, religion, and popular morality of the nations in Amos 1-2 are largely unknown, it is reasonable to assume that each nation knew that its rebellious deeds were against their own norms of conduct. If the nation guilty of the offense had been the offended party, certainly each nation would have felt that it had been wronged. All peoples believe that breaking a treaty is wrong, that kidnapping and selling innocent people for personal economic gain is reprehensible, that the incomprehensible brutality of killing defenseless pregnant women is barbarous. The morality of war and the treatment of foreigners is never determined by the exact same code of conduct which regulates every day life within the kinship family, but even in war there are basic norms of human conduct which regulate behavior. One who submits or surrenders to a foreign army is treated different from one who fights; noncombatants are not treated the same as troops.[104] God holds each nation guilty of rebelling against the moral norms of conduct which governed its morality. These crimes were a purposeful rebellion against all concepts of humanity and the laws of conscience which God gives to each man. These two aspects of general revelation gave each nation the ability to make decisions for which they are accountable. Amos announces that God will hold each nation responsible, and the moral sensitivity of the people of Samaria would have caused them to agree with God's condemnation of the sins of the nations.

"I will send fire"

Each oracle contains an announcement of punishment by Yahweh. There is no reference to other gods punishing the nations; it is Yahweh who stands as the protector of the weak and helpless, the establisher of justice, and the judge of the powerful. As the sole God and ruler of all nations, Yahweh directs judgment particularly on "the secure palace-fortresses," the "one who holds the sceptre" (1:5, 8), and the "king and his princes" (1:15; 2:3). The

---

[104]Eichrodt, *Theology of the Old Testament* 323, seems to suggest from biblical examples that war was outside the domain of popular morality. But the text does not approve of Abram's lying about his wife (Genesis 12, 20), the crime of Simeon and Levi against the men of Shechem (Genesis 34), the oppression of the Israelites by the Egyptians (Exodus 1-5) or the misuse of the Levite's concubine in Judges 19-21. Instead Israel honored the spies' oath to Rahab in a time of war (Joshua 2, 6), kept the treaty with the deceitful Gibeonites (Joshua 9), and David considered Joab guilty for killing Abner (2 Samuel 3). Barton, *Oracles Against the Nations* 51-61, points out rules of international morality from international treaties, from diplomatic relations, and records of wars which describe the conduct of various kings. See K. Barth, *Church Dogmatics* IV, 2, *The Doctrine of Reconciliation* (New York: Scribners, 1958) 443-52, for a discussion of inhumanity and Amos.

chief cities, their walls, and their inhabitants will be destroyed and many will be taken captive. The abuse of power enables the strong leaders to put themselves above norms of conduct; might becomes the rule of conduct. Personal gain, revenge, and total humiliation of the helpless were the goals of the leaders; because they were secure and powerful any means was used to attain and maintain their position. The removal of these secure palace-fortresses and the judgment of the nations is not a judgment on any institution (kingship or cities), but on the misuse of power and rejection of humane conduct. Because Yahweh has seen these rebellious acts, he will judge each nation.

Yahweh is pictured not only as a judge but also as a warrior who has universal sovereignty over all nations. The holy warrior declares war on those who displease him. Fate is not the cause of a nation's judgment; even the employment of some foreign army remains in the background. The fire of God's wrath is the primary weapon; Yahweh will fight and destroy the powerful within each nation. There is clearly no limit to his power, nor boundary which delineates its use. His fire goes out equally on all with a similar result. The concept of God as a judge and a warrior are not new with Amos. This understanding of God is found in earlier Israelite traditions (according to Amos 2:9-10; 4:11).

The Theological Background of Amos

Although Amos begins a new stage in the prophetic movement, his proclamation of the message "Thus says Yahweh" is in line with the prophecy of Samuel (1 Sam. 15:2), Nathan (2 Sam. 7:4, 8; 12:7, 11), an unidentified prophet (1 Kings 13:21), Elijah (1 Kings 17:14), and other prophets (1 Kings 20:13, 28, 42). His announcement of God's demand for accountability is similar to ancient traditions about the universal responsibility which stands behind the flood narrative (Genesis 6) and the judgment of the foreign Amorites (Gen. 15:16), Sodomites (Genesis 18-19), Egyptians (Exod. 9:27; 10:16-17), and Amalekites (1 Sam. 15:2-3). God's role as a judge is not a new concept, and the description of Yahweh as a warrior goes back to the very early Red Sea tradition (Exod. 15:3). When foreign nations are judged by God, it is because of the iniquity of the Amorites, Sodomites, Egyptians, and Amalekites, not because they have broken a covenant law.

This continuity with earlier traditions indicates that Amos is not presenting a new theological understanding of a prophet, morality and ethics, God's sovereignty over the nations, or of Yahweh's role as a judge and warrior. Amos re-emphasizes and reaffirms a theological tenet which the Israelites in Samaria were partially aware of from their traditions. He proclaims a theological cause-and-effect relationship which the people of Samaria could easily understand and affirm. The self-evident truth of the message is important to his overall purpose in the final oracle. The rhetorical effect of his highly stylized oracles hammers home the message in a way which cannot be avoided. God has spoken; the nations have committed great sins; they will be held accountable for their inhumanity to man; God will destroy these centers of power and the leaders who do such things. Having established his theological base, Amos is now ready to apply these accepted ideas to his audience in the final paragraphs.

The Oracles Against the Nations

_____ *Amos 2:4-16* _____

Introduction

The oracle against Judah forms a natural bridge between those against the foreign nations and Israel itself. Judah, Israel's sister nation, was a frequent rival against Israel; thus its judgment would have sparked a special smile of approval. Having captured the sympathy and approval of his listeners, Amos moves to address his audience. At this point the audience expected to hear a positive climax about Israel's future victories. But Amos transforms the traditional, final salvation oracle into a judgment speech against Israel. Because the theological principles adduced in the earlier oracles have been firmly substantiated as legitimate guidelines for interpreting God's activity in history, the audience cannot escape the inevitability of the conclusion which Amos draws. The rhetorical advantage of surprise heightens the dramatic effect of the conclusion and burns the word of God deep into the listener's conscience. Israel is not only guilty of inhumanity like the ungodly nations, it treats its very own people with the same disrespect and barbarity that the nations save for foreigners. Because of their transgressions, they too will suffer destruction.

Background

The setting for 2:4-16 is the same as 1:3—2:3. Although war imagery is used throughout Amos 1-2, in these final verses the audience discovers that the prophet is not calling the nation to war against its neighboring enemies. What had appeared to be a war oracle by an Israelite sympathizer now turns out to be a judgment speech by a foreigner.

The ritual setting, which was rejected earlier,[1] is not particularily convincing for these final oracles either. The religious references in 2:6-8 are subordinate to the social evils which are the primary focus of the prophet's condemnation. Reventlow has hypothesized a cursing ritual associated with a covenant renewal ceremony, but Wolff has pointed out the inadequate line of evidence for this setting.[2] The reference to the law of Yahweh (2:4), stretching out beside every altar, drinking in the house of their gods (2:8), and the reci-

---

[1] See the section on Background for 1:3—2:3.

[2] Wolff, *Amos* 147 finds the linguistic parallels too inexact and the covenantal cultic festival too hypothetical to support Reventlow's theory.

tation of an ancient traditional confession (2:9-10) do not by their mere presence presuppose a cultic setting. Although some of these traditions may be used in the worship of Israel on other occasions, the ritual use of them is not evident in this context. These traditions demonstrate that Judah and Israel have a distinctive religious background which effects the degree of their responsibility, but they do not point to a setting different from 1:3—2:3.

The theological background of Amos and his audience includes their knowledge of the law of Yahweh, the exodus, wilderness, and conquest traditions. The historical and theological references to these concepts in several of the early prophetic books demonstrate that these were fundamental to the nation's understanding of its past. Isaiah knew of Sodom and Gomorrah (Isa. 1:9; 3:9) and so did Amos (4:11). Isaiah makes allusions to Gideon's defeat of the Midianites (Isa. 9:4 [Heb. 9:3]; 10:26), the detailed stipulation of the sacrificial system (Isa. 1:11-15), and sins which were a rejection of the law of Yahweh (Isa. 5:24).[3] Hosea knew that the people had ignored the significance of God's gracious acts to Israel in the past (Hos. 8:13; 9:3; 11:1-5; 12:9 [Heb. 12:10]; 13:4), refers to the stipulations of the law (Hos. 4:2, 6; 8:1, 12), and makes some clear references to the language of the covenant (Hos. 1:9-10; 2:19, 23 [Heb 2:21, 25]; 8:1).[4] Micah knew of the exodus (6:4-5; 7:15), and Amos mentions the plagues in Egypt (4:10), sacrifices in the wilderness (5:25), David's ability to play the harp (6:5), sabbath laws (8:5), the exodus and conquest (2:9-10; 9:7), and reveals some knowledge of the legal code in Exodus.[5] The argument of Amos assumes that the people know and generally accept the law of God as part of their cultural heritage. The covenant idea is implied at some points, but for the most part it seems to remain in the background.[6]

---

[3]Vriezen, "Essentials of the Theology of Isaiah," 135.

[4]N. W. Porteous, "The Prophets and the Problem of Continuity," *Israel's Prophetic Heritage*, ed. B. W. Anderson and W. Harrelson (New York: Harper and Row, 1962) 17; G. H. Davies, "The Yahwistic Traditions in the Eighth-Century Prophets," *Studies in Old Testament Prophecy*, ed. H. H. Rowley (New York: Scribner's, 1950) 40-42; C. N. North's survey of prophetic references to earlier tradition in *Old Testament Interpretation of History* (London: Epworth, 1946) 42-53, includes the prophet's knowledge of (1) the patriarchal tradition, (2) exodus and conquest, (3) the covenant, (4) settlement and (5) monarchy; W. Zimmerli, *The Law and the Prophets* (Oxford: Blackwell, 1965) 67-75, surveys the references to the law and covenant in the eighth-century prophets.

[5]Zimmerli, *The Law and the Prophets* 68-69 follows Würthwein, "Amos-Studien," 40-52, who derives Amos's accusation concerning the mistreatment of the poor from Exod. 22:26 (25), interest from Exod. 22:25 (24), and false weights from Lev. 19:35 or Deut. 25:13-16. See Zimmerli's "Prophetic Proclamation and Reinterpretation," *Tradition and Theology in the Old Testament*, ed. D. A. Knight (Philadelphia: Fortress Press, 1977) 76-87 for the early prophet's use of fundamental traditions.

[6]In recent years many see the covenant ideas under every phoneme. See F. M. Seilhamer, "The Role of Covenant in the Mission and Message of Amos," *A Light unto My Path: Old Testament Studies in Honor of J. M. Myers*, ed. H. N. Bream et al., (Philadelphia: Temple Univ., 1974) 435-51 or G. Snyder, "The Law and Covenant in Amos," *Restoration Quarterly* 25 (1982) 158-66.

The social setting in these final oracles is not one of military exploitation of the weak, massive slave trade, or the desecration of the dead, but the abuse of the weak by the strong remains the fundamental theme of the accusation in 2:6-8. The social context observed elsewhere in Amos (3:15; 4:1; 5:10-13; 6:1-7; 8:4-6) points toward the existence of various power groups in Israel which employed economic and legal means to take advantage of weaker members of society.[7] Some have reconstructed the social setting as a class conflict brought about by the gradual Canaanization of the economic system and the increased urbanization of the nation during the monarchy. These forces led to the stratification of society and a departure from the nomadic, agrarian, and egalitarian ideals on which the nation was founded.

This sociological analysis reconstructs an idealistic classless society which probably never existed in Israel. The very existence of positions of responsibility like the priest, the elder, the judge, the commander of thousands, and the officials of the monarchy argue against an egalitarian society.[8] Both the oppressed and the oppressor were determined by circumstances at different points in time. Merchants, landowners, the wealthy, the crown, and even the poor themselves were able to bring different levels of economic oppression on others. It was also possible for each segment of society to be oppressed by higher authorities or foreign governments. Amos does not argue for a peasant revolt, nor does he offer a program of social reform which will eradicate systemic evil from the fiber of Israelite society.[9] He does not condemn the wealthy per se, nor are the poor identified as the righteous who will be saved from the destruction that threatens to engulf the nation. Amos attacks various socio-economic means of gaining wealth because they are contrary to the accepted traditions known in the law of Yahweh. Aspects of a prebendal system, rent capitalism, or a patrimonial domain system may have been in place in different segments of the nation, producing no detrimental effects at one time or very harsh results at another. Whatever the complex of economic factors, Amos narrows in on the exploitation of the weak in ways contrary to the law of God. The socio-economic systems are being misused by Israelites to abuse their Israelite neighbors. God's anger will bring judgment on the nation because Israel's ways are no longer the ways of God.

---

[7]B. Lang, "The Social Organization of Peasant Poverty in Biblical Israel," *JSOT* 24 (1982) 48, believes that rent capitalism was the primary system that led to the problem that Amos condemns.

[8]M. Fendler, "Zur Sozial kritik des Amos," *EvT* 33 (1973) 32-53, sees several groups oppressing the poor rather than one homogeneous group, unlike H. Donner, "Die Soziale Botschaft der Propheten in Lichte der Gesellschaftordnung in Israel," *Or An* 2 (1963) 229-45.

[9]H. B. Huffmon, "The Social Role of Amos' Message," *The Quest for the Kingdom of God: Studies in Honor of G. E. Mendenhall* (Winona Lake: Eisenbrauns, 1983), 111-13.

Structure and Unity

Structure

The syntactical outline of Amos 2:4-16 below contains both similarities and differences when compared to the first six oracles. The outline derived from the content of the oracles will be followed in the exegesis of the verses later.

Oracles Against the Nations
2:4-16

2:4   G. God's judgment against Judah

Thus says Yahweh,
  because of 3 rebellious acts of Judah
  and because of 4,
I will not vacillate about it,
  because they rejected Yahweh's law,
   and did not keep his statutes;
    but their liars[a] lead them astray,
     the ones after which their fathers went.

    1. Source of the message
    2. Indictment against Judah
     a. Because of great sinfulness
     b. Accountability is demanded
     c. Specific sins described

2:5   3. Punishment of destruction

I will send fire upon Judah,
  and it will devour the palace-fortresses of Jerusalem.

     a. On the secure palace-fortresses

2:6   H. God's judgment against Israel

Thus says Yahweh,
  because of 3 rebellious acts of Israel
  and because of 4,
I will not vacillate about it,
  because they sell the innocent for money,
   the needy for a pair of sandals;

    1. Source of the message
    2. Indictment against Israel
     a. Because of great sinfulness
     b. Accountability is demanded
     c. Specific sins described
      (1) Sell the poor

they trample[b] the head of the weak into the dust of the earth
and manipulate the afflicted's way of life;
also a man and his father go into the same maid
  in order to profane my holy name.

      (2) Oppress the weak
      (3) Misuse the defenseless
      (4) Profane God's name

---

cThey stretch out on garments which were pledgedc beside every altar. They drink wine which was tribute in the house of their gods.	**2:8**	(5) Exploit the destitute for pleas- ure
Yet I myself destroyed the Amorites before themd which height was like the height of cedars, and who were strong like oaks. I destroyed his fruit abovee and his root below.	**2:9**	d. God's acts for Israel are re- jected (1) God de- stroyed their ene- mies
And I myself brought you up out of the land of Egypt, I led you forty years in the wilderness fthat you might possess the land of the Amorites, and I raised up some of your sons as prophets and some of your young men as Nazirites. Is this not so, sons of Israel declares Yahweh.	**2:10** **2:11**	(2) God re- deemed and cared for them (3) God gave them spir- itual leaders (4) Challenge to accept God's sov- ereignty
But you caused the Nazirites to drink wine, and you commanded the prophets saying, "You shall not prophesy."	**2:12**	(5) Israel rejected God's sov- ereignty
Behold, I will make (the ground) cleaveg under you as a wagon cleaves (the ground) when fully loaded with sheaves.	**2:13**	3. Punishment of destruction a. God will bring an earthquake
Then flight will vanish from the swifth and the strong will not strengthen his power, the mighty will not save his life.	**2:14**	b. Escape is impossible
Then the one who holds the bow will not stand, the swift of foot will not escapei and the one who rides the horse will not save his life;	**2:15**	
jeven the bravest warriors will flee nakedj in that day, declares Yahweh.	**2:16**	4. Confirmation Formula

2:4a. The Old Greek translated "their liars" with "their follies, idols" and adds "which they have made," which is not in the Hebrew.

2:7b. The Massoretic Text has one verb here, but the Old Greek gives two: "Those who are treading," which goes with "upon the dust of the earth," and "they are beating," which is connected to "upon the head of the weak." The first verb translates the verb *šûp* "to crush, trample" rather than *ā'āp* "to yearn, desire," which is the spelling in the Hebrew here. These two roots are also confused in Amos 8:4. In this verse the rarer *šûp* fits the context better and is consistent with the accusation in Amos 4:1. See A. Szabo, "Textual Problems in Amos and Hosea," *VT* 25 (1975) 502.

2:8c-c. The Old Greek contains numerous variations in 2:8a. The Old Greek omits "upon," resulting in the translation, "they stretch out their garments" rather than "they stretch out on their garments," which is in Aq., Sym., the Targ., and the Hebrew. "Pledged" is "bundled with cords" in the Old Greek while Aq. has "corrupt."

2:9d. Several MSS have "before you" instead of "before them." The third person agrees with the plural verbs in 2:6-9. The change of person to second person does not begin until 2:10. By continuing the third person of 2:6-8 into 2:9 the author identifies the "they" in 2:6-8 with the "they" in 2:9. The "they" of 2:9 and the "you" of 2:10-12 are identified thematically as the same group.

2:9e. For the Hebrew "I destroyed" the Old Greek has "I dried up," which fits the metaphor of the tree better. Aq. agrees with the Hebrew text.

2:10f. The Syriac adds "and I brought you to this place" before the last line to give the verse a line parallel to 10a.

2:13g. The Old Greek has "I roll, turn," Aq. "I will clatter," Targum "distress," and Syriac "I will press." The Hebrew hiphil participle from *'uq* may be an Aramaism of the Hebrew *ṣuq* "press, crush," the Arabic *'aqa* "creak, groan," Aramaic *puq* "shake, totter," or the Ugaritic *'qq* and Arabic *'aqqa* "split." H. Gese, "Kleine Beiträge zum Verständnis des Amosbuches," *VT* 12 (1962) 417-24 gives a full discussion of the various options and concludes that the last suggestion is best. See also H. P. Müller, "Die Wurzeln *'yq, y'q* and *'uq*," *VT* 21 (1971) 556-64.

2:14h. The Old Greek has "from the runner" while Aq. and Theod. have "from the light, swift."

2:15i. The Old Greek has a passive "he will not be saved" instead of the active "will not escape."

2:16j-j. Greek translators seem to have read *mṣ'* "to find" instead of *'myṣ* "brave" and thus ended up with the translation "the strong shall not find his heart [confidence] in power, and the naked will flee in that day." Several Greek traditions omit the negative in the first clause and some omit "the strong" at the beginning of the clause. Aq. and Sym. confirm the reading in the Hebrew text.

The structure of the final two oracles is closely related to the earlier prophecies against Israel's neighbors. Both 2:4-5 and 2:6-16 have: "Thus says Yahweh" and the regular indictment formula "because of three rebellious acts and because of four, I will not vacillate about it, because they have." Only the Israel oracle has a final divine confirmation formula. The expansion of the Israel speech draws the emphasis to this climax.

In spite of these similarities, the final two prophecies are quite unique. The Judah oracle has a long indictment, short punishment, and no final divine confirmation formula, thus it matches the rhetorical structure of the Tyre and Edom oracles and supports the pairing design that the author built into the first seven oracles. The Israel oracle is more complex and difficult to analyze. To the long indictment clause in 2:6-8 is added a supplementary paragraph about God's acts on behalf of Israel and her rejection of God (2:9-12). This strengthens the persuasive force of the accusation and demonstrates that Israel is without excuse. In place of the usual punishment clause, there is a long paragraph on the magnitude of the total defeat of Israel's army (2:13-16).

The first paragraph of the indictment against Israel (2:6-8) begins with the usual structural markers: "because of " plus an infinitive construct. The paragraph is rhetorically held together by repeated descriptions of ways in which the poor and helpless were abused. Almost paradoxical to this emphasis, Amos 2:9-12 relates how God ("I") has graciously redeemed and cared for Israel when it was poor and helpless (2:9-10). A topical division of this material would separate 2:9-10 (the exodus and wilderness period) from 2:11-12 (the prophets and the Nazarites), but the formal contrast between the "I"

(2:9-11) and the "you" (2:12) and the final clause, "Is this not so, O sons of Israel, declares Yahweh," at the end of 2:11 are stronger divisional markers. This structural design points to the unity of 2:9-11, while the final rhetorical question in 2:11 and the accusation in 2:12 are needed to transform the recital of God's gracious deeds into an accusation for which Israel carries full responsibility.

The final paragraph begins in 2:13 with the introductory "behold" and returns to the theme of the destruction of people. The destruction of Israel in 2:13-16 stands in bold contrast to the nation's destruction of the poor and weak in 2:6-8, and to God's destruction of the Amorites for Israel in 2:9-10. The description of the defeat of Israel is a rhetorical masterpiece with word-play, paradox, and repetition. This section is unified by: the repetition of "swift" in 14a and 15b; "flee" in 14a and 16b; "to be strong" in 14b and 15a; "mighty" in 14c and 16a and "he will not escape" in 14c, 15b, and 15c; and the overall parallelism of the negative clauses in 2:14-16.[10]

Unity

The unity of 1:3—2:16 is questioned because of doubts about the authenticity of the Judah oracle in 2:4-5, the central section of the Israel oracle (2:10-12), and a few other scattered words and phrases. The genuineness of 2:4-5 is examined on the basis of: (1) a form-critical comparison of this oracle with earlier oracles; (2) linguistic and stylistic factors; and (3) other supplementary evidence. The evaluation of these factors has led some to conclude that all of 2:4-5, only 2:4b, or none of 2:4-5 is secondary.

The amount of weight given to each of the arguments is quite diverse. Form-critical considerations based on the structure of 2:4-5 are very important to some,[11] but others, who also reject part or all of 2:4-5, conclude that the difference in form is not significant.[12] The later view is more convincing, for the prophets were not robots who could not change and adapt a form to their own purpose. The earlier examination of the formal structure of the oracles (see the section on Structure and Unity for 1:3—2:3) concluded that the variation in form was designed so the oracles could be grouped into pairs; thus the Judah oracle follows pattern B.

The primary criteria for determining the authenticity of 2:4-5 is the linguistic or stylistic argument. Three points are raised to demonstrate a change in style: (a) the use of "deuteronomistic" terms which date from a period later than Amos; (b) the introduction of a prose gloss (2:4b) into a poetic section; and (c) the vague or general description of religious sins instead of a specific

---

[10]H. N. Richardson, "Amos 2:13-16: Its Structure and Function," *SBL 1978 Seminar Papers* (Missoula: Scholars Press, 1978) 363-65.

[11]Wolff, *Amos* 140 and Schmidt, "Die deuteronomistic Redaktion des Amosbuches," 174-78.

[12]Mays, *Amos* 41 and Rudolph, *Amos* 118-22.

social sin.[13] The "deuteronomistic" terms in 2:4*a* include "law of Yahweh," "his statutes," "they have kept," and "went after." Although no one doubts the importance of these terms to the theology of Deuteronomy (Deut. 4:40; 6:17; 7:11; 11:32; 16:12; 17:19; 26:16), to determine a "deuteronomistic" influence, a clear dependence, which cannot be explained on other grounds, must be established. Since all the early prophets demonstrate some knowledge of early Israelite traditions (see the section on Background), it is difficult to affirm this position. Isaiah, a contemporary of Amos, even uses the term "law" to describe prophetic speech (1:10) and the "law of Yahweh" to refer to the word of God in Isaiah 5:24 and 30:9.[14] These terms are used not only in early prophetic texts but also in Levitical, hymnic, and wisdom texts.[15] Because of their wide use before the time of Amos, an exact quotation of a particular phrase limited only to Deuteronomy would be required to show direct dependence. Rudolph and Driver properly conclude that Amos 2:4a is not a late "deuteronomistic" addition.[16]

The criteria for denying the authenticity of 2:4*b* depend heavily on the conclusion that "their lies, liars" refers to "their false gods, idols," but this meaning is not attested elsewhere using this term. This idea is foreign to the context of the present and previous oracles against the nations. "Lie, liar" *czb* is not used in Deuteronomy and only three times (Judg. 16:10, 13; 2 Kings 4:16) in all of Joshua—2 Kings. If this text were "deuteronomistic," the term *hbl* "emptiness" would have been used (Jer. 2:5; 14:22; 2 Kings 17:15; 1 Kings 16:13; Deut. 32:21). The context of Amos 2:4 is similar to the situation in Isaiah 3:12, "your leaders have led you astray (*t'h*—the same root is used for the verb in 2:4) and confuse the course of your path"; Isaiah 9:15-16 "the prophet who teaches lies (*czb*)...those who lead this people astray (*t'h*)"; Isaiah 28:15 "we have made lies (*czb*) our refuge"; Jeremiah 23:14 "the prophets in Jerusalem . . . they commit adultery and walk in lies (*czb*)"; Jeremiah 23:32 "I am against those who prophesy lying dreams, says Yahweh, and who tell them and lead my people astray (*t'h*)." The problem is not false gods but leaders, priests, and prophets who lie and lead the nation away from the law of God. Once the phrase "to follow after" is placed in a context other than "following after other gods" (Deut. 4:3; 8:19; 11:28; 13:2 [Heb. 13:3]; 28:14), there is no reason why social sins should be excluded from the prophets' thoughts (see Isaiah 3:12-15 and 5:8-25).

---

[13]Fosbroke, *Amos* 785-86; Harper, *Amos* 44; Wolff, *Amos* 140; Mays, *Amos* 41; Schmidt, "Die deuteronomistiche Redaktion des Amosbuches," 174-78.

[14]Hammershaimb, *Amos* 45-46.

[15]Lev. 3:17; 6:18, 22; 7:34, 36; 10:9, 11, 15 and especially Lev. 18:4-5, 26; 19:19, 37; 20:8, 22; 25:18; 26:15, 17; or Ps. 18:21[Heb 18:22]; 37:34; 78:56; 89:31; 99:7 or Prov. 7:1, 2; 8:32; 19:16; 28:4; 29:18.

[16]Rudolph, *Amos* 120-21; Driver, *Amos* 120; See also Hammershaimb, *Amos* 45-46; Haran, "Empire of Jeroboam ben Joash," 274 and S. Wagner, "Überlegungen zur Frage nach den Beziehungen des Propheten Amos zum Südreich," *TLZ* 96 (1971) 653-70.

Supplementary evidence brought against 2:4-5 includes: (a) Amos had no call or commission to Judah, but there is no evidence that he was called to preach against Damascus, Philistia, Ammon, and the other nations; (b) the treatment of Judah would weaken the climax against Israel in 2:6-16, but this ignores the strong distinctive nationalism which existed in Israel and the independence of Israel for close to two hundred years; and (c) Amos likely treated Judah as a part of Israel within 2:6-16 (as in 3:1-2) rather than with a separate oracle, but this criticism overlooks the distinctions which Amos makes in the book between "the whole family" in 3:1, which includes both Israel and Judah, and his use of "Israel" (3:13), "house of Jacob" (3:13), "house of Israel" (5:1), and "house of Joseph" (5:6), which are limited to Israel.

Amos 2:10-12 is another passage which sometimes is attributed to someone other than Amos. The evidence for this conclusion is based on: (a) the shift from third to second person in verse 10-12; (b) the incorrect order of the conquest before the exodus in 2:10-11; and (c) the stereotyped "deuteronomistic" phraselogy.[17] The shift in person from third (2:9) to second (2:10-12) serves to strengthen the contrast between what God did against the Amorites and what God did for the Israelites,[18] while maintaining the continuity of identity between the third person in 2:6-8 and the new section beginning in 2:9. Chronological order is not important to the purpose of Amos at this point and is not a sign of lateness unless this order can be found in late writings. The "deuteronomistic" evidence in 2:10 is based on Amos' use of the verb 'lh "to go up, bring up" but this term is used elsewhere in the early prophets (Hos. 2:15 [Heb 2:17]; 12:13 [Heb 12:14]; Amos 2:10; 3:1; 9:7). Only one (Deut. 20:1) of the twenty-seven uses of 'lh in Deuteronomy is related to the exodus. Deuteronomy discusses the exodus twenty-one times but has the verbs ys' "to go out" instead of 'lh "to go up."[19] This is a strong indication that the book of Amos was not relying on the book of Deuteronomy.

Rudolph maintains the authenticity of 2:10-11 but does question verse 12.[20] Although the rhetorical question at the end of verse 11, "Indeed, is it not so, O sons of Israel, declares Yahweh" might appear to be more appropriate at the end of a section, and verse 8 seems to be the end of the accusations against Israel, neither factor excludes the addition of another accusation in verse 12. The question at the end of 2:11 draws the audience into the argument and forces them to agree that God acts on behalf of his people and

---

[17]Wolff, *Amos* 112-13, 141-42, 169; R. F. Melugin, "The Formation of Amos: An Analysis of Exegetical Method," *SBL 1978 Seminar Papers* (Missoula: Scholars Press, 1978) 384-85; and Schmidt, "Die deuteronomistic Redaktion des Amosbuches," 178-82 omit all of 2:10-12. Harper, *Amos* cxxxii, 54, has doubts about parts of verse 12 and changes the order of verses 9 and 10.

[18]Rudolph, *Amos* 146.

[19]T. R. Hobbs, "Amos 3:1b and 2:10," *ZAW* 81 (1969) 384-87 and B. S. Childs, "Deuteronomic Formulae of the Exodus Tradition," *VT* 17 (1967) 30-39.

[20]Rudolph, *Amos* 146-48.

against those who reject him. Amos 2:9-11 by itself is incomplete and lacks a clear application or accusation. Verse 12 draws the section to a close, by showing that God's sovereignty over their lives was rejected when his messengers were rejected.

Other pre-exilic prophets (Hos. 11:1-4; 13:4-6; Isa. 1:2; Mic. 6:3-5) recite God's great act of grace toward Israel to demonstrate the nation's ungratefulness or rejection of God, so the appearance of similar verses in this indictment is not unique or unusual.

Finally, a few commentators have raised questions about the amount of repetition within the various parallel clauses in 2:13-16.[21] The importance of repetition to the structure of 1:3—2:3 is a warning against solutions which alter or delete parts of verses on the basis of repetition, a rhetorical device which Amos frequently uses.[22]

Interpretation

G. God's Judgment Against Judah: 2:4-5

1. The source of the message (2:4a)

"Thus says Yahweh" identifies the source and authority behind the message Amos proclaimed concerning Judah.

2. The indictment against Judah (2:4b-c)

a. Because of great sinfulness (2:4b). "Because of three rebellious acts and because of four" repeats the indictment formula employed in the earlier accusations. Although Judah and Israel were once one nation, rivalry between the tribes existed before the reign of David (2 Samuel 2-3), and eventually the nation split after the death of Solomon (1 Kings 12). Bitterness and mistrust resulted in open war between the two brother nations (1 Kings 12:18-24; 14:30; 15:7, 16-21, 32; 2 Kings 14:8-14). The introduction of the calves at Bethel and Dan, and the acceptance of Baalism and other cultic innovations (1 Kings 12:28-33) widened the gap between Judah and Israel. In many ways the Israelites in Samaria considered Judah a foreign nation, and the audience greeted Amos' condemnation of Judah with a good deal of pleasure and smug self-righteousness.

b. Accountability is demanded (2:4b). "I will not vacillate about it" demonstrates Yaweh's determination to hold Judah responsible for her guilt. His wrath will not cease; the decree will be carried out; Judah will be pun-

---

[21]Wolff, *Amos* 134-35 questions the authenticity of 2:14a or b, while Rendtorff ("Zu Amos 2:14-16," *ZAW* 85 [1973] 226-27) keeps all the lines but places 15a after 14a. H. N. Richardson's ("Amos 2:13-16: Its Structure and Function in the Book," *SBL Seminar Papers* [Missoula: Scholars Press, 1978] 361-65) examination of the structure shows how the stichs are locked into a compact rhetorical unit by their present structure.

[22]Paul, "Concatenous Literary Pattern," 397-403.

ished for her many rebellious acts. Any privilege which Judah enjoyed through her special relationship to God is ignored. The possibility of excuse is not even mentioned; instead the advantage of Judah increases the weight of her guilt.

c. Specific sins described (2:4c-d). The indictment against Judah is structurally similar to the longer indictments against Tyre (1:9) and Edom (1:11). Some conclude that 2:4 was added by a later "deuteronomistic" editor, but these formal and linguistic arguments are insufficient to establish an exclusive "deuteronomistic" influence.[23] Amos and the other eighth century prophets knew about the "law of Yahweh,"[24] and his condemnation of Judah is based on their responsibility to follow God's revealed will. Some traditions came through the medium of Moses and the prophets, while others were derived from the law courts, the priests, and the wise men. Through these servants of God, the nation was taught to despise the evil ways of the nations around about them and remain loyal to a distinctively Israelite way of life. Amos charges Judah with repudiating and rejecting these divine guidelines on life. These accusations are more specific than the earlier oracles, because the law that Judah rebelled against is given. On the other hand, the oracles against the earlier nations are more specific, because the specific rebellious act is given. This shift emphasizes Judah's responsibility to God by contrasting their action with the high standards that God revealed to them. The other nations were judged on the basis of common sense and a popular sense of morality; these were the statutes and laws which guided them.

The final lines of 2:4 are often interpreted to refer to Judah's worship of "false gods, or idols." On the basis of this interpretation, a specific sin against Judah is identified, but it is a crime against Yahweh rather than a social sin as in earlier oracles. But the root meaning of czb is "to lie," and there is no case in Deuteronomy where this root clearly means "false gods, idols."[25] The prophets do describe the people as being "led astray" by the "lies" (czb) of the false prophets and leaders of the nation (Isa. 3:12; 9:15-16; 28:15; Mic. 3:5; Jer. 23:14, 32). These leaders deceived the people of Judah and caused perversion in the moral, civil, ceremonial, and personal behavior or attitudes of the people. The leaders of Judah are not that different from the kings who lead the other nations astray (1:15; 2:3).

"Follow after" is normally used with persons (Gen. 37:17; 24:5, 8, 39, 61; Numb. 16:25; Josh. 3:3) rather than objects, thus the contrast is between following Yahweh or following liars.[26] The sins of Judah's forefathers are many; but if Isaiah's description of the way in which Jerusalem has been led astray by false leaders and liars is at all related to the accusation here, then social

---

[23]See the section on Unity, pp. 77-78.
[24]See the section on Background, pp. 70-71.
[25]See the section on Unity, pp. 77-78.
[26]For the construction of the relative clause see GKC 138a-b; 155c-d.

sins against the poor may be in view (Isa. 3:12-15). The general nature of the accusations in 2:4 argues against interpreting the sin too specifically.

By agreeing with Amos' accusations against Judah, the Israelite audience is admitting the validity of God's law as a standard for the judgment of his people. Judah knew God's will (and so did Israel), but she failed to follow him. Although failure to follow Yahweh's law is never specifically mentioned in the following oracle against Israel, most agree that the Israelite legal code is the backdrop for the accusations against Israel. Therefore, the establishment of its authority immediately before the Israelite oracle is significant. The specific sins of Israel (2:6-8) are contrary to the traditions which Judah and Israel received and the proclamation of the prophets (2:11). By getting Israel to support the judgment against Judah on the basis of the law of Yahweh, Amos has prepared the nation for God's word against the northern tribes.

3. The punishment of destruction (2:5)

a. On the secure palace-fortresses (2:5). The punishment against Judah is stated in the briefest terms. The long indictment clause, short punishment clause, and the absense of any final divine confirmation formula follows the pattern used in the Tyre and Edom oracles (1:9-12). The lack of any reference to the walls is similar to 1:11 and 2:2 where territories rather than cities are mentioned. The use of an identical punishment formula against Judah demonstrates that Judah will suffer the same punishment as the other nations; God will send judgment upon the secure palace-fortresses where the evil "liars" live. Those who lead the people astray will be destroyed because they have caused the nation to reject God's way.

H. God's Judgment Against Israel (2:6-16)

1. Source of the message (2:6a)

"Thus says Yahweh" identifies the source of this new message. Yahweh has again revealed his word to the prophet Amos. His divine authority is the power behind the words proclaimed.

2. Indictment against Israel (2:6b-12)

a. Because of great sinfulness (2:6b). Using the same phrase which was employed to describe the excessive sinfulness of all the other nations, Amos points his finger at the rebellious acts of Israel, his audience. There is no indication that this oracle includes more than the northern nation.[27] The inclu-

---

[27]The term Israel is ambiguous, and its meaning must be determined by its context. In 2:6, "Israel" is not a general designation for the "people of God" (Wolff, *Amos* 164-5), for "Israel" or "my people Israel" in 7:8, 15, 16, 17 are the "house of Isaac" in 7:9, 16, the "house of Jeroboam" in 7:9, or the "house of Israel" in 7:10; and these do not include the southern kingdom of Judah. "People of Israel" in 3:1 is broader than the northern nation because it specifically identifies this group as the "whole family which I brought up from Egypt." The judgment of Israel in 3:14 is in the context of Samaria (3:9, 12) and Bethel (3:14), and these contextual factors

sion of the Israelites in the list of nations which have rebelled against God must have surprised the prophet's audience, for many of his listeners had probably concluded that Israel under Jeroboam II would be the instrument God would use to punish Edom, Tyre, Ammon, and the other nations. With the Syrians and Assyrians in a weaker political position and with some initial taste of victory in their blood (2 Kings 13:25), many must have expected Amos to make an announcement of salvation, to predict the great day of Israel's victory over all its enemies—the Day of Yahweh (5:18-20).

    c. Specific sins described (2:6c-8)

    (1) Sell the poor (2:6c-d). The sins of Israel in verse 6 have been interpreted in two quite different ways. Selling people for money may refer to the miscarriage of justice by bribing judges or the abuse of debtors by creditors. Although buying and selling is related earlier to slave trade (1:9, 11), the context of 2:6 is distinct. The traditional understanding of these activities has related them to the judicial system in Israel because:[28] (a) "righteous" is a forensic term related to a legal declaration (cf. 5:12); (b) the "pair of sandals" is an idiom used in the transfer of property in a court situation (Ruth 4:1-10); and (c) the law (Exod. 23:6-8; Lev. 19:15; Deut. 16:18-20), the prophets (Isa. 1:23; 3:14; 5:23; 10:2; Jer. 5:28; 22:3; Micah 3:9-11; 7:3) and Amos (5:12) speak out against injustice in the courts through bribery. Others believe the abused persons are the "innocent" who are sold into slavery for a very small debt.[29] There is no bribery or court injustice required with this understanding. Both interpretations provide insight into abuses which Yahweh would condemn, but the latter seems preferable in this verse because of the term "to sell" of the needy is always in the context of debts and slavery (Exod. 21:7-8; Lev. 25:39-40; Deut. 15:12-14).[30] Although court action may sometimes be involved, the prime evil described in 2:6b is the merciless selling of destitute people who have done no wrong. Instead of allowing the poor peasant time to earn enough to pay off his loan, his rich creditor insisted on immediate payment. This demand could be satisfied only by the debtor selling himself into slavery. The reference to "a pair of sandals" attests to the small amount of money owed.[31] Honest citizens in need of a small amount of

---

also determine the meaning of "sons of Israel" in 4:5 (the ones who go to Bethel in 4:4). Amos 9:7 seems to use the term more broadly of the people within both nations for historical reasons.

    [28]Cripps, *Amos* 140; Driver *Amos* 151; Mays, *Amos* 46; E. A. Speiser, "Of Shoes and Shekels," *Oriental and Biblical Studies,* ed. J. J. Finkelstein and M. Greenberg (Philadelphia: Un. of Penn., 1967) 151-59.

    [29]Harper, *Amos* 49; Rudolph, *Amos* 140-41; Wolff, *Amos* 165. A. S. Kapelrud, "New Ideas in Amos," *VT* 16 (1966) 200-04 believes these are the "righteous" who stand for just and righteous action. Formerly the "righteous" were blessed and wealthy, now they are poor.

    [30]Lang, "Social Organization of Peasant Poverty," 47-63; E. W. Davies, *Prophecy and Ethics* (Sheffield: *JSOT,* 1981) 66-69, 76-80; R. North, *Sociology of the Biblical Jubilee,* AnBib (Rome: Pontifical Biblical Institute, 1954) 135-90.

    [31]The preposition *b* is instrumental in giving the price by which one can purchase something; GKC 119p.

assistance to meet the necessities of life are treated uncompassionately by the more powerful citizens of Israel. Amos defends the rights of the poor as defined in the legal traditions (Exod. 21:2-11; Deut. 15:12-19) and condemns the nation's attitude toward the destitute. The proper attitude toward the poor is to maintain them, to take no interest, but fear your God, for Israel was once a slave in Egypt (Lev. 25:35-38; Exod. 22:25-27). Instead of following the law of Yahweh, Israel treated its own poor like Tyre treated foreign slaves.

(2) Oppress the weak (2:7). Amos 2:7 does not describe the economic enslavement of the poor, but instead, emphasizes the physical oppression of the helpless and weak. Textual, lexicographic, and syntactic problems have led to several divergent interpretations to each line. If the root šā'ap means "to be eager, yearn" the first line refers to the desires of the rich; but if it is a variant spelling of šûp "to trample, crush" as most conclude, then the verb describes the actions of oppressors. The reference to "the dust of the earth" may be symbolic of mourning (1 Sam. 1:2; 15:32), a metaphor of humiliation (Gen. 3:15), a synonym for the seed of Abraham (Gen. 13:16),[32] or a gloss which should be omitted.[33] Three distinct interpretations exist because of these difficulties: (1) the Israelites are eager to secure for themselves everything that the poor have, even the dust which they throw on themselves (an hyperbole for everything); (2) the Israelites are eager to bring the dust of the earth (a sign of misery and sorrow) upon the head of the weak;[34] (3) the Israelites trample upon the head of the weak.[35] The final option is widely accepted, and its imagery is similar to Amos 4:1 "who crush the needy" and Isaiah 3:15 "What do you mean by crushing my people, by grinding the face of the poor?" The powerful were walking all over the weak (Ps. 94:3-6). This clause does not indicate what method is being used to take advantage of the helpless. Psalms 72:12-14 and 82:3-4 encourage proper treatment of the poor and helpless and assures them of God's protection from mistreatment.[36] The early legal traditions (Exod. 22:20-23; Deut. 16:11, 14; 24:19-21) required sharing and proper regard for the poor, and the early prophets (Isa. 1:17; Micah 3:1-12; Amos 5:10-11; 8:4-6) condemn the oppression of the weak.

"Manipulating the afflicted's way of life" may be a general accusation of persecution and oppression[37] or a specific accusation of perverting justice in

---

[32]Szabo, "Textual Problems in Amos," 502.

[33]Harper, *Amos* 48; Mays, *Amos* 42; Wolff, *Amos* 133.

[34]Beek, "Religious Background," 134-35, retains "to yearn" but omits "upon the dust of the earth" and translates "on the head of" as "at the cost of" on the basis of 1 Chron. 12:19.

[35]Other verbs like šûp are sometimes spelled with an aleph. qûm can be q'm, rûš can be r'š: GKC 23g. š'p and šûp are variant spellings of the same root in Ps. 56:2 [Heb. 56:3]; 57:3 [Heb. 57:4]; Ezek. 36:3 and Amos 2:7; 8:4.

[36]The protection and care for the weak, orphans, and widows was part of a common ancient Near Eastern morality. F. C. Fensham, "Widow, Orphan and the Poor in Ancient Near Eastern Legal and Wisdom Literature," *JNES* 21 (1962) 129-39 and E. Hammershaimb, "On the Ethics of the Old Testament Prophets," *Congress Volume, Oxford, 1959*, SVT 7 (Leiden: Brill, 1960) 75-101.

[37]Driver, *Amos* 152; Harper, *Amos* 51; Rudolph, *Amos* 139.

the courts.[38] Certainly the powerful did oppress the poor through the misuse of the legal system. Amos 5:12, Isaiah 10:2, and Prov. 17:23 use the verb "turn away" to describe illegal injustice in the court, but in doing so each makes some sort of reference to a legal setting, thus qualifying the more general idea within the verb. Since the verb in Amos 2:7 is without any legal qualification, a legal setting should not be implied.[39] Their brutal oppressors "turn them aside from the way" that they would usually follow by putting all kinds of difficulties in their path. Those who are forced to do things against their desires are called the afflicted. The powerful push them around, control their life, determine how they will live, and deprive them of their rights (Prov. 22:22; 30:14). The afflicted are not free human beings but manipulated in inhuman ways.

The oppressed are also called the "poor, thin, weak"[40] and the "humble, meek, afflicted." The first term is used of those who are militarily weak (Judg. 6:6; 2 Sam. 3:1) as opposed to the strong, and the economically poor as opposed to the rich (Exod. 30:15). Some derive this concept of the poor from wisdom usages in Proverbs,[41] but some of the poor in Proverbs are characterized by laziness (Prov. 12:11, 24; 13:4; 24:33) and negligence (18:9; 19:15). The main contact with wisdom thinking, and this is common with the legal traditions as well, is the condemnation of the oppression of the poor and the weak (Prov. 14:31; 22:16, 22-23; 28:3). Although Amos has contact with wisdom, cultic, and legal traditions, there is nothing distinctive about his conception of the weak which enables one to connect his thinking with any specific literary tradition. These people are pictured as oppressed, helpless, weak, and unable to defend themselves against the rich and powerful. An hypothetical land reform to squeeze out the small farmers[42] is less likely than a slow, long-term policy by large land owners to buy up property, to charge high taxes to renters, and to use the court legally and illegally.[43]

(3) Misuse the defenseless (2:7b). The second half of 2:7 describes the sexual abuse of women. The clause may relate to immorality with prostitutes at a baalistic place of worship,[44] incestuous relations with the same woman,[45]

---

[38]Mays, *Amos* 46; Wolff, *Amos* 166.

[39]A more general use of "to turn aside" is found in Job 23:11; 24:4; Isa. 30:11; Mal. 3:5.

[40]For a full discussion of the etymology, use, and bibliography on *dl* see H. J. Fabry, "*dl*," *TDOT* III (Grand Rapids: Eerdmans, 1978) 208-30.

[41]Wolff, *Amos* 166. Kapelrud ("New Ideas in Amos," 200-04) believes the Psalms provided the background for the meaning of these terms.

[42]K. Koch, "Die Entshehung der sozialen kritik bei den Propheten," *Probleme biblishcher Theologie,* ed. H. W. Wolff (München: Chr. Kaiser, 1971) 236-57.

[43]G. J. Botterwerk, "'Sie verkaufen den Unschuldigen um Geld'. Zur socialen Kritik des Propheten Amos," *Bibel und Liturgie* 12 (1971) 215-31.

[44]Cripps, *Amos* 142; Hammershaimb, *Amos* 48-49; H. M. Barstad, *The Religious Polemics of Amos,* SVT 34 (Leiden: Brill 1984), 11-36 denies the sexual overtones, but sees the maiden at a *marzah* banquet (cf. 6:1-7).

[45]Wolff, *Amos* 167; Keil, *Amos* 253.

or the exploitation of a helpless female servant by her master and his son.[46]

The identity of the "maiden" and the place where the sexual relationships take place are not given. Some conclude from the reference to the "house of their gods" and "laying down beside every altar" in 2:8 that the sin in 2:7 took place at temples of Baal. Hosea 4:14 describes the adultery being practiced in Israel with temple prostitutes.

Others believe that "the same maiden" is in view (GKC 126b). The woman is not a cultic prostitute, for she was called a "holy one, dedicated one" (Hos. 4:14). Since *na'arāh* "maiden" can describe a servant (Ruth 2:5, 8, 22, 23; 1 Sam. 25:42; Esther 4:4, 16), this accusation probably condemns the violation of a defenseless female servant by both a father and his son. The old legal traditions forbids a father or a son from having sexual relations with the other's wife and provides protection for a female household slave (Exod. 21:7-9). The slave was protected by law because she was frequently abused,[47] but the maiden *na'arāh* was of higher status.[48] The oppression of the maiden instead of the slave is therefore a sign of how far the oppressive measures of the powerful have gone. The faithful household employee is misused and treated as if she had no rights. She was not a slave without legal status, but she was inhumanly treated by the powerful men within society.

(4) Profane God's name (2:7c). The final line of 2:7 is sometimes considered a secondary addition because of its similarity to phrases in Leviticus and Ezekiel,[49] but this theological statement is used in the context of abusing slaves in Jeremiah 34:16 and of sexual abuses in Genesis 49:4 (cf. Gen. 35:22); Leviticus 19:29;1 Chronicles 5:1, and not just in a priestly setting. The introductory *lm'n*[50] may indicate purpose "in order to"[51] or consequence "so that."[52] Thus two options are available: the preposition points to the consequence of their action, or the statement is a rhetorical and ironic evaluation of the people's motives. This latter, more shocking and penetrating understanding of the implications of the corrupt action is more in keeping with the

---

[46]M. A. Beek, "The Religious Background of Amos II: 6-8," *OTS* 5 (1948) 136; Mays, *Amos* 46.

[47]L. Duerr, "Altorientalische Recht bei dem Propheten Amos und Hosea," *BZ* 23 (1935/36) 153, notes that a father and son could legally have sexual relations with the same slave in many nations.

[48]J. Macdonald "The Status and Role of the *NA'AR* in Israelite Society," *JNES* 35 (1976) 147-70 and B. Cutler and J. Macdonald, "Identification of the *NA'AR* in the Ugaritic Texts," *UF* 8 (1976) 27-35, conclude that this type of person was very different from a slave and with a higher social status.

[49]Wolff, *Amos* 133-34; Schmidt, "Die deuteronomistische Redaktion des Amosbuches," 179 point to its use in Lev. 18:21; 20:3; 22:2, 32; Ezek. 20:39; 36:20-22. Mays, *Amos* 46 joins this phrase with the next verse, while Harper, *Amos* 48 put verse 7 after 8.

[50]H. A. Brongers, "Die Partikel *lm 'n* in der biblisch-hebräischen Sprache," *OTS* 18 (1973) 84-96, translates 2:7 with *wodurch* "by which means" (89), but this takes much of the sting out of the statement and expresses an idea which the prophet would probably put in different words.

[51]Driver, *Amos* 153; Rudolph, *Amos* 139.

[52]Cripps, *Amos* 142; Harper, *Amos* 51; Mays, *Amos* 46.

forcefulness of a conclusion and the other cutting ironic remarks of Amos
(3:2, 10; 4:4-5; 5:18-20, 21-24; 6:6-7). The holy reputation of Yahweh is destroyed and his honor outraged because of Israel's action. Although some
may have considered these sins as acceptable practices, God, who defends the
poor and helpless, considers them an attack on himself and a repudiation of
the holy traditions which the nation has inherited.

(5) Exploit the destitute for pleasure (2:8). The interpretation of verse
8 largely depends on how one understands the cultic references elsewhere.
Driver and Hammershaimb envisage a Canaanite drinking feast with the participants involved in immoral relationships upon garments taken from the
poor (cf. Hos. 4:11-14).[53] It is also possible to take the "stretching out" to refer to reclining at a banquet or feast held at a temple (Amos 6:4-6), without
any suggestion of immoral sexual behavior.[54] In keeping with the overall context, Amos first describes how debtors are exploited. Then, to illustrate that
this profanes God's name (2:7b), Amos reminds his audience of how they
have the audacity to use these objects in their joyous feasts.

Exploitation is the primary emphasis of the verse. The legal traditions in
Exodus 22:26-27 and Deuteronomy 24:12-13 permit a creditor to take a
man's garment in pledge (but not a widow's—Deut. 24:17), but it must be returned before nightfall. The garment in this case is a legal instrument used as
security against a debt. By keeping the garment gained through legal means,
the rich misuse the system in order to further their own enjoyment of life.
The Yabneh-yam letter records a nearly contemporary (735-625 B.C.) misuse
of this practice in Judah.[55] The frequency of this practice is implied by the
fact that it regularly happened at "every altar." The irony of the situation is
obvious; the rich go to "worship" at the feast with garments that legally
should be returned to the poor.

In a similar vein, they take wine given as payment for fines and use it for
their own pleasure. This does not refer to money or goods collected by the
priest (Lev. 5:14-16; 6:5 [Heb. 5:24]; 2 Kings 12:4-16) but the payment of
civil fines prescribed by judges.[56] Some believe the wine was pawned or for-

---

[53]Driver, *Amos* 153; Hammershaimb, *Amos* 49; M. Dahood, "To pawn one's cloak," *Bib* 42
(1961) 359-66, believes the reference to pawning one's cloak in the tomb of Apollophanes from
150 B.C. is a pledge that a man left with a harlot and therefore interprets Amos 2:7 in a similar
manner.

[54]Mays, *Amos* 47.

[55]J. Naveh, "A Hebrew Letter from the Seventh Century B.C." *IEJ* 10 (1960) 129-39; F. M.
Cross, "Epigraphic Notes on Hebrew Documents of the Eighth-Sixth Centuries B.C.: II The
Murabba'at Papyrus and the Letter Found Near Yabneh-yam," *BASOR* 165 (1962) 34-46; L. De-
lekat, "Ein Bittschriftenwurf eines Sabbatschänders," *Bib* 51 (1970) 453-70. The text says
"When I had measured this harvest of mine in the regular way, he took the garment of thy servant; and all my brethren will testify for me, those who were harvesting with me in the heat of
the sun; all my brethren will testify for me. Truly I am innocent of any guilt." The garment was
taken presumably because the reapers did not fill the quota which the owner of the land required.

[56]R. J. Thompson, *Penitence and Sacrifice in Early Israel Outside the Levitical Law* (Leiden:
Brill, 1963) 167.

feited to creditors by those who were unable to pay their tribute, debts, or taxes.[57] Such a setting would demonstrate the heartless nature of the rich. In spite of their questionable legal practices, the rich drank the wine in their joyous feasts in the house of their gods. These offenses took place at the major temples at Dan and Bethel as well as at local shrines.

d. God's acts for Israel are rejected (2:9-12). The indictment against Israel takes a new twist in this paragraph. A direct accusation concerning some social evil is absent; instead, the emphasis falls on God's sovereign intervention over Israel's past history. God's past deeds for Israel stand in bold contrast to the nation's present action (2:6-8) which profanes his holy name. By rejecting the prophets (2:11-12), the people were rejecting the basis of the prophetic message of God's sovereignty over their lives.

Initially the recitation of God's great acts of salvation were national confessions or songs of praise (Exodus 15; 20:1-2; Deuteronomy 32; Josh. 24:3-13) and in some of these (Deut. 32:15-29; Josh. 24:14-24) there is a warning against rejecting God and forgetting his acts of grace. This sets the pattern for the pre-exilic prophets (Hos. 11:1-4; 13:4-6; Isa. 1:2; Mic. 6:3-5) who recited the great acts of God to reveal the seriousness of the nation's infidelity.[58] In Hosea 13:6 and Micah 6:4 these traditions are employed to show that the people forgot God's acts of grace, while Isaiah 1:2-3 and Hosea 11:3, 5 fault the nation for its rebellion. Amos 2:11-12 is used in a way that is similar to this later group, but 2:9-10 seems closer to the emphasis in the first two passages.

(1) God destroyed their enemies (2:9). In 2:9 God's past acts are interpreted theologically to emphasize his destructive power over the mighty. The Amorites originally occupied the area that the Israelites conquered. Genesis 15:16 promises the defeat of the Amorites, a term which broadly includes all the people of the land. Numbers 13:29 and Deuteronomy 1:18-20 locate the Amorites in the hill country of Palestine. Numbers 21:13, 21, 26 include the kingdom of Sihon in Transjordan within the Amorite camp, and Joshua 13:4-5 places the Amorites to the north of Palestine.[59] Amorite is not a technical term but a general reference to those who lived in Palestine before the Israelites. The chief characteristics are the legendary height and strength of the Amorites. He compares their height to the cedars and their strength to the oaks. This agrees with the tradition concerning the spies' report, "they are stronger than we...men of great stature. And we saw the Nephilim (the sons of Anak, who came from the Nephilim); and we seemed to ourselves like

[57]Fosbroke, *Amos* 288; Rudolph, *Amos* 144-45.

[58]G. E. Wright, "The Conquest Theme in the Bible," *A Light Unto My Path* (Philadelphia: Temple Univ. Press, 1974) 509-18.

[59]Akkadian sources refer to the *Amurru* as nomads living to the west of Assyria and Babylon. Sumerian *Martu* is an identical term which has the same geographic (west) and ethnic connotations. M. Liverani, "Amorites," *Peoples From Old Testament Times* (Oxford Univ. Press, 1966).

grasshoppers." (Numb. 13:31-33; Deut. 1:28; 2:10, 21-22). Amos does not use the old traditional metaphors but substitutes appropriate illustrations which are faithful to the earlier perspective. In contrast to this figure of power is the metaphor of complete destruction in the next clause. The destruction of the fruit and the root emphasizes the totality of the Amorite defeat.[60] Isaiah 37:31 uses similar figures in a positive way to promise the nation that it will take root and bear fruit, and Ešmun'azar's curse on his enemies who disturb his sarcophagus contains the line "May they have no root below and no fruit up on top, and may they be cursed among the living under the sun" (*ANET* 662).

The action of uprooting and destroying the strong cedars and oaks is attributed to God. In the first half of 2:9 God says "I myself destroyed"; this emphasis is repeated again in the second half in "I destroyed." The mighty are nothing before his power; he is in control of the history of his people and can destroy the strong for the sake of the weak. His past action serves as a demonstration of grace toward Israel as well as a witness to destructive power over those who profane his name (Gen. 15:16; Deut. 9:1-5; 1 Kings 21:26). The recollection of God's gracious deeds is used (in Deut. 29:1-9; Josh. 24:8; and Ps. 105:43-45) as a challenge to faith, devotion, and obedience to God, "for he is a holy God; he is a jealous God; he will not forgive your transgressions or your sins" (Josh. 24:19). Although a similar challenge to faith may underlie the material here, this is not the main purpose of Amos at this point.

(2) God redeemed and cared for them (2:10). Chronological order is ignored for the sake of emphasizing the contrast between God's destructive power against the powerful Amorites (2:9) and his redemptive power toward the weak Israelites in Egypt and the wilderness (2:10). Through the addition of the emphatic personal pronoun "I myself," Amos focuses on God's acts of grace. The change to second person "you" from third person "them" in 2:9 makes the rhetorical appeal to remember the past more direct. The formulation of Israel's confession of faith is uniquely structured (cf. 3:1; 9:7) and should not be seen as a later redactional addition (see the section on Unity). The unusual order, the emphatic style, and the chaiastic appearance of references to the Amorites reveal a distinctive treatment of these traditional themes. God has acted powerfully on behalf of the nation by delivering it from Egypt, and this liberation was at the heart of the people's concept of their identity and origins. No memory or symbol was more central to the faith than the exodus (Josh. 24:5-7). Although the wilderness was seen as a testing of their faith (Deut. 8:1-3) and was filled with times of rebellion (Exod. 16:3; 17:2; 32:1-6; Numb. 14:1-4; 16:3) it was also a time in which God cared for

---

[60]H. L. Ginsberg, " 'Roots Below and Fruit Above' and Related Matters," *Hebrew and Semitic Studies Presented to G. R. Driver,* ed. D. W. Thomas and W. D. McHardy (Oxford: Clarendon, 1963) 59-71.

them and led them so that they might take possession of the land of the Amorites (Deut. 8:1-10). The land was God's gift, and his mighty power over the inhabitants of the land of the Amorites was the key to who possessed the land.

(3) God gave them spiritual leaders (2:11a). The stress on what God has done ("I raised up") maintains the continunity with 2:9-10 and counteracts the tendency to see the reference to prophets as the beginning of a new paragraph. The rising up of prophets and Nazirites enabled God to direct the nation's political, economic, social, and religious affairs. Moses, the nation's earliest prophet, was used by God to lead the nation out of Egypt, guide them through the wilderness, and direct them in the ways of God. The Nazirites who consecrated themselves to Yahweh were examples of holy living to the rest of the nation (Numbers 6).[61] Amos does not identify any individuals in either class, nor does he associate either group with any specific duty or institution.[62] At this point he is merely drawing the connection between God's sovereign workings with the nation through word (the prophets) and deeds (the exodus).

(4) Challenge to accept God's sovereignty (2:11b). Although it might seem more fitting to have this appeal to the audience after the accusation in verse 12,[63] Amos is more concerned that his listeners give allegiance to their own spiritual heritage. His question, "Is this not so?" would have encouraged a positive response. By giving consent to their own traditions, they are faced with the truth that God has had his sovereign hand on the nation since its beginning. If this is so, as God declares it is, then certain implications naturally follow. They must evaluate their treatment of the weak and poor to see if it is consistent with God's words and deeds on their behalf.

(5) Israel rejected God's sovereignty (2:12). The recital of deeds of grace is the basis of the indictment in 2:12. Amos uses the Day of Yahweh (5:18) and election (3:1) traditions in a similar way. Once the audience has identified itself with the orthodox confessions of beliefs, Amos turns the truth against them. Once the people have agreed that God has guided the nation from the beginning, Amos demonstrates that they have rejected God's will as it was modeled and spoken by the prophets and Nazirites. By corrupting the Nazirites with wine, contrary to God's Word (Num. 6:1-6; Judg. 13:14), Israel set itself in direct opposition to God's sovereign design. Rather than encourage men and women to separate themselves to God, to live holy lives of humility and obedience, these young people were encouraged to

---

[61]Absolom was not a Nazirite, but Samuel (1 Samuel 1) and Samson (Judges 13) were two prime examples which Amos may have had in mind. See G. B. Gray, "The Nazirites," *JTS* 1 (1900) 206.

[62]Eichrodt, *Old Testament Theology* I, 304-06 connects the Nazirite to Holy War traditions and sees them as a force against the Canaanization of Israelite culture. T. W. Overholt, "Commanding the Prophets: Amos and the Problem of Prophetic Authority," *CBQ* 41 (1979) 523, connects the condemnation with the nation's worship of false gods, but this seems unlikely.

[63]Harper, *Amos* 57.

drink wine and ignore the traditional requirements of the Nazirite vow.[64] The presence of a truly dedicated Nazirite was an embarrassment because the Nazirite was a living example of what God desired and thus stood as a stark reminder of how far Israel had strayed from God.

The people also exercised some control over the prophetic voice in their midst. Certainly, the nation was not against all prophets, so either Amos is speaking only of the true prophets of God or he is exaggerating his point. Micaiah ben Imlah (1 Kings 22:8) who was imprisoned because he tended to give only negative prophecies to the sinful Ahab is an example of stifling only the words of the true prophet.[65] The personal experience of rejection by Amos in 7:10-17 is a testimony to the accuracy of the charge, for he himself heard Amaziah say, "you shall not prophesy."[66] Amos 2:12 uses a plural verb while 7:16 has a singular verb, thus 2:12 is not merely autobiographical, but the experience in 7:10-17 may have influenced the words Amos chose to use when he put 2:12 into written form.

Opposition to the words of the prophets was equivalent to rejection of the will of God. Because the nation's social order was contrary to the law of God, because they did not recognize the sovereignty of the God of the exodus who delivered them from the oppression of slavery, because they rejected God's ways and words by perverting the Nazirite and quieting the prophet, the nation is guilty and stands condemned just like the other nations.

3. Punishment of destruction (2:13-16)

a. God will bring an earthquake (2:13). The punishment clause is divided into two sections: what God will do to the nation (2:13) and what effect this punishment will have on the nation (2:14-16). The stereotyped clauses like "I will send fire . . . and it will destroy the palace-fortresses" are missing, but the military defeat of a nation is the focus in all cases. Those responsible will have their security and power removed when God himself intervenes in the nation's history with acts of judgment instead of grace.

The judgment is introduced by the particle "behold" which introduces a new paragraph (cf. 6:11, 14; 9:9). The emphatic personal pronoun "I myself" forcefully makes the point that Yahweh's sovereign will is the power behind the nation's future.

Now God stands in opposition to Israel, as he once stood against the Amorites (2:9). The act of God against the nation is expressed in a metaphor com-

---

[64]The hiphil of *šqh* implies a causative influence could have taken the form of social pressure or vocal encouragement which seduced the Nazirite into believing that it really did not matter if the old way of life was abandoned. Compare Jeremiah 35 where the Rechabites refuse wine and are an example to the nation.

[65]Other examples include 1 Kings 13:4; 18:4; 19:2; Isa. 30:11f.; Jer 11:21; 20:7-10; Micah 2:6 and of course Amos 7:10-17.

[66]Amaziah's words in 7:12-13 say the same thing as Amos' quotation of his words in 7:16, but they are not identical words. Amos 2:12 is not completely identical to either.

paring God to a cart or wagon full of sheaves. The metaphor is unique, surprising, and confusing. The image is drawn from the prophet's agricultural background, but the choice of a very rare word to describe the main action has resulted in a multitude of interpretations. The root '*uq* can be derived or connected to different roots in Hebrew, Aramaic, Ugaritic, Arabic, and Akkadian which do not have the same meaning.[67] A growing consensus is leaning toward the meaning "to split, open, rend, cleave."[68] Thus, just as an overloaded wagon cuts open the soft earth with its wheels, so God will cleave or open up the ground in judgment. The imagery describes an earthquake which will destroy the nation's fortresses and send its people into a panic-stricken state. The connection of harvest with punishment (8:1-2) and the references to earthquakes elsewhere in Amos (1:1; 4:11; 6:11; 8:8; 9:1, 5) seem to fit the judgment motifs used by Amos. If an earthquake is intended, it is an act of God no one can deny. There is no escape from it and no one can defend against its power. The fulfillment of this prediction of an earthquake two years after Amos spoke this message (1:1) gave new force and canonical status to his words in later years. God did act in power as Amos predicted; his hand of judgment did shake the foundations of the northern nation. Amos spoke the words of God.

b. Escape is impossible (2:14-16*a*). The results of God's judgment will be devastating. The prophet draws what appears to be a battle scene with troops, archers, and horsemen. There is no mention of any enemy, for the foe is Yahweh himself, and his weapon is the earthquake. In this Holy War Israel's speediest troops will not be swift enough, its strongest and bravest will not escape death, its well-armed archer and charioteer will be useless. The strong military forces will totally collapse in terror when God shakes the earth in anger. The army of Israel will be crushed "in that Day" of Yahweh (1:16; 5:18-20) when he passes through their midst. The phrase "he will not save his life" is used twice and to it is added "he will not escape." Death and naked shame await the army and the nation. By the repetition of the parallelism Amos emphasized the awesomeness of God's terror upon the powerful. If these cannot endure the day of God's judgment, the rich and powerful who oppress the weak have no chance of survival and are not even worthy of mention in this context.

4. Confirmation formula (2:16*b*)

Amos ends this shocking and passionate confrontation against Israel with two simple but powerful words, "declares Yahweh." Yahweh has spoken

---

[67]See the textual note for 2:13.

[68]Gese, "Kleine Beiträge zum Verständnis des Amosbuches," 417-24; Mays, *Amos* 54; Rudolph, *Amos* 148-49; Wolff, *Amos* 171. Since so many options are available, no absolutely positive conclusion is possible. Since several possibilites make sense, the original intention is somewhat unclear. The parts of the metaphor should not be identified (sheaves equal sins, etc.).

words of terror against his enemy Israel. He knows about their guilt and he
will utterly devastate the nation as he has said. Because it is God's word it
will happen.

Theological Developments

The theological implications of 1:3—2:3 form the backdrop for the message within 2:4-16. Its consistent structure, focus on abuses of the weak, and
prediction of God's determination to judge every nation because each is accountable for sins, caused the Israelite audience to agree with God's acts of
destruction. In the final two oracles against Judah and Israel, Amos brings
his audience to the realization that they themselves stand condemned if the
same principles are applied to their situation.

The theological background for both the Judah and the climactic Israelite
oracle is based on the people's knowledge and acceptance of the law of God
and the early traditions about God's sovereign acts on behalf of his people.
The other early prophets testify to the importance of these themes in the people's understanding of their past (Mic. 6:4; Hos. 11:1-4; 12:9; 13:4), even
though the nations had drifted far from Yahweh and had accepted many cultural and theological influences from the baalistic religion of the Canaanites
(see especially the book of Hosea). The people still would give assent to the
view that Yahweh could and should judge the other nations for their barbarous deeds against the weak. Their ideals about right and wrong were in some
sense still related to the legal heritage derived from the law. Their worship included traditional sacrifices (5:21-23) and traditional songs and confessions
which celebrated the past (Amos 2:9-10). Amos does not focus condemnation
on their false theological traditions but on their rejection of their true national
heritage and its theological implicatons. Amos no longer argues on the basis
of a common sense of morality which all people have through conscience, but
condemns both nations for their rejection of a divine revelation and divine activity on their behalf. If God's judgment was valid on the basis of acts contrary to conscience, how much greater is the responsibility for those people
who have received a specific divine revelation on how to live. Accountability
and the severity of justice are both related to the degree of responsibility.
God's chosen people had received the truth and had enjoyed the benefit of
God's sovereign acts; therefore the rejection of these traditions and his continued guidance of the nation through his prophets is a rejection of God's sovereign control over them.

The accusation against Israel includes a strong judgment of the nation's
socio-economic policy and its implication on how the weak and poor are
treated. The oppressors in Israel do not take advantage of some foreign individual in a time of war but turn their own brothers into slaves, their own servants into objects of abuse for their own pleasure, and their legal system into

a shameful affair (2:6-8). These acts profane the holy name of God. God's name is profaned and his holy reputation is shamed because his people who are called by his name do not honor God in their lives. They do not separate themselves from those who treat the poor with injustice; they do not live in gratitude to God for his acts on their behalf while they were poor and helpless slaves (2:10). God totally destroyed the Canaanites and intervened into the events of history for the sake of his helpless and weak people who were slaves. He destroys the strong and takes on the cause of the abused and needy. The shocking reality which Amos portrays is the metamorphosis of God's poor people into a strong and abusive power which stands in opposition to God.

The results of God's past grace will not preclude their future judgment. Amos announces the coming of a day of inescapable military defeat. Human power and abilities will be nothing in that day. No one will escape. Even the fastest and those well equipped for battle will perish. No military foe is identified because the destroyer will be the Divine Warrior, God himself. Not a word of hope enters the oracle and no exceptions to the judgment are apparent. Amos is not just announcing the defeat of the army in an upcoming battle; he is predicting the end of a nation.

PART TWO

THE VERIFICATION OF GOD'S WARNINGS OF PUNISHMENT ON SAMARIA

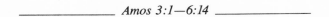

Amos 3:1—6:14

This new unit is introduced by "Hear" which also delineates some of its sections—3:1, 9, 13; 4:1; and 5:1. The introduction to the visions in 7:1, 4, 7, "Thus the Lord Yahweh showed me, and behold," points in a new direction and indicates the beginning of the following major unit.

The structure of the individual oracles in chapters 3-6 are distinct from the regular formula (for three/for four) found in Amos 1-2. Amos 3-6 builds the case against Israel by developing the issues raised in 1-2. Some connect chapters 2 and 3 so closely that the climactic oracle against Israel in 2:6-16 ends after 3:2 or 3:8.[1]

The implications of Amos 1-2 underlie the new prophecies against Israel. The foreign nations have sinned in their violent treatment of other nations (1:3—2:3), but Israel treats its helpless fellow citizens in the same manner (2:6-8). Violence and oppression rule in Samaria (3:9-10). Therefore, God will deal with all sinful people according to their rebellion (Amos 1-2), and he will deal with Samaria exactly according to the privileges she has enjoyed (3:1-2). The fire of destruction which will destroy the foreign nations in Amos 1-2, will spread to Israel's palace-fortresses (3:15; 4:3; 5:6, 9; 6:8) and the people will go into exile.

The long unit of chapters 3-6 can be divided into smaller segments. Chapters 5-6 are unified by the common theme of lamentation and woe (5:1-2, 16-20; 6:1-7), references to the audience as the "house of Israel" (5:1, 3, 4, 25; 6:1, 14) and the threat of death (5:1-3, 16-17, 18-20; 6:7-11). Koch makes the break between chapters 4 and 5 a major division between units, thus 5-6 are connected with 7:1—9:6.[2] His observations support the division of 3-4 from

[1]K. Budde, "Zu Text und Auslegung des Buches Amos," *JBL* 43 (1924) 75-76; W. A. Smalley, "Recursion Patterns and the Sectioning of Amos," *BT* 30 (1979) 123, 201, put 3:1-2 with the previous section. Motyer, *Day of the Lion* 69, puts 3:1-8 with chapter two, while A. van der Wal, "The Structure of Amos," *JSOT* 26 (1983) 109, makes 2:6—3:2 a paragraph, but 1:2—3:8 becomes the major divisional unit.

[2]Koch, *Amos* 107-11 begins a new unit at 5:1 because (1) new addresses are identified (the house of Israel), (2) 5:1 follows the doxology in 4:13 which brings the previous unit to a close, and (3) because 5:1 is syntactically constructed (with a relative clause) like 3:1 which begins the previous unit.

5-6, but the themes in 5-6 have more in common with 3-4 than 7:1—9:6.

The thematic continuity which brings chapters 3-6 together include: (1) the charge against Samaria, her fortresses, and her lavish homes in 3:9-11, 15; 4:1; 5:9; 6:1, 8, 11; (2) the luxury of the upper class in 3:15; 4:1; 5:11; 6:4-6; (3) the perversion of justice and righteousness in 3:9-10; 5:7, 10-13, 24; 6:12; and (4) the punishment of exile in 3;12; 4:2-3, 5:5, 27; 6:7, 14. The repetition of questions (3:3-8; 5:18; 6:2, 12), imperatives (3:1, 9, 13; 4:1, 4-5; 5:1, 4-6, 14-15; 6:2), participles (3:10; 4:1, 13; 5:8; 6:1, 4-6), and other grammatical forms add to the sense of unity within the larger section.

Several of the paragraphs within 3:1—4:13 (the first half of the major section 3:1—6:14) are marked by the introductory "hear" (3:1, 9, 13 and 4:1). In the first paragraph Amos uses a series of rhetorical questions to demonstrate that there is a cause for the punishment he announced in chapter 2. In 3:9—4:3, Amos verifies and expands his earlier message. Because Israel is full of violence (3:9-10), God will destroy the nation (3:11-12), remove the security of religion and luxury (3:13-15), and send the oppressive leaders of the nation into exile (4:1-3). The final paragraphs in 3:1—4:13 center around Israel's failure to return to God and worship him in purity (4:4-13).

The references to Samaria (Amos 3:9; 4:1; 6:1, 4-6) suggest that the location for the oracles in 3:1—6:14 was the capital city where the rich and powerful lived in their luxurious palace-fortresses.

The Cause of Divine Punishment
Versus the Results of Divine Election

_____ *Amos 3:1-8* _____

Introduction

God's election of Abraham and the nation of Israel resulted in the promise of a good land, many children, prosperity, protection and the presence of God with them (Gen. 12:1-3; 18:18; 24:18). The privileges of election were enormous, but the responsibilities of living according to the standards of being a holy nation were very high. Unfortunately many Israelites seemed to concentrate more on the eternal blessing than on the conditional nature of God's blessings. When Amos announced the destruction of Israel at the end of his oracles against the nations, his audience stood in shock and disbelief. For the nation to respond positively to the word of God concerning the destruction of Israel, the prophet must overcome the illogical nature of supposing that the God who chose Israel would now destroy her. This paradox which was created because the people rejected God's ways (2:6-8) and forgot his grace (2:9-12) must be restated in a convincing way to persuade the audience that God will judge Israel. The cause of God's judgment is directly related to the fact that God had elected them to be his people. This fact does not exclude his judgment.

Amos attempts to convince his audience by demonstrating how even the most commonly observed results have a cause, that every cause has an effect. This is true in nature as well as in the relationship between God and Israel. The prophet's announcement of the end for Israel was caused by God's desire to warn the nation, the cause of the warning was the nation's disregard for its elect status.

Background

Since Amos is having a disagreement with his audience over the validity of God's judgment, the backgrounds of a prophetic lawsuit or a disputation speech from a wisdom setting have been linked to the structure and background of 3:1-8. The structure and content of neither form is fully represented in this section, but vocabulary and stylistic imitations of similar literary pieces are reflected at several points.

A covenant lawsuit from the divine council is found in 3:1-2, with 1*a* being the imperative call to court, *1b* the historical prologue, *2a* the statement of the covenant relationship, and *2b* the indictment.[3] Covenant motifs like the exodus and "know" support this view.[4] Additional evidence is derived from the judgment scene in 3:9-12.[5] The covenant lawsuit pattern is applied to all of 3:1—4:13 and often seen as the background to 4:4-13.[6] The absence of many structural parts of the covenant lawsuit, the lack of any reference to a *rîb* "lawsuit" or the covenant makes this interpretation suspect. Although the covenant relationship is assumed, the form of the speech is unique when compared to the covenant lawsuits in the other early prophets (Hosea 4; Micah 6).

Wolff prefers a "call to attention" form in 3:1 and a didactic disputation in 3:3-8. He derives both from a wisdom context.[7] The "call to attention" is related to similar calls to learn in wisdom texts (Prov. 8:32; 2 Sam. 20:17) and the interrogative questions concerning observations about cause and effect in nature are associated with the rhetoric of the sages.

Wisdom and non-wisdom disputation speeches are found in Isaiah, and several of these are joined with other genres.[8] Disputation took place in court, between enemies, and even friends. Issues varied from the price of a horse to politics and the fine points of theology. The variety of themes, settings, and structures indicates that no one fixed structure was used in disputation speeches. Most prophetic disputes are centered around their understandings of God. These theological disputes frequently are related to a prophet's new revelation which runs contrary to the popular understanding of some tradition.[9]

The range of analogies in 3:3-8 are derived from the common experience of a shepherd. Amos knew the habits of the lion and probably had personal experience with traps and snares. Insights into the relationship between cause and effect are a natural result of observation and do not require training in a wisdom school. The context of this dispute is found in Amos 1-2 where Amos

---

[3]F. M. Cross, "The Council of Yahweh in Second Isaiah," *JNES* 12 (1953) 274-77 and H. W. Robinson, "The Council of Yahweh," *JTS* 44 (1943) 151.

[4]H. Huffmon, "The Treaty Background of *YADA'*," *BASOR* 181 (1966) 33-34; F. H. Seilhamer, "The Role of the Covenant in the Mission of Amos," 440-43.

[5]L. A. Sinclair, "The Courtroom Motif in the Book of Amos," *JBL* 85 (1966) 351-53, finds a call of witnesses in 3:9, an accusation in 3:10; and the sentence in 3:11-12.

[6]M. O'Rourke Boyle, "The Covenant Lawsuit of the Prophet Amos: III:1—IV:13," *VT* 21 (1971) 338-62; W. Brueggemann, "Amos 4:3-13 and Israel's Covenant Worship," *VT* 15 (1965) 1-15; and G. Snyder, "The Law and Covenant in Amos," 158-66.

[7]Wolff, *Amos* 93, 183 or Wolff, *Amos the Prophet: The Man and His Background* (Philadelphia: Fortress, 1973) 6-10; S. Terrien, "Amos and Wisdom," *Israel's Prophetic Heritage*, ed. B. W. Anderson and W. Harrelson (New York: Harper and Row, 1962) 111-12.

[8]R. F. Melugin, *The Formation of Isaiah 40-55*, BZAW (Berlin: de Gruyter, 1976) 31. He derives some disputes from psalms of lament (40:27-31), hymns (44:24-28), and other genres (48:1-11). In 45:9-13 he finds a disputation transformed into a prophetic messenger speech.

[9]A. Schoors, *I Am God Your Savior: A Form Critical Study of the Main Genres in Isaiah XL-LV*, SVT 24 (Leiden: Brill, 1973) 294-95.

announced the destruction of the nation Israel. His Israelite audience knew that the nation was very strong at this time, and they found the prophet's message offensive, unreasonable, and theologically undefensible. God had chosen them to be his people and promised to bless them. News of their total destruction (2:13-16) made no sense. Amos and the people disagree; thus a dispute arose.

Structure and Unity

Structure

The syntactical structure of clauses and the poetic parallelism of words are highlighted in the outline of the text. The exegesis of the text will follow the flow of thought in the English outline.

The Cause of Divine Punishment versus the Results of Divine Election
Amos 3:1-8

3:1 A. Privilege carries responsibility

Hear this word
  which Yahweh speaks concerning you,
    Oh, sons of Israel
    (concerning the whole clan
      which I brought up from Egypt),
saying:

     1. The call to hear God's word
     2. The recipients of the message

3:2
     3. The elect will be punished
      a. The privilege of election
      b. Punishment because of privilege

"Only you did I select out of all the clans of the earth,
Therefore I will punish you according to your iniquity."

3:3 B. Every effect has a cause, every cause an effect

Do two walk together[a]
  if they do not agree?[b]

     1. What is the cause of unity?

Does a lion roar from the bush   **3:4**
  when there is no prey?
Does a young lion raise his voice[c] from his hiding place
  if he captures nothing?

     2. What is the cause of warning of destruction?

Does a bird fall into a trap[d] on the ground when there is no snare?[e] Does a trap spring up from the ground if it actually captures nothing?	**3:5**	3. What is the cause of destruction?
	3:6	C. God's causes and their effects
Or does a trumpet blow in a city and the people are not afraid?[f] Or does a disaster happen in a city and Yahweh has not acted?		1. Does a warning cause fear? 2. Is a disaster caused by God?
Surely the Lord Yahweh has not acted if he has not revealed his plan[g] to his servants the prophets.	**3:7**	3. God causes prophets to warn of disaster
	3:8	4. The effects God's warning should have.
A lion roars![h] Who will not fear? The Lord Yahweh speaks![h] Who will not prophesy?		a. The people should fear b. The prophet should warn

3:3a. The Old Greek adds "generally, at all" after the verb.

3:3b. The verb y'd "meet, agree" is confused with yd' "know" in the Old Greek. Aq. "they agree together" and Theod. "they meet together" follow the Hebrew order of the consonants. See D. W. Thomas, "Note on nô'adu in Amos 3:3," JTS 7 (1956) 69-70.

3:4c. The Old Greek adds "generally, at all" here.

3:5d. The word "trap" is omitted in the Old Greek and by some modern commentators because it lengthens the line too much. See Mays, Amos 59; Wolff, Amos 180.

3:5e. "Snare" is translated "birdcatcher, fowler" in the Old Greek, thus focusing on the person rather than the object which catches the bird.

3:6f. The Old Greek has a passive verb.

3:7g. The Old Greek translates "his plan" as "his teachings" while Aq. has "his secrets" and Theod. "his plan."

3:8h. Both verbs are put in the future tense in the Old Greek, but a present tense is a better understanding of the Hebrew perfect verbs in this context.

This structural outline of 3:1-8 is determined by the following syntactic and semantic distinctions between its various parts. Amos 3:1 is set off from the rest by its lack of poetic parallelism and its introductory formulas which identify the speaker and the audience. Amos 3:2 begins the poetic section, but the absence of the question form as in 3:3-4 and the presence of "therefore" suggests that 3:2 ends the first paragraph rather than starting a new paragraph.[10] Amos 3:1 and 3:2 are also topically related.

[10]Gese, "Kleine Beiträge zum Verständnis des Amosbuches," 425, connects 3 to verse 2, but its structural connections with 3:4-8 are stronger. The verse does have a transitional role and does link 3:1-2 to the conclusion in 3:6-8.

The parallelism within the structure of 3:3-6 is:

3:3 do.... if not
3:4 does... when no
    does... if... nothing
3:5 does... when no
    does... if... nothing
3:6 or.... not
    or.... not

Amos 3:3 is syntactically distinct because it has only one line; it is semantically distinct because it does not deal with animals or destruction. Thus 3:3 helps make the transition from 3:1-2 to 3:4-8. Verses 4 and 5 are almost exact parallels, and both use the verb "capture." Verse 6 uses 'm "or" instead of h (the question marker) and deals with the destruction of a city instead of animals. The pattern is broken in 3:7, and the poetic parallelism is not as synonymous as 3:4-6. The declarative statement in 3:7 is closely connected to the context of 3:6b, "Yahweh has not acted," and the issue of prophecy in 3:8b. The final verse in the paragraph uses synonymous parallelism, and it contains distinctive statements and questions that call for a response to God's message of destruction.

The repetition of "to say, speak" in 3:1 and 8; "to roar" in 3:4 and 8; "lion" in 3:4 and 8; "prophecy" in 3:6 and 8; "to do" in 3:6 and 7 and the two different words for "fear" in 3:6 and 8 draw the unit together. The question form aids in this process.

Unity

The unity of 3:1-8 is questioned because the style, topic, and connection between 3:1-2 and 3:3-8 are unclear and in tension. The disputation style with its rhetorical questions seems foreign to the brief announcement of judgment in 3:1-2. Individual phrases within each section are identified as later redactional insertions.

Melugin believes all of 3:1-2 is redactional, Schmidt objects to 3:1, Wolff pinpoints only 3:1b as a supplementary addition by a deuteronomistic redactor, while Harper considers just the short phrase "sons of Israel" a gloss.[11] The unusual character of 3:1-2 is indeed striking, but Melugin's objection to "Hear" which is so essential to the structuring of Amos 3-5 (see 3:1, 9, 13; 4:1; 5:1) is not convincing. The use of 'lh "to bring up" in 3:1b instead of ys' "to go out," which is used in Deuteronomy, argues strongly against the deuteronomistic source of Wolff and Schmidt (see 2:10-12).[12] Most of the

[11]R. F. Melugin, "The Formation of Amos" SBL 1978 Seminar Papers I (Missoula: Scholars Press, 1978) 380-81; Schmidt, "Die deuteronomistische Redaktion des Amosbuches," 173; Wolff, Amos 175; Harper, Amos 65-66.

[12]Hobbs, "Amos 3:16 and 2:10," 384-87 and Rudolph, Amos 152, properly deny any deuteronomistic connection.

other arguments are even less compelling.[13] The major problem is the reference to God in the third person in 3*a* but first person in 3*b*. A textual emendation to third person or the interpretations of 3:1*a* as a messenger speech formula could solve the difficulty.

Within 3:3-8, the authenticity of 3:7 is questioned.[14] Its rather prosaic style, its reflection of a deuteronomistic view of the prophets as the servants of God, its repetition of ideas in 6*b* and 8*b*, the lack of flow from cause to effect, the absence of the question form, and the reference to the prophets in the council of God produce doubts about the authenticity of 3:7. These peculiarities must be weighed on their syntactical, lexical, and contextual merits.[15] (1) Syntactical changes present in 3:8 bring the section to a conclusion. These syntactical changes begin in 3:6 where the interrogative particle is missing. Thus the statement in 3:7 is in line with the two statements in 3:8 and are part of the prophet's method of bringing his speech to a climax. The statement may be judged authentic if it functions significantly in the prophet's attempt to persuade his audience. (2) The lexical repetition of ideas similar to those in 6*b* and 8*b* is a sign of the style of Amos (see 2:14-16; 3:1-2; 3:4-5), and references to the prophets as servants who receive messages from God's divine council are not solely deuteronomistic in origin and use.[16] The deuteronomistic view of prophecy was concentrated on the fulfillment of the words of the prophets which is not the focus of 3:7. (3) The contextual problems are partially caused by the view that Amos is defending his own authority to speak. It seems that Amos is more interested in defending God's announcement of judgment to bring the nation to a point where it will fear God. Amos 3:7 has a significant rhetorical function in this process. The exe-

---

[13]The repetition of "all the clans" in 3:1*b* and 3:2 and "concerning you" and "sons of Israel" in 3:1*a* seems unusual, but the style of Amos in 1:3-2:16 was full of repetition. The objection to "saying" in 3:1*b* because it is rare in Amos (2:2; 7:10; 8:4) is hardly adequate, because elsewhere Amos always introduces quotations. Melugin claims that the accusation within the prophetic oracle of judgment (his definition of 3:1-2) differs from 3:2*a*, but that is exactly the distinctive and creative style that Amos uses throughout the book. He uses an old accepted tradition in a totally new way to reverse the expected conclusion. The paradox or dispute would not have arisen if the tension between 3:2*a* and 3:2*b* was not present.

[14]Gese, "Kleine Beiträge zum Verständis des Amosbuches," 425, also rejects 3:3, but his analysis has not gained acceptance. S. Mittmann, "Gestalt und Gehalt einer prophetischen Selbstrachtfertigung (Am. 3:3-8)," *Theologische Quartalschrift* (1971) 136, also rejects 3:3. Wolff, *Amos* 180 rejects this position.

[15] Wolff, *Amos* 181; Mays, *Amos* 61-52; Melugin, "The Formation of Amos," 381-82; Schmidt, "Die deuteronomistiche Redaktion des Amosbuches," 183-88; G. Pfeifer, "Unausweichliche Konsequenzen. Denkformenanalyse von Amos iii:3-8," *VT* 33 (1983) 341-47. Among those who do not see 3:7 as secondary are Driver, *Amos* 162; Harper, *Amos* 71-73; Hammershaimb, *Amos* 59-60 and Y. Gitay, "A Study of Amos's Art of Speech: A Rhetorical Analysis of Amos 3:1-15," *CBQ* 42 (1980) 304-05.

[16]The concept of the divine council exists in ancient Near Eastern writings and is present in the Micaiah story (1 Kings 22:19-28) in Psalm 82, 89:6-8, and in Proverbs. It is not just a late idea from the time of Jeremiah (23:18, 22). The concept of the prophet as a servant is based on early traditions about Moses (Josh. 1:1-15), Samuel (1 Sam. 3:9-10), and Elijah (1 Kings 18:36-43).

gesis of 3:7 will demonstrate how the text is used to confirm God's message of disaster on Israel.

Interpretation

A. Privilege carries responsibility (3:1-2)

1. Call to hear God's word (3:1a)

The oracle is introduced with a strong imperative summons, "Hear this word." This formula announces the beginning of an important message and exhorts the audience to pay special attention to what follows. Messengers used this device to gain attention when delivering a royal decree (2 Kings 18:28-29),[17] and in some prophetic announcements it is an integral part of the message that God wanted delivered.[18] This introduction also identifies the source of the message. The exclusion of this phrase would weaken or destroy the authority the passage contains. If it were missing the dispute would degenerate into a mere difference of opinion between Amos and his audience. The real issue of debate is: Will God destroy Israel, his chosen people?

2. Recipients of the message (3:1b)

The oracle is addressed to the "sons of Israel."[19] The designation "sons of Israel" in the context of the following clause, "the entire clan which I brought up from the land of Egypt," is much broader than the "house of Israel," which specifically refers to the northern kingdom in passages like Amos 7:10. This phrase includes the whole people because it is based on God's acts of grace to the entire nation. This historical reason is the primary basis for avoiding a distinction between Samaria and Judah in this text, but the broader reference to the whole nation also removes any accusations of blind political nationalism toward Judah.

The basis of the prophet's message was a tradition which was dear to all the people and the reason for their existence. Amos uses the exodus tradition three times (2:10; 3:1; 9:7) to emphasize the saving grace of God on their be-

---

[17]The interpretation of many examples is unclear, but the use of "hear" by the messenger is probably found in Amos 7:16; 2 Kings 7:1; 18:28-29 (but notice the contrasting use in 18:19); Isa. 66:5 (note the use of "his word"); Jer. 9:20-22 ("his mouth"). Westermann, *Basic Forms of Prophetic Speech* 100-28, discusses the messenger speech in some detail with examples from Mari.

[18]In most instances the call to attention is a divine call and includes (1) the call to attention; (2) the identification of the source or speaker; and (3) a reference to the topic or the recipients of the message. The secular messengers frequently use this introductory formula as the first part of the sender's message: 1 Sam. 22:7, 12; 2 Sam. 20:16; 1 Chron. 28:2; 2 Chron. 13:4; 15:2; 20:20. Prophetic speeches have "hear" as an integral part of the divine call to attention: 1 Kings 22:19; 2 Chron. 18:18; Isa. 7:13; 48:1 and especially clear are Isa. 44:1-2; Jer. 7:2-3; 17:20-21; 19:3; 21:11-12; 22:1-2, 29-30.

[19]"Sons of Israel" occurs in 3:1, 12; 4:5, while "house of Israel" is found eight times in chapters 5-6.

half. The patriarchal traditions include this promised deliverance (Gen. 15:13-14; 46:4; 48:21; 50:24), and it was accomplished under the leadership of Moses (Exod. 3:1-16). The exodus was a proof of God's love and faithfulness and the basis of the nation's faithfulness and love to God.

This deliverance which gave the people a common identity was used against them in Amos 2:9-11. In light of what God did (destroyed the Amorites; brought them up from Egypt; led them in the wilderness; and raised up prophets) the national transgressions are almost unbelievable (2:6-8). The return to these themes shows that the people do not understand the relationship between God's act of redemption and this new prophecy of doom. The repetition of the phrase "which I brought up from the land of Egypt" demonstrates, on the one hand, that both the prophet and Israel hold to the centrality of the exodus event. Amos is not denying that they are God's people; but on the other hand, it is clear from what follows that the lasting significance of the exodus event is being questioned. In the end, God's previous announcement of judgment is verified: What God said is true *because* they were redeemed from Egypt.

This setting and connection with 2:10 is lost if 3:1*b* is omitted as a secondary gloss (see the section on Unity). If all of 3:1 is part of God's message (instead of a prophetic introduction) one of the major reasons for omitting 3:1*b* is removed. If God is calling on Israel to hear (3:1*a*), then he would naturally use the first person singular in 3:1*b*.[20] The canonical relationship of 3:1*b* and 2:10 (which is against Samaria) argues against the suggestion that 3:1*b* was added so that this material could be applied to a Judean audience at a later date.[21]

3. The elect will be punished (3:2)

a. Privilege of election (3:2*a*). The magnitude of the message of grace goes beyond the deliverance from Egypt. The first half of verse 2 reveals how Israel was different from the other nations that God moved from place to place (Amos 9:7). By quoting an earlier tradition which describes the Israelite understanding of the relationship between God and the nation, the contradiction between what God said in the past (which the people believe) and

---

[20]The first person singular "which I brought up" appears out of place if the quotation of God's words begin only after "saying" at the end of 3:1. The incongruity is not eased by blaming it on a redactor who should have seen the problem just as clearly as Amos. Several solutions are conceivable: (1) Mays, *Amos* 55 believes it may be due to the fact that Amos is quoting a fixed cultic statement; (2) Harper, *Amos* 66 points to the close identification between the words of God and the prophet; (3) the first person singular could be a transcriptional error for a third person verb, but the Old Greek agrees with the Hebrew reading; (4) or as seems best, the whole of 3:1 is part of God's message. The introductory messenger-speech formula introduces the message in a manner similar to Jacob's message to Esau in Gen. 32:5, where "Thus says your servant Jacob" is the first part of the message. He continues with a first person singular in the next part of the message.

[21]Wolff, *Amos* 175; Hobbs, "Amos 3:16 and 2:10," 384-87 has shown that the vocabulary is not deuteronomistic.

God's new message through Amos (which they question) is set forth.

The verb "I have known" is not God's knowledge of their existence but points toward an intimate relational knowledge which exists between the two parties.[22] The exclusive term "only" plus the partitive use of *min* "out of" emphasize the unique position of Israel.[23] The emphatic position of "only you" at the beginning of the sentence contrasts with "all the clans of the earth" to portray the selective relationship that God established with Israel.[24]

This privileged position may be based on any one of several different traditions: (1) Deuteronomy 7:7 and 14:2 differ slightly from 3:2*a* in vocabulary (using "choose" instead of "know") and correlate "choosing" with the establishment of the covenant (compare Exod. 19:3-6); (2) Deuteronomy 10:15 uses the same vocabulary as Deuteronomy 7:7, 14:2, and adds "only" like Amos, but connects this act to the selection of the patriarchs and their descendents; (3) Genesis 12:3, 18:18-19 and 28:14 are Bethel traditions used by Amos in 3:2.[25] Mays believes Amos 3:2*a* is essentially covenantal and that Amos has read the covenant theme back into the Abraham incident in Genesis 18:18-19. By this means Amos compares God's requirements of "righteousness and justice" on Abraham with God's requirements on Amos' audience.[26] But Amos 3 does not capitalize on these themes, and a twisted interpretation of Genesis 18:18-19 seems an unlikely base for Amos to build a logical argument. The patriarchal connection as well as the giving of the land and the conquest traditions are not directly implied in 3:2*a*.[27]

Amos 3:2*a* maintains contact with several traditions, yet it remains distinct from all of them. The central focus is the election of Israel to be the people of God. Thus the verse has strong covenantal overtones without actually mentioning the covenant.[28] The importance of the exodus and election were well known, for these were the foundation stones on which the whole status and existence of Israel was built. Amos agrees that Israel is a most privileged peo-

---

[22]God knows and understands all things (Job 28:23-26; Job 38—42:3), makes known or reveals himself and his ways Numb. 12:6; Isa. 44:23 his glory; Ps. 77:15 his strength; Numb. 18:5; Jer. 11:18. He knows through a relationship (2 Sam. 7:20-21; Exod. 33:12; Nah. 1:7) and selects or elects people to be his (Gen. 18:19; Jer. 1:5; Hos. 13:5; Amos 3:2).

[23]GKC 119w and note: "Out of"separates the object from a larger general class. To know one out of a group indicates a selective choice.

[24]GKC 142f: The variation from the normal verb-subject-object order, giving "you only" the first position, creates this emphasis.

[25]Th. Vriezen,"Erwägungen zu Amos 3:2," *Archäologie und Alte Testament: Festschrift für K. Galling* (Tübingen: Mohr, 1970) 255-58.

[26]Mays, *Amos* 57.

[27]Wolff, *Amos* 176-77 connects this with the giving of the land as in 2:9-10 or with the revelation of God's will, which contained regulations concerning justice that Israel failed to keep. Fosbroke, *Amos* 792 sees a more direct association with the conquest theme.

[28]Huffmon, "The Treaty Background of YĀDA'," 34, sees Amos 3:2 as a remarkable parallel to the Hittite Treaties and translates "know, select" in the technical sense of "you only have I recognized by covenant."

ple, but his rhetorical use of this tradition and his understanding of the implication of the exodus and election are surprising and devastating.

b. Punishment because of privilege (3:2b). Directly contrary to privilege is punishment. In Amos 3:2b, God declares with straightforward clarity that the privileged people will be punished. This announcement creates a paradox that is completely contrary to the unique position of Israel. This startling thesis reaches back to pick up the tension left by the prophecy of punishment in Amos 2:13-16. It echoes the same theme because the earlier message was not understood or believed. The dispute is summarized in 2a and b: Israel is elect; Israel will be punished.

"Therefore" marks the abrupt transition to a strong conclusion. Since it is not preceded by a list of sins like the normal prophetic accusation, it has the rhetorical effect of catching the listener somewhat by surprise. It introduces a judgment that is contrary to the concept of election in 3:2a without giving any reason. Since no cause is given, the conclusion appears to be rather questionable. But the proximity between election and punishment is saying that judgment will come because of privilege. Contrary to this conclusion is the more popular belief that Israel's elect status will guarantee protection from judgment. The populace wonders how this new message of punishment can be from God.

Amos 3:2b does not amplify the reason for the coming punishment. The final prepositional phrase, "concerning all your iniquities," only hints at the evidence marshaled in 2:6-16. Instead, Amos states that God will "visit, pay attention to, punish" them.[29] The primary concern of Amos at this point is not their sin but their mind and will. They must come to realize that the prophecy of punishment is the result of a cause (it is a warning from God) and is meant to cause a result (it is to bring fear).

B. Every effect has a cause, every cause an effect (3:3-5)

The significance of 3:3-8 is all too frequently centered around the prophet's justification of himself. The next two paragraphs (3:3-5, 6-8) are seen as the prophet's answer to the protester's question: Where did the prophet get his authority to speak?[30] But the emphasis is not on the messenger's authority but the message of destruction.[31] This fact is sometimes missed because 3:3-8 are not read in the context of 3:1-2. Amos 3:3-8 is an

---

[29]*pqd* may relate to God's: (1) observation of or attention to "something evil" in Exod. 3:16; 4:31 or good in Ps. 8:4[Heb 8:5]; 80:14[Heb 80:15]; (2) positive "visiting, blessing" in Gen. 21:1; 50:24-25; Jer. 15:15; (3) negative "visiting, punishment" in Hos. 1:4; 2:13[Heb 2:15]; Exod. 20:5; Isa. 10:12; or (4) "appointment, setting someone over" in Jer. 1:10; Ezra 1:2. The reference to iniquities at the end of 3:2 and the similar negative context in 3:14 determines the meaning here.

[30]Wolff, *Amos* 183, 187; Hammershaimb, *Amos* 57, 59; and Mays, *Amos* 59, believe that Amos is answering those who deny his authority.

[31]Harper, *Amos* 64.

answer to the paradox in 3:1-2. The people object to the prophecy of punishment on Israel in 3:2b and 2:13-16.[32] The prophet is involved only because he is transmitting a message of warning and because God has caused him to speak (3:8). The message is what makes the prophet important and the message is what the people reject. The message is defended because it has a cause and because it was given to bring about a result.

The flow of the argument in 3:3-8, which is step one in the total overall argument of the section (3:1—4:13), is marked by several semantic, syntactical, and structural difficulties. The parts of 3:3-8 are: (3:3) one question about unity; (3:4-5) four questions about warnings and destruction among animals; (3:6) two distinct questions concerning warnings to cities and God's role in the capture of a city; (3:7) one prose statement that identifies the prophet's message as a warning which precedes God's action; and (3:8) a final call to respond to God's message. This material divides itself into two parts: 3:3-5 and 3:6-8.[33] Each small point is contructed around cause and effect relationships. This rhetorical masterpiece convincingly demonstrates that God's prophecies of punishment in Amos 2:6-16 and 3:2b did not just happen by chance. They were sent by God as a warning of danger and should result in the response of fear within the people.

1. What is the cause of unity (3:3)?

The structure of the initial question identifies verse 3 as part of the logical argument in 3:3-8 and not the conclusion to 3:1-3.[34] But this syntactical relationship with what follows does not presuppose a total semantic disunity with what precedes. The setting of 3:3 after 3:1-2 implies that the relationship described in 3:3 is between Yahweh and Israel. Although some believe 3:3 describes the relationship between God and Amos (3:7), 3:7-8 has not been spoken. Therefore the relationship between God and Amos would not enter the discussion at this point.

The rhetorical question is formed in such a way that the listener will immediately arrive at a negative answer. The imperfect verb and the proverbial nature of the saying indicate that the relationship of walking together is not an accidental association but a state of continuous unity.[35] Those who repeatedly

---

[32]C. J. Labuschagne, "Amos' Conception of God and The Popular Theology of his Time," *Studies of the Book of Hosea and Amos* OTWSA 7-8 (Potchefstroom: Rege-Pers Beperk, 1965) 126 and Cripps, *Amos* 152-53 relate 3:3-6 to God and Israel and 3:7-8 to God and the prophet. This ignores the close connection of the total paragraph. S. Daiches, "Amos III:3-8" *ExpT* 6 (1914-15) 237, makes additional observations which are not vital to the overall message.

[33]Two basic approaches to 3:3-8 are evident: (1) 3:3-6 only illustrate the principle of cause and effect, and 3:8 applies this to the prophet; or (2) 3:3-8 are about the relatonship of God and Israel.

[34]Harper, *Amos* 67 and Gese, "Kleine Beiträge zum Verständnis des Amosbuches," 425, relate 3:3 to 3:1-3. It is mainly these commentators who have seen the relationship between God and Israel in 3:3.

[35]GKC 107a-b, e: The imperfect represents action as continuing or being repeated. Proverbial expressions describe what customarily happens on the basis of long experience and observation

walk together do so because of unity, not just a scheduled appointment. If the latter were intended, the proverb would not necessarily be true to life, for many walk together without a prior appointment. The prophet persuasively argues that there was an original cause for Israel's relationship to God (the exodus and election; 3:1-2), but the continuation of that relationship is not guaranteed by its initial creation.

2. What is the cause of warnings of destruction (3:4)?

If agreement is the cause of unity (3:3), what is the cause of destruction? Amos approaches this topic in a roundabout way by drawing on analogies of destruction from nature. These were readily understood by all. The logic of the cause-and-effect relationship was used to convince the audience of the cause of the announcement of destruction in 3:2.

The first illustrations investigates the cause of warnings of destruction using the same syntactical construction employed in 3:3.[36] This linkage brings out the contrast and requires the listener to give the same answer to both questions. To illustrate his point, Amos inquires about the cause of a lion's roar. It is a sign that the lion has leaped from his hiding place in the bush and is in the process of seizing his prey.[37] The roar is an announcement of an attack, a sign that destruction is only a split second away. Would a lion roar and scare all the animals away if it were not making a kill?[38] No! The same point is made in the second half of the verse. It does not describe a later event after the kill when the adult has brought the kill to its young.[39] The "young lion," known as the *kepîr,* is not confined to the den, as the "cub" *gur,* but goes out with the adult to hunt (Ezek. 19:2-3). The young lion learns to be quiet before the kill and attempts to copy the roar of its parent when the prey is seized. The lion's "hiding place" is in the wild rather than the den.[40] The answer to the questions were clear to the audience, even those who were not shepherds like Amos. When a warning of destruction is given, it is because something is going to be attacked. Amos will build on this illustration later in 3:8.

3. What is the cause of destruction (3:5)?

The analogies in this verse are developed around the practice of captur-

---

(107g). D. R. Hillars, *Covenant: The History of a Biblical Idea* (Baltimore: Johns Hopkins, 1969) 131, finds covenantal overtones in "walking together."

[36]The second half of 3:4 has an identical syntactical structure to 3:3. The interrogative with an imperfect verb, plus "if...not" with a perfect verb. Amos 3:4a is parallel to 3:5a.

[37]May, *Amos* 59 and Wolff, *Amos* 180 treat "from his hiding place" as a gloss because it upsets the meter. The phrase is in the Old Greek translation and creates a good parallel to "from the bush."

[38]"If, when" translates the conjunctive "*vav,*" which introduces a circumstantial clause that is contemporaneous with the action of the main verb: GKC 141e, 142d, and 156.

[39]As claimed by Harper, *Amos* 69 or Fosbroke, *Amos* 793-94.

[40]the root *m'ôn* describes the "dwelling place" of God, humans, and animals. God also roars from his holy "dwelling place" (Jer. 25:30). In Job 38:39-40 the lion hunts from his "hiding place," not from his den.

ing animals by snares. Amos concludes that an animal is captured because it enters into a snare. Although this much is fairly clear, there is a great deal of uncertainty about what kind of hunting methods are being described. Some see a hunter throwing a boomerang or a net,[41] while others picture a bird being caught in a net-trap on the ground because it tripped the snare when it tried to eat the bait.[42] The uncertainty is caused by "trap" in the first line, which many reject as secondary, and "bait, snare, boomerang, hunter" *môqēš,* which is very hard to define.[43]

The second example states that a trap will not spring shut if nothing is in it. The certainty of this fact is emphasized by the addition of an infinitive absolute before the finite verb.[44] The use of *lkd* "capture" at the end of verse 4 and 5 draws the illustrations together so that the point cannot be missed. When you see or hear certain signs (the lion roaring or the trap shutting), you know something is being captured.

Since Amos applies these principles to Israel in the following verses, at this point the illustrations should be left as simple illustration. The bird is not identified with Israel or the snare with sin. The rhetorical questions are used to drive home a point. The questions allow the listener to respond with his own answer, instead of being told what is right. They also give the clever speaker the opportunity to pre-determine the answers his audience will give.

C. God's causes and their effects (3:6-8)

With a slight change in form (the interrogative *h* is dropped) and emphasis, the flow of thought is interrupted and the conclusion is begun in verse 6. Even within the conclusion, the verses are not evenly constructed. Verse 6 is a question, verse 7 is a statement, and verse 8 contains both a statement and a question. By using these divergent forms, Amos is able to draw the listener into his rhetorical trap so that they cannot escape the snare of his logic. The conclusion progressively unfolds the significance of what Amos is saying. Once the overall picture is perceived, the thematic interconnections become more striking.

1. Does a warning cause fear (3:6a)?

Anyone who had lived in a walled city during a time of seige knew the fear that came when the watchman blew the warning to signal the approach of an enemy army (Hos. 5:8-9). When the trumpet blew, the people heeded the warning and feared for their lives. This was a natural result, for people react just like animals when they hear the roar of an attack. But the parallelism be-

---

[41] Wolff, *Amos* 185 hold the first view, while Mays, *Amos* 61 has the second.

[42] Driver, *Amos* 161.

[43] H. Gehmen, "Notes on *Môqēs,*" *JBL* 58 (1939) 277-81 and G. R. Driver, "Reflections on Recent Articles," *JBL* 73 (1954) 131-36, discuss the biblical and extra-biblical material in detail.

[44] GKC 113q.

tween those in the city and the animal is not exact yet, for Amos has only described the result of warnings and not their cause, as in verse 4. By introducing a question concerning the destruction of a city without naming the city, the listener is led to agree with the principle without realizing, until later, that the principle applies to the earlier prophecies of punishment on Israel.

2. Is a disaster caused by God (3:6b)?

The second half of the verse gives the reason why a city is captured.[45] Just as the ultimate reason for the capture of an animal is the existence of the snare, so also, the ultimate cause of a political disaster is God.[46] To this the people had already agreed in chapter 1-2. Although the people were accustomed to thinking that God always gives success to his chosen people, they could not deny that God brings judgment on some nations. Amos has shown that the God who elects and blesses is also the God who punishes. What other cause could produce such results? In light of the prophet's announcement of judgment in 3:2b, the implications of this speech begin to crystalize. This verse springs the trap and foreshadows the final climax in 3:8.

3. God causes prophets to warn of disaster (3:7).

Amos 3:7 is unique because it answers, instead of asks a question, but its authenticity should not be denied (see the section on Unity). It is an important part of the overall flow of thought because it interprets and ties together the two questions in verse 6 with the prophecy of 3:2b. God never sends defeat on a city (his action in 3:7a which is connected to 3:6b and 3:2b) unless he sends a warning (3:7b and 3:6a). The prophecy of punishment in 3:2b (and 2:6-16) is a trumpet blast of warning because God is about to act. Amos is revealing God's plan of action that was decided in the divine council.[47] These plans have not been kept secret but are graciously communicated to people for a purpose.

Amos is not defending himself in this verse, for the main clause is about what God does.[48] He is not attempting to vindicate his own authority or declare his own point of view. He is merely a servant who discloses the policy that Yahweh, the God of Israel, has determined. The revelation of God's decisions to a prophet does not limit God's sovereign freedom to take a contrary

---

[45]The calamity is a political disaster, the defeat of a city (Amos 3:11, 15 and 6:3; 9:4, 10) and not the temporary chastenings in 4:6-11 as maintained by Wolff, *Amos* 182. See A. Kapelrud "New Ideas in Amos," *SVT* 15 (1965) 196-98.

[46]The New English Bible translates 3:6b as "If their is evil in a city, will not the Lord act." See M. J. Mulder, "Ein Vorshlag zur Übersetzung von Amos III.6B," *VT* 34 (1984) 106-08.

[47]Early references to the divine council during the period of Ahab and Micaiah (1 Kings 22:19-28); Isaiah (Isa. 6:1-12); Psalm 82; 89:6-8 and in the ancient Near East argue against those who see this idea beginning at the time of Jeremiah. Robinson, "The Council of Yahweh," 151-57; Cross, "The Council of Yahweh in Second Isaiah," 274-77.

[48]This view is accepted by most. See Wolff, "The Irresistible Word (Amos)," *CurTM* 10 (1983) 5.

course of action if people repent (Amos 7:1-6; Jonah 3:1—4:3). The prophet's later call for the nation to "seek God and live" (5:14-15) is not a vain, or misguided bit of hope; it is the heart of God calling on men to fear God's warning and repent.

4. The effect God's warnings should have (3:8)

a. The people should fear (3:8*a*). Half of the dispute is settled already. The audience knows that the punishment announced in 3:2*b* is a warning of what God will do. But the dispute for human hearts, which are the object of the dispute, is still to be settled. If there is no positive response to the mind's understanding of the message, the dispute will fail to cause its intended results. Thus Amos calls for a personal decision of the heart and will. This shift is revealed in the change in style which contrasts a statement of fact (3:7) with a call for a response (3:8). In the process Amos integrates earlier images (3:4-6) and applies them to the present human situation. The hypothetical attack of a lion becomes reality, and the sound of the trumpet warning is heard. God's word is the warning and God is the lion (1:2). Since he has roared, he must be in the process of attacking his prey (3:4). This roar is like a trumpet blast which warns a city (3:5); this roar is the prophet's message of judgment that precedes God's action (3:6). Is it possible that people will not fear? What other results could this cause? A response of fear is necessary if the two parties are to walk together in unity again (3:3).

b. The prophet should warn (3:8*b*). To encourage this response, Amos identifies the source of his message. This message of punishment is what God has spoken. It is impossible for a person to ignore such a warning and not proclaim it. Amos responded in fear and gave this unpopular prophecy. Now he calls on the nation to respond in fear. The context implies (3:6) that this fear is a trembling before the almighty power of God which determines each person's destiny. In later chapters he will call for a fuller response. At this point Amos is calling on the people to take the first step and accept the fact that God has announced the judgment of Israel.

Theological Development

In the Near Eastern world it was commonly believed that all events were causally related. If Ur was destroyed by an enemy, the gods were angry (*ANET* 455); if there was a victory in war, the gods brought it about. Babylonian records indicate that every event was significant. The shape of rising smoke could predict the future, the acts of wild animals were omens of good or bad fortune, and the appearance of the stars and the shape of the moon affected one's fate.[49] Israel also looked for and saw cause-and-effect relation-

---

[49]R. R. Wilson, *Prophecy and Society in Ancient Israel* (Philadelphia: Fortress, 1980) 89-98, describes some of the interpretations of omens found in the *šumma alu* (over ten tablets on the

ships between events. God was not a theological abstraction that had no contact with or power over the history of natural and human events.[50]

As people gain financial security, social acceptance, status, political independence, and greater pleasure, their need for dependence on God tends to evaporate. Religion can become a dead acceptance of traditions. The maintenance of the social and political status quo can soon replace the theological implications that true faith has. A person's concept of responsibility before God and neighbor can be perverted because God no longer affects the events of daily life. Although everyone knows that every effect has a cause, the time delay between an act and its effect can deceive some into forgetting this basic law of life.

Tradition taught that Israel was elect (2:10; 3:2). God elected and redeemed his people from Egypt (2:9-10; 3:1), but Amos announced a contrary message of punishment and destruction (2:13-16; 3:2). This paradoxical reaction by God is fundamentally rejected by Amos' audience because it is contrary to their orthodoxy. This happened because their orthodoxy eliminated the dynamic of a trusting relationship and substituted a static nonrelational guaranteed benefit. In order to persuade his audience, Amos first redefines the rational contact between cause and effect in nature. After he applies the cause-and-effect principle to God's action, he concludes by challenging his audience to allow the cause (God's roar) to have an effect (fear) in their lives (3:8).

Although theology does not always seem logical to the unbeliever, rationality is a part of the process that helps people understand the nature of the relationship between God and the world. Although God irrationally acts in grace to elect a favored people, God does not irrationally inspire a prophet to deliver a message of destruction on his chosen people unless there is a cause. In fact, God limits his activity to a prophet's prior announcement of his action (3:7). Therefore, even the roar of God through the prophet's mouth is an act of grace that warns Israel of God's impending judgment. The cause of Amos's prophecy is God's roar. Who knowing God's word can help but proclaim it (3:8)? Only those who do not fear God. Only those whose deadened orthodoxy has removed God from the relational, cause and effect world of reality can dare ignore the roar of the lion.

---

behavior of insects, snakes, cattle, dogs, fire, wild animals, and houses); the *summa izbu* (about the meaning of malformed children or animals; and the *enuma Anu Enlil* which deals with the sun, moon, and placement of stars. A. L. Oppenheim, *The Interpretation of Dreams in the Ancient Near East* (Philadelphia: American Philosophical Society, 1956) discusses dreams.

[50]Formerly it was believed that the Hebrew view of God's purposeful activity in history was very distinct from other nations' view of their god's activity in history (See C. F. Whitley, *The Genius of Ancient Israel* (Amsterdam: Philo Press, 1969), p. 64-85), but A. Albrecktson, *History and the Gods* (Lund: Gleerup, 1967) has shown that Israelites and non-Israelites saw a very close cause and effect relationship in history.

Confirmation of God's Punishment

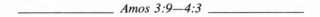

Introduction

In the second section of this speech Amos presents additional evidence to verify the announcement of punishment in 2:6-16 and 3:2*b*. In order to impress the message on the hearts of the people, Amos develops three paragraphs that confirm his earlier proclamation of punishment. These oracles expand the basis and the nature of God's judgment. God's action in 2:14-16 (the army will be destroyed) and 3:2*b* (you will be punished) are due to the open violence within Samaria's fortresses (2:6-8; 3:9-10; 4:1). Because of this, a nation will come and completely destroy these places of violence (3:11-12). God will remove the security of religion and luxury (3:13-15) and exile the oppressive upper class in Samaria (4:1-3).

Background

The setting of the three paragraphs in 3:9—4:3 is clearer than 3:1-8. The location of Samaria is mentioned in 3:9, 12 and 4:1. References to the palace-fortresses (3:10, 11), winter and summer homes, ivory homes and great homes (3:15), and signs of oppression and violence (3:10; 4:1) indicate that Amos is castigating the rich and powerful members of the economic and political aristocracy. To convince his audience, Amos returns to discuss the oppression described in 2:6-8. He confirms the validity of his evidence by suggesting that barbarous foreigners testify of its truth. After he verifies his accusation of the nation's violence against the poor, Amos reaffirms the punishment of destruction and exile for Samaria (3:13-15).

These oracles draw a sharp contrast between the wealthy class and the poor. The specific abuses found in 2:6-8 are absent in this section, although the references to "oppression of the poor" and "crushing the needy" in 4:1 are lexically and thematically connected to 2:6-8. The oppressors in 2:6-8 were left unidentified. From the accusation one can surmise that they were the wealthier and more powerful members of society, for 3:9—4:3 describes the guilty in more detail.[51] Those condemned are "those who store up violence and destruction in their palace-fortresses" (3:10). Their expensive and large homes will be destroyed (3:15) with only a "corner of a couch or part of

---

[51]Lang, "Social Organization of Peasant Poverty," 53-55.

the leg of a bed" left (3:12). The elite women of society received a special sarcastic diatribe for their luxury and excesses (4:1).

Although Amos is primarily against oppression, the richly furnished homes of the powerful members within society stand as symbols for their abuse of the poor. The maintenance of the status quo within these lavish and secure homes was the preoccupation of the wealthy. Their feasts were legendary for their drunkenness and waste (6:4-8). Their concern was not for the ruin of the nation or the plight of the weak; they were only concerned about indulging themselves in pleasures. Because of these evils, it appears that they have lost their sense of right and wrong (3:10); therefore, God will judge the rich and powerful by destroying their prized homes and sending them into exile in shame.

Some find the literary background for these oracles in the covenant lawsuit, but the comparisons with this genre are not particularily convincing.[52] Amos 3:9—4:3 is much more than a "call for witnesses to hear and testify." It contains both accusations and announcements of judgment well before the supposed introduction of the case in 4:4-5. The form is so distinct from the covenant lawsuit in structure that it is best to describe these three paragraphs as prophetic judgment speeches that confirm the verdict given in 2:13-16 and 3:2b.[53] Each oracle begins with the verb šm' "to hear, proclaim," but only the first and third have accusations that outline the reason why the charges are being made against Israel. All three contain the announcement of punishment, and the last two end with the divine confirmation formula "declares Yahweh." The absence of some declaration of guilt in the second oracle is probably due to the close relationship 3:13-15 has with 3:9-10.[54] Each oracle has unique structural features which are defined in the next section on structure.

Structure and Unity

Structure

The syntactical diagram reproduces the structure and flow of the message within 3:9—4:3. The English outline will be used in the exegesis of the text.

---

[52]Boyle, "The Covenant Lawsuit of the Prophet Amos: III:1-IV:3," 343-49; Sinclair, "The Courtroom Motif in Amos," 352; Seilhamer, "The Role of the Covenant," 443; Snyder, "Law and Covenant in Amos," 162.

[53]Mays, Amos 63, 71; Wolff, Amos 191, 200, 205; Melugin, "The Formation of Amos" 378-79 calls these oracles "proclamations of disaster."

[54]Wolff, Amos 200, 205.

The Confirmation of God's Punishment
Amos 3:9-4:3

<table>
<tr>
<td></td>
<td></td>
<td>A. An enemy will destroy the places of violence</td>
</tr>
<tr>
<td></td>
<td></td>
<td>1. Even foreigners recognize Samaria's oppression</td>
</tr>
<tr>
<td>Call out to the fortresses[a] in Ashdod,[b]
and to the fortresses[a] in the land of Egypt,
and say,
Assemble yourselves on the mountains[c] of Samaria,
and observe the great terror[d] within it
and the oppression within it.</td>
<td>3:9</td>
<td>a. Summons foreigners to Samaria
b. Instruction to confirm Samaria's violence</td>
</tr>
<tr>
<td>They do not know how to do what is right,[e]
declares Yahweh,
those who store up violence
and destruction in their fortresses.</td>
<td>3:10</td>
<td>c. Violence has destroyed morality</td>
</tr>
<tr>
<td></td>
<td></td>
<td>2. An enemy will oppress the land</td>
</tr>
<tr>
<td>Therefore, thus says the Lord Yahweh,
An adversary[f] will be[g] around about the land,
it will tear down your strong places from you,[h]
your fortresses will be plundered.</td>
<td>3:11</td>
<td>a. God announces destruction on the palace-fortresses</td>
</tr>
<tr>
<td>Thus says Yahweh,
As a shepherd recovers from the mouth of a lion,
two leg bones
or a part of an ear,
so the Israelites dwelling in Samaria will be recovered,
consisting of a corner of a couch[i]
or part of the leg[j] of a bed.[k]</td>
<td>3:12</td>
<td>b. God proclaims total destruction</td>
</tr>
<tr>
<td></td>
<td></td>
<td>B. God will destroy the places of security</td>
</tr>
<tr>
<td>Hear and solemnly warn the house of Jacob,
declares the Lord Yahweh, God of hosts.</td>
<td>3:13</td>
<td>1. Summons to confirm God's punishment</td>
</tr>
<tr>
<td>Surely on the day
when I punish Israel for its transgressions
I will punish the altars of Bethel,
the horns of the altar will be cut off
and they will fall to the ground.</td>
<td>3:14</td>
<td>2. God will remove their religious security</td>
</tr>
<tr>
<td>I will smite[l] the winter house,
the house of ivory will disappear,
the great house shall come to an end,[m]
declares Yahweh.</td>
<td>3:15</td>
<td>3. God will remove their social status
4. Divine confirmation formula</td>
</tr>
</table>

		C. God will exile the wealthy oppressors
Hear this word, O cows of Bashan,	4:1	1. God's accusation against the oppressors
who are on the mountains of Samaria,		
those who oppress the poor,		
those who crush the needy,		
those who say to their[n] husbands:		
bring that we may drink.		
The Lord Yahweh has sworn by his holiness,	4:2	2. God's oath of exile for Samaria
Behold, days are coming upon you[o]		
when one shall take you[o] away with hooks,[p]		
and the rest of you[o] with fish hooks.[q]		
And you shall go out[r] through breaches,[s]	4:3	
each one straight before her,		
and you shall be cast[t] to Harmon,[u]		3. Divine confirmation formula
declares Yahweh.		

3:9a. The Old Greek translates "fortresses, strongholds" with "country" here and in 3:10, 11 and 6:8. The error may be a confusion between *'armnôt* "fortresses" and *'arṣôt* "land." In Amos 1:4, 7, 10, 12, 14; 2:5 the Old Greek translates this word with "foundations." See P. Heawood, " *'rmnôt* and *'rm*," *JTS* 13 (1912) 66-73.

3:9b. "In Ashdod" is read "in Assyria" by the Old Greek. Wolff, *Amos* 189 thinks the parallelism between Egypt and Assyria in Hosea (7:11; 9:3; 11:5, 11; 12:2) may have influenced the Greek translators, but G. R. Driver, "Abbreviations in the Masoritic Text," *Textus* (1960) 121, thinks the word was abbreviated "As" in the Hebrew, thus the confusion.

3:9c. Syriac and Old Greek have the singular "mountain" as in 4:1 and 6:1.

3:9d. For "terror, tumult" the Old Greek has "astonishing things," and Sym. has "famines."

3:10e. "To do what is right" is translated "what will be against her" in the Old Greek.

3:11f. "An adversary" *ṣar* is understood to be *ṣōr* "Tyre" in the Old Greek and Aq. and "beseiged" in Symm.

3:11g. The Old Greek adds the verb "he shall be made desolate," which is not in the Hebrew.

3:11h. M. Dahood, "Hebew-Ugaritic Lexicography II," *Bib* 48 (1967) 425 connects "from you" with the Ugaritic *mmk* "sinkhole," but this interpretation is unlikely since the text makes sense as it is.

3:12i. The Old Greek has "over against a tribe," while Aq. and Sym. have "in the corner of a couch." The root *mth* is associated with two different roots, one meaning "couch," the other "tribe."

3:12j. The word *ubdmšq* is understood to be a reference to Damascus in the Old Greek, Syriac, Aq., Sym., and Theod. which Mays, *Amos* 66 accepts. If the text is emended by dividing the present consonants into two words *ubd mšq* as I. Rabinowitz, "The Crux of Amos 3:12," *VT* 21 (1961): 228-31 suggests, then the parallelism of "a part of a leg" gives a more consistent parallel with the leg and ear of the lamb.

3:12k. "Bed" is "priests" in the Old Greek, and it is placed at the beginning of v. 13 instead of at the end of v. 12.

3:15l. The Old Greek uses two verbs, "I will crush and smite," while Aq. has "I will buffet" and Sym. "I will smite."

3:15m. The verb *sûp* "to end" in the Hebrew was understood to be from the root *ysp* "to add" by the Greek translators. They also took *rabîm* "great houses" to refer to "many other houses," a very legitimate understanding of the Hebrew word.

4:1n. The suffix "their" is masculine, but the subject is feminine.

4:2o. The masculine plural suffix is used in the first two lines, but the feminine plural appears in the last line.

4:2p. "Hooks" is translated as "weapons" in the Old Greek, "spears" by Theod., and "shields" by Aq. and the Targum.

4:2*q*. The Old Greek has nothing for "fish" at the end of the verse, unless "burning plague" is an attempt to give it some meaning. They also had trouble with "hooks" and seem to have given "seething pots" as its equivalent.

4:3*r*. The Old Greek has a passive verb to match the passive verb later in the verse.

4:3*s*. "Breaches" is "woman" in Aq. and Theod. and "naked" in the Old Greek.

4:3*t*. The Hebrew active hiphil form should be revocalized to a passive hophal.

4:3*u*. "To Harmon" is read "the mountain of Rimmon" in the Old Greek, "Armenia" in Aq. and Sym., and "on a high mountain" in Theod.

The paragraphs within the long section 3:9—4:3 are divided into separate units by: (1) the repetition of "hear, proclaim" in 3:9, 13 and 4:1; (2) the direction of each section to different groups (to call foreigners to observe violence, 3:9); to proclaim judgment against Bethel and the stately homes (3:13); and to call the oppressive women to hear God's oath (4:1). The amount of emphasis on the accusation and the judgment also varies. Nevertheless, these three announcements of judgment have much in common when compared to the material which precedes and follows. Most group these prophecies together, although some deny that they were originally connected (see the section on Unity).[55] A number of commentaries do not group 4:1-3 with chapter 3.[56]

The first paragraph (3:9-12) is divided into two parts by the "therefore," which begins the announcement of judgment in 3:11. The first part (3:9-10) includes a group of imperatives which summon and instruct. The themes of oppression, violence, and fortresses bring the verses together to form a unified accusation. The second half of the paragraph (3:11-12) is divided into two sayings by the introductory "thus says the Lord" before each verse and by the tight parallelism in 3:11 and the comparison in 3:12, "as he recovers...so they will be recovered." The tearing down of the palace-fortresses in 3:11 is pictured by the useless scraps recovered in 3:12.

The second paragraph (3:13-15) also begins with an imperative summons (3:13*a*). The first person singular verbal forms bring verses 14-15 together. Verse 15 is unified by the four references to houses and is related to 14 by its similar development of the destruction theme against the "house of God," "Bethel."

The last paragraph (4:1-3) begins with the imperative summons in 4:1 and is divided into two parts by the introduction of an oath in 4:2. Amos 4:1 is built around three masculine plural participles which describe the audience, while 4:2-3 is characterized by its animal imagery (cows were also mentioned in 4:1). The participles and the oath are unique, but thematic continuity with the preceding oracles draws the parts of the unit together.

---

[55]Harper, *Amos* 74; Rudolph, *Amos* 162-63; Wolff, *Amos* 200; van der Wal, "The Structure of Amos " 109.

[56]Driver, *Amos* 167; Koch, *Amos* I, 107-08; R. Gordis, "The Composition and Structure of Amos," *HTR* 32 (1940) 239, 248.

Unity

Although some have connected 4:1-3 to 4:4-5 or the whole of chapter 4, this analysis: (1) ignores the thematic unity of 3:9—4:3 and the discontinuity of subject matter between 4:1-3 and 4:4-5, (2) ignores the relationship of "hear this...; proclaim" in 3:1, 9, 13 and 4:1, and overplays the relationship between 3:1, 4:1 and 5:1; and (3) misinterprets the "cows of Bashan" in 4:1 by giving them a cultic significance.[57]

Others treat each paragraph as a separate unit and deny or ignore the unity within the larger section. Consequently 3:9—4:3 is divided into several more or less independent utterances (3:9-11, 12, 13-15; 4:1-3).[58]

One significant point of discontinuity is the lack of an accusation in 3:13-15. To solve this problem, some have joined 3:12b to 3:13-15, but this creates a very abnormal syntactical construction and results in the people of Samaria witnessing against themselves.[59] Amos and other prophets do give oracles of doom with little or no emphasis on the accusation (5:1-3; 8:9-14), so this phenomenon is not unique to the passage. The lack of an accusation in 3:13-15 means that the accusations in 3:9-10 serve both 3:11-12 and 3:13-15. The reference to transgressions in 3:14 refers to the sins that the author has previously mentioned and are a summary accusation.

Interpretation

A. An enemy will destroy the places of violence (3:9-12)

The first paragraph is rhetorically designed to confirm what Amos has already said. The message of punishment (2:6-16; 3:2) is true and its destruction will be caused by God (3:3-8) even though Israel is God's chosen people (3:1-2). The violence that characterizes the foreign nations (Amos 1-2) has infiltrated the Israelite society. Since the same accusation resulted in God's destruction of their palace-fortresses in chapters 1 and 2, it is not surprising to find that God will also cause Samaria's fortresses to be plundered and destroyed.

1. Even foreigners recognize Samaria's oppression (3:9-10)

---

[57]Koch, *Amos* II 76-77, 107-08, 124, believes 3:9-4:3 was originally one unit, but because of the cultic association in 4:1-3 (in its present form) it now goes with 4:1-13. J. Watts, "A Critical Analysis of Amos 4:1ff," *SBL 1972 Seminar Papers* (Cambridge: Society of Biblical Lit., 1972) II, 495-98 believes "declares the Lord" in 4:3 is a later addition which has caused 4:1-3 and 4:4-13 to be cut apart; Melugin, "The Formation of Amos" 377-78 follows Koch.

[58]Mays, *Amos* 62-73 does not address the issue in his exegesis. Fosbroke, *Amos* 799 questions the editorial placement of 3:13-15; Harper, *Amos* 74-75 puts 3:15 after v. 11; but Wolff, *Amos* 200, 205 is more balanced, seeing diversity within a basic continuous unit.

[59]Maag, *Amos* 17 and Weiser, *Amos* 127 take this view, but Wolff, *Amos* 197; and Mays, *Amos* 67 reject it (see the exegesis of 3:12).

a. Summons foreigners to Samaria (3:9). The first part of the prophetic judgment speech is hidden within the instructions to summon a group of foreign dignitaries. With unusual boldness Amos invites the upper class from other nations to verify the sinfulness of Samaria. The prophet is willing to allow an "impartial" audience the right to examine and evaluate the behavior of the rich and powerful inhabitants of the palace-fortresses in Samaria. To bring these witnesses to Samaria, Amos sends messengers to invite them.[60] It is pointless to speculate about who was sent to invite the foreign emissaries to Samaria.[61] Since their testimony is never recorded, it is best to understand this summons as a rhetorical device.[62] The hypothetical coming of immoral barbarians from neighboring states to judge the morality of Samaria is used because of the dramatic effect it will have on the listener. The prospect for a positive evaluation is very remote.

The invitation is to be announced in the strongholds and palaces in Egypt and Ashdod (not Assyria). The choice of these two states is probably due to some historical, military, or cultural factor which made them particularily appropriate. Perhaps Samaria had recently taken unfair advantage of these nations.

b. Instruction to confirm Samaria's violence (3:9b). The instruction to these visitors must have produced a strong reaction. The observers from Egypt and Ashdod are to assemble together on the hills around Samaria to find out what is going on within the city.[63] From this vantage point they can witness the daily activities of its citizens and learn how the occupants of the palace-fortresses treat the other half of society. They are particularily instructed to notice the "great terror" and "oppression" that dominates life in the capital. This terrorism involves anarchy and bloodshed; it destroys human perception of reality and the value of human life.[64] Amos 2:6-8 also describes the oppression of the weak by those who rule by might and terrorism. It is an extreme depravity bred by a lust for power.[65] This is what the imaginary foreign diplomats will see when they come to Samaria.

c. Violence has destroyed morality (3:10). The accusation probes deeper

---

[60]Messengers are commissioned to proclaim warnings of destruction in Jer. 4:5, 16; 5:20; 46:14 and Joel 3:9 (Heb. 4:9), or to announce good news in Isa. 48:20 and Jer. 31:7.

[61]Who is being addressed in the second person plural imperative? Amos, a group of prophets, the foreign nations, or a group of heralds could receive this command, but these are all hypothetical. Since the message is given to the people of Samaria, they are the ones who are addressed.

[62]Mays, *Amos* 63; Rudolph, *Amos* 163.

[63]The niphal imperative "assemble yourselves together" has a reflexive sense: GKC 51c-e.

[64]This terror is the tumult, confusion, and panic caused by God's curse upon a people (frequently its army) in Deut. 28:20; 1 Sam. 5:9, 11; 14:20; 1 Chron. 15:5; Isa. 22:5; Zech. 14:13. It is the opposite of the state of joy (Ezek. 7:7) or peace (2 Chron. 15:5). The word describes acts rather than emotions. The plural form may express an intensification of the idea (GKC 124c) or the frequency of this type of behavior (GKC 124f).

[65]See the pictures which immortalize violence in J. Pritchard *ANEP* figure 319, 348, and 373 or the idealization of violence in battle reports in Grayson, *Assyrian Royal Inscriptions*

into the sins of the nation by looking for some of the underlying causes for the anarchy within the palace-fortresses. God's evaluation of their hearts pinpoints one of the nation's basic problems. The Israelites "do not know how to do what is right." They have practiced injustice against their fellow Israelites so long that it has become part of their normal behavior. Although "right" does have a mild legal connotation (Prov. 24:26; Isa. 26:10), most of the time it is found within the broader context of doing what is good, honest, and proper.[66] This accusation is a general summary of all their behavior. The norms of common sense and fair play no longer enable their conscience to guide them. A sense of humanitarianism and mutual responsibility is foreign to their thinking. This deterioration caused by the "good life" has persisted so long and gained such a dominant force in determining behavior that the people are unable to do what is right and proper.

The second half of the verse identifies the group that has lost its moral consciousness. They are categorized by what they do and where they live. By the misuse of power, they amass greater wealth and gain more influence. Their houses are full of the profits obtained through "violence and destruction." These twin vices are treasured like diamonds and rubies; through them the rich rulers furnish their palace-fortresses with the best that crime can buy. Each beautiful table, each bed and each sofa was purchased at the cost of someone's life or through legalized robbery.[67] In fact, business was so good that the people were forced to stockpile and hoard their violently-obtained treasures. This type of behavior may be due to the acceptance of Canaanite ways into Israelite culture, but the focus of attention is on the guilt of Samaria, not the source of their corrupt ways.

Amos' purpose throughout is to convince the people of Samaria of God's punishment because they have sinned. The violent means by which the powerful maintain their wealthy status is open for all to see. God condemns it and the wealthy from Egypt and Ashdod would condemn it.

II, 126: "I felled with the sword 800 of their combat troops, I burnt 3,000 captives...I made a pile of their corpses. I burnt their adolescent boys and girls...I cut off of some their arms and hands; I cut off of others their noses, ears, and extremeties. I gouged out the eyes of many troops. I made one pile of the living and one of the heads. I hung their heads on trees around the city."

[66]The wisdom background of this word, which Wolff, *Amos* 193, and Terrien, "Amos and Wisdom," 452 see, is not particularily impressive, as J. L. Crenshaw, "The Influence of the Wise on Amos," *ZAW* 79 (1967) 46, has shown.

[67]Violence and destruction are pairs together in Isa. 60:18; Jer. 6:7, 20:8; Ezek. 45:9; and Hab. 1:3. The words are probably not synonymous but are used together to describe two factors which make up a single way of life. "Violence" is associated with strife in Ps. 55:9 (Heb 55:10), physical mischief in Ps. 7:16 (Heb. 7:17), but chiefly bloodshed and murder in Judg. 9:24; Hab. 1:9; 2:8, 17; Joel 3:19 (Heb. 4:19); Jer. 51:35, 46. Robbery can refer to physical violence or murder in Jer. 5:6; 47:4; Ezek. 32:12, but the noun and verb are frequently found in connection with the devastation or ruin of a city (Isa. 15:1; 23:1; Jer. 48:1; 49:3), a nation (Jer. 4:20; 9:18; 49:10), or other objects. The context of the metaphor seems to demand the unusual sense of "robbery" in Amos 3:10, for the objects are not destroyed but stored up in the fortresses.

2. An enemy will oppress the land (3:11-12)

a. God announces destruction on the palace-fortresses (3:11). The announcement of punishment in 3:11-12 completes the prophetic judgment speech. Just as the rich inhabitants of the fortresses have oppressed, so they will be oppressed. God will accomplish this by sending an adversary upon them in the form of an unidentified enemy army. The defeat of Samaria is described in three stages in verse 11. First the adversary will encompass the land, then it will tear down the nation's strong places (probably its cities), and finally it will plunder the palace-fortresses. The first phase involves the whole land. The invading army will destroy the nation as a whole and not just replace the present dynasty. The encompassing position of this foe cuts off Samaria from all outside help and emphasizes the tremendous power that the enemy wields. The primary targets of the invading forces are the large fortified cities. The thick walls and towers of a city are the strength and security of the wealthy because they provide protection from a superior division of enemy troops outside.[68] The adversary will bring these massive defensive monuments down to the ground. The personalization of "your strong places" and the separative prepositional phrase "from you" suggest that the people were trusting in these walls.[69] Once the walls were destroyed, the lovely palace-fortresses were ready to be dismantled. Those who oppressed and plundered others will now be oppressed and plundered.[70]

b. God proclaims total destruction (3:12). Verse 12 should not be treated as an isolated oracle which is foreign to the present subject matter. The graphic illustration is directly related to the destruction and plunder of the wealthy who live in the fortresses of Samaria (see the section on Structure and Unity). Since it has a proverbial form, its style is different from verse 11.[71] These changes are normal in a simile and only indicate something of the prophet's ability to use a variety of rhetorical forms. The comparison presents a balanced and rhythmic parallelism in word ("recover" is repeated) and thought.

God's announcement of defeat in 3:11 is confirmed by God's proclamation of the total destruction of the luxury in the fortresses of Samaria. Their lavish

---

[68]Details of the defensive walls of Samaria with its five-foot-thick inner wall and its outer casement wall about thirty feet wide are described in G. Risner, C. Fisher, and D. Lyons, *Harvard Excavations at Samaria* (Cambridge: Harvard Un., 1924) I, 43:122; J. Crowfoot, K. Kenyon and E. Sukenik *Samaria-Sebaste I: The Buildings at Samaria* (London: Palestine Exploration Fund, 1942) 9-20.

[69]Even Ashur-Nasir-Apli II knew the folly of trusting in strong walls and armies: Grayson, *Assyrian Royal Inscriptions* II 126, 140.

[70]The Assyrian Royal Inscriptions are full of the exploits of the army. After each battle a long list of tribute, which was plundered from the palace-fortresses is listed. Grayson, *Assyrian Royal Inscriptions* II 118-147 is packed full of examples; *ANET* 275-76 describes the furniture Ashurbanipal II took on one of his campaigns.

[71]The imperfect verb expresses what customarily happens in a proverbial form: GKC 107g. Other examples are found in 3:3-8; 5:19; 6:12.

dwellings will be stripped to the bone. The prophet makes this point by giving an example drawn from the everyday experience of a shepherd who cares
for the herd of his master. Amos and his audience knew that the shepherd
could not protect the flock from every wild beast that roamed the hills of Samaria. When a sheep was killed, the shepherd was required by Israelite law to
recover the remains and return them to the owner: "If it is torn by a beast, let
him bring it as evidence" Exod. 22:10-13 (Heb. 22: 9-12).[72] Although God
enabled David to deliver a sheep from the mouth of a bear and a lion (1 Sam.
17:34-37), most shepherds had to be satisfied with taking back a few bits and
pieces to their masters (Isa. 31:4). The verbs "rescue, deliver" may be used
ironically since there is really nothing to rescue, or the semantic field of the
verb may be related to the idea of "recovery" (Judg. 11:26; 1 Sam. 30:18,
22). The recovery of two leg bones and a small part of the ear emphasizes the
totality of the destruction, not that something of value will be left after the
lion has finished his meal. Only a very small part remains; there is no hope
that the life of the sheep will be saved.

The second half of the verse applies this comparison to what will be left
when the wealthy fortresses are attacked and plundered. The passive verb,
"will be recovered," avoids identifying who will do the recovering and directs
attention toward what will be recovered. No counterpart for the lion is given
(it could be God as in 3:4, 8 or the foe as in 3:11),[73] but the sheep do corre-
spond to the upper class in Samaria who own magnificent beds (Amos 6:4).
The destruction and plunder of the fortresses will be so complete that only a
few scraps of a bed will be recoverable.

This interpretation is dependent on several difficult lexical and syntactical
factors. The last two lines end with parallel words for a "bed." The part of
the bed that remains is debated. Some believe the word *p't* means "splendid,"
but "footboard" or "corner" are more likely.[74] In the light of the meager remains of the sheep, the portion of the bed that remains is probably no more
than a single portion from the corner post of a couch or the corner of a blanket.

The last phrase has raised greater controversy because of the difficulty in
understanding "part of a leg" (see the textual notes). The word probably does
not refer to Damascus for the spelling is incorrect, it does not give a suitable

---

[72]The same principle is found in the Code of Hammurabi, a Mesopotamian legal code about
one thousand years before Amos. "If a visitation of a god has occurred in a sheepfold, or a lion
has made a kill, the shepherd shall prove himself innocent in the presence of god, but the owner
of the sheepfold shall receive from him the animal stricken in the fold," *ANET* 177, code 266.
This custom lies behind the defense of Jacob in Gen. 31:39.

[73]S. Mittmann, "Amos 3:12-15 und das Bett der Samarier," *ZDPV* 92 (1976) 149-67, believes
the lion was a protective symbol used on the beds.

[74]Gese, "Kleine Beiträge zum Verständnis des Amosbuches," 430, believes Akkadian *putu*
"foot board" is the root of this word. This may be similar to the Ugaritic *p'* "corner, forehead."
C. Gordon, *Ugaritic Textbook* (Rome: Pontifical Biblical Institute, 1965) glossary no 1994.
Mays, *Amos* 66 derives the word from the root *yph* "to be beautiful."

parallel for the previous line, and a reference to Damascus is foreign to the overall context of the destruction of Samaria.[75] The interpretation which understands this word as "damask" (silk) is equally problematic for the word "damask" comes from Arabic, there is no evidence that this product was manufactured in this area until long after the time of Amos, and this rendering gives a very poor parallel to "the corner of a couch" in the preceding line. Several emendations are suggestive, but Rabinowitz has offered an excellent solution which maintains the Hebrew text and parallelism. By simply dividing *bdmsq* into two words he arrives at the meaning "a part of a leg" *bad mšq*.[76]

Before these lexical conclusions can be put together, some syntactical questions must be answered. The first relates to the translation of the plural participle "dwelling, sitting" and the connection it has with what precedes and follows. Some translate this participle "those who are sitting" and connect it with what follows.[77] But the relationship between "sitting on a bed" and being rescued is rather obscure. The parallelism between 12a and 12b becomes very peculiar with this interpretation.

The reconstruction of Rabinowitz translates the participle "those who dwell" and connects it with what precedes. This analysis has the advantage of making the last two lines parallel. On the other hand this reading of the text has a problem with the preposition "in" which precedes the last two phrases. Rabinowitz solves this issue by identifying the preposition as a *beth essentiae*.[78] The sheep will be recovered in the form of a leg or part of an ear while the Israelites will be recovered in the form of a corner of a couch or a piece of the leg of a bed.[79] This simile dramatically conveys the idea that the plundering of the fortresses will be so complete that only a few worthless fragments will be left. This graphic description of God's judgment is God's response to violence and robbery (3:9-10) which has enabled the fortress dwellers to store up their riches.

B. God will destroy the places of security (3:13-15)

The second paragraph within the larger section, 3:9—4:3, is marked with

---

[75]Damascus has a double *m* and a *ś* instead of a *š*. Mays, *Amos* accepts the translation Damascus.

[76]Rabinowitz, "The Crux in Amos III:12," *VT* 11 (1961) 278-31 and H. Moeller, "Ambiguity in Amos 3:12," *BT* 15 (1964) 31-34. Other emendations are: "on the edge" by G. R. Driver, "Difficult words in the Hebrew Prophets," *Studies in Old Testament Prophecy*, ed. H. H. Rowley (Edinburgh: T. and T. Clark, 1957) 69, by changing the text to *bmqrš*; or "headboard" in Gese, "Kleine Beiträge zum Verständnis des Amosbuches," 431 by changing the text to *b'mšt*. See also O. Loretz, "Vergleich und Kommentar in Amos 3, 12," *BZ* 20 (1976) 122-25.

[77]Wolff, *Amos* 196; Rudolph, *Amos* 158; Mays, *Amos* 66; Driver, *Amos* 164.

[78]Rabinowitz, "The Crux of Amos III: 12," 220. See GKC 119i where this use of *b* means "as, in the capacity, in the form, consisting of."

[79]These beds may be similar to the ones Ashurbanipal is lounging on in a relief found at Nineveh. Pritchard, *ANEP* fig. 451.

the characteristic summons, "hear," but this paragraph introduces new topics and a structure which does not include a full accusation like 3:9-10. Because 3:13-15 are temporally and topically related to the canonical context of 3:9-11, a full repetition of the accusation seems unnecessary.[80] The paragraph expands and develops God's message of doom so that even the "sacred structures" are included. The rhetorical purpose of this focus is to remove any hope or security the rich have. Neither the horns of the altar nor their great luxurious homes will protect them from God's punishment. This emphasis on total destruction is picked up from 2:14-16 and applied to new areas of life to strengthen the force of the message.

1. Summons to confirm God's punishment (3:13)

A summons is sounded by two introductory imperatives. As in 3:9, this rhetorical call is given for the dramatic effect it will have on the listeners in Samaria. They themselves verify the warning by their reception of God's words.[81]

The recipients are "the sons of Jacob" (Amos 6:8; 7:2, 5; 8:7), a specific reference to the ten northern tribes. The source of the message is "the Lord Yahweh, God of hosts."[82] Verse 13 is not just a messenger formula added by Amos or some later redactor but God's solemn warning to the nation. The title emphasizes the power and might of God.[83] When he fights against his enemies, he has the power to destroy everything completely. This reminder of the power of God is an incentive to take God's warning seriously and not trust in one's elect status (3:2) or in any other religious and social institutions for protection.

2. God will remove their religious security (3:14)

The force of the warning is heightened by the initial particle "surely, indeed"[84] and the introductory temporal clause which allows for a double em-

---

[80]Wolff, *Amos* 200, 205; Mittmann, "Amos 3, 12-15 und das Bett der Samarier," 149-67 maintains that 3:13-14 are a later prose insertion, while Fosbroke, *Amos* 799 sees a close connection between 3:13-15 and 4:4-5.

[81]"To witness" is used in a legal context where one witnesses against another (Deut. 17:6; 1 Kings 21:10, 13) and in the context of official business to seal a transaction before witnesses (Jer. 32:10, 25, 44). In these and other situations the function of the witness is to affirm or attest to the truth. When someone verifies something about the future his testimony becomes a warning, exhortation, or admonition (Gen. 43:3; Exod. 19:21; 1 Sam. 8:9; 1 Kings 2:42).

[82]The identity of the "hosts" is still debated. See Cripps, *Amos* 330; Wolff, *Amos* 287; Eichrodt, *The Theology of the Old Testament*, I 192-94; B. Wambacq, *L'epithète divine Jahve Seba'ôt* (Bruges: DeBrouwer, 1947).

[83]Wolff, *Amos* 199 considers the title to be a later addition, but Rudolph, *Amos* 160 objects only to the length on metrical grounds and drops "Lord" to bring the title into line with 4:13 and 6:14. Mays, *Amos* 68 objects to the use of "God of hosts," but this phrase, which is so unusual in the early prophets, occurs so frequently in Amos (4:13; 5:14, 15, 16, 27; 6:8; 9:5) that it must be based on a genuine tradition (Fosbroke, *Amos* 799). If it were added, it is very difficult to understand why it was added so inconsistently and why the redactors did not add the phrase to other early prophetic books.

[84]GKC 159ee. 148d. The absolute certainty of a result is emphasized by the insertion of *ki* "indeed."

phasis on "I will bring punishment."[85] The reference to "punishment for transgressions" connects this paragraph with the vocabulary of Amos 2:6 and 3:2. The transgressions are not repeated again since they were given in Amos 2:6-12 and 3:9-10. The results of these sins will be a "day" of God's visitation. This new idea, which is inconspicuously introduced here, plays a fundamental role in Amos' understanding of God's relationship to the history of Israel. Someday, on the Day of Yahweh (Amos 5:18-20), the divine judge will interrupt the course of history to punish Israel.

To convince the people of this fact and to remove all false hopes, the disaster is prescribed in yet another way. The transgressions of the nation include crimes of violence and murder, the types of crimes that require the death penalty (Exod. 21:12; Lev. 24:17; Numb. 35:30-1). These same laws provide protection from punishment in cities of refuge (Exod. 21:13; Numb. 35:10-15, 22-28; Deut. 19:1-33) or on the horns of the altar (Exod. 21:14; 1 Kings 2:28). But if the party is guilty, the person can be removed from the horns of the altar and punished. These customs are employed by Amos to explain how God will remove the security of the horns of the altar.[86] The altars will be destroyed. Their last hope will disappear; their security will be dashed to the ground. The destruction of the holy places at Bethel is a sign of the impotence of their faith and the gods they serve.[87]

3. God will remove their social status (3:15)

The first person verb expresses God's own involvement in the devastation of Samaria, but this verse does not say how the "smiting" will be accomplished. It could be caused by a military force (3:11-12) or possibly an earthquake (2:13; 8:8; 9:1). The intention of the verse is to persuade and convince the rich and powerful of God's devastating action. God's judgment will destroy their socio-economic security as well as their religious security (3:14).

By their oppression the upper class was able to gain and maintain their economic status. This economic base made it possible for them to construct for themselves elaborate homes with expensive furniture. Archaeologists have discovered house foundations with several rooms off a central courtyard. These demonstrate a large distinction between the rich and the poor in the eighth century B.C.[88]

The summer and winter homes may refer to two-story homes, the lower

---

[85]The preposition *b* "on" (before "day") indicates a temporal use of the infinitive construct: GKC114b, d-e. The first person suffix on *pāqdî* "I bring punishment" functions as the subject of the infinitive construct: GKC 115e.

[86]The actualization of this prophecy may come through enemy activity or an earthquake (Amos 9:1). See Rudolph, *Amos* 165; H. W. Wolff, "Das Ende des Heiligtums in Bethel," *Archäologie und Altes Testament, Festschrift für K. Galling* (Tübingen: Mohr, 1970) 287-98.

[87]J. Hyatt, "The Deity Bethel and the Old Testament, *JAOS* 59 (1939) 81-98 and I. Eissfeldt, "Der Gott Bethel," *Kleine Schriften* I (1962) 206-33, believe that the Elephantine god "Bethel" is described here, not the city of Bethel, but this hypothesis is very unlikely.

[88]H. Beebe, "Ancient Palestinian Dwellings," *BA* 31 (1968) 49-57, discusses these structures and their sociological significance.

heated floor being for winter (Jer. 36:22) and the upper, cooler chamber designed to catch the summer breezes (Judg. 3:20). On the other hand "house" normally is not used to describe two different rooms or parts of one house. The Barrakkab Inscription from Zenjirli, which comes from the period of Amos, refers to the fact that the kings of Sam'el had no suitable palace. They had only one palace which had to serve both as their winter and summer palace. This text indicates that Barrakkab now has a separate palace, but his fathers had to stay year round in one palace.[89] One middle Babylonian period document, two late Babylonian texts, and Zenophon's description of the palaces of Cyrus substantiate the view that kings had separate houses at different locations.[90] In Samaria, the wealthy were able to enjoy the luxury that kings normally enjoyed. But newly attained social security will not last long, for these homes are about to be destroyed.

These luxurious villas are described as "houses of ivory" and "great houses" in the second half of the verse. Ahab's house was known for its beautiful ivory (1 Kings 22:39). Jeroboam II and the rich people of Samaria seemed to have a similar ability to flaunt their wealth. The excavation of Samaria has produced a massive number of beautiful ivory reliefs that testify to the abundant use of ivory within the palace area.[91] The word *rabîm* may describe the number of houses, but "great, chief, important" presents a better parallel.[92] The repeated emphasis on the destruction of the houses of the rich removes any doubt about God's intentions. The warning is shocking: God is sending total destruction!

4. Divine confirmation formula (3:15)

C. God will exile the wealthy oppressors (4:1-3)

The final paragraph of 3:9—4:3 confirms God's punishment by describing the last stage of his judgment. After an enemy comes and destroys the fortresses (3:9-12), and God removes their places of security (3:13-15), his final act will be the total humiliation of the cultured elite (4:1-3). Those who have gained power and wealth through acts of violence and oppression (3:9-10; 4:1) will be oppressed and treated like animals. The oath form in the second

---

[89]J. Gibson, *Textbook of Syrian Semitic Inscriptions II: Aramaic Inscriptions* (Oxford: Clarendon, 1975) 87-91.

[90]S. Paul, "Amos III: 15—Winter and Summer Mansions," *VT* 28 (1978) 358-59. Ahab also had a palace at Jezreel and Samaria (1 Kings 21:1; 21:18); B. Napier, "The Omrides of Jezreel," *VT* 9 (1959) 366-78.

[91]J. Crowfoot and G. Crowfoot, *Samaria-Sebaste II: Early Ivories from Samaria* (London: Palestine Exploration Fund, 1938) contains photographs and a description of these ivories, or *Encyclopedia of Archaeological Excavations in the Holy Land* IV, 1044-46 and the plate on 1039.

[92]Driver, *Amos* 167; Harper, *Amos* 78 and Wolff, *Amos* 199, 202, on the basis of "the great house" in Amos 6:11 take this to be a reference to many houses; see G. Glanzman, "Two Notes: Amos 3:15 and Os. 11:8-9," *CBQ* 23 (1961) 227-29.

half of the paragraph is incontrovertible evidence that the punishment of exile will be accomplished.

Amos 4:1-3 is connected to what precedes by the introductory summons, "hear," by its structure of an accusation plus an announcement of punishment, and by various thematic motifs. These assocations aid in determining whether the "cows of Bashan" are a symbol of wealth and luxury or the symbol of a fertility cult in Samaria.

1. God's accusation against the oppressors (4:1)

The accusation contains a call to attention, an identification of the audience and a list of accusations which describe the sins of the recipients. The initial summons, constructed similarly to 3:1 and 5:1, is distinct in its use of participial instead of relative clauses.[93] The masculine plural imperative "hear" would not cause one to expect a condemnation of women, but the feminine "cows" and the reference to their "husbands" have traditionally led most to identify the audience with the wealthy women of Samaria.[94] Because of the mixture of genders, the Targum identified the audience as the leaders of the nation who made requests to false gods, "their lords."[95] Some interpreters believe the "cows of Bashan" are a symbol of a fertility cult in Samaria. The connection with the Baal cult is based on the context of 4:1-3 (next to 4:4-5) and the identification of various words within the paragraph with concepts related to Baalism.[96] The evidence from context is weak. A judgment on the rich oppressors fits the context of 3:9-12, 15 and the prophet's emphasis in 2:6-7; 5:10-13; 6:1-7; and 8:4-6. Although Amos condemns false worship, he seldom refers, like Hosea, to the worship of other gods (but cf. Amos 5:26).

The fertility motif is related to Bashan, but it is difficult to know how Amos is using this symbol in Amos 4:1. Bashan is the fertile area located east of the Jordan River and north of the Yarmuk River. This Transjordan plain was noted for its beautiful oaks (Isa. 2:13; Ezek. 27:6), its good pastures (Jer. 50:19; Mic. 7:14) and its fine cattle (Deut. 32:14; Ps. 22:12 [Heb. 22:13]; Ezek. 39:18; Micah 7:14), but there is no biblical tradition which connects it

---

[93] The differences in the syntactical construction of these introductions suggests that 4:1 should not be seen as a major division between sections.

[94] The Hebrew Bible has numerous examples where a feminine subject is used with a masculine verb. GKC 110k; 145o.

[95] Calvin and Luther consider the cows to be the wealthy men of Samaria and their "lords" to be a reference to their kings.

[96] H. M. Barstad, "Die Basankühe in Amos IV:1" *VT 25* (1975) 286-97; J. D. Watts, "A Critical Analysis of Amos 4:1ff" 489-500; A. J. Williams, "A Further Suggestion about Amos IV:1-3" *VT* 29 (1979) 206-11. They believe "cows" is a technical term drawn from fertility cult practices. The existence of the Baal cult on Bashan is derived from Ps. 68:15-16 [Heb. 68:16-17], while terms like "their lords" are associated with the title of Baal. "Let us drink" is connected with the new year's feast within the cult. The comparison of the nation with animals in a baalistic context in Jer. 2:20-24 and Hos. 4:15-16 is used to support this position. See also P. F. Jacobs, "Cows of Bashan—A note on the Interpretation of Amos 4:1," *JBL* 104 (1985) 109-10.

with the Baal fertility cult.[97] If this association is not firmly established, attempts to relate "lord" to Baal or "drinking" to a Baal feast are inconclusive.

This figure of speech probably was used because of the shocking effect it would have on the listener.[98] The oaks of Bashan symbolize the proud and haughty in Isaiah 2:13, the bulls of Bashan symbolize violence and strength in Psalm 22:12, and Bashan itself is a sign of fatness and fertility. These ideas fit the negative context of a group of wealthy women who oppress the poor and concern themselves only with selfish desires (4:1b). This is the same type of person who has both summer and winter homes decorated with ivory (3:15). These are the people who cause violence and oppression from their palace-fortresses (3:9-10).

The second half of the verse describes the selfish behavior which enabled these women to maintain their high social status. The two active participles portray their continual abuse and oppression of others.[99] This exploitation strengthened their control over the nation and provided funds to support their eccentricities. The text is silent about the methods used, but Amos 2:6-7; 3:9-10; 5:12 and 8:4-6 describe how some groups oppressed the poor and needy.[100] This helpless segment of society which had no wealth was subjugated further and forced to produce greater wealth for those who already were rich. There is no mercy or compassion for the weak; instead they are crushed and broken. "Lord, husband" appears to be a mockery of the nagging of the women as well as a derogatory remark about the husband's au-

---

[97]Jeremiah 2:22 uses Bashan in a political not a religious sense. The nation's lovers refer to political allies of Jehoiakim. Ps. 68:15-16 is difficult to interpret, but there is no evidence that an important Baal cult was located in Bashan. Barstad's inability to prove the connection between Bashan and Baal weakens his whole hypothesis in "Die Bashankühe in Amos IV:1," 293. K. Koch, "Die Rolle der hymnischen Abschnitte des Amos-Buches," ZAW 86 (1974) 514, connects the "hills" and "high places" which God will destroy in 4:13 with the "cult hill of Samaria" in 4:1, but this hypothesis is questionable.

[98]Mays, Amos 72 thinks "cows of Bashan" has a positive connotation of quality and fatness which would amount to flattery instead of insults, while Speiser sees this as a reference to the voluptuous stature of the women ("Bemerkungen zu Amos" VT 23 [1953] 306).

[99] In GKC 116a the active participle indicates a continual uninterrupted exercise of an activity. "To crush" is found parallel to "to oppress" in Deut. 28:33; 1 Sam. 12:4; Hos. 5:11 and is parallel to "to break in pieces" in Ezek. 29:7; "to oppress" in Judg. 10:8; "to break" in Eccl. 12:6 and Isa. 58:6. It describes the "breaking, crushing" of the head of Abimelech (Judg. 9:53) and of Leviathan (Ps. 74:14). War involves "crushing" by the enemy (Deut. 28:33; Judg. 10:8; Hos. 5:11). In time of peace the wicked and the rich "crush" the poor (1 Sam. 12:4; 2 Chron. 16:10; Job 20:19) by defrauding them and taking their property.

[100]"Needy" 'ebyôn, which is used 61 times in the Old Testament, describes those who should be treated with compassion and justice (Deut. 15:4, 7, 9, 11; 24:14) but who are often neglected (Jer. 5:28; Ezek. 16:49), persecuted, robbed, or murdered (Ps. 109:16; Jer. 2:34; Ezek. 18:12; Amos 2:6; 5:12; 8:4-6). These people are often godly people (Ps. 37:14; 74:21), and God promises to help them (Ps. 9:18[Heb 9:19]; 12:5 [Heb 12:6]; 35:10; 69:33 [Heb 69:34]). 'āni (74 times) is a parallel term which describes the "poor, afflicted, humble." dāl (48 times) refers to the "weak, low, poor." In Akkadian "dullu" refers to those who are pressed into forced labor, and this idea is not far from the position of the poor in Israel. G. Botterweck " 'ebyôn" TDOT I 27-41 and H. Fabrey "dāl" TDOT III 208-30.

thority.[101] The last line "bring that we may drink" may also be an example of the indulgent life of the rich.[102] Drinking, feasting, and the throwing of parties were some of the chief concerns of the women. These pictures are opposite the ideal woman protrayed in Proverbs (31:4-7, 20) and reminiscent of the behavior of Jezebel (1 Kings 21:5-15) and the leading women in Jerusalem (Isa. 3:16-4:1).

2. God's oath of exile for Samaria (4:2-3)

The announcement of punishment takes the form of an oath. The present oath to remove Israel from the land is just as true as God's earlier oath to give the land to the seed of Abraham (Deut. 6:10, 18, 23). The oath is irrevocable because it is based on God's divine holiness. Similar expressions are found in Amos 6:8 and 8:7, but the closest parallel is Psalm 89:35 (Heb. 89:36). Parallel to the oath in Psalm 89 is the thought that God does not violate, change, or lie about his word. When God swears an oath "by his holiness" he commits his character and the reality of his essence to his word. Holiness is in some ways an almost undefinable quality that distinguishes God from people. It is synonymous with divinity itself and is associated with the idea of God's majestic power and purity.[103]

The seriousness of the oath is heightened by "for truly, surely" and the imminent expectation of a new period of history. The phrase "the days are coming" signals the approach of a new era. It became a prophetic formula which introduced new events in the coming eschatological era as well as the dynamic action of God in the present history. Both positive and negative events follow this formula (1 Sam. 2:31; 2 Kings 20:17; Isa. 39:6; Amos 8:11; 9:13; Jer. 7:32; 9:25; 16:14; 19:6; 23:5, 7; 30:3), but the negative context indicates the intention here.

The general picture relates to the destruction of the walls of a city and the deportation of its inhabitants. The exact impact of the symbols in verse 2 are still rather obscure because of the meaning of ṣinôt and ṣîrôt. The first term could mean "shields," but this meaning is always attached to a masculine noun (these are both feminine). Some picture the enemy dragging out the corpses of the women of Samaria on shields, but in 4:1-3 deportation rather than death is the lot of the women.[104] Other commentators think ṣinôt is a feminine form of "thorn" and believe it refers to some sort of barbed hook used to fasten prisoners to a rope. A few Assyrian reliefs picture captives

---

[101]Rudolph, *Amos* 176. "Lord" is used for husband in Gen. 18:12; Judg. 19:26, 27, but it is unusual. The word has the connotation of master.

[102]"Bring" is an imperative (the final *h* is sometimes added: GKC 48i), while "that we may drink" is a cohortative which expresses the speaker's intention: GKC 108d.

[103]O. Procksch "*hagios*" *TDNT* I 88-97; Eichrodt, *Theology of the Old Testament*, I 270-79.

[104]Targum and the Old Greek have "arms, shields"; Snaith, *Amos* 69-71 believes the people will be removed on shields and in fish pots. S. M. Paul, "Fishing Imagery in Amos 4:2," *JBL* 97 (1978) 183-86 reviews the five ways that this word has been translated.

being marched into exile by means of a ring through their nose or lip.[105] Schwantes and Wolff relate this Hebrew term to the Akkadian *ṣerretu* or *ṣinnatu* "nose rope, halter, rein" but this proposal is rejected by Rudolph and Williams.[106] Since *ṣinôt* is parallel to *ḥôḥ* "brier, ring, hook" in passages that refer to the capture of a sea monster (Ezek. 38:4; Job 41:2 [Heb 40:26]), the translation "hooks" seems reasonable in a context that deals with the exile of prisoners using the imagery of animals.[107] The last two lines appear to be synonymous, but the understanding of the second object is also problematic. The word has been translated fish hooks, boat, pot, harpoon, cattle prod, and spear.[108]

Although there is still some confusion about the identity of the way the women will be taken into exile, these symbols of defeat and humiliation show how the tables will be turned. They have treated the poor as animals, now they are in line for a similar type of treatment. Violence and inhumanity will be a part of the punishment that every last one of them will suffer. The luxurious living will end and the rich oppressive women will shamefully go into exile.

Verse 3 may continue the analogies of verse 2, but there are no explicit references to animals. The humiliation of capture in verse 2 presupposes the defeat of the city of Samaria. The breaches in the wall are those made by an enemy army (1 Kings 11:27) or an earthquake.[109] "Each one before her" may indicate the extent of the destruction of the walls; thus the destruction of the walls is so extensive that one can exit at almost any point.[110] As prisoners of

---

[105]G. Rawlinson, *The Five Great Monarchies of the Ancient Eastern World* (New York: Dodd, 1881) I, 243 and *ANEP* 152, fig. 440.

[106]S. Schwantes, "Notes on Amos 4:2*b*," *ZAW* 79 (1967) 82-83; Wolff, *Amos* 207; see also the Enuma Elish I, 72, "He seized Mummu, holding him by a nose rope..." *ANET* 61. On the other hand A. J. Williams, "A Further Suggestion about Amos 4:1-3," *VT* 29 (1979) 206-11 and Rudolph, *Amos* 161, reject this view because the Greek and Hebrew never use the meaning "nose rope" for this word in other passages. They prefer to derive the meaning from comparative Hebrew material.

[107]Williams connects the people in Amos 4:2 with imagery of the sea monster by interpreting "Bashan" as a serpent or dragon. He believes Amos is dependent on an ancient monster myth in 4:2, but these suggestions are unlikely. Military and fishing imagery (Hab. 1:14-15; Jer. 16:16; Ezek. 29:4) explains the symbols; there is no need to introduce mythology into the text.

[108]Paul, "Fishing Imagery in Amos 4:2," 186-90, reviews the several ways that this word has been translated. Paul prefers the translation "pots" based on imagery used in a Mari text about taking captives in a fisherman's basket.

[109]"Breaches" is the object of the sentence (GKC 118d-f) and should be translated "through breaches" to fit the verb. Watts, "A Critical Analysis of Amos 4:1ff," 495 n 19, believes this word has fertility connotations and that *rmn* is the name of a god. See also J. J. Glück "The Verb *PRS* in the Bible and in Qumran Literature," *RevQ* 5 (1964-65) 123-27.

[110]If the animal imagery continues into verse 3, one might picture the captives connected to a rope, being led off through a breach in the walls like a line of cows going through a hole in the fence like Hammerschaimb, *Amos* 67 and Driver, *Amos* 168. Joshua 6:5, 20 uses a similar phrase in the description of the fall of Jericho to picture the completeness of the destruction of the walls.

war the indulgent ladies will be forced to leave the protection of their homes and forsake their life of luxury and privilege.

Although the meaning of *harmônāh* is in doubt, the word is clearly a reference to exile or disgrace. Amos 5:27 ends with a reference to the exile of the nation "beyond Damascus," and this word may point in a similar direction to Armenia or Mount Hermon (see the textual notes.)[111] The fat cows of Bashan will be disgracefully thrown out of Samaria like a seasoned corpse (Amos 8:3; Jer. 22:19).[112] Ezekiel 16:5 uses this imagery of a child that is rejected, unpitied, and abhorred. God despises the luxurious oppressors and will totally humiliate them. Their experience will be as vile and inhuman as the atrocities they inflict upon the poor and helpless within Israel.[113]

3. Divine Confirmation Formula (4:3)

Theological Development

The rational arguments concerning cause and effect in Amos 3:1-8 reminded the nation that privilege carries responsibility, that election may bring God's blessing on those who fear him, or judgment on those who fail to walk together in unity with God. If the logic of this approach is accepted, there still is a need to prove that Israel has failed to carry out the responsibilities of God's elect people. Amos announced disaster in 3:2, but the basis for this judgment and the extent of God's punishment (2:6-16) need some additional verification and reinforcement to cause the audience to fear God.

Amos verifies the charges against the nation in 3:9-10 and 4:1. The oppression described in 2:6-8 is confirmed by hypothetical foreign witnesses from the ungodly nations around Israel. Since Israel has just finished judging the deeds of these nations who commit transgressions worthy of punishment (1:3—2:3), it is only fair play for Amos to ask these impartial visitors to evaluate what is happening in Samaria. The evil within Samaria is violence, anarchy, and no sense of right and wrong (3:9-10; 4:1). Those accused of these evils are the powerful and wealthy inhabitants of the palace-fortresses (3:10-12; 4:1).

---

[111]D. N. Freedman and F. I. Andersen, "Harmon in Amos 4:3," *BASOR* 198 (1970) 41, connect Harmon with Hermel, the home of Dan'el in the Ugaritic texts. If the text were emended slightly from *harmônah* to *'armônah*, the familiar "palace-fortresses" would be the place from which they were cast.

[112]The final *h* on "and you shall be the thrown" is unusual and may be an example of dittography (GKC 44), but similar forms are sometimes found (GKC 32i; 44g, m; 47c).

[113]Watts, "A Critical Analysis of Amos 4:1ff," 497-500, attempts to trace the historical growth of 4:1-5 by attributing part of the section to: (1) Amos's words against the fertility cult; (2) a later editorial process to support the reform of Josiah in 621 B.C.; (3) a post-exilic liturgical usage which introduces several introductory formulas; (4) a fifth-century redaction of the speech against Samaria instead of Bethel; and (5) the addition of the accusations of social injustice during the time of Nehemiah. This hypothetical reconstruction is imaginative, speculative, and full of unsupported methodology and conclusions.

Violence, oppression, and anarchy were the social evils present in the days of Noah (Gen. 6:11-13), and oppression and affliction describe the Egyptian enslavement of the Hebrews before the the the exodus (Exod. 3:7-9; 5:14-16, 21). The law forbids the oppression of the poor and needy (Deut. 15:7-18; 24:15; Lev. 25:35-43). The poor were to be cared for with generous provision to meet their needs. A strong warning against a hardened heart is coupled with an admonition to give to the needy according to the degree that God has blessed. The constant theological motivation which transforms this obligation into a joy is the remembrance that Israel was once a poor slave in Egypt. They were redeemed from oppression by Yahweh when he chose them to be his people (Deut. 15:15; 24:18; Lev. 25:38, 42). To rule over someone oppressively was a sign that an individual did not fear God (Lev. 25:43). The violence within the palace-fortresses and the crushing of the needy by the wealthy women of Samaria verify the nation's rejection of its traditions and status as the redeemed and elect people of God (2:9-10; 3:1-2). They are worse than their neighbors who commit acts of barbarity and oppression against foreigners. Their foreign neighbors would be astonished to see how the nation of Samaria oppresses its own people.

Ezekiel, in a similar manner, evaluates the sins of Sodom as less than the sins of Judah (Ezek. 16:44-52). God's own people have lost all sense of humanitarianism; they seem to have no conscience to distinguish right from wrong behavior. Their criteria for decision making are determined by their own selfish desires for power and wealth (Amos 3:10; 4:1). The wealthy enjoy their security and luxury within their beautifully furnished palace-fortresses because of oppression; therefore, their central concern is to maintain this position of power and advantage. Amos confirms his earlier accusation in 2:6-8 and explains the cause of God's punishment of the elect (3:1-2). God swears an oath to strengthen the nation's understanding of God's decision (4:2).

The effect of God's judgment will bring about the destruction of the people and places that cause violence (3:11-12, 15, 4:2-3). The strong city walls will be breached (3:11; 4:3); the palace-fortresses will be looted for booty and destroyed (3:11-12, 15). The powerful oppressors themselves will be oppressed, treated like animals, and sent into exile (4:3). Power and wealth will not buy security, and neither will the altar or temple at Bethel (3:14). These proclamations of destruction verify God's intention to bring about the end of the nation.

Israel is Unwilling to Return to God

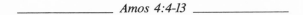
Introduction

God's rejection of the chosen nation has been substantiated and its sinfulness confirmed. Because of the nation's sin, God will bring an enemy to destroy the places of violence (3:9-12), remove the religious and social places of security (3:13-15), and send the wealthy and oppressive citizens into exile (4:1-3). This confirmation of the prophet's earlier messages (2:6-16; 3:1-2) could have produced a number of responses from the audience: true repentance (cf. Jonah 3:1-10), a denial of the accusations, arguments of self-defense, or suggestions on how to avoid God's punishment. No public reaction is recorded (cf. Amos 7:10-17), but if the response was anything other than a move to repent, Amos would need to persuade his audience that their actions were inadequate.

The criticism of the nation's worship at Bethel and Gilgal (4:4-5) and its failure to truly return to God, suggests that Amos perceived the response of the audience to be the traditional: "We will go over to Bethel and offer some sacrifices to gain the favors of God." The prophet's ironic mockery of these meaningless acts of contrition and worship (4:4-5) demonstrates that the people are unwilling to turn to God with their whole heart. Things are no different from earlier years when God chastened the nation. The people continually refuse to return to God (4:6-11). Therefore, they must now prepare to meet Yahweh, the Lord God of Hosts, the creator and judge of the world (4:12-13).

Background

Because of the ritual themes in 4:4-5, the use of ideas similar to the levitical curses in 4:6-11, and the presence of a hymn in 4:13, many have found the setting for this section in the worship of Israel. Although some do not refer to any specific festival, Reventlow believes Amos was a cultic prophet who borrowed ideas from a ritual cursing ceremony.[1] Brueggemann accepts Reventlow's basic approach to 4:6-11 and interprets 4:12 "prepare to meet your God" as a liturgical call for the nation to reinstate the covenant at the annual renewal ceremony. This key clause is taken to be both a threat and a call to

---

[1]Mays, *Amos* 74 only refers to some festival, but Reventlow, *Amos* 90 hypothesizes a covenant renewal ceremony; Watts, *Amos* 51-67 points to the New Year's ceremonies at the fall equinox.

repentance. It is derived from the tradition where God calls the people to meet him on Sinai for the giving of the law (Exod. 19:11, 15, 17) and from holy war traditions (Prov. 21:31; Jer. 51:12). According to this interpretation, Amos 4:4-5 is the prophetic denouncement of the nation for trying to renew the covenant without having a proper relationship to God.[2]

Ramsey points to a similar setting but maintains that Amos is using the form of a prophetic lawsuit because the nation has fallen into idolatry. The conclusion to the lawsuit in 4:12 is a radical announcement of inevitable judgment and not an offer of repentance as Brueggemann suggests.[3] Boyle connects 4:6-11 to the curses in Deuteronomy 28 rather than those in Leviticus 26 and interprets all of 3:1—4:13 as a prophetic lawsuit. Amos 4:4-5 is an introduction of the case which demonstrates how Israel has violated the terms of the covenant through its cultic abuses. She compares this to sections of other lawsuits that describe the futility of ritual sacrifices (Isa. 1:13-15; Micah 6:6-7). Amos 4:6-11 is compared to the benevolent acts of God in Amos 2:9-11 and other lawsuits (Micah 6:3-4), thus it does not function as a series of curses. The conclusion in 4:12 is not an offer of repentance but a sentence which calls the nation to prepare to receive the execution of God's judgment. Most interpreters find a hymnic style in 4:13, but various settings are proposed (cultic and legal). Many of these suggestions are problematic.

The background of Amos 4:4-13 is not only based on the biblical traditions or the forms of speech used by Amos but also on how Amos uses the traditions he has inherited. Amos 4:4-5 with its imperative instructions to come to worship is thematically connected to activities at the sanctuary and stylistically developed around a priestly call to worship (Lev. 23:2, 4, 21, 37, 44; Joel 1:14; 2:15-16). This sarcastic parody employs Israelite traditions but transforms their normal meaning through the use of exaggeration, the charge of false motives, and the statement that this "worship" is actually sinful. Initially, Amos identifies with the audience's desire to go to Bethel or Gilgal to seek the favor of God, but the list of cultic abuses functions as an indictment in its present setting. The religious activities are not overtly identified with covenant renewal as Brueggemann maintains.[4]

The second paragraph of Amos 4:6-11 is characterized by a series of five catastrophic acts of God against his people and the five-fold refrain, " yet you did not return to me." The refrain emphasizes how useless it is for the people to run off to Bethel or Gilgal to offer more sacrifices. These sacrifices have not included a true turning to God in the past; therefore, this solution is mocked. The nation's history is a disastrous record of unwillingness to truly

---

[2]Brueggemann, "Amos IV:4-13 and Israel's Covenant Worship," 1-15.

[3]G. W. Ramsey, "Amos 4:12-A New Perspective," *JBL* 89 (1970) 187-91 and R. Youngblood, "*Lkr't* in Amos 4:12," *JBL* 90 (1971) 98.

[4]Brueggeman, "Amos IV:4-13," 9-10 draws a connection between "on the third day" in Exod. 19:11, "the morning" in Exod. 19:16; 24:4; 34:2, "burnt offering and peace offering" in Exod. 24:5 and similar words in Amos 4:4-5. This evidence is far from conclusive.

worship God. Even though God sent the calamities in Amos 4:6-11, these curses (cf. Leviticus 26; Deuteronomy 28 or 1 Kings 8) did not cause the nation to turn to God. Much attention has been given to the lexical connections between the covenant curses and Amos 4:6-11. Most suggest the use of covenantal traditions, but the relationship is not extensive enough to hypothesize a direct literary dependence.[5] The series of calamities is not given in a curse form with future verbs as in Leviticus or Deuteronomy, thus their function here is not to curse but to report how God has brought curses on the nation in the past. Boyle makes 4:6-11 a series of "paradoxical saving gestures" to induce the nation to faithfulness. This view seems forced because these calamities function as evidence of what God has done to those who were unwilling to worship him; they are the accusation in this oracle of judgment. It is also apparent that these deeds of Yahweh are not the classical series of salvation events which were proclaimed in temple services at festivals. Since no existing structure contains the elements Amos displays in this oracle, the present speech must be seen as a rather unique reconstruction of a series of curses using Amos' particular style of repetition.

The refrain "you did not return to me" indicates that the expected result of punishment (repentance) did not happen. The repetition of this clause draws the focus of attention to the unwillingness of Israel to return to God, rather than on the various chastenings of God. This repeated phrase is the concluding word for each unit in the series, and it gives a theological evaluation of the nation's inadequate ritual response to each of God's chastenings. This rhetorical emphasis was designed to heighten the people's perception of the futility of their numerous self-serving sacrificial activities. Thus Amos 4:6-11 is primarily the prophet's attempt to convince the audience that their response to God's announcement of punishment and exile (2:13-16; 3:2, 11-15; 4:2-3) is the wrong response. "Let us go down to Bethel and Gilgal to offer more sacrifices to gain the favor of God" is not necessarily the same as having a real meeting with God. Their behavior after previous punishments and sacrifices was not a true turning to God.

Having pointed out the uselessness of the people's worship, Amos surprisingly calls the nation to meet God in 4:12. "Prepare to meet your God" is drawn from priestly instructions that call the nation to worship (Exod. 19:11, 15, 17; 2 Chron. 12:14; 19:3; 20:33; 27:6; 30:19; 35:4-16) and is much like 4:4-5. Here also Amos transforms the call to worship and turns it into a message of judgment. Since preparation to meet God is also used in holy war settings, Amos is able to twist the focus from encouragement to worship to a warning of war with God. The final doxological hymn, which celebrates and praises God for his creative power and judgment on Israel's enemies, sud-

---

[5]Mays, *Amos* 80. Mays finds only a loose connection to the curses and the festival. Most commentators focus too heavily on the curses and do not pay enough attention to the refrain and its significance in the context of 4:4-13.

denly becomes an awesome warning that this all-powerful God will meet Israel in combat. This hymn is a blending of holy war and theophany tradition.[6]

Structure and Unity

Structure

The English outline will be used to structure the exegesis of the text.

Israel is Unwilling to Repent and Worship God
Amos 4:4-13

		A. Israel's unacceptable worship
[a]Go to Bethel and transgress,[a]	**4:4**	1. It is a transgression
[b]to Gilgal, transgress more,		
[a]Bring your sacrifices every morning,		2. It is mere ritual
your tithes every third day.		
Offer up the thank-offering[c] of leavened bread.	**4:5**	3. It is for personal recognition
Announce the freewill-offering.[d]		
Shout,		
for so you love to do,[e]		
O sons of Israel,		
declares Yahweh.		
		B. Israel did not turn to God when chastened
I myself even gave[f] you cleanness[g] of teeth	**4:6**	1. Famine produced no return to God
in all your cities,		
and lack of bread		
in all your places,		
yet you did not return to me,		
declares Yahweh.		
I myself even withheld the rain from you,	**4:7**	2. Drought produced no return to God
when it was three months until harvest.		
Then I sent rain on one city,		
and on another city I sent no rain.[h]		
One field received rain,[h]		
another field which had no rain[h] dried up;		
then two or three cities staggered[i] to another city	**4:8**	
to drink water,		
but they were not satisfied,		
yet you did not return to me,		
declares Yahweh.		

---

[6]J. L. Crenshaw, "Amos and the Theophanic Tradition," *ZAW* 80 (1968) 203-08 draws on the Exodus 19 and 34 theophany tradition concerning the nation's preparation to meet God at Sinai.

I afflicted you with scorching wind and mildew;
  locusts were eating your many[j] gardens and vineyards,
    your fig trees and olive trees
declares Yahweh.
	4:9	3. Crop failures
		   produced no
		   return

I sent a plague[l] on you, like on Egypt;
I slew your young men with the sword
  and your captured horses;
I caused a stench[m] of your camp to go up
  even into your nostrils,[n]
yet you did not return to me,
declares Yahweh.
	4:10	4. Military defeat
		   produced no
		   return to God

I overthrew you
  like God overthrew Sodom and Gomorrah,
 ¶ and you were like fire brands snatched from burning,
yet you did not return to me,
declares Yahweh.
	4:11	5. Near destruction
		   produced no
		   return to God

Therefore, thus I will do to you, Israel,
  and because I will do this to you
  prepare to meet[o] your God, O Israel,
	4:12	C. Israel will meet
		   God in judgment
		   1. Announcement of
		     a meeting with
		     God

for behold, he who forms the mountains[p]
  and creates the wind,
  who declares to humans
    what are their thoughts,[q]
  who makes the dawn, darkness,[r]
  who treads on the high places of the earth,
  Yahweh, God of Hosts is his name.
	4:13	2. A reminder of
		   the power of the
		   God of hosts

4:4a. The Greek translators missed the ironic nature of these verses and made the verbs aorists (thus accusations, "you went to Bethel") instead of ironic imperatives.

4:4b. The Hebrew has no preposition before Gilgal since it and the verb are implied from the preceding parallel line. The Greek translation and the Targum insert the preposition instead of leaving it implied.

4:5c. The infinitive absolute acts as an imperative since it continues the function of the preceding plural imperatives in 4:4 (GKC 113z). The Old Greek makes the verb plural. The "thank offering" *tôdāh* was read *tôrāh* "law," a common mistake in reading and writing Hebrew because the *d* and *r* look almost identical. Aq. has "thank offering" in agreement with the Hebrew. The Targum substitutes "from violence" for "from leaven."

4:5d. Freewill offerings is translated "professions, confessions" in the Old Greek and "vows" in the Syriac.

4:5e. The Old Greek puts this clause in indirect discourse, "proclaim that the sons of Israel loved these things."

4:6f. The Old Greek translates the verb as a future instead of a past like the Hebrew.

4:6g. For "cleanness of teeth" the Old Greek has "toothache." Sym. and Theod. confirm the Hebrew text reading "purity," while Aq. has "blow, wound."

4:7h. These verbs are future in the Old Greek because the Hebrew verbs are imperfect. These imperfects should be understood iteratively, referring to the repeated rains that came.

4:8i. The Old Greek believes the cities "will be gathered together" rather than "staggering." The Greek verb is a future passive.

4:9j. "Many" was understood as a verb, "you multiplied" in the Old Greek, thus a contrast is developed between what you did and what the locusts did.

4:9k. The Old Greek makes the contrast stronger than the Hebrew with "and not even then" in verse 9, 10 and 11.

4:10l. The Old Greek has "death" similar to Exod. 5:3; 9:3 while Aq. has "plague."

4:10m. *br'ōš* "stench" was read *br'ēš* "fire" by the Greek translators.

4:10n. *'p* can mean "nose" or "anger." The stench of the dead will affect their nose, but when the translators misread stench as fire, "anger" fit the context better.

4:12o. The Old Greek has "to call" while Theod. has "to meet."

4:13p. The line reads, "I am the one who makes the thunder strong" in the Old Greek.

4:13q. "What are his thoughts" which are two words in Hebrew are put together by the Greek translators and thus read "his anointed one, his messiah." Aq. has "his instruction," Sym. "his utterance," and Theod. "his word."

4:13r. "Darkness" is rendered "mist" in the Old Greek, "flood" in Aq. and "evening" in Sym.

Amos 4:4-13 is divided into three diverse but interrelated paragraphs. Plural imperatives related to temple worship characterize the first unit of 4:4-5. The verse shows a good deal of regular parallelism, and the paragraph is closed with the traditional "declares Yahweh." Although some have connected 4:1-3 directly with this unit, the themes in 4:1-3 are more closely connected to the oppression in 3:9-15 than the worship motifs in 4:4-13.[7]

The second paragraph (4:6-11) contains a series of five punishments by God. Each punishment begins with a first person singular perfect verb and concludes with the refrain, "you did not return to me, declares Yahweh." The whole series has regularity similar to the patterns of repetition found in Amos 1-2.[8] Although Wolff and a few others extend this unit through 4:12, the absense of the concluding formula and the introduction of *lākēn* "therefore" provide sufficient evidence to warrant a new paragraph in 4:12.[9] The whole paragraph is connected with 4:4-5 by *w⁵gam* "and even." The individual units vary in the amount of parallelism and in length.[10] While Mays sees no development or intensification within the series and Reventlow emphasizes the monontony of the series, Crenshaw sees a steady intensification from one punishment to the next.[11] The first three punishments relate to the destruction of crops while the last two describe the destruction of people.

The third paragraph (4:12-13) is made up of two quite distinct parts. Amos 4:12 continues the use of the first person singular verb, but in this case it is imperfect, referring to God's future actions. The final verse is characterized by a series of participles. The hymn-like character of 4:13 and unique themes

---

[7]See the discussion on Structure and Unity for 3:9—4:3.

[8]A similar use of a refrain is found in Isa. 9:12, 17, 21; 10:4.

[9]Wolff, *Amos* 211 or Melugin, "The Formation of Amos," 385.

[10]Amos 4:6, 7b and 9 have clear parallelism, while 4:7-8 is unusually long. Wolff, *Amos* 212 considers 4:8 and 11 to be prose, but this conclusion ignores the regularity within the verses.

[11]Mays, *Amos* 78; Reventlow, *Amos* 84; and J. L. Crenshaw, "A Liturgy of Wasted Opportunity," *Semitics* 1 (1970) 31.

demonstrate that the two verses do not come from the same tradition. The syntactical connector "for" and the descriptions of the characteristics of God who will meet his people in judgment draw the two together. Because of the distinct style and themes within 4:13, many question its authenticity.

Unity

Signs of disunity are found in 4:4-13 because: (1) 4:7 contains redundancies, 4:8 has a rather prosaic style, and the total length of the second punishment is greater than any of the others in the series; (2) the charges of unwillingness to return to God in 4:6-12 are not found in any other genuine oracles in Amos; and (3) the style, theme, and theology of the hymn in 4:13 is unusual when compared to the rest of Amos. Redactional activity is sometimes associated with the connecting word "even" at the beginning of 4:6 and the repetition of "I will do this to you" in 4:12.

Harper raises a question about the phrase "while there were yet three months until harvest" because it disturbs the parallelism of 4:7 and is out of character with the general references to rainfall in 4:7-8.[12] Others question the unnecessary duplication in 4:7c or the nonpoetic style of 4:8.[13]

Reventlow solves these problems by reconstructing an exactly balanced parallelism which satisfies his demands for uniformity, but this solution puts unrealistic strictures on the prophet's freedom to creatively develop his rhetorical argument.[14] It is also difficult to build literary criteria to evaluate Amos' style and the accepted structural patterns of that day. Since rain is extremely important to a shepherd and the livelihood of an agricultural economy, the focus on rain is not surprising.

Wolff challenges the authenticity of the whole unit of 4:6-12 by comparing it with the series of oracles against the nations (Amos 1-2) and the series of visions (Amos 7-9). He finds in Amos 4:6-12 less regularity in structure, with more of an emphasis on accusations instead of punishments. Wolff distinguishes this section from Deuteronomic sources and identifies it with Josiah's destruction of the altar at Bethel in 2 Kings 23:15-20 over one hundred years after the time of Amos.[15] These conclusions seem to be motivated more by Wolff 's hypothesis that 4:12 pictures someone standing at Bethel pointing at its destroyed altar than by a comparison with the other series of oracles. The series against the nations and the series of visions are not uniform in structure or content and have varying degrees of emphasis on punishment.

---

[12]Harper, *Amos* 96.

[13]Harper, *Amos* 96 considers 4:7b-8 an interpolation; Rudolph, *Amos* 169, 178 only has trouble with 4:7b; and Mays, *Amos* 77 finds the prosaic style of 4:8 suspicious.

[14]Reventlow, *Amos* 75.

[15]Wolff, *Amos* 212-217 follows E. Sellin on this point. Maag, *Amos* 24 also thinks the accusation that Israel is unwilling to turn to God is uncharacteristic of the prophet and added by another hand. See Rudolph, *Amos* 173-75 for criticisms.

Although the length and structure of 4:7-8 are problematic, Wolff's whole-sale rejection of the section as a later addition at the time of Josiah's destruction of the altar at Bethel goes far beyond the evidence and the conclusions of most commentators.[16]

The hymn in 4:13 has been attributed to a later editor because it: (1) does not smoothly flow from its context; (2) has an elevated theology of God as creator; and (3) uses participles and the title "Yahweh, God of hosts, is his name" which gained popularity after the time of Amos. Although the hymn does not have the same style, structure or content as 4:6-12, Boyle, Brueggemann, Crenshaw, and Watts fit 4:13 into the context of 4:12b, because 4:13 describes the greatness and power of Yahweh who will meet the nation in a theophany.[17] The argument based on the theology of God as creator can no longer be connected solely to late theological writings, for creation is discussed in Egyptian, Ugaritic, and Mesopotamian texts well before the time of Amos. The expression of this theme of creation in 4:13 shows a strong sense of poetic parallelism and the participles have their closest parallels in hymnic literature. This may indicate that Amos is quoting a traditional hymn his audience would recognize. The date of the hymn is difficult to establish, but the final phrase, "Yahweh, God of hosts, is his name" is similar to the early, "Yahweh is his name" used in Exodus 15:3, Psalm 68:4, and 83:18. The reference to "Yahweh of hosts" can be traced back to holy war traditions (Josh. 5:13-15; 1 Sam. 15:2; 17:45; 2 Sam. 5:10) and the ark (1 Sam. 1:3, 11; 4:4; 2 Sam. 6:2, 18; Ps. 24:10) well before the time of David.[18] Although some prefer to date this hymn later than Amos, the evidence does not demand this conclusion.[19]

If the hymn has a significant function in Amos 4, a strong case can be made

---

[16]Factors which weaken Wolff's position are: (1) Amos was not the man of God in 1 Kings 13 whose words were fulfilled by Josiah in 2 Kings 23:15-20; (2) Amos 3:1—6:14 were probably spoken at Samaria not Bethel (Amos 3:9, 12; 4:1; 6:1); (3) unwillingness to turn to God in 4:6-11 is not substantially different from Israel's unwillingness to listen to its prophets (Amos 2:11-12; 3:6-8; 7:10-17; 9:10) or unwillingness to truly worship God (4:4-5; 5:4-5, 21-26); and (4) 4:6-12 does not display the influence of a later prophetic development of the themes of hunger, sword, or repentance one would expect if this portion were written at the time of Josiah.

[17]Wolff, Amos 52-54; Brueggemann, "Amos 4:4-13 and Israel's Covenant Worship," 10-13; Boyle, "The Covenant Lawsuit," 358-62; J. L. Crenshaw, Hymnic Affirmation of Divine Justice (Missoula: Scholars Press, 1975) 6; Kapelrud, Amos 39 finds no real difference in the concept of God in the hymns and in the rest of Amos.

[18]See Wambacq, L'epithète divine Jahve ṣebā'ôth 195-99; J. L. Crenshaw, "YHWH Sebā'ôt šemô: A Form-Critical Analysis," ZAW 81 (1969) 156-75.

[19]W. Berg, Die sogennanten Hymnenfragmente im Amosbuch (Frankfurt: Peter Lang, 1974) 322-26; F. Horst, "Die Doxologien im Amosbuch," ZAW 47 (1929) 45-54; Crenshaw, Hymnic Affirmation 24; Cripps, Amos 66; and Wolff, Amos 217 date the hymn later than Amos, but those who propose a date before the time of Amos include Boyle, "Covenant Lawsuit" 360; Brueggemann, "Amos 4:4-13 and Israel's Covenant Worship," 10-13; Hammershaimb, Amos 74-75; Kapelrud, Amos 38-39; Rudolph, Amos 182-83; Watts, Amos 54; C. Story, "Amos—Prophet of Praise," VT 30 (1980) 67-68; W. Rudolph, "Amos 4:6-13," Wort, Gebot, Glaube: Beiträge zur Theologie des Alten Testament, ed. J. J. Stamm (Zürich: Zwingli, 1970) 27-38, argues convincingly for the unity of 4:6-13.

for its importance to the original message of Amos. Frost compared this hymn with statements of thanksgiving and believes its purpose is to affirm the certainty of God's judgment. Drawing on the practice of sacred law where people are called upon to glorify God (Josh. 7:19; 1 Sam. 6:5; Job 5:9-16; Jer. 13:15), Horst concludes that the hymn affirms the validity of God's judgment. Brueggemann interprets the hymn as a support for the prophet's call to covenant renewal. By describing the God the nation would encounter, Amos motivates the nation to repent, to praise God, and renew the covenant.[20] Although these and other studies came from various angles, each in its own way concludes that the description of God's power and greatness in 4:13 confirms that this sovereign God will meet Israel. The background of the hymn is the worship of the nation, not the legal system. The theophany motif of the holy warrior is evident in 4:12-13, but God will come in judgment not salvation. The final phrase "Yahweh, God of hosts, is his name" confirms in almost oathlike fashion the authority of these statements.[21] Amos has used well-known traditions earlier in the book (2:9-11; 3:1-2) but reconstructed them in unique ways to convince his audience. In a manner similar to 4:4-5, Amos uses this priestly hymn concerning God's powerful theophany judgment but directs it against Israel instead of their enemies.

Interpretation

A. Israel's unacceptable worship (4:4-5)

1. It is a transgression (4:4a)

Amos begins this section with another plural imperative (cf. 3:1, 9, 13; 4:1), but in this instance the prophet does not call the people to attention, he calls them to go to the places of worship at Bethel and Gilgal. This signals a movement in the argument to a new topic, away from accusations and punishments because of oppression and violence against the poor. Amos confronts the popular belief that God will remove their punishment if they go to one of their national shrines and zealously offer some additional sacrifices to please him. Once Amos understands the response of the audience, he launches into a sarcastic parody of a priest calling the nation to worship and praise God (cf. Ps. 95:1, 6; 98:1, 4; 100:1, 2, 4). The shocking irony of the prophet's instruction becomes immediately apparent when Amos encour-

---

[20]S. B. Frost, "Asseverations by Thanksgiving," *VT* 8 (1958) 380-90; Horst, "Die Doxologien im Amosbuch," 45-54; Brueggemann, "Amos 4:4-13 and Israel's Covenant Worship," 10-11.

[21]Crenshaw, *Hymnic Affirmation* 75-114, makes this phrase the key to understand the whole of 4:13. Its importance cannot be denied, but this phrase should not take total precedence over the setting of the hymn itself and the context of worship in 4:4-13. Watts, Wolff, and Crenshaw link 4:13 to a struggle with idolatry, but this goes well beyond the main message that God will come and judge the nation.

ages the people to transgress and transgress more.[22] God's evaluation of the cultic activities at Bethel and Gilgal depicts a sinful cult.

Although unanimity on the location of Bethel does not exist, Bethel was one of the locations where Jeroboam I set up an alternate place of worship for the Israelites (1 Kings 12:25-33).[23] This was probably the same site where Jacob worshiped God after receiving the promise of Abraham from God (Gen. 28:10-22; 35:1-15). Here Jeroboam stationed a golden calf in a temple, so that people would maintain loyalty to the northern nation and not return to worship in Judah at Jerusalem. It was a national temple (Amos 7:13) and probably more important than Gilgal. Although Gilgal, which is near Jericho, was the significant site where Joshua set up the twelve stones taken from the Jordan after the children of Israel crossed over into the land (Josh. 4:19-20; 5:1-10), its status as a place of worship is masked by some mystery. Saul was anointed king at Gilgal, and sacrifices were offered to the Lord on an altar there (1 Sam. 11:15; 13:8-12), but Hosea (4:15; 9:15; 12:11) pictures the site as a place of evil, harlotry, and Baalism.[24] Amos does not make reference to these factors but points to the people's focus on ritual activity and ego satisfaction instead of love for God (4:5).

2. It is mere ritual (4:4b)

The reason for going to Bethel or Gilgal is explained in the command to bring sacrifices and tithes. The sacrifice (zbḥ) is a general term for any animal sacrifice. Most commentators connect this sacrifice to the peace offering (Lev. 3:1-17; 7:11-18) because the thank and freewill offerings in 4:5 were types of peace offerings, because these sacrifices provided a sumptuous meaty meal for the offerer, and because these sacrifices were condemned by some prophets (Hos. 8:13; Jer. 7:21). The offerings were brought once a year (1 Sam. 1:3, 7, 21) to the temple as optional offerings to celebrate the peace that God had provided the worshiper in all areas of life.[25] The tithes were a tenth (Gen. 14:20; 28:22; Lev. 27:30-33; Deut. 12:6, 17; 14:22-29; 26:12-15) which were paid every three years from the produce of the field and the flock. Part of it was eaten while rejoicing "in the presence of the Lord," so

---

[22]The infinitive construct introduces the main verb and the finite verb describes the manner. See GKC 120a, g or Jer. 1:12 "you have seen well," for a similar example.

[23]Traditionally archaeologists have identified Bethel near Beitin, but see D. Livingstone, "Location of Bethel and Ai Reconsidered," WTJ 33 (1970) 20-44; A. F. Rainey, "Bethel Is Still Beitin," WTJ 33 (1971) 175-88

[24]H. J. Kraus, Worship in Israel (Oxford: Blackwell, 1966) 146-65 and "Gilgal: Eine Beitrag zur Kultgeschichte Israels," VT 1 (1951) 181-99; W. J. Dumbrell, "The Role of Bethel in the Biblical Narratives from Jacob to Jeroboam," Australian Journal of Biblical Archaeology 2 (1974) 65-76; On the problem of locating Gilgal see J. Muilenburg, "The Site of Ancient Gilgal," BASOR 140 (1955) 11-27; or B. M. Bennett, "The Search for Israelite Gilgal," PEQ 104 (1972) 111-22; On the nature of the sin see Barstad, Religious Polemics of Amos 54-57, who suggests that the worship of other gods is involved. This took place at these sites, but Amos does not seem to condemn those kinds of sins here.

[25]M. Haran, "zebaḥ hayyamîm," VT 19 (1969) 11-22, discusses the yearly sacrifices.

that the people would learn to fear the Lord, and part was given to the Levites (Numb. 18:21-32). The ironic tone of the oracle appears in the description of these sacrifices and tithes as "yours" rather than God's. The exaggerated demand that the sacrifices be brought every morning, instead of once every year, and the tithe every day, instead of every third year, shows that significance was based on the number and frequency of these ritual acts rather than the quality of their worship in the presence of God.[26] Hosea taught that God was more interested in loyalty than sacrifices (Hos. 6:8) and Micah indicated that God required justice, love and humility, not a thousand rams or ten thousand rivers of oil (Micah 6:6-8). God's desire is to meet with the person whose heart is at peace with God, not with the person who is merely performing repetitions and meaningless ritual.

3. It is for personal recognition (4:5)

Continuing with imperatives, Amos mockingly encourages the people to "offer or burn" a thank offering with leavened bread.[27] The levitical regulations (Exod. 23:18; Lev. 2:11; 7:12-13; 22:29-30) do not permit leavened bread to be burnt as a thanksgiving offering but do allow leavened bread to be eaten at the peace offering meal. The freewill offering, like the thank offering, was one of the peace offerings and was to be a spontaneous act of joy and devotion to God (Exod. 35:6-7; Lev. 7:16; 22:18; Deut. 12:6-7). It was not a means of parading your generosity and good deeds before your friends (Matt. 6:2) but was the inner expression of love by a person who loved God with all his heart. The verse ends with the charge that the children of Israel love to shout about their activities at the temple. This analysis of their sacrifices expresses the people's real love. Their "worship" has nothing to do with God, his desires, his will, or his service. They are honoring themselves. They do not confess their sins and worship in the presence of God (Amos 5:21-24). This rhetorical call to worship thus becomes another accusation against the nation. Their desire to offer more sacrifices to win God's favor and avoid his punishment was a waste of time. This is God's word and his view of their impious religiosity.

B. Israel did not turn to God when chastened (4:6-12)

The regular pattern developed in this series of five oracles includes: (1) a description of God's chastening of the people through punishment; (2) Isra-

---

[26]The distributive use of *l* "every" morning (GKC 134q) illustrates the exaggeration. Mays, *Amos* 75; Hammershaimb, *Amos* 69; and Wolff, *Amos* 219, reject this view and see the offerer bringing his offering on the first day, after he arrives at the temple, and his tithe on the third day.

[27]"Offer" is an infinitive absolute used as an imperative (GKC 113bb). G. J. Wenham, *The Book of Leviticus* (Grand Rapids: Eerdmans, 1979) 74-81 describes the Levitical regulation for the peace offering. Amos does not condemn the use of leaven as baalistic, but this may be true (Hos. 3:1).

el's unwillingness to return to God; and (3) a closing formula of divine confirmation that verifies that this was the word of the Lord. Although each
chastening was significant, the last two involved the loss of life and were
more serious. Together they stress the guilt and stubbornness of the people
and justify the climactic movement by God to bring a final judgment (4:12).

1. Famine produced no return to God (4:6)

The new paragraph is connected to 4:4-5 with the connecting participle
"even."[28] The emphatic personal pronoun "I myself" constructs a strong contrast between the unacceptable worship of the nation (4:4-5), the acts of God
(4:6-11), and the unwillingness of Israel (4:6-11). God's sovereign control of
nature and the history of his people are intertwined when he sends a famine
upon "all your cities."[29] The famine is described as a time of "lack of bread"
and "shining teeth" because there was no food. The date of the famine and
the relationship of this calamity to the following lack of rain is unknown.
These factors were probably self-evident to the audience and did not require
clarification. Although some connect these disasters to the covenant curses in
Leviticus 26 and Deuteronomy 28, Amos' composition shows a great deal of
independence from these texts and makes no direct reference to the covenant.[30] The repeated refrain directs greater focus on the unwillingness of the
nation to repent and truly worship God. The purpose for the disaster was to
bring the nation to its knees before God, but the divine intention was not
achieved. "They did not return to me," places the nation in direct opposition
to the will of God. Amos does not describe what the people are to turn from,
but the context of 3:9—4:3 and 4:4-5 suggests that God wanted the people to
turn from their oppressive social treatment of the poor and their selfish and
ritualistic worship practices.

2. Drought produced no return to God (4:7-8)

The first-person verbs directly connect God to the action of sending or
not sending the rain. This was not luck or a quirk of meteorological forces.
God's control over the rain not only had a severe effect on the city wells and
cisterns but also on various fields. The seriousness of the drought was due
both to its length and its timing during the last three months before harvest
(February-April) when the heads of grain were filling out. The lack of rain at
this crucial time would have brought disaster on the farming community.
When a few drops of rain did fall, the moisture fell in very uneven patterns.

---

[28]Some question the original connection between 4:4-5 and 6-11, because 6-11 do not discuss
the cult, but the use of the phrase "return to me" is directly connected to the purpose of worship
at the temple. See A. Weiser, "Zu Amos 4:6-13," *ZAW* 46 (1928) 49-59.

[29]M. Dahood, "Hebrew-Ugaritic Lexicography," *Bib* 48 (1967) 431, takes "places" to be a reference to their "homes."

[30]Mays, *Amos* 79-80; Brueggemann, "Amos 4:4-13 and Israel's Covenant Worship," 6-8; while
Boyle, "The Covenant Lawsuit," 352-57 concludes that the curses function similar to the saving
acts of God in Amos 2:9-11. Barstad, *Religious Polemics of Amos* 61-74 rejects the covenant
background and opts for a fertility cult background.

One city would repeatedly receive a small amount of rain while another would frequently receive nothing. To alleviate these problems people from cities that had no water traveled to other cities to get enough water to live. In verse 8, Amos pictures whole cities staggering in exhaustion to find water to satisfy their thirst, but their needs were never fully met. The description of the plight of those without water may involve some rhetorical characterization to emphasize the seriousness of the situation. It makes the nation's unwillingness to turn to God even more remarkable.

3. Crop failures produced no return to God (4:9)

The third chastening sent by God to discipline the nation adds to the destruction of the crops which produced food for the nation. Fields on rocky or high ground were quickly dried up when the rains did not come (4:7). Fields in a valley had more sub-soil and were closer to the water table. But even the crops and the trees that reach deep into the earth to draw their strength were affected by this new disaster. Blight caused by a blasting hot wind (cf. Gen. 41:6, 23, 27) scorched the vitality right out of the leaves and caused them to wither. The heat along with an attack of mildew turned the crops a sickly yellow or brown color, and this destroyed all hopes of getting any food for the coming year. As if this were not serious enough, God sent a plague of locusts to devour anything that may have received special attention and survived.[31] These grasshoppers continually devastated their many gardens and vineyards as well as their orchards of olive and fig trees.[32] The proportions of God's judgment were enormous. There will be no grain to plant or feed their animals, no olive oil for fuel, cooking or medication, no wine to drink, and no fresh vegetables from the garden. This is a curse from God (Deut. 28:22; 1 Kings 8:37), but the people were still unwilling to turn to God in true worship. They no doubt went to the temple to go through the ritual but there was no real meeting with Yahweh, the God of Israel.

4. Military defeat produced no return to God (4:10)

The fourth punishment was a plague associated with a military defeat and the slaughter of many of the nation's finest young men. The larger military context of 4:10 argues against identifying this plague with the fifth plague which fell upon the livestock of Egypt (Exod. 9:3-7). The death of the young men is more comparable to the death of the firstborn (Exod. 11:4-7; 12:29-

---

[31]Driver, *Amos* 84-93 and Wolff, *Amos* 27-28 have detailed discussions of locust, their various stages of development, the names given to them in the Bible, and some observations from scientists who have studied locusts. Joel 1 gives a fuller exposition of the destruction caused by the gnawing teeth of the locust.

[32]Mays, *Amos* 76; Harper, *Amos* 99-100; Cripp, *Amos* 173; Wolff, *Amos* 210; and Rudolph, *Amos* 169 change "many" to a first person singular verb "I ravaged, dried up." This makes good sense and matches the focus on God's acts in the other verses, but it is not required by the syntax of the verse.

30).[33] Assyrian records mention plagues during this general time period, but there is no way of making a connection with those described here.[34] The allusions to wars are probably those with Syria before the time of Jeroboam II (2 Kings 10:32-33; 13:7) or possibly during Jeroboam's wars to extend the borders of Israel (2 Kings 14:25-28). These wars cost the lives of many promising young men and resulted in the loss of many horses and chariots to their enemy. Because of the unburied corpses of men and animals, a terrible stench of decaying bodies filled the air (Isa. 34:3). Three times Amos makes the point that God caused these things to happen, yet in spite of these clear reminders of death, the nation failed to return to God. The seriousness of the chastening and the presence of that unavoidable and sickening smell of death should have caused a change in heart, but Israel remained unwilling.

5. Near destruction produced no return to God (4:11)

The fifth chastening is described by comparing it to the overthrow of Sodom and Gomorrah (Gen. 19:24-29). The phrase has almost a proverbial tone to it, and its use in other texts suggests that the traditions about these two cities were well known (Deut. 29:23 [Heb. 29:22]; Isa. 1:7; 13:19; Jer. 49:18; 50:40). The destruction in Genesis 19 probably included an earthquake which may have caused Amos to draw the comparison here. Some think this does not refer to an earthquake, but possibly to the nearly total destruction of Israel by Syria (2 Kgs. 10:32-33; 13:7). It does not refer to the political destruction of the nation in 722/1 B.C. by the Assyrians as Wolff maintains.[35] The destruction was almost complete like Sodom's, but deliverance came at the last moment and many were saved from destruction. The nation should have recognized this as the hand of God and turned to him and changed its ways, but again the prophet reemphasizes the fact that the nation was unwilling to return to God and truly worship him.

C. Israel will meet God in judgment (4:12-13)

1. Announcement of a meeting with God (4:12)

Few verses in Amos have caused more speculation or diversity of opinion than this climactic ending to Israel's unwillingness to return to God. These differences in 4:12 relate to varying understandings of: (1) the text itself; (2) the meaning of "thus" and "this"; (3) the background of the clause, "prepare to meet your God"; and (4) the positive or negative meaning of "prepare to meet your God."

---

[33]Harper, *Amos* 100 reviews the various approaches: (1) it came from Egypt; (2) it came suddenly like the plagues in Egypt; (3) it came with the severity of the Egyptian plagues; (4) it came on the armies' way to Egypt. Snaith, *Amos* 77 and others drop the clause, thinking it is a gloss. Rudolph, *Amos* 179 connects this plague with the death of the firstborn and sees a play on *bahur* "young men" and *b'kôr* "firstborn."

[34]Cripps, *Amos* 174; Rudolph, *Amos* 179.

[35]Wolff, *Amos* 221; Harper *Amos* 101 identifies 4:11 with the earthquake in Amos 1:1.

Cripps and Weingreen suspect that the second line, "because I will do this to you" is a marginal variant of the first line that was added to the text. Sellin changes *kh* "thus" to *klh* giving "I will make a complete end to you"; Morgenstern proposes, "as you have done to me"; and Rudolph reconstructs, "you have done to yourself."[36] Each solution attempts to get around the problem of repetition and the lack of concreteness, but none of these are convincing. Any solution must first determine what the words "thus" and "this" mean. Wolff imagines the author pointing as he speaks. By doing this, the author clarifies that he is referring to the destroyed altar at Bethel.[37] A less imaginative approach is to suggest that Amos purposely left the issue vague to raise greater anxiety. Mays refers "this" and "thus" to the concrete moment of judgment when Israel will meet God.[38] If one follows a somewhat similar line and connects 4:12 to the initial statement of punishment in 3:2 (which is reinforced in 3:11-12, 13-15; 4:2-3) the overall unit is tied together (3:1— 4:13) and a consistent approach to what God has already said is maintained. The second line emphasizes that it is precisely because God is going to do "this" (punish you), that the nation will now meet God. The background to this statement is derived from the worship of the nation. It is not an offer of covenant renewal or a call to repentance but an announcement of a face to face confrontation.[39] Using theophany motifs similar to those used at Sinai (Exod. 19:11, 13, 17), and probably employed by priests on many worship occasions, Amos parroted an announcement of the divine presence. But the context clearly indicates that the blessings of the divine presence have been transformed into a fearful event of punishment. Amos uses holy war images, where the divine warrior prepares for battle to meet and destroy his enemies, to reverse the usually positive expectations into one of awful terror.[40] Since they will not return to God and will not properly prepare themselves to meet him in true worship, God will meet the nation in a theophany of judgment. He will bring destruction on the temple (9:1) and on the nation when he passes though their midst (5:17). The meeting does not refer to the appearance of his glory at the temple (Exod. 40:34-35; 1 Kings 8:11) but to his destructive power in the history of the nation (Mic. 1:3-4; Nah. 1:2-6).

2. A reminder of the power of the God of hosts (4:13)

This verse stands apart from its context with regard to (1) its parallelism, (2) its stylistic use of several participles, and (3) the theological themes under

---

[36]Cripps, *Amos* 176; J. Weingreen, "Rabbinic Type Glosses in the Old Testament," *JSS* 2 (1957) 159; Morgenstern, "Amos Studies IV," *HUCA* 32 (1961) 318; Rudolph, *Amos* 171.

[37]Wolff, *Amos* 217; Hammershaimb, *Amos* 74 follows a similar interpretation but does not relate the hand gesture to the fall of Bethel over one hundred years after Amos.

[38]May, *Amos* 82; while Harper, *Amos* 105 thinks the general reference is more threatening.

[39]See the section on Background for 4:4-13.

[40]Ramsey, "Amos 4:12—A New Perspective," *JBL* 89 (1970) 187-91, believes God should refer to the nation's gods.

consideration. Although some maintain that this discontinuity points to the conclusion that the hymn-like verse was added later, it is just as reasonable to conclude that Amos quoted a well-known hymn his audience used.[41] Elsewhere in this section Amos takes the priestly traditions and uses them against his audience (4:4-5, 12). If 4:12 pictures a theophany, it would be natural for Amos to borrow a traditional hymn which glorifies the power of God. In this context though, the presence and power of God in Israel have a negative function. Amos transforms the good news of God's glorious might into a fearful warning of judgment because his power will be used against rather than for Israel.[42]

A connection with 4:4-12 is made in the phrase "who declares to man what are his thoughts." God understands the true motivation behind Israel's sacrifices and freewill offerings. He knows that they did not return to him with all their hearts after repeated chastenings. On the basis of his knowledge of the thoughts of his people (Ps. 94:11), God has declared to the nation through Amos their unwillingness to meet him.[43] His powerful abilities insure that his action is just and leave man without a defense. These powers are possible because God is the creator of man as well as the one "who forms the mountains and creates the wind." Isaiah also celebrates God's creative powers, but Amos makes no reference to God as a redeemer as Isaiah.[44] Instead, the hymn which Amos quotes focuses on the fact that God is a mighty judge. The turning of dawn into darkness describes how God can turn the positive potential of dawn into a dark and dismal night (4:6-11). As he comes in judgment he will tread down the high places of the earth (Mic. 1:3). Nothing can stand before the power of his theophany, and certainly the capital city of Samaria will not escape his wrath when he comes to meet his people in judgment.

The hymn ends with an identification of the name of Yahweh. Wolff, Crenshaw, and others see this as an implicit attack on other gods, but this use is foreign to the context here.[45] "Yahweh of hosts" recognizes the power of the divine warrior and in almost oath-like fashion closes the hymn with the certainty that Yahweh's authority and character stand behind it.

Theological Development

The Old Testament and ancient Near Eastern documents contain numerous

---

[41]Crenshaw, *Hymnic Affirmation* 119 and Maag, *Amos* 57-58 also believe the prophet has reversed the regular meaning of an ancient hymn. See the section on Structure and Unity for 4:4-13, concerning the authenticity of 4:13.

[42]Wolff, *Amos* 222-23 finds a liturgical directive to cause the remnant at Bethel after 722/1 B.C. to sing praise to God, but this view is extremely hypothetical and unnecessary, since the verse can make good sense in its context.

[43]Rudolph, *Amos* 181-82; the meaning of this clause has confused the ancient translators and still presents confusion because it is in a series of statements about God's sovereignty over nature. H. P. Müller, "Die Hebräische Wurzel *śîh* " *VT* 19 (1969) 361-71.

[44]Story, "Amos—Prophet of Praise," 67-69.

[45]Wolff, *Amos* 224; Crenshaw, *Hymnic Affirmation* 109-14, 123.

references concerning temples, priest, and sacrifices. [46] The worship of the gods in other nations often took place at temples, was conducted by priests, and included sacrifices, but each nation had its own distinctives and its own special gods. The biblical traditions about sacrifice can be traced back to the Cain and Abel story (Genesis 4), but no regulations from God are known from these early attempts to thank and worship God. In the human struggle to live in a hostile world, there was a strong desire to gain the blessing of the gods. Consequently sacrificial gifts were seen as a method of gaining expiation, of saying thank you, of expressing communion and unity with the divine, and of worship. A certain amount of ritual was involved with the ceremony of offering sacrifices and some of the Psalms seem to suggest that liturgical prayers, songs, confessions, or laments become part of temple worship (Psalm 24; 26; 28; 100). The unfortunate tendency to concentrate on performing the proper ritual was a constant threat to the real purpose of the sacrificial system. The ritual, the sacrifice, and the liturgy were instituted to aid the offerer in his meeting with God. These graphic symbols visualized the most significant principles which determine a person's relationship to God. A substitute may take the place of the sinner; the sinner confesses his sin with his hand on the substitute; the death of the substitute is the penalty for the sin; atonement and forgiveness of sin is the result. The heart of the whole process is the worshiper's understanding of the symbols, his humble confession, and his true desire to seek God for forgiveness (Lev. 23:27; 16:29-31; Ps. 51:16-17 [Heb 51:18-19]; Isa. 66:2; 2 Chron. 7:14). A request for forgiveness would be meaningless if there was no turning of the heart from its desire to commit the sin (Jer. 3:22—4:4; 26:3; 36:3); a request for cleansing would be a mockery if there was no true desire to remain pure from the iniquity (Ps. 51:1-13). The sacrifice of a wicked heart was rejected by God (Prov. 21:27).

The heart of the theology of sacrifice is related to the idea that the offerer has a meeting with God, who dwells in the temple. The sinner comes "before the Lord" to present his offering "to the Lord." The presence of God in the holy of holies was real and at times seen in a very dramatic and visible way (Exod. 40:34). It dwelt in the "tent of meeting" where men met with God to commune with him and worship him (Exod. 33:15).[47] When individuals, families, or the whole nation came to the temple to meet with God, they were to seek the Lord and call upon his name out of a pure heart (Isa. 55:6-7; 58:9; Ps. 139:23-24). Without proper motives and proper preparation of the heart, there would be no meeting with God.

---

[46]Studies which research the origins of the priesthood and sacrifices include: A. Cody, *A History of Old Testament Priesthood*, AnBib (Rome: Pontifical Institute, 1969) who has a lengthy bibliography on pp. xvi - xxvii; H. H. Rowley, *Worship in Ancient Israel: Its Forms and Meaning* (London: SPCK, 1967); and Wenham, *Leviticus* 37-44, for more bibliography.

[47]S. Terrien, *The Elusive Presence: The Heart of Biblical Theology* (New York: Harper and Row, 1978) 161-226; M. Haran, "The Nature of the *'Ohel Mo'edh* in Pentateuchal Sources," *JSS* 5 (1960) 50-65.

Amos 4:4-5 describes a worship which is judged to be a transgression. There is an emphasis on many sacrifices (cf. Mic. 6:6-7), a certain ignoring of ritual symbolism in the use of leaven, and a total lack of humility. Their freewill offerings were opportunities to demonstrate their "spirituality" and to pat themselves on the back. Elsewhere Amos proclaims that God hates Israel's sacrifices; he despises their feasts and songs (5:21-24). He challenges the nation to "seek God and live" (5:4). The refrain, "they did not return to me" (4:6-11), dramatically emphasizes the unwillingness of the nation to repent of its evil and turn to Yahweh for forgiveness in true worship. Although they offered sacrifices at Bethel and Gilgal, in the process they did not turn with all their hearts to seek God. There was no meeting with Yahweh. Amos and the other early prophets repeatedly criticize worship at the temples in Judah and Israel because it is a sham that God rejects (Isa. 1:11-18; Hos. 6:6; Mic. 6:6-8), but they do not reject the sacrifices offered out of a pure heart.[48] Because the people of Israel refuse to properly prepare their hearts, no divine meeting takes place. Therefore, God will come to meet the rebellious nation in judgment (4:12). The fearful and powerful theophany of God will meet his enemy Israel and execute his judgment. The promise of the joy and peace of God's presence will be transformed into punishment, destruction, and exile (3:2, 11-15; 4:2-3).

Amos ends this oracle with a hymn of praise to God which magnifies his creative power and his execution of judgment (4:13). This worship hymn is in fact a threat of judgment to Israel, because God knows the thoughts of all people, and he knows that the hearts of the Israelites are not pure before him. Now the mighty power of God, the divine warrior whose name is Yahweh the God of hosts, will accomplish his task by bringing the ultimate curse of death upon the nation.

---

[48]Rowley, *Worship in Ancient Israel* 144-75. Amos does not condemn the temple or the sacrifices because of Baalism, like Hosea does, nor does he take a Judean nationalistic position and defend Jerusalem as the only proper temple.

Lament Over Israel

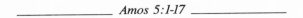

Amos 5:1-17

Introduction

Amos has given his message of judgment and exile for Israel (2:13-16; 3:2, 11-15; 4:2-3, 12) and has identified the reason for this punishment (violence and oppression—2:6-8; 3:9-10; 4:1). He has mocked the people's empty ritual and pointed to their unwillingness to turn in true worship to meet God (4:4-11). Because of this, God almighty will meet the nation in judgment (4:13).

The last half of the long section 3:1—6:14 is made up of a lament (5:1-17) and two woe oracles (5:18-27; 6:1-14). These sections focus on death and laments for the dead (5:1-3, 16-17; 6:9-10) and on removing the people's false sense of security in their worship (5:4-6, 14-15, 21-26), their future hopes of blessing (5:18-20), their luxury (6:1-7), and their military strength (6:13). Military defeat will destroy the nation (6:8, 11), and the people will go into captivity (5:27, 6:7). These prophecies are particularly addressed to "the house of Israel" (5:1, 3, 4, 25; 6:1, 14) or Joseph (5:6, 15; 6:6) and were probably given at Samaria (6:1-11) rather than Bethel.[49]

Amos 5:1-17 laments the results of the judgment announced in 3:1—4:13. Since God will destroy Israel, what can the prophet do but cry out in despair at the death of these people. The lament is structurally complex, with antithetical announcements of death followed by exhortations to live (5:1-3 and 4-6, or 5:14-15 and 16-17). Commentators are divided on the amount of weight to give each portion. Consequently, some picture Amos as a prophet of doom, while others believe his primary role was to call the nation to repentance. The presence of another hymn (5:8-9) separates the thematically related accusations in 5:7 and 10-13, thus various reconstructions of the text propose to bring greater continuity to the flow of the message in 5:1-17.

Background

The main literary traditions evident in 5:1-17 are derived from four different backgrounds: (1) the lament (5:1-3, 16-17); (2) the exhortation (5:4-6, 14-15); (3) the hymn (5:8-9); and (4) the announcement of judgment (5:7,

---

[49]Hammershaimb, _Amos_ 76 puts Amos in Bethel at a feast. Watts, _Amos_ 61 believes Amos is at the autumn festival during the fall equinox. See also Morgenstern, _Amos Studies,_ I 428.

10-13). In addition, some find minor influences of: (a) a covenant tradition behind the punishment in 5:11 and the call to seek good and not evil in 5:14-15;[50] (b) a wisdom background for the admonitions in 5:4-5, 14-15 and the statement about the "prudent" in 5:13;[51] (c) a "woe oracle" at the beginning of 5:7; and (d) theophany traditions behind 5:14, 17 and the hymn in 5:8-9.[52]

(1) The formal announcement of a dirge in 5:1 and the presence of lamentation themes in 5:2-3, 16-17 confirm the centrality of this literary tradition for 5:1-17. The *qinah* rhythm in 5:2-3 also provides evidence for a lamentation. These verses describe the death of the nation and the destruction of the army (5:2-3). The grief associated with the lament is particularily evident in the last paragraph (5:16-17). Elsewhere laments, wailing, and mourning are connected with the funeral services for a loved one (Gen. 23:2; 50:1-4; 2 Sam. 1:17-27; 2 Chron. 35:25) or the approaching threat of death due to sickness or an enemy (Psalm 6, 13, 60; Esther 4:1-3; Jer. 11:18-23).[53] These songs of grief were employed by the prophets to mourn the death of a nation (Lamentations 1-4) or to dramatically predict the approaching fall of a nation (Isa. 15:1-9; Jer. 7:29; 9:17-22; 48:36-44; Ezek. 26:17-18; 27:26-36; 28:12; 32:2). Activities related to lamenting death include the shaving of the head bald, the wearing of sackcloth, and the employment of professional mourners.[54] The discovery of similar patterns of lament in cultures and writings of other ancient Near Eastern peoples reveals that it was common practice to lament both the death of a loved one as well as the death of a nation or city state.[55] The unusual circumstance for the lament in Amos 5 is that Israel, the nation he is lamenting, is a strong and powerful nation which is very much alive. Some later prophets mockingly lamented the fall of other nations and in the process brought a message of comfort to Israel (Isa. 15:1-9; Ezek. 26:15-

---

[50]Mays, *Amos* 94 finds the covenant curses of Deut. 28:30-38 behind the judgment in 5:11, while Seilhamer, "Role of Covenant in the Mission and Message of Amos," 446, sees covenant language in 5:4-6, 14-15.

[51]Wolff, *Amos* 232-33, 242-45, 250 identifies wisdom motifs in 5:4-5, 14-15, and reconstructs a woe-oracle in 5:7, 10-11. Mays, *Amos* 98 connects 5:13 to wisdom sayings in Proverbs. T. M. Raitt, "The Prophetic Summons to Repentance," *ZAW* 83 (1971) 30-49, gives six reasons why the wisdom background for 5:4-5, 14-15 is inappropriate. He finds a convenantal background (Exod. 19:5-6; Josh. 24:20).

[52]Wolff, *Amos* 241-45; E. Gerstenberger, "The Woe-Oracles of the Prophets," *JBL* 81 (1962) 249-63; R. J. Clifford, "The Use of HOY in the Prophets," *CBQ* 28 (1966) 458-64; J. G. Williams, "The Alas-Oracles of the Eighth Century Prophets," *HUCA* 38 (1967) 75-91; W. Janzen, *Mourning Cry and Woe Oracle* BZAW (Berlin: de Gruyter, 1972); Mays, *Amos* 90; Rudolph, *Amos* 194. The theophany background is emphasized by Crenshaw, "Theophanic Traditions," 206-07.

[53]C. Westermann, *Praise and Lament in the Psalms* (Atlanta: John Knox, 1981) 261 describes the laments of the afflicted and laments for the dead.

[54]G. Stahlin, "*kopetos*" *TDNT* III 836-41 gives a general overview of mourning in the Old Testament as well as in the ancient Near East and the New Testament.

[55]The god Marduk lamented the destruction of Babylon as L. Cagni, *The Erra Epic* (Malibu: Undena, 1977) 50 describes. The lament over the destruction of UR (*ANET* 455-63) and other ancient Near Eastern laments are reviewed by Janzen, *Mourning Cry and Woe Oracle* 6-16.

18). When the prophets lamented the fall of their own nation, it is assumed that they gave heart-felt laments to awaken the nation to the reality that their death would soon take place. Thus the wailing chant of Amos over the "dead" nation of Israel was designed to send shock waves through the crowd of listeners. The nation is dead, its military is defeated (5:2-3), people will be wailing everywhere because God will pass through the midst of the nation in judgment.[56]

(2) The relationship of the catastrophic messages of doom in the laments (5:1-3, 16-17) to the hopeful exhortations that are directly next to them (5:4-6, 14-15), produces antithetical tensions and nearly opposite interpretations. One approach to the dilemma is to treat the laments merely as warnings that were intended to bring the nation to repentance. The call to seek God fits in well with this view of the lament, but it does not give adequate weight to the numerous clear announcements of the end of Israel found throughout Amos.[57] The opposite extreme treats the announcements of judgment and the lament with such seriousness that the exhortation to repent is not a real offer of repentance which could avert God's destruction of the nation.[58] Others suppose that the contradictory messages were given at different time periods or to different audiences.[59] Finally, there are a group of commentators who see the death of the nation as unavoidable, but at the same time they believe the gift of life is seriously offered to the remnant who will seek God.[60] The problem of understanding the exhortation is multiplied by the fact that some deny its authenticity, think it is spoken ironically, or believe part of the torah instructions (5:4) are quoted from what priests were teaching at the local shrines.[61]

---

[56]Barstad, *Religious Polemics in Amos* 82-88 connects the lament with fertility themes and Baalism, but this goes far beyond the emphasis in the text.

[57]A. Heschel, *The Prophets* 12, or J. M. Berridge, "Zur Intention der Botschaft des Amos. Exegetische Überlegungen zu Am. 5," *TZ* 32 (1976) 340; N. J. Tromp, "Amos 5:1-17: Toward a Stylistic and Rhetorical Analysis," *OTS* 23 (1984) 72-73, take the laments to be hyperbole or an extreme formulation intended to shock the audience.

[58]J. M. Ward, *Amos and Isaiah* (Nashville: Abingdon, 1969) 47.

[59]Wolff, *Amos* 238 summarizes the view of A. Alt, "Die Heimat des Deuteronomiums," *Kleine Schriften zur Geschichte des Volkes Israel* 2 (1953) 269; Also Raitt, "The Prophetic Summons to Repentance," 40-41, 47-48 draws the summons to repentance from the covenant curses and blessings; the summons is a call to renew the covenant.

[60]May, *Amos* 90; F. Hesse, "Amos 5, 4-6.14f.," *ZAW* 68 (1956) 1-17, sees the remnant as a key factor but concludes that the antithetical ideas are irrational parodoxes of the reality of God which even Amos did not understand. See A. V. Hunter, *Seek the Lord! A Study of the Meaning and Function of the Exhortations in Amos, Hosea, Micah, and Zephaniah* (Baltimore: St. Mary's Seminary, 1982) 61-65 surveys these approaches to the problem.

[61]Wolff, *Amos* 231-34 rejects 5:6 and 14-15 and makes 5:4 a call to seek God through the prophet Amos; Rudolph, *Amos* 190-01 takes 5:4 as a quotation; Weiser, *Profetie* 191-92 sees 5:14-15 as ironic like 4:4-5 and rejects the authenticity of 5:6 and 14-15. Rudolph and Mays see Amos imitating instruction from priestly torah, which is reversed; thus they give it a mild ironic twist because of what follows. K. W. Neubauer, "Erwägungen zu Amos 5:4-15," *ZAW* 78 (1966) 292-316, sees all of 5:4-15 to be the prophet's polemic against worship at the temples in Israel. Raitt, "The Prophetic Summons to Repentance " 33-35 gives a two-part structure to the summons to repentance: the appeal and the motivation. The appeal may include a messenger for-

The phrase "seek me and live" does not seem to be derived from a wisdom setting, or from a call to seek God through a prophet but is from the worship setting at the temple.[62]

The reference to the remnant in 5:14-15 alleviates the tension between death and life. This small ray of hope is not based on easy promises but on a spiritual and social change. It does not involve the prophet in creating false hopes, for the lament in 5:16-17 is an overwhelming witness to God's judgment of the nation in spite of the response of the remnant. The exhortations also function on another level as accusations, because they reveal why the punishment of God will come: no one has sought Yahweh and practiced justice.

(3) The third literary tradition is the hymn in 5:8-9. The hymn is closely related to 4:13 and functions in a similar manner. It reminds the audience again of the character of the God they will meet. Its location at the central pivitol point of the chiastic structure heightens its rhetorical effectiveness. The participles in the hymn honor God for his sovereign and majestic power and create a clear contrast to the participles in 5:7, 10. In the context of the accusation of changing justice to bitterness in 5:7, the descripton of God as one who changes light to darkness and changes the location of the waters of the sea by bringing them on the land has a threatening tone. This hymn of praise to the name of God celebrates his destructive power over the strong and their fortress (5:9); these are the people who oppress the poor and live in expensive houses (5:10-13).

(4) The accusations and announcements of judgment in 5:7, 10-13 reveal why the nation needs to seek God (5:7), why it needs to seek good and establish justice in the gate (5:15), and why death and lamentation are coming on the nation. Although several suppose that 5:7 begins a woe oracle, the initial "woe" being lost due to haplography, this solution has no textual evidence and is unnecessary.[63] Since the cries of woe come from the background of a funeral setting, it is easy to see how such a hypothesis would fit in with the theme of lament in 5:1-3, 16-17. Nevertheless, this conclusion seems contrary to the present organization of the material. The use of participles in 5:7, which are characteristic of woe oracles, can more readily be explained as purposely designed rhetorical contrasts to the existing participles in the hymn in 5:8-9.

The two judgment speeches in 5:10-11 and 12-13 each contain an accusation, plus "therefore" and a result statement. Although some refuse to con-

---

mula, vocative, and an admonition, while the motivation may contain a promise, accusation, and a threat.

[62]Wolff, *Amos* 232, 238, 250; J. Lust, "Remarks on the Redaction of Amos 5:4-6, 14-15," *OTS* 21 (1981) 141-42, derives "and live" from Deuteronomy and "seek me" in 5:4-5 from the context of seeking God at the temple.

[63]Wolff, *Amos* 233, 241-44; Mays, *Amos* 90-01; Rudolph, *Amos* 194, 197; and Neubauer, "Erwägungen zu Amos 5:4-15," 312-13, adds "woe" at the beginning of 5:7.

nect 5:10-11 together or put 5:12 with 16-17, the form of the judgment speech is well represented and need not be destroyed because of a slight shift in topic or a change in pronouns.[64]

These traditions from a variety of backgrounds are uniquely set one against the other to produce the contrasts and tensions that Amos is trying to convey. By such harsh contrasts and antithetical statements the prophet is able to transform the unexpected lament into a serious challenge to the nation's theological expectations. The use of any one form or tradition by itself would not have created the effect that the present masterpiece displays.

Structure and Unity

Structure

The exegesis of the text in the next section will follow the outline derived from the analysis of the structure that is displayed below.

A Lament Over Israel
Amos 5:1-17

		A. Lament over the death of Israel
Hear this word,[a] which I am taking up concerning you, a lament concerning the house of Israel.[b]	**5:1**	1. Call to hear the lament
She is fallen, the virgin Israel[c] shall not rise again; she lies forsaken on her land, there is no one to raise her up.	**5:2**	2. Lament over the dying
For thus says the Lord Yahweh: the city that goes out with a thousand, shall have left[d] a hundred; the city that goes out with a hundred, shall have left[d] ten of the house of Israel.	**5:3**	3. Extent of death
		B. Warnings about life and death
For thus says Yahweh to the house of Israel: Seek me and then you shall live!	**5:4**	1. Seek Yahweh for life, not temples
Do not seek Bethel! Do not go to Gilgal! Do not cross over to Beersheba![e] For Gilgal will surely go into exile, and Bethel will have sorrow.[f]	**5:5**	

---

[64]Wolff, *Amos* 233; Neubauer, "Erwägungen zu Amos 5:4-15," 313.

Seek Yahweh and then you shall live!
   Lest he burst forth like a fire
     against the house of Joseph,
    and it will devour,
    and there will be no quenching of Bethel.[g]

5:6   2. Seek God or he will destroy

They are the ones who change[h] justice
   into a bitter thing,[i]
and have laid righteousness to rest[j] in the ground.

5:7   C. No justice is the reason for death

5:8   D. A reminder of Yahweh's power to bring judgment
    1. God's power to bring change

But[k] he is the one who made Pleiades and Orion,[l]
   who changes darkness to morning,
    and darkens day to night;
   who calls the waters of the sea,
    and pours them on the face of the earth,
Yahweh[m] is his name!
He is the one who flashes[n] destruction on the strong,
   and brings destruction on the fortress.

5:9   2. God's power to destroy

E. Oppression is the reason for judgment

The one who reproves in the gate, they hate,
  and the one who speaks the truth, they abhor.
Therefore,

5:10   1. They reject legal justice

5:11   2. Riches of oppression will not be enjoyed

   because you tread[o] on the poor,
    and keep taking grain-tax[p] from him;
   you will build houses of hewn stones,
    but you will not live in them;
   you will plant splendid vineyards,
    but you will not drink their wine.
Indeed, I know of your many transgressions,
   and your numerous sins:
  by oppressing the innocent
  and accepting bribes,
they turn aside the poor in the gate.

5:12   3. God knows their oppressive acts

Therefore, the prosperous[q] will be silent at that time
  for it will be a disastrous time.

5:13   4. Results of oppression will end in disaster

F. Exhortation about life and justice

Seek good, not evil,
  so that you may live;
it may be that Yahweh, God of Hosts,
  will be with you,
   as you have said.

5:14   1. Seek good, God may be with you

Hate evil and love good![r]
Establish justice in the gate!
  Perhaps[s] Yahweh, God of Hosts
   will be gracious to the remnant of Joseph.

5:15   2. Do good, God may be gracious

		G. Future laments when God visits Israel
Therefore thus says Yahweh God of hosts, the Lord:ᵗ	**5:16**	1. Everywhere, they will mourn
In every square there will be wailing,		
in every street they will say, Alas! Alas!		
They will call the farmer to mourning,		
the skilled mourners to lamentation,		
in every vineyardᵘ there will be mourning,	**5:17**	2. God's presence will bring mourning
for I will pass through your midst,ᵛ		
says Yahweh.		

5:1a. The Old Greek adds "of the Lord."

5:1b. "The house of Israel" is made the subject of the verb "fallen" by the Greek translators.

5:2c. "Virgin Israel" is the subject of "forsaken" in the next line in the Old Greek.

5:3d. The Greek translation makes these verbs passive, "there shall be left a hundred."

5:5e. The name Beersheba is transliterated in the Old Greek in 8:14, but here it is translated "the well of the oath" as in Gen. 21:14, 31; 26:31.

5:5f. The Old Greek read or interpreted *'wn* "sorrow, grief" as *'ayin* "nothing," which does make good sense in this context. The Targ. matches the reading in the Greek, and several English translations follow these translations, but the MT is more consistent with the lament theme.

5:6g. The final reference to Bethel is "the house of Israel" in the Targ. and the Old Greek.

5:6h. The Hebrew has participles in 5:7-9, so the Greek translators believed all three verses were about God, which is clearly the case in 5:8-9. Thus, the Hebrew idea of the people of Israel "changing" justice refers to God "executing" justice in the Old Greek (using the same verb "to do" in 5:8).

5:7i. "Bitter thing, woodworm" is "on high" in the Old Greek.

5:7j. The verb *nuh* "to rest" is "to establish" in the Old Greek since God is the subject.

5:8k. The verse seems to be lacking a word or phrase at the beginning. The Targ. has "Let there be fear in the presence of him who..." at the beginning of the verse, but a simple contrast is implied by the parallel structure of 5:7-8.

5:8l. "He who makes Pleiades and Orion" is "He who makes everything and changes them" in the Old Greek. Sym. has "Pleiades and the stars," Theod. reads "Pleiades and the evening star," while Aq. gives "Archturus and Orion."

5:8m. The Old Greek adds to Yahweh, "God, the all powerful one" which makes this phrase parallel with "Yahweh, God of hosts" in 4:13.

5:9n. The Greek, "He who distributes, dispenses" implies *hammapliĝ* instead of our present *hammabliĝ*, which is difficult to fit into this context. Aq. "smile" and Sym. "laugh" indicate that *hammabliĝ* "smile, shine" was in the text in their day.

5:11o. The Old Greek has "because you smite the poor with your fists."

5:11p. "Grain-tax" is "choice gifts" in the Old Greek, an apparent confusion of *bar* "grain" and *bḥ r* "to choose."

5:13q. The root *kŝl* can mean "clever, successful, prosperous" or "prudent." The Old Greek and many commentators interpret it positively, thinking the reference is to the prudent, but this does not fit in a statement of punishment.

5:15r. The Greek translators make the verbs first common plurals, "we"; thus the verse becomes a confession.

5:15s. Instead of "perhaps" the Old Greek has "so that, in order that."

5:16t. The final word "Lord" does not appear in the Old Greek.

5:17u. The Old Greek has the lamentation in "all the ways, roads" instead of "all the vineyards."

5:17v. The Targ. translates this line, "I will reveal myself to perform vengeful judgment."

The structure of 5:1-17 is complicated by the appearance of material from several different literary backgrounds. The identification of a chiastic structure within the unit has opened the door for a new evaluation of the structure and unity of these diverse forms.[65] The structure of the chiasm is:

A. 5:1-3 lament
   B. 5:4-6 exhortation
      C. 5:7 accusation of no justice
         D. 5:8a-c hymn
            E. 5:8c Yahweh is his name
         D'. 5:9 hymn
      C'. 5:10-13 accusation of no justice
   B'. 5:14-15 exhortation
A'. 5:16-17 lament

Although this discovery has uncovered new possibilities for seeing the design of 5:1-17, there still are many problems in understanding how these parts fit together and how the meaning is developed within the chiastic structure.

Before de Waard's analysis the hymn in 5:8-9 was seen as an intrusion into the context because it separated 5:7 and 10. Consequently, 5:8-9 were rejected as later additions, and 5:7 and 10 were put together.[66] In addition 5:4-6 and 14-15 were sometimes brought together as one unit, and 5:13 was omitted as a later addition.[67] Even the structural unity within individual units was in doubt (5:1-2, 3); therefore, the more recent rhetorical and structural studies have made major breaks with the analysis of the past.[68]

The introductory and concluding focus on lamentation and death set the tone for the whole unit. The prediction of captivity, destruction, and warnings within the exhortations supplement this focus. The announcements of judgment (5:11, 13) and the destructive power of God (5:8b, 9) support the central theme of death and destruction for Israel. The relationship between the chiastic pairs evidences progression and expansion. In 5:1-3 the prophet

---

[65]J. de Waard, "The Chiastic Structure of Amos 5:1-17," *VT* 27 (1977) 170-07, fits everything into the structure except 5:13; Lust, "Redaction of Amos 5:4-6, 14-15," 154, suggests a chiastic arrangement which covers 4:1—6:7, but he omits 5:7, 8-9, 13 and seems unaware of the work of de Waard; Tromp, "Amos 5:1-17: Stylistic and Rhetorical Analysis," 63-71, follows de Waard's chiastic structure but gives a more detailed picture of the intricate connections within and between the individual paragraphs; R. F. Melugin, " 'Form' Versus 'Formation' of Prophetic Books," *SBL 1983 Seminar Papers* (Chico: Scholars Press, 1983) 24-27, follows a slightly different outline of the structure of 5:1-9, while Story, "Amos—Prophet of Praise" 74, finds a structural relationship between 4:1-13 and 5:1-9.

[66]Rudolph, *Amos* 194-98; Mays, *Amos* 90; Crenshaw, *Hymnic Affirmation* 6-10.

[67]Rudolph, *Amos* 189-94; Lust, "Redaction of Amos 5:4-6, 14-15," 129-31; Hesse, "Amos 5:4-6:14f," 1-17; Crenshaw, *Hymnic Affirmation* 124-31.

[68]See the section on Unity below for additional information on factors which cause questions about the unity of 5:1-17.

laments because Israel has fallen and its army is destroyed, but 5:16-17 pictures Israelites everywhere lamenting because God will pass through their midst. The exhortation in 5:4-6 is cultically oriented, while those in 5:14-15 are more directly related to moral issues of behavior. Even the hymn celebrating the powerful sovereignty of God over nature in 5:8 is refocused in 5:9 on how God's power brings destruction on the strong who are guilty of injustice (5:7, 10-13). These differences give a greater emphasis on death and destruction in the first half of the chiastic poem and more focus on the reason for destruction in the second half.

The structure of the individual paragraphs, and their connection to one another, illustrate the skill employed in putting the total unit together. Notice how various repetitions have cemented Amos' oracle: The initial lament contains an introductory summons to hear a lament (5:1), a lament over a dead nation (5:2), and a vivid substantiation of the lament in a description of a defeated army (5:3). The prose of 5:1 introduces the *qinah* poetry of 5:2-3. Each verse is centered around the lament for the dead with ABAB line parallelism in 5:2-3. The exhortations using imperatives, set 5:4-6 apart from what precedes. Warnings of death, destruction, sorrow, and exile in the two subordinate clauses in 5:5 and 6 connect the section to 5:1-3. The specific reference to "the house of Joseph" and "Bethel" in 5:6 match the final reference to the "house of Israel" at the end of 5:3. The initial participle in 5:7 reveals the reason why destruction is coming, but it also sets up the contrast between the "changes" of God (5:8) and the people (5:7). Bitterness and putting something to rest in the ground (in 5:7) are drawn from funeral traditions. The hymn continues the theme of death and destruction in its flood motif in 5:8 and the destruction of the strong in 5:9 (cf. 5:3). The participles of 5:7-9 continue into 5:10 where the author returns to the theme of 5:7. The theme of injustice is expanded in 5:10-11 and the evils of the strong whom God will destroy (5:9) are catalogued. Two parallel accusations (5:10, 12) and clauses of punishment (5:11, 13) continue the themes of injustice in the gate and destruction of houses (5:9). The call to "seek good, not evil" interrupts the accusations of injustice (5:10-13) with a call to establish justice (5:14-15). The two verses are structurally parallel with initial exhortations followed by subordinate clauses about the possibility of grace (instead of warnings of destruction as in 5:5-6). The final paragraph (5:16-17) returns to the theme of lament and closes with the awesome warning that God will pass through the midst of the nations.

These pieces all fit together in a somewhat complicated manner, but the rhetorical building blocks, the repetition of themes and structural balances are too frequent to be accidental. Some have seen the repetition as a sign of secondary redactional activity and have had trouble following the logical progression of the lament, thus the unity of the lament has been questioned at some points.

Unity

A few commentators assign 5:6, 14-15 to a secondary level of redaction because the verses merely expand the original message of 5:4-5, interrupt the connection between 5:12 and 16-17, and offer hope for a remnant.[69] Wolff dates 5:6 to the time of Josiah and 5:14-15 to a period after 733 B.C., but most maintain that Amos wrote this material.[70]

The major difficulties surround the hymnic fragment in 5:8-9 and the result clause in 5:13. Doubts about 5:8-9 arise because it seems to interrupt the context by separating 5:7 from 10, uses late theological themes about God creating the constellations, and is hymnic in nature with several participles.[71] But within the chiastic structure of 5:1-17, 5:8-9 fits well as the central pivotal section. The participles in 5:7 and 10 go well with those in 5:8-9 and the thematic connections between "change" in 5:7 and 8 and destruction of the houses of the strong in 5:9 and 10-11 demonstrate how skillfully the hymn was interwoven into its context. If Amos borrowed a hymn of praise that his audience accepted and recognized from the worship at the temple, it would have provided a powerful witness concerning the character of God.[72] He is not only a sovereign who blesses, he uses his might to bring judgment on the strong who reject justice.

The traditional translation of 5:13 relates the text to the silence of the prudent person in this evil time when injustices were rampant in the land. While this idea could describe the righteous persons in verse 12, it is peculiar to find this emphasis where a statement of punishment would be expected.[73] If the root *kšl* is understood in its negative sense and refers to the "cleverness, prosperity" of the wicked, and if "to be silent" means silence because of death, then 5:13 would be a statement of punishment which fits into the context very well.[74]

Phrases like "pass over to Beersheba" in 5:5, "the house of Israel" in 5:3, or "Bethel" at the end of 5:6, and "God of hosts" in 5:14 and 15 are identified as editorial expansions by a few, but there is little evidence to support these proposals other than some preconceived feeling concerning the proper length or structure of poetic parallelism.[75]

---

[69]Wolff, *Amos* 231-34; Weiser, *Prophetie* 185.
[70]Rudolph, *Amos* 190; Hesse, "Amos 5.4-6.14f." 1-17; Mays, *Amos* 89-90, 99-102; Neubauer, "Erwägungen zu Amos 5, 4-15," 292-316.
[71]This view is held by most commentators. See Crenshaw *Hymnic Affirmation* 5-24; Mays, *Amos* 83, 95.
[72]G. L. Botterweck, "Zur Authenzität des Buches Amos," *BZ* 2 (1958) 182-86.
[73]Mays, *Amos* 98 and Wolff, *Amos* 250 propose a wisdom background for 5:13 (cf. Prov. 24:21-22; 25:9-10).
[74]G. V. Smith, "Amos 5:13: The Deadly Silence of the Prosperous," *JBL* 107 (1988) 289-91.
[75]Mays, *Amos* 84, 86, 99; Wolff, *Amos* 228, 231.

Interpretation

A. Lament over the death of Israel (5:1-3)

The previous chapters have emphasized that God will punish Israel (3:2), defeat its army (2:13-16), destroy their houses and temples (3:11-15), and send them into exile (4:2-3) when God meets the nation face to face (4:12-13). Since the end has already been announced, it is somewhat natural for the prophet to lament the death of the nation. The prophet's deep concern for the welfare of the nation is displayed in his call for God to be merciful in the first two visions (7:1-6), so there is every reason to believe that Amos truly is in great sorrow over the future of Israel.

1. Call to hear a lament (5:1)

Amos begins this new section with another imperative call to attention similar to those used to begin new sections or paragraphs in 3:1, 9, 13; 4:1.[76] The subordinate relative clause identifies the addresses as the house of Israel, the northern nation. The references to places of worship in Bethel, Gilgal, and Beersheba cause some to identify the audience as a group of worshipers at the temple at Bethel, but the capital city of Samaria seems more likely since 3:1—4:13 was given there (3:9; 4:1) and 6:1-14 is tied to the wealthy in Samaria. The message is not immediately identified as the word of Yahweh, as in 3:1, 13, but the connection is clearly proclaimed later in the lament (5:3, 4, 16). The content of the message is drawn from the common practice of lamenting the death of a loved one (Gen. 23:2; 2 Sam. 1:17-27). The dirge at the funeral was filled with emotions; its short sobbing phrases were interspersed with cries of grief and hopelessness. Although the context of Amos 1-4 may have naturally led the prophet to see the need to lament the fall of Israel, his listeners were probably sent into a state of shock by this outrageous pessimism. Israel's army was strong, Jeroboam II had brought prosperity to the nation, and there were no major threats from the Syrians or Assyrians at this time. Because of this situation, the audience was not very inclined to accept the prophet's lament; therefore the lament is expanded to include the reason for the lament. The purpose of the prophet is to convince the nation that death is at their doorstep. This obituary will hopefully awaken the nation to its true status: it is dead.

2. Lament over the dying (5:2)

The lament does not predict the future destruction of Israel but its present state of collapse.[77] The theme of "fallen" is common in laments (2

---

[76]Wolff, *Amos* 235 derives this call to attention from the wisdom school, but the summons was commonplace in the home, in the temple, in politics, and any place where instructions were given.

[77]Harper, *Amos* 106, 109 takes the perfect verb to be a prophetic perfect, which predicts with certainty a future event (GKC 106n). Many translations use a perfect tense "has fallen," but a present tense is more consistent with the imagery in the rest of the verse.

Sam. 1:19, 25, 27 "How the mighty have fallen," 3:34; Lam. 2:21) and immediately signals the death of someone. This grief is concerning "the virgin
Israel," a metaphor which heightens the sense of tragedy.[78] The personifica-
tion of the nation as a young virgin in the prime of life, unconquered and unfulfilled in her role as wife or mother, indicates the waste of her life (Jer.
18:13; 31:4, 21).[79] This untimely death is made sure in the verb "she shall not
rise again."[80] The nation has no hope because it lies "forsaken" on the land
like a dead corpse, abandoned after a battle. The military defeat spoken of in
3:11; 4:3 is implied at this point. Her allies among the nations, her pagan
gods and even Yahweh have forsaken her and refuse to come to raise her up
(contrast Hos. 6:1-3). The finality of the event is drawn in bold figures full of
pathos. They express the bitterness of grief and the loneliness of death. The
rhetoric is not to be explained as mere hyperbole.[81]

3. Extent of death (5:3)

Verse 3 pinpoints why there is no hope. The cities of the nation will send
forth their troops in thousands or hundreds, and only a tenth will survive.
The organized military units (1 Sam. 8:12; 18:13; 22:7; 2 Sam. 18:1, 4;
2 Kings 11:4, 19) will be decimated by an undefined enemy when they go
out to war. The focus is on the death of almost everyone rather than on the
life of a few. In 5:14-15 the prophet does develop the remnant theme, but
there it is limited to those who seek God and establish justice.

B. Warnings about life and death (5:4-6)

1. Seek Yahweh for life, not temples (5:4-5)

The unexpected lament is followed by an equally surprising summons to
seek Yahweh and live. The paradox of death (5:1-3) and an offer of life (5:4,
6) demands explanation.[82] One could interpret "for" at the beginning of 5:4
as an introduction to the reason why the nation will die. This reason could be
God's earlier command which has been ignored, or it might be based on
some current command from God,[83] neither of which offers grace to the people. Perhaps it is an ironic statement,[84] or could Amos be calling the nation
to seek God through the prophet himself or to seek God through worship at
Jerusalem.[85] Several perceive that Amos is quoting or mimicking a slogan or

---

[78]Other laments praise the former state of the deceased to heighten the sense of tragedy (cf.
Lam. 1:1; 4:1-2; 2 Sam. 1:23; Ezek. 27:4-9, 26-29; 28:12-15; 32:2.

[79]Virgin is also used of other nations: Lam. 1:15; 2:13; Jer. 18:13; 46:11; Isa. 37:22; 47:1.

[80]The second verb *qum* "to rise" is the principal verb, while the first verb describes the manner of the action. See GKC 120a, g.

[81]Tromp, "Stylistic and Rhetorical Analysis," 73 believes it is hyperbole.

[82]See the review of the three major positions in the section on Background.

[83]Harper, *Amos* 109-10; Cripps, *Amos* 180.

[84]Weiser, *Profetie* 190-02; Wolff, *Amos* 239; Hesse, "Amos 5.4-6.14f." 7-10.

[85]Kapelrud, *Amos* 50; Lust, "Redaction of Amos 5:4-6, 14-15," 139-40; Wolff, *Amos* 238;
Hunter, *Seek the Lord* 172-73 follows Westermann's conclusions.

an exhortation given by priests at a temple in 5:4.[86] If the phrase was common in the worship of the nation and understood to mean that the people were to turn to God, it received a mild ironic twist when it is coupled with the command not to seek God at Bethel (5:5). Although they go through the right ritual and believe everything is fine, there is a major difference between going to Bethel, Gilgal, or Beersheba and seeking Yahweh.[87] Thus, what initially appears to be an exhortation is actually a warning against a deceptively popular conception of worship.

The prohibition concerning worship at the popular shrines is antithetical to the encouragement to seek God.[88] No reason is given for not seeking God at these places, but some suspect it was because other dieties were worshiped at these temples.[89] The exhortations imply that people were not seeking God but were receiving false promise of life and blessing. Bethel was the state temple controlled by Jeroboam II (cf. 7:10-17; 1 Kings 12:25-33) which contained one of the golden calves. Gilgal was located near Jericho and was condemned by Hosea (4:15; 9:15; 12:11 [Heb. 12:12]).[90] Beersheba lies in the southern part of Judah; thus the people from Israel had to cross over their border and travel far to the south to reach Beersheba. It was a famous site where Abraham made a treaty with Abimelech (Gen. 21:31-33) and later lived (Gen. 22:19). Jacob received God's blessing, built an altar, and worshiped God there (Gen. 26:23-25). The pilgrimages to Beersheba were in some way related to these traditions, but little is known about the sanctuary or its worship. The repetition of the negatives and the naming of three popular places of worship creates a strong warning. These clauses color the initial call to seek God and reveal its rhetorical nature.

The rest of verse 5 fills out a chiasm using the names of towns, and in the process demonstrates why it is useless to go to Bethel and Gilgal.[91] These places are destined for destruction and exile (cf. 3:14). The word play on Gilgal uses the "g" and "l" sounds to build alliteration between the place, the verb, and the infinitive absolute.[92] There is no question about it; Gilgal's population will be exiled, and Bethel will be turned into a place of sorrow and grief.[93] The theme of lament and the results of military defeat (cf. 5:2-3) are

---

[86]Rudolph, *Amos* 190; Wolff, *Amos* 238; Mays, *Amos* 87; Hunter, *Seek the Lord* 56-67.

[87]The second imperative "and you shall live" gives a direct assurance that the consequences will take place if the condition is met. See GKC 110f.

[88]The first two negatives are milder, while the third is stronger. See GKC 107o, 109c, e.

[89]Kapelrud, *Amos* 50; Barstad, *Religious Polemics in Amos* 77-79, 82-88 also connects the lament to the worship of a fertility god.

[90]See the articles listed under the references to these places in 4:4-5. Lust, "Redaction of Amos 5:4-6, 14-15," 142-44 takes Gilgal as a reference to the "stone circle" or the sanctuary at Bethel, but this is unlikely.

[91]J. de Waard, "The Chiastic Structure of Amos 5:1-17," 172; Wolff, *Amos* 239 suggests that the line with Beersheba is a later addition, but it fits well into the chiastic structure.

[92]*haggilgāl gālōh yigleh*. The infinitive absolute strengthens the verbal idea to describe how certain the idea is. See GKC 113n.

[93]Many translate the last line, "Bethel will come to naught" following the Targum and Old

again brought forward. These places will not be protected because God has forsaken them to the enemy. To seek God at these temples is useless; it will only bring the worshiper into the danger of being swept away into exile.

2. Seek God or he will destroy (5:6)

The initial call to seek God so that you may live is repeated, but this time instead of a contrast as in 5:4-5, there is a conditional "lest" clause following it. This formulation of destruction repeats the previous threat in a way that opens the possibility of choosing life. "Seek Yahweh and then you shall live" sets the conditions down and lays out one option. Life may be chosen or the people can suffer death because of the unquenchable fire of God's destruction. This possibility of grace should not be watered down but should be understood as a real exhortation (in contrast with 5:4) to seek God in light of the conditional sentence. The offer is made, but it is not developed or emphasized (see 5:14-15 for the development of the idea). The main purpose of the prophet in this context is to warn the people of impending doom so that they will seek Yahweh.

The "lest" clause is used in several Psalms of lament (7:2 [Heb 7:3]; 13:4 [Heb 13:5]; 28:1; 38:17; 50:22) when a worshiper calls upon God to save him, lest his enemies destroy him. In some cases the "lest" clause is followed by a "there is none to" clause as in Amos 5:6 (Ps. 7:2 [Heb 7:3]; 22:11 [Heb 22:12]; 50:22).[94] Thus it appears that Amos is employing terminology of lament to make his point in this verse.

They must seek Yahweh "lest he bursts forth like a fire" against them.[95] Fire itself was the instrument of God in the oracles against the foreign nations in Amos 1-2, but here God himself is pictured as a devouring fire that destroys everything (cf. 7:4-6). The threatening warning is heightened by the verb "burst forth, rush forth," a figure which suggests the nearness of the judgment and the quickness of its coming. This idea is supported by the final clause, "there will be no quenching of Bethel." Once the decree is given, God will destroy the nation. Prayers, sacrifices, wailing, and armies will not help. At this point, there is no hope. Even Bethel, that sacred site that many believed was above destruction, will be devoured. The only hope for life is Yahweh!

C. No justice is the reason for death (5:7)

To this point Amos has concentrated on death and warnings of death. The only implied reason given in 5:1-6 is Israel's failure to seek Yahweh. Many in

---

Greek. Hosea refers to Bethel (the house of God) as Beth-awen (house of idolatry) (Hos. 4:15; 5:8; 10:5), so some feel Amos is using that pun here. Neither solution is necessary since the text fits the context as it presently stands.

[94]Hunter, *Seek the Lord,* 76-78.

[95]H. Tawil, "Hebrew *slh/hslh,* Akkadian *ešēr/šušuru*: A Lexicographic Note," *JBL* 95 (1976) 405-13, makes a strong case for the semantic range of this root to include "to burn."

his audience no doubt objected, claiming to be loyal in their sacrifices and prayers. Why then does God reject the seeking that presently exists? In the briefest terms possible, the prophet points to injustice. Again the issue is not developed (cf. 5:10-13), for it would detract from his efforts to move to the heart of the issue: Yahweh himself and his sovereign power (5:8-9).

The ideas of justice and righteousness could be defined in social, legal, or cultic terms. In verses 10-13 a social context is clear, but here the undefined concepts could be descriptive of all the nation's relationships. The quality of its response to God is not characterized by right relationships consistent with expected norms of the covenant or God's character. Naturally their relationships with one another were equally void of righteousness and justice. If the context of 5:4-6 is determinative, this is a critique of the nation's worship. The transformation of righteousness into bitterness was a fundamental reversal of God's intended order.

The relationship between 5:7 and the preceding and following verses have caused some to introduce a woe oracle here or to place 5:7 just before 5:10. Both of these suggestions seem unneccessary, for 5:7 uses imagery of lament to tie it to 5:1-6 ("lay to rest in the ground" and "bitterness") and contains lexical ("change") and syntactical (the participle) connections with 5:8-9. The result is a strong contrast between those in the house of Joseph who change justice and Yahweh, the powerful Creator, who can change all the forces of nature and bring about justice through the destruction of the strong who in fact pervert justice.

D. A reminder of Yahweh's power to bring judgment (5:8-9)

1. God's power to bring change (5:8)

Although Watts expands the hymn to include 5:6-7, omits parts of verse 8, and relates verse 9 to the stars rather than God's destruction of the strong, these suggestions require numerous emendations that are unnecessary in light of the linguistic connections between the verses and the chiastic structure of the lament in 5:1-17.[96] The prophet has borrowed a hymn of praise of Yahweh (cf. 4:13) to remind his audience of the power of Yahweh. Its placement after 5:7 creates an antithesis between the men "who change justice" and God "who made...and changes darkness to morning and darkens day to night." Human injustice threatens to destroy the world, but God is the creative owner who made and providentially controls the natural powers within the world. The reference to God's creation of the stars and constellations is unusual, although Job 9:9, 38:31 and Isaiah 40:26 use these themes in somewhat paral-

---

[96]Watts, *Amos* 54-57; Crenshaw, *Hymnic Affirmation* 47-74 gives a full review of many reconstructions of this hymn as well as various interpretations of the difficult words within the hymn. The section on Structure and Unity summarizes some of the reasons for questioning its position in 5:1-17 as well as ways of seeing how the prophet has fit the hymn into its context.

lel ways.[97] His unlimited power is presented in positive affirmations which the
audience would accept as their own confession. But the God who created the
stars, who changes night to day and day to night, also has sovereign power
over the waters and can bring them with destructive power over the land
(9:6). This reference should not be minimized or softened into the idea that
God graciously sends rain from heaven to the earth (Job 36:28).[98] God's acts
in history remain in the background, but the contrasts between the way of
people and God are clearly drawn. Yahweh is God, Yahweh is his name, Yahweh alone has the power to change the forces of nature and direct their influence on the earth. The contrast is awesome and the hymn of praise becomes a
doxology of judgment in light of the nation's injustice and God's prediction of
death.

2. God's power to destroy (5:9)

The hymnic style continues in the participles which describe God's
power over the strong who live in the nation's strongholds. The picture of
God's activity in history is clouded by the use of *blg* which usually means "to
shine, to be glad" (Ps. 39:13 [Heb 39:14]; Job 9:27; 10:20).[99] The root can
describe the "flashing forth" of the power of Yahweh using the picture of the
light.[100] The final line of 5:8 introduces the power of God's judgment in nature; thus the application of that destructive power against the strong who
carry out injustices (5:10-12) is in tune with the context. The focus on the
strong and their fortresses is consistent with the emphasis earlier in Amos 1-
2; 3:11-12, 15; 4:1-3. The original hymn may have been modified by Amos to
direct his attack against the wealthy and powerful members of his society.[101]
In this setting the hymn of praise is transformed into a fearful recital of the
awesome power of God to judge. God the warrior will bring destruction, and
therefore the nation should lament.

E. *Oppression is the reason for judgment (5:10-13)*

1. They reject legal justice (5:10)

If the rejection of righteousness and justice in 5:7 is a more general state-

---

[97]Crenshaw, "The Influence of the Wise upon Amos," 49-50. It is unlikely that these stars represent the summer and winter seasons or that some ancient myth is being remembered.

[98]May, *Amos* 96; Story, "Amos-Prophet of Praise," 72 believes this is a description of rain, but
Harper, *Amos* 116 and Crenshaw, *Hymnic Affirmation* 128, properly see it as a destructive
reference, possibly drawing on the Noah traditions.

[99]J. J. Glück, "Three Notes on the Book of Amos," *Studies on the Book of Hosea and Amos*
OTWSA 5-6 (Potchefstroom: Rege-Pers Beperk, 1965) 115-16 emends the text to *bl'* "to bring
about," while others have suggested *bld* "to appoint" or *plg* "to bring destruction."

[100]Numerous attempts are made to find names of stars in 5:9. See G. Hoffmann, "Versuche
zu Amos," *ZAW* 3 (1883) 110-11; G. R. Driver, "Two Astronomical Passages in the Old
Testament," *JTS* 4 (1953) 208-12; Watts, *Amos* 54-57; Crenshaw, *Hymnic Affirmation* 47-60.

[101]Speculation on the original content and form of the hymn has only produced several unsub-
stantiated guesses. Modifications by Amos are not recoverable, but the major redactional activity

ment relating to all areas of life, or a specific accusation concerning the inadequacies of the temple worship, then 5:10 is a movement to expand the accusation to a new area. A lack of righteousness and justice is still the key theme, but in the following verses its application is to the social behavior of the powerful and wealthy over the poor and weak members of society (cf. 2:6-8). This emphasis on the accusation of injustice changes the focus of the second half of the lament. Although death, destruction, and lamentation are present (5:11, 13, 16-17), justice in the gate (5:10, 12, 15) and the need for moral changes are given greater prominence.

The gate of the ancient city was the site where local trade and business was carried out (2 Kings 7:1, 18), group meetings were held (Neh. 8:1; 2 Chron. 32:6) and the elders of the city sat to decide matters of justice (Gen. 23:10; Deut. 21:19; 22:15; Job 29:7; Prov. 24:7; Ruth 4:1-12). At certain times judges were appointed to decide cases (Exod. 18:13-26; Deut 16:18-20; 17:8-13; 2 Chron. 19:4-11) and sometimes priests (Ezek. 44:23-4; 1 Chron. 23:4; 26:29) and judges like Samuel (1 Sam. 7:16; 8:2) exercised judicial authority. The exact way in which the courts worked is not fully explained. The root *ykḥ* "the one who reproves" has been identified with the role of a judge who executes justice (Isa. 11:3), the one who argues a case (Job 13:3), or the one who supports right and condemns evil in the court's decision-making process (Job. 32:12; Isa. 29:21).[102] Justice was important in each of these aspects of the court system, and it is possible that none of them was functioning in the role that God intended.

The accusation in 5:10 reveals a concerted effort to control and manipulate the legal process to the advantage of special interests instead of justice. In light of the context of 5:9-13, those who hated justice in the court were the powerful and rich who used the courts to gain advantage over the poor. Through bribes, false witnesses, social pressure, and intimidation (5:12) injustices were multiplied. The few that did support proper and fair legal judgments were hated with a passion because they spoke the truth. The law condemned false witnesses (Exod. 20:16; Deut 19:15-19), but this did not prevent people from attempting to pervert justice (Prov. 12:17; 1 Kings 21:10).[103] The abhorrence of people who witnessed truthfully, who spoke judgments according to the principles of the law of God, reveals a deep-seated and intentional striving to overturn justice. Their character and way of life was contrary to God's justice; therefore God's destructive power will bring ruin to the strong ones who have built comfortable palace-fortresses with the gains from court decisions (5:9).

---

was probably related more to the choice of a hymn, which would fit the purpose of the prophet, rather than a major reshuffling of the verses in the poem.

[102]Harper, *Amos* 119 suggests that the prophet himself could be included, but this seems unlikely.

[103]R. de Vaux, *Ancient Israel: I Social Institutions* (New York: McGraw-Hill, 1965) 143-60, gives a summary of various aspects of the judicial system in Israel.

2. Riches of oppression will not be enjoyed (5:11)

"Therefore" introduces the announcement of punishment, but before the punishment itself is described, a more direct explication of the accusation is offered using second person pronouns. It is no longer the indefinite "one who" or "they," but it is "you" who tread on the poor. The verb *bôs*, which is found only here, appears to be related to *bôs* "to tread, trample" rather than the Akkadian *šbš* "to levy, extort taxes."[104] This is similar to the accusations in 2:6, 4:1, and 8:4, but in each case a distinctive means is used to subvert the poor. The courts were corrupted to further the economic gains of the rich, and the very institution which was designed to protect the weak now functions to destroy them. Amos 2:6 describes the selling of the poor for next to nothing, while this statement reveals why the poor were poor. The poor through heavy loans and taxes were driven into bankruptcy and eventually into slavery. The peasant farmers were gradually driven from the land and then forced to pay heavy percentages of their grain in rent to work land owned by the wealthy. The law forbids the charging of interest, requires a compassionate attitude of care for the poor (Lev. 25:35-43), and demands the return of his land in the year of jubilee (Leviticus 25). These laws were ignored in order to increase the land holdings of the rich.

Through these lucrative taxes the landlords were able to build for themselves elaborate and expensive homes of hewn stones. The common brick or rough stone walls of the average Israelite home were despised. Cut stones were extremely costly and usually limited to the king's residence and temples (1 Kings 6:36; 7:9, 11). In Israel the wealthy were literally living like kings because of their abuse of the poor.[105] In addition to their enjoyment of splendid homes, the rich and powerful had planted beautiful vineyards to supply themselves with abundant wine.

The punishment clauses remind these people that God's curse will be upon these undeserved luxuries. What they have built, they will not live in; what they have planted, they will not eat. This pattern is found elsewhere (Deut. 28:30; Mic. 6:15; Zeph. 1:13). God's laws of justice will now go into effect and his curses will remove these blessings. This curse will some day be reversed to produce an opposite effect in the day of God's blessing of the nation (9:14), but for now only destruction and lamentation will be heard.

3. God knows their oppressive acts (5:12)

A second oracle of punishment is found in 5:12-13.[106] The accusation in

---

[104]Wolff, *Amos* 230 follows H. Torczyner's suggestion and accepts the Akkadian meaning, which makes a good parallel to 5:11b. The present form is a poel form with *š* arising through the process of dissimilation.

[105]H. Beebe, "Ancient Palestinian Dwellings," *BA* 31 (1968) 49-57.

[106]Wolff, *Amos* 248; Mays, *Amos* 96-97; Rudolph, *Amos* 194 believe the announcement of judgment in 5:16-17 completes the accusation in 5:12. These and others throw out 5:13 as a later addition from a wisdom context, but both of these conclusions seem unnecessary if 5:13 is related to the death (silence) of the "prosperous, clever" who abuse the poor.

5:12 is similar to 5:10, denouncing the social practices which the powerful use to take advantage of the weak and poor. The second accusation responds to a denial of the facts brought forward in the first accusation. God himself surely knows the facts, he is aware of how many sins are being committed. It is useless to claim to be innocent and without guilt before God, for he sees the heart of every person and keeps track of their sins (Job. 22:12-14; 11:11; 28:24; Ps. 73:11; Ezek. 8:12). By the repetition of "many" and "numerous," attention is drawn to how frequently these sins are committed and how many people are involved with rebellious acts against God. Three specific sins are catalogued and each is related to the judicial system in Israel (5:10).

The first two charges employ plural participles similar to 5:7. The first charge is that of oppressing the innocent who are not guilty of any legal wrong. This kind of person obeys the law, practices righteousness, and is blameless of any charges. In spite of such innocence, these individuals are oppressed in various ways (2:6; 3:9-10; 4:1). The type of hostility or persecution may have revealed itself in many overt acts, but taxation and the court context of 5:10-12 suggests some very concrete areas in which an advantage was gained over the innocent. The second charge is directly connected to court procedures. The *kpr* "atonement" usually is a sum of money paid to ransom someone guilty of a crime (Exod. 21:30). The word is also used of a bribe (1 Sam. 12:3) which is given to sway the opinion of the judge who is deciding a legal case. This is one example of how the innocent were persecuted by the wealthy who could afford to buy off a judge to get a favorable decision on a questionable or illegal act. Because the courts were not protecting these people, the needy were "turned aside" from the right. This third charge gives the result of this legal sham. The law specifically warned against perverting the justice due the poor person (Exod. 23:2-3, 6; Deut. 16:18-20) and connected the pursuit of justice in the court with life and possession of the land. Prophecies in Isaiah indicate that similar legal perversions were present in the courts in Judah (Isa. 1:23; 5:23; 10:1-2).[107] Such acts are directly contrary to God's command to protect the needy (Deut. 10:18; Ps. 146:9).

4. Results of oppression will end in disaster (5:13)

After the accusation of 5:12, an announcement of judgment would be expected. Verse 13 begins with "therefore," the usual introduction to a statement of punishment; but then 5:13 is commonly assigned to a later editor who expanded the text using wisdom motifs.[108] This conclusion seems almost inevitable in light of the peculiarities of the verse. A new look at the meaning

---

[107]E. W. Davies, *Prophecy and Ethics* (Sheffield: JSOT, 1981) 90-112, examines the administration of justice in Isa. 1:21-6 and discusses the problems of bribery, the right of appeal and the rights of the poor. Some believe Isaiah used Amos 5:7-12, but a common erosion of the principles of justice in the courts of both nations is a more likely explanation.

[108]Wolff, *Amos* 233, 248; Mays, *Amos* 98 and the earlier section on Unity.

of *kšl* "prudent, prosperous, successful," *dmm* "silence," and *r'h* "evil, dis-
asterous," opens up a fresh interpretation of this verse as an announcement of
punishment against the wicked in Israel. If the root *kšl* is not taken as a reference to the innocent in 5:12 who are "prudent" by keeping silent, but understood as a reference to the "prosperous, successful, or clever" wealthy
inhabitants who oppress the innocent, the verse begins to make sense.
These will be punished and silenced by God, a term that describes a person's response of grief at a time of disaster (Lam. 2:10; 3:28) or metaphorically refers to silence because of death (Jer. 8:14; 48:9; Ps. 31:17 [Heb
31:18]; 1 Sam. 2:9). In either case, themes of destruction and lament are
intertwined with a statement of punishment which will take place on that
disastrous day when God judges the nation. God will reverse the plight of
the wealthy who silence the poor through bribery and injustice. Although
the wicked have prospered and become quite successful through their prudent influence on the important people at the proper time, they themselves
will soon be silenced when God's disastrous day comes upon them (3:14;
4:2; 6:3). That day will be a day of punishment and darkness and not a day of
salvation (5:18-20).

F. Exhortations about life and destruction(5:14-15)

1. Seek good, God may be with you (5:14)
     Verses 14-15 form a well-balanced paragraph, made up of imperatives,
conditional clauses, and chiastic relationships between good and evil. The
exhortation is directly related to the themes and structure of 5:4-6 and need
not be denied to Amos.[109] The call to "Seek good and not evil" is significantly different from 5:4, 6. The implications of truly seeking Yahweh (5:6)
are related to moral behavior in 5:14-15. Hating evil and establishing justice
are the only ways to escape the judgment of death and receive life. These motifs are common in wisdom literature, but no new setting is necessary.[110]
Amos 5:14-15 move beyond the context of temple worship in 5:4 to give the
second half of the chiastic lament a slightly different flavor than the first. Although death and destruction are still in focus (5:11, 13, 16-17), more attention is given to injustice and the pursuit of what is good and just. These
provide hope for the few who will respond to the challenge.[111]
     In a manner similar to 5:4-6, Amos quotes a traditional promise, "Yahweh,
God of hosts will be with us," to show that this hope is conditional on moral

---

[109]See the section on Unity.
[110]Wolff, *Amos* 250; Mays, *Amos* 100.
[111]Lust, "Redaction of Amos 5:4-6, 14-15," 137-40; W. H. Schmidt, "suchet den Herrn, so
werdet ihr Leben," *Ex Orbe Religionum I; Festschrift für Widengren,* ed. J. Bergman *et al.*
(Leiden: Brill, 1972) 127-40; C. Westermann, "Die Begriffe für Fagen und Suchen in AT," *Ke-
rygma and Dogma* 6 (1960) 2-30.

behavior. This phrase of assurance of salvation might come from holy war traditions used at the temple or is possibly from salvation oracles spoken by cultic prophets in the worship of the temple.[112] The promise of life, God's presence, and his protection (cf. 9:10) were unconditionally understood as eternal grants of divine favor which were not connected to morality.[113] Amos offers only conditional promises based on a radical change in behavior, but even then he hedges God's response with "perhaps" in 5:15. The prophet's purpose is not to deny totally the validity of all hope in God; his purpose is to explain the basis for expecting the fulfillment of their dreams. The military success of Jeroboam II and the economic prosperity of the upper class enhanced the perception that God was now giving the good life to his people. Amos explodes this deceptive idea by reminding them that the privilege of God's presence must be preceded by an acceptable relationship with God and one's fellow citizens. The elect status of Israel was not insurance against punishment (3:1-2).[114] Although Amos does not focus on punishment, it is assumed from the context. His emphasis is on the possibility of God's presence, if the right changes are made.

The search for, and commitment to a life of goodness and justice is opposite to one centered around evil. The result of the proper direction of life leads to the anticipation of life rather than death. Then "it may be" that God will be with them. A person's devotion and free choice are keys to understanding the potential of the future. Yet the future is never sure, since God is also free to deal with people according to his wisdom.[115] Nevertheless, within the boundaries of freedom, justice is a compass which points to the future and is a guide to a daily walk that avoids that disastrous day of judgment.

2. Do good, God may be gracious (5:15)

The imperatives sound the call for moral change, using hate and love as opposites. The renunciation of all desires and inclinations to be involved with evil is the high standard set by God. For Amos, proper worship at the temple is intrinsically identical with seeking Yahweh (5:4-6), and this is unified with loving good (5:14-15) and establishing justice. Loving good and hating evil are part and parcel of loving God with all your heart (Deut. 6:5). The specific identification of loving good with the concrete action of establishing justice

---

[112]Wolff, *Amos* 250; Neubauer, "Erwägungen zu Amos 5, 4-15," 295-308; Hunter, *Seek Yahweh* 82, but Lust, "Redaction of Amos 5:4-6, 14-15," 131-32, argues against Neubauer because of the work of H. D. Preuss, " '...ich will mit dir sein,' " *ZAW* 80 (1968) 139-73. Crenshaw, "Amos and the Theophanic Tradition," 207-08, connects the phrase with the protective role of the theophany in Israel's holy wars.

[113]C. J. Labuschagne, "Amos' Conception of God and the Popular Theology of his Time," *Studies on the Book of Hosea and Amos,* OTWSA 7-8 (Potchefstroom: Rege-Pers Beperk, 1965) 128-30.

[114]Raitt, "The Prophetic Summons to Repentance," 30-49, sees a covenant tradition behind the prophetic summons to repentance, and Lust, "Redaction of Amos 5:4-6, 14-15" 141, thinks the offer of life was derived from the covenant promises in Deuteronomy.

[115]Hesse, "Amos 5, 4-6.14f.," 6-7, 11-13; Mays, *Amos* 102.

connects the conditionality of 5:15 with the accusations in 5:10-13. Devotion and morality are not alternatives open to selective acceptance or rejection. To make Amos a social critic and ignore his unification of these matters with devotion to Yahweh would be senseless, for the presence of God with us is the only sure hope of establishing justice.

The "perhaps" is parallel to "it may be" in 5:14. The summons is to seek God, to hate evil, and establish justice regardless of the outcome. God may be gracious to the ones who respond, but there is no promissory note in the subjunctive tone of the result clause.[116] In spite of the unsure consequence, the need for change is pressing, and the likelihood of a major change in God's judgment is indefinite. The graciousness of God is not directed to the nation but to the remnant. Thus no hope for national resurgence is envisioned, only mercy for those few who seek God. It is assumed that only a remnant will hear the prophet's call and respond.

The remnant motif is not to be rejected as a concept inconsistent with the thought and message of Amos.[117] The faithful remnant idea is found in 1 Kings 19:18, and a remnant who escapes destruction is related to the use of this root in Genesis 45:7, Amos 1:8, and 5:3. The word does not have an eschatological meaning as in Micah 4:7 and 5:6-8; for the immediate context does not describe God's gathering of the remnant and the establishment of his kingdom.[118] Although these ideas were present in Israel and Judah at the time of Amos, and though the words of the prophet have implications for the nation's view of God's care for it on the Day of Yahweh (5:18-20), the specific concern of Amos is to exhort individuals to change their behavior instead of trusting in false promises of the presence of God with them. The remnant of Amos is not based on some ancient promise, but is a matter of the grace of God. Amos is setting down the qualifications for the remnant concept; it will not include all Israel or the ones who are faithful in temple worship, but only those who evidence a moral transformation in their lives. Thus the remnant motif is given theological significance. It is not just the group of people left after the destruction of Israel, a view which conveys more hopelessness than hope. The prophet is giving hope for the near future, explication of the basis for hope, and by implication the reason why so many will be judged.

---

[116]Wolff, *Amos* 251 has difficulty with this concept, but Mays, *Amos* 102 willingly accepts the idea that God's sovereignty includes a freedom to act in ways people do not understand.

[117]G. Hazel, *The Remnant: The History and Theology of the Remnant Idea from Genesis to Isaiah* (Berrien Spring: Andrews University, 1972) 173-215; Wolff, *Amos* 250 dates this verse after 733 and the campaigns of Tiglath-pileser III to Palestine. Many give the word an eschatological slant and credit the verse to a later editor after the time of Jeremiah. See Lust, "Redaction of Amos 5:4-6, 14-15," 134-37.

[118]Hasel, *The Remnant* 393 sees this as the first use of the term in an eschatological sense, but the absense of many of the eschatological themes in other prophets argues against this.

G. Future laments when God visits Israel (5:16-17)

1. Everywhere, they will mourn (5:16-17a)

In a new paragraph the prophet returns to the theme of lament from 5:1-3. The conclusion warns against taking the hope in 5:14-15 too optimistically. Because the nation has committed injustices (5:10-13), the nation will be punished and everyone will lament.

A vivid picture of national mourning is emphasized by the repetition of lamentation three times. He speaks of mourning, skilled mourners, and the cry of the mourner. The grief of that day will be overwhelming. Death will be everywhere and everyone will be involved. The open squares, the side streets, and the vineyards will be filled with people wailing for their loved ones.[119] The magnitude of the catastrophe stresses its effect on the whole land. The cry will be heightened by the inclusion of professional mourners (Jer. 9:17 [Heb. 9:16]).

2. God's presence will bring mourning (5:17b)

The reason why there will be death everywhere is explained cryptically in the final line, "I will pass through your midst." No intermediate army or plague is envisioned as the real cause of death. God himself will be the force which Israel will have to deal with. He will meet them (4:12) and he will judge them. The terminology is drawn from the exodus experience when God passed through the midst of Egypt (Exod. 11:4; 12:12) in a theophany of judgment.[120] This time God will not pass over Israel and deliver them, he will destroy them as he devastated the Egyptians. They will grieve like the Egyptians when God's hand of death falls upon them. The contrast between the nation's origin and establishment through God's grace in Egypt, and its end at this time, effectively communicates God's final decree. Later Amos indicates that this judgment will be God's last, for he will not pass by them again (7:8; 8:2).

Theological Development

The intention of Amos was to cause the nation to re-evaluate some of its traditional theological beliefs. His issues were not peripheral items to the faith of the people. His questions reached to the very heart of Israel's relationship to God. Amos and his audience knew that God had chosen Israel, delivered them from Egypt, and given them the land (2:9-10; 3:2). These traditions carried with them implications of a special relationship with Yahweh and special responsibilities to maintain loyalty to Yahweh. Amos had already

---

[119]Gese, "Verständnis des Amosbuches," 432-35 interprets "vineyard" as "vinedresser," while Glück, "Three Notes on the Book of Amos" 116-19, believes the word means "grave-digger," derived from the root *krh* "to dig."

[120]Crenshaw, "Amos and the Theophanic Tradition," 206-07.

predicted that the nation's unwillingness to turn to God in true worship will result in God's coming to meet the nation in judgment (4:12-13). The result of judgment will be destruction and death instead of life and God's blessed presence with them. The antithesis between life and death is developed in two rather complicated ways. One thread of thought examines life and the theological means of maintaining life. The other investigates the threat of death and the theological reason for its presence. Central to both questions is the character of God (5:8-9) and a person's relationship to him.

Life was connected to seeking Yahweh, the establishment of justice, the graciousness of God, and God's presence. Life in all its fullness was centered around Yahweh, the Creator and Lord of nature and history (5:8-9). Its potential was available for those who lived in the presence of God. The presence of God was particularily connected to the holy place in the temple, the place where the people came to seek God's forgiveness and fellowship. His presence symbolized nearness, power, protection, good welfare, and the assurance of life. His presence was an act of grace. It could not be bought by magic or bribery, and it was not an eternal possession that could be manipulated to advantage. God's presence and the life it bestowed was a blessing of the covenant relationship, not a consequence to be earned by good behavior. Purity in moral behavior and complete devotion to Yahweh in worship were synonymous with life in the presence of Yahweh. The demise of a unified understanding of a person's relationship to God's presence led Amos to dispel the popular religious voice in Israel. By disassociating God's presence and life itself from true seeking after God in worship, the establishment of justice, and the grace of God to the faithful, there arose a false religion in Israel. The summons of the prophet were warnings concerning false beliefs, exhortations to accept God's way, and challenges to commitment to the grace of God's presence.

The seriousness of the exhortations was appreciated only to the extent that the people understood why the alternative to life was death. Death is the result of the withdrawal of God's protective presence (5:14) and his passing through the midst of the nation in judgment (5:17). The freedom of God allows him to change and bring forth destruction (5:9) and break forth like an unquenchable fire upon those who refuse to seek him (5:6). When he forsakes Israel, there will be none to save her (5:2), for her army and her fortresses will be nothing (5:3). The reason for God's judgment of death and withdrawal of his presence is clearly linked to the nation's failure to seek God (5:4). The worship at Bethel, Gilgal, and Beersheba has no reality; therefore these places will be destroyed (5:5-6). When the people came to God, there was no change in their behavior. Instead of promoting justice and righteousness, these were buried, perverted, and hated (5:7, 10). The poor were treated unfairly, the courts were corrupted through bribes, and honesty was a thing abhorred (5:10-12). Because of these many sins the gains of injustice will be destroyed and the prosperous will be silenced with death (5:11, 13). A person's relationship to death was determined on the basis of one's relationship to God and the adoption of godly behavior in relationships with others. God controls both life and death.

The reality of hope in a time of severe judgment seems to create antithetical expectations. But neither result is unjust, for God sees and knows the heart of each person. National defeat and destruction are unavoidable once God forsakes the nation, but an individual response to the exhortation to seek God, establish justice, and love good, provides hope to the remnant who heed God's word. God's grace may be poured out again and life may be given, but only to those who truly seek Yahweh and live righteously. For these the praise of God will not be a threat but a joy and a strength for the disastrous days ahead.

Woe Oracle Concerning False Hopes

Introduction

Amos has just finished a lament over the death of the nation, Israel (5:1-17). The obituary reveals that the nation is in a hopeless state. Its worship is not true seeking after God (5:6), and there is no seeking after good or hatred of evil (5:14-15). This view is supported by the absence of justice and righteousness in the temple and in the way the wealthy upper class treats the poor (5:7, 10-13). Consequently, God will burst forth with judgment on the strong (5:9), eliminate the nation's powerful army (5:3), destroy the beautiful homes built by the rich through oppression (5:11), and bring such a disastrous day on the nation that there will be wailing everywhere (5:16-17). Only a small remnant may escape when God passes through the nation in power and in judgment (5:17b).

The audience response to this announcement of death was no doubt as dramatic as their response to the prophet's message of death and destruction in Amos 1-2. The prophet is crazy; these things cannot be; our theology tells us that God is for us. They felt secure in their faith, knowing God's promises were true. The prosperity and military might of Jeroboam II was only a confirmation that God was on their side. God's presence with them (5:14) was their assurance that the Day of Yahweh would be bright and glorious.

Amos attempts to deal with these false hopes in the two woe oracles of 5:18-27 and 6:1-14. Their hope in the salvation of God on the Day of the Yahweh is a false hope (5:18-20); their security in their offerings and worship in the temples is a false hope (5:21-27); and their trust in the affluence and security of Samaria is a false hope (6:1-14). Both woe oracles lament the nation's false hopes and end with a prediction of exile. With supurb rhetorical skill the prophet attacks the sacred dreams of a people who have let conservative theological tradition and affluence destroy reality.

Background

Three areas of background information significantly influence the content of 5:21-27: (1) the setting and use of woe oracles; (2) the origin and theological beliefs surrounding the Day of Yahweh idea; and (3) the nature of worship practiced in Israel. When Amos spoke, people had a general knowledge of what he was talking about; therefore it was not necessary to go into a long description of what the people expected on the Day of Yahweh. The audience was aware of the images and gods described in 5:26 and had heard woe oracles before. Unfortunately, the small amount of information on these points has caused a considerable amount of confusion on each issue.

(1) The cry of woe is clearly associated with lamentations for the dead in 1 Kings 13:30, Amos 5:16, Jer. 22:18, and 34:5. In some instances it merely serves to call people to attention (Isa. 55:1; Zech. 2:6 [Heb. 2:10]; 2:7 [Heb. 2:11]). In a few cases a woe is in contrast to a blessing, thus suggesting a blessing-curse contrast between the words (Eccl. 10:16-17; Isa. 3:10). Because of these different usages, three different settings for the woe oracle have been proposed. Westermann compared the woe oracle to the covenant curses in Deut. 27:15-26. A salvation oracle was pronounced for Israel and then a curse in the form of a woe oracle would be directed at Israel's enemies. This emphasis is particularily strong in the exilic and post-exilic usages of "woe."[1] Gerstenberger and Wolff pointed out some of the weaknesses of Westermann's view and have traced the woe oracle back to wisdom literature. They derived the saying from the "popular ethos" of clan wisdom about acceptable or "blessed" conduct and unacceptable or "woe" conduct (Eccl. 10:16-17). This proposal seems most unlikely since there is only one example of a "woe" in the wisdom literature of the Old Testament.[2] The third setting for the woe oracle is the funeral lament. Several scholars have persuasively demonstrated that the actual origin of the woe oracle was the funeral lament.[3] Janzen illustrates the use of woe statements in a context of funeral lament in the Erra Epic where Marduk laments the fall of Babylon,[4] in the Poem of the Righteous Sufferer (ANET 436), in the Prayer of the Raising of the Hand to Ishtar (ANET 384), in the Lament over the Destruction of Ur (ANET 460), the Ugaritic Tale of Aqhat (ANET 154-55) and other Akkadian, Egyptian, and Greek texts.[5] These include laments after the death of individuals, cities, or nations. Although the original setting of the woe is the funeral lament, the use of it in the prophets may move beyond that narrow context. Thus Clifford finds a change in syntax, a more bitter curse-like tone, and a closer association with the taunt in the eleven imprecations of woe in Jeremiah and Habakkuk. Some exilic texts, and particularily Zechariah 11:17, are closer to a

---

[1]Westermann, *Basic Forms of Prophetic Speech* 190-98.

[2]Wolff, *Amos* 242-42; E. Gerstenberger, "The Woe-Oracles of the Prophets," *JBL* 81 (1962) 249-63.

[3]R. J. Clifford, "The Use of *HŌY* in the Prophets," *CBQ* 28 (1966) 458-64; G. Wanke, " *'ōy* and *hôy*," *ZAW* 78 (1966) 215-18; J. Williams, "The Alas-Oracles of the Eighth Century Prophets," *HUCA* 38 (1967) 75-91; W. Janzen, *Mourning Cry and Woe Oracle* (Berlin: W. de Gruyter, 1972) 1-39; Mays, *Amos* 103.

[4]Cagni, *The Erra Epic* (Malibu: Undena, 1977) 50, translates the text, "Ah Babylon, whose top I had made as luxuriant as that of a palm tree, but which the wind has scorched; Ah Babylon that I had replenished with seed like a pine cone, but whose fulness I could not sate myself; Ah Babylon..." Woe is translated "ah."

[5]Janzen, *Mourning Cry and Woe Oracle* 6-18.

curse.[6] There is a natural, grieving movement from the lament to the desire for revenge in both biblical and non-biblical uses of woe.[7] The funeral context of Amos 5:1-3, 16-17, the use of woe in 5:16, and the pre-exilic setting of Amos argue for a funeral lament setting for the woe oracle beginning in 5:18. This also fits the negative reversal given to the Day of Yahweh concept in 5:18-20 and the prediction of exile in 5:27.

(2) The setting of the Day of Yahweh concept is equally confused, with a variety of possible options: (a) Gressmann, drawing on many of the ideas of his teacher, H. Gunkel, traces the Day of the Lord back to a common ancient Near Eastern mythical conception of cosmic and earthly catastrophies. It was common to divide history into periods, each ending with a great destruction. These eschatological ideas were connected to the movement of the sun and stars. Well before the time of the prophets, Israel borrowed these ideas and developed their own eschatological day of judgment on Israel's enemies and salvation for themselves.[8] This view is weakened because of its derivation of Israelite eschatology from a non-Israelite source.

(b) Mowinckel derives the Day of the Lord from the worship at the great autumn New Year's festival, when Yahweh was enthroned as king. From this cultic day of the Lord, an ideal eschatological day was projected into the future when God's manifestation or epiphany will bring salvation for his people. He does not see this as a borrowing of ancient Near Eastern eschatology; instead eschatology is an Israelite phenomenon.[9] Variations of this basic approach have been promoted by several critics.[10] The weakness of this theory is the hypothetical nature of Israel's celebration of a Babylonian festival, which contained mythology distinct from Israelite beliefs.

(c) A third group of scholars finds a firmer origin for the Day of the Lord in the concept of holy war. Von Rad did not base this conclusion on Amos 5:18-20, because it was too fragmentary. Instead he looked for fuller texts like Isaiah 13 and 34, Ezekiel 7 and 30, and Joel 2. These prophecies were filled with wars, the desolation of the land, and many of the other motifs connected with war. Thus he concluded that the Day of the Lord describes the sacred war of Yahweh when he gains victory over his enemies. This was an ancient Israelite tradition which was not originally eschatological but became

---

[6]Clifford, "The Use of HŌY in the Prophets " 461-63.

[7]Janzen, *Mourning Cry and Woe Oracle* 27-34.

[8]H. Gressmann, *Der Ursprung der israelitisch - jüdischen Eschatologie* (Göttingen: Vandenhoeck and Ruprecht, 1905) 141-43. C. van Leeuwen, "The Prophecy of the YŌM YHWH in Amos 5:18-20," *OTS* 19 (1974) 119, criticizes this view because not all the Day of the Lord passages are of future eschatological events, the mythical connections are most improbable, and this explanation ignores some of the historical and social conditions related to the idea.

[9]S. Mowinckel, *He that Cometh* (Oxford: Blackwell, 1959) 125.

[10]Kapelrud, *Amos* 71-75; Watts, *Amos* 68-76, 81-4; J. Morgenstern, "Amos Studies," *HUCA* 11 (1936) 124; 15 (1940) 304; J. Lindblom, *Prophecy in Ancient Israel* (Philadelphia: Fortress, 1962) 316-19; J. Gray, "The Day of Yahweh," *SEA* 39 (1974) 5-37; Clements, *Prophecy and Covenant* 107-10.

eschatological in the prophets as it was given cosmic significance. He did not see this as an idea borrowed from Israel's neighbors.[11] This approach has gained many adherents but is weakened by the critique of Weiss. He criticized von Rad because one-third of the passages about the Day of the Lord do not mention war, many passages which do describe God's war do not refer to the Day of the Lord, and the early (Amos 5:18-20; Isaiah 2) references and numerous later Day of the Lord prophecies can be better explained as developments of the theophany theme.[12]

(d) A fourth suggestion is that the Day of the Lord developed from the covenant, with blessing for Israel and curses for her enemies. Fensham and Héléwa see the Day of the Lord as a day of battle, with connection to holy war traditions. For breach of the covenant Israel will be judged, and curses will fall on the enemies of God. Curses on a day of the Lord may vary; sometimes it will be war, but at other times darkness, plagues, or some other method will produce justice.[13]

(e) A fifth view derives the Day of the Lord from the theophany of Yahweh. Černy understands the Day of the Lord in a full-blown eschatological sense when God intervenes in power. Weiss also believes the Day of the Lord is the theophany appearance of God, but he maintains that Amos introduced the term. Hoffman draws the idea from the theophany where God appears to save or judge a people. He thinks the idea existed before Amos, was not used eschatologically by Amos, but was given eschatological significance by later authors.[14] Others combine the theophany traditions with the covenantal, cultic, or holy war traditions.[15]

This later opinion seems to fit the evidence best. The Day of the Lord is always pictured as a divine appearance of God. Although that manifestation frequently is related to a holy war event where Israel or some other nation is

---

[11]G. von Rad, "The Origin of the Concept of the Day of Yahweh," *JSS* 4 (1959) 97-108; He is followed by K. D. Schunck, "Strukturlinien in der Entwicklung der Vorstellung vom 'Tag Yahwes,' " *VT* 14 (1964) 319-30; Wolff, *Amos* 34, 255; Mays, *Amos* 104; R. W. Klein, "The Day of the Lord," *CTM* 39 (1968) 517-25.

[12]M. Weiss, "The Origin of the Day of Yahweh Reconsidered," *HUCA* 37 (1966) 29-72.

[13]F. C. Fensham, "A Possible Origin of the Concept of the Day of the Lord," *Biblical Essays*, OTWSA 7-8 (Potchefstroom: Rege-Pers Beperk, 1966) 90-97; F. J. Héléwa, "L'origine du concept prophétique du 'Jour de Yahvé'," *Ephemerides Carmeliticae* 15 (1964) 3-36.

[14]L. Černy, *The Day of Yahweh and Some Relevant Problems* (Prague: Univ. Karlovy, 1948); Weiss, "Day of Yahweh Reconsidered," 29-72; Y. Hoffman, "The Day of the Lord as a Concept and a Term in the Prophetic Literature," *ZAW* 93 (1981) 37-50.

[15]Fensham, "Day of the Lord," 92 uses theophany and covenant curses; S. Mowinckel, *The Psalms in Israel's Worship* I (Nashville: Abingdon, 1962) 116 n. 35, connects theophany with the cultic enthronement of Yahweh; von Rad, "Day of Yahweh," 104 says that in its wars "Israel experienced something like a theophany, a personal entry of Yahweh." Although van Leeuwen, "The YOM YHWH in Amos 5:18-20" 127-31 tends to agree with Fensham's covenant curse idea, he concludes that the common denominator of the Day of the Lord is the theophany; Barstad, *Religious Polemics of Amos* 89-108, finds the holy war the predominant theme in the Day of the Lord, but he finds the life setting in the prophetic lament, which was probably part of a cultic event at the temple.

destroyed in battle, a number of passages, including Amos 5:18-20, make no reference to war. The term was known in pre-exilic times to Amos and his audience, but it was commonly accepted as the day of God's salvation of Israel. There is little to suggest that Amos used the Day of Yahweh in an eschatological sense. Some prophets do give a cataclysmic and universalistic application which is clearly eschatological (Isa. 34:8; 63:3; Zech. 14:1), but this kind of language is absent from Amos 5:18-20. Consequently, Amos is predicting a disastrous day of death, darkness, and mourning (5:3, 13, 16-17) when God passes through their midst (5:17) to meet them (4:12). The context of several passages (2:13-16; 3:11-15; 4:2-3; 5:3, 5-6; 5:27) suggests that war may be involved, but 5:18-20 envisaged the real cause of death, the passing of the Lord (in theophany) through their midst as at the time of the exodus (Exod. 12:12; Amos 5:17). The context of war (in 5:2-3, 5, 9, 27) is related to the Day of the Lord, but this aspect is not emphasized in 5:18-20.

(3) The third area of background assumed in these paragraphs relates to the worship described in 5:21-26. The annual pilgrimage feasts of Unleavened Bread, Weeks, and Tabernacles (Exod. 23:14-18; Lev. 23:4-44; Deut. 16:10-16), as well as the various sacrifices and songs of worship made up the rich heritage of Israel's temple traditions. These worship patterns were well established long before the time of Amos. The rejection of Israel's worship by Amos is quite parallel to Isaiah's condemnation of worship at the temple in Jerusalem (Isa. 1:10-17). This is because the prophets made a strong connection between God's demand for justice and his acceptance of worship (Micah 6:6-8; Hos. 6:6). A unique aspect in Amos' accusation is that the nation has worshiped Assyrian astral dieties. A great deal of uncertainty surrounds the text and the nature of this worship. It is clear that the people worshiped man-made images, that these gods were related to the stars, and that they were venerated as king. These practices were forbidden in the ten commandments (cf. Deut 4:15-19), for Yahweh alone was to be honored as king (Exod. 15:18; Judg. 8:23; 1 Sam. 8:7-8; 12:12; Psalm 99).[16]

Structure and Unity

Structure

The structural relationships between the clauses and parallel words are reproduced in the diagram of the text. The English outline describes the flow of thought and will be used later in the exegesis of the text.

---

[16]G. V. Smith, "The Concept of God/the gods as King in the Ancient Near East and the Bible," *Trinity Journal* 3 (1982) 18-38.

A Woe Oracle Concerning False Hopes
Amos 5:18-27

		A. Woe, the Day of Yahweh will bring no hope
Woe, those who desire the Day of Yahweh! What will the Day of Yahweh be for you? It will be darkness and not light.	**5:18**	1. Expectations concerning the Day of Yahweh 2. It will be dark, not light

For example,[a] a man will flee from a lion,
    and a bear will meet him;
or he will go[b] home
    and lean his hand against the wall,
    and a snake will bite him.
	5:19	

Surely, it will be a day of darkness, not light, and gloom with no brightness in it.	**5:20**	B. Ritualistic worship is rejected, it offers no hope
I hate, I despise[c] your festivals; I do not delight in your assemblies,	**5:21**	1. God rejects their festivals

even though you offer to me burnt offerings
      and your grain offerings,
    I will not accept them.
Your peace offerings
    from your fat calves,[d]
I will not look at them.
	5:22	2. God rejects their sacrifices

Remove from me the noise of your songs; I will not listen to the sound of your harps.	**5:23**	3. God rejects their praise
Instead, let justice flow like water and righteousness like an ever-flowing stream.	**5:24**	4. God accepts justice
		C. False worship will bring exile, not hope

Did you offer to me only sacrifices and grain offerings
    for forty years in the wilderness,
    O House of Israel?
	5:25	1. The presence of true worship

And will you now lift up Sakkuth[e] to be your king,[f]
    Kiyyun[g] to be your image,
    a star to be your god,
    that which you made for yourself?
	5:26	2. The presence of false worship

Therefore, I will exile you beyond Damascus, Says Yahweh, the God of Hosts is his name.	**5:27**	3. The result will be exile

5:19a. "Like, when, for example" at the beginning of the verse is made more hypothetical in the Old Greek by adding "if" plus a subjunctive verb, "if a man should flee."

5:19b. The Hebrew "he will go" appears to begin a second example which is not directly connected to the first example. The Old Greek translators saw them closely connected and therefore translated the verb "he ran," implying that he was escaping from the bear.

5:21c. The Old Greek adds "sacrifices" before "your festivals."

5:22d. "Fat calves" *mî rî'ēkem* was read as *mr'* "appearance" by the Greek translators.

5:26e. For "Sikkuth" the Syriac, Sym. and the Old Greek have "tent" which is merely a different vocalization of the same three radicals *skt.* Theod. has "sight, appearance" from *skh.* Acts 7:43 reproduces the Old Greek.

5:26f. Sym. and Theod. have "your king," but Syriac, Aq., the Old Greek, and Acts 7:43 read the three radicals *mlk* as a reference to the god Moloch.

5:26g. A confusion between Greek *k* and *r* led to the spelling "Raifan" in the Old Greek and Acts 7:43, but Aq. and Sym. have the *k* at the beginning of the word. The emendations of the verse are many. A recent attempt to create a poetic oracle by combining the Greek and Hebrew readings is found in C. Isbell, "Another Look at Amos 5:26," *JBL* 97 (1978) 97-99. Harper, *Amos* 130 and Rudolph, *Amos* 206-08 give extensive examples of past attempts to solve the textual problems of 5:26. The Qumran, Damascus Document 7.13-19 is closer to the Hebrew but does have some peculiarities.

The structure of this woe oracle can be identified by observing the changes in its thematic and syntactical indicators. The first paragraph has the Day of Yahweh, darkness, and no light as its key motifs. Third person verbs are predominant in 5:18-20. The limits of the second paragraph are defined by the first person verbs with a negative. Terms relating to worship tie together 5:21-24. Although 5:24 does not have any of these characteristics, it functions as a strong positive antithetical conclusion to the preceding negative statements about the nation's worship. In the final paragraph, 5:25-26 are centered around worship, while 5:27 has a final announcement of judgment. In a sense, 5:25-26 summarize 5:21-24, while 5:27 describes the darkness of 5:18-20 in very concrete terms. The common denominator between the paragraphs is the inadequacy of the nation's theological understanding. Their confidence was placed in their beliefs about the Day of Yahweh, and their hopes were based on pleasing God through their worship. The prophet reveals that their expectations concerning the Day of Yahweh and the value of their sacrifices are false. Both expectations are reversed; there will be no light; there will be no acceptance of sacrifices. The final questions focus on the inadequacy of their worship and confirm the predicted judgment (5:26-27).

The internal characteristics of the first paragraph (5:18-20) include an initial inquiry concerning "the day" and a conclusion about the nature of that "day." Both beginning and end employ the antithetical light and darkness contrast. Between these two poles are two fairly balanced examples of future events that depict this dark day. The internal characteristics of the second paragraph (5:21-24) include a series of first person singular verbs and paired nouns with pronominal suffixes ("your festivals...your assemblies"). Justice and water are the parallel themes in 5:24, but no nouns with personal pronouns are present. Therefore, its relationship to the paragraph is not as tightly developed. The third paragraph (5:25-27) is more loosely constructed. Verse 25 returns to the theme of offerings, and verse 26 has second person plural pronominal suffixes on nouns related to the issue of worship. The two verses are held together by parallel verbs that contrast their true worship in the past with their present false worship. The question form of verse 25 is also found in 26. The final verse stands by itself, being an announcement of punishment.[17] The lack of unifying connections in 5:25-27 has resulted in several proposals which raise questions about the unity of this paragraph.

Unity

Although there are a few objections to individual lines or phrases in 5:18-24, the primary difficulties in understanding the unity of this section relate to 5:25-26.[18] Some find evidence of a later deuteronomistic edition in 5:25-26 because (1) 5:25 questions the offering of sacrifices in the wilderness similar to Jeremiah 7:21-23, and (2) the astral dieties in 5:26 were probably only introduced into Israel after the Assyrian conquest of Israel in 722/21 (2 Kings 17:30-31).[19] Alternate understandings of the content of these verses relieve much of the tension. At the present time it is impossible to accurately pinpoint when Assyrian astral dieties were introduced into Israel. Amos 8:14 witnesses to the presence of other gods before the fall of Samaria. Given the problematic nature of the text and the uncertainties about the meaning of 5:25-26, the evidence pointing one way or another is not sufficient to allow very firm conclusions on these issues.

Interpretation

A. Woe, the Day of Yahweh will bring no hope (5:18-20)

1. Expectations concerning the Day of Yahweh (5:18a-b)
   This paragraph begins as a woe oracle, lamenting the false hopes placed in the nation's concept of the Day of Yahweh.[20] Following the lament in 5:1-17 and the repeated emphasis on wailing and mourning in 5:16-17, the woe ora-

---

[17]Mays, *Amos* 110 translates 5:26 as a future statement of punishment, thus connecting it with 27, Fosbrooke, *Amos* 821 connects verse 25 with 21-24 and puts 26-27 with Amos 6:1-14, since both refer to a future judgment.

[18]Harper, *Amos* 129 believes "What will the Day of Yahweh be for you?" in 5:18 is a later interpolation and Wolff, *Amos* 253 thinks "It will be darkness and not light" in 5:18 prematurely announces the conclusion in verse 20. Harper, *Amos* 129 attributes "Your peace offerings of fatted calves, I will not look at them" in 5:22 to a later hand, while Mays, *Amos* 105 and Rudolph, *Amos* 205-06 contend that a line has dropped out of 5:22.

[19]Wolff, *Amos* 264-65; Schmidt, "Redaktion des Amosbuches," 189; E. Würthwein, "Amos 5, 21-27," *Wort und Existenz. Studien zum Alten Testament* (Göttingen: Vandenhoeck and Ruprecht, 1970) 65-67; Mays, *Amos* 112-13; L. Rector, "Israel's Rejected Worship: An Exegesis of Amos 5," *Restoration Quarterly* 21 (1978) 175.

[20]The beginning of the woe oracle follows the regular pattern of woe plus a plural participle (cf. 6:1). The question form is also used in 6:2. Amos 5:20 describes judgment but is an unusual statement of punishment; consequently, 5:27 serves as a description of their punishment.

cle is a continuation of the same perceptions (see the section on Background). If the audience reacted negatively to the prophet's announcement of death and destruction (5:1-17), based on their hopes for salvation on the Day of the Lord, then this paragraph would be a direct response to such spoken or unspoken hopes. His audience is made up of some who "long for, desire, look forward to" the Day of the Lord. Their expectations are that it will be a positive day of joy and salvation (see the section on Background) with God's presence in their midst. The prophet's lament for those who desired to see the Day of the Lord must have appeared to be rather heretical. Why lament concerning this day of joy? The prophet's lament is related to the people's expectation. "What will the Day of Yahweh be for you?" This rhetorical question suggests that the answer is something other than a day of joy. The tone of lament already hints that this day will be something very different.

2. It will be dark, not light (5:18c-20)

Amos takes this well-known concept and reverses the fate of Israel; instead of salvation and light, there will be darkness and defeat. This transformation of the Day of the Lord is centered around theophany motifs, but the preceding military imagery (2:13-16; 3:1, 11-15; 4:2-3; 5:2-3, 5-6, 9, 11) and the concluding threat of exile (5:27) put that day in a context of war. Destruction and death will ultimately be caused by God's passing through their midst in judgment (5:17), but a military defeat will be only one of the ways God will accomplish this. It is not clear if the darkness is metaphorical of an evil day or if the prophet expected signs in the heavens (Joel 2:10). Amos 8:9 suggests that Amos knew about such traditions, but he does not focus on these specific manifestations of darkness in 5:18. The audience understood the traditions Amos was describing, but they expected darkness for their enemies, not for themselves.

To drive his point home, the prophet illustrates with two examples drawn from the experience of rural living (cf. 3:3-6; 6:12; 9:9). A man is fleeing from a lion and soon finds himself face to face with a bear. In the second example, a man enters the peace and safety of his home and is bitten by a snake. These folksy, proverbial sayings portray a situation where death is everywhere and inescapable. When a person thinks he has escaped and is secure, then death will strike in a most unexpected manner.[21] To emphasize the darkness of this day, the end of the paragraph (5:20) repeats the initial statement twice: it will be darkness not light, it will be darkness not light!

B. Ritualistic worship is rejected, it offers no hope (5:21-24)

1. God rejects their festivals (5:21)

A causal connection between God's rejection of the nation's worship and

---

[21]The rather allegorical interpretation of Wolff, *Amos* 256 reads too much into the imagery.

the Day of the Lord is not overtly made, although it is implied in the conclusion in 5:27. The main connection between the two paragraphs is that both describe traditions within Israel that provide false hopes for the people. They believed that their festivals, their sacrifices, and their songs of praise would be accepted by God and that he in response would pour out his blessings on the nation.

The first person verbs in verses 21-23 carry an extremely powerful renunciation of the nation's most significant expressions of love and devotion to God. In very harsh and forthright terms God announces, "I hate, I despise...I do not delight." Earlier Amos condemned those who hate the person who reproves in the gate (5:10) and calls for the nation to hate evil (5:15). God's hatred is directed against those who are boastful and do evil (Ps. 5:5 [Heb. 5:6]; 45:7 [Heb. 45:8]; Amos 6:8). This statement bristles with intense pathos because of the forcefulness and the depth of resolve behind a word like hate. To despise is equally intense, for it contains images of divine rejection and repudiation. These terms convey more than an attitude of the mind; they include activity that expresses itself in destructive ways. "I will not delight" reverses God's normally positive response to worship. The expectations of the worshiper are false, God has no pleasure in these rituals. These words are amazingly similar to Isaiah's (1:10-17), but there is no sign that these prophets have borrowed a type of priestly instruction which informed the offerer concerning the acceptance or rejection of his sacrifice. Their words arise out of their own experience with God's pathos, for they express a vehement rejection which is too intense and critical to be copied from a regular part of a worship service.[22]

God rejects all aspects of the nation's worship (cf. 4:4-5; 5:4-6). First he attacks their joyful festivals and assemblies. The festal gatherings at the annual pilgrim festivals may have included the traditional Feast of Passover and Unleavened Bread, the Feast of Weeks or Harvest, and the Feast of Booths or Ingathering.[23] First Kings 12:32-33 records the institution of a unique feast at Bethel in the eighth month, but is silent about whether the old feasts were continued or omitted. The special attention given to the Feast of Passover and Unleavened Bread by Hezekiah and Josiah (2 Chron. 30:1-3, 26; 35:16-18) suggests that the feasts were not always celebrated, even in Judah. Amos does not chide the people for not celebrating feasts; he condemns the feasts they

---

[22]The priests were given the responsibility of rejecting or accepting sacrifices (Lev. 1:3-4; 22:18-19). J. Begrich, "Die priesterliche Tora," *Gesammelte Studien zum Alten Testament* (München: Kaiser, 1964) 245-46 does derive these from the priestly instructions while E. Würthwein, "Amos 5, 21-27" 143-52, relates this negative response to the acceptance or rejection of a worshiper's petition in a lament. P. J. Budd, "Priestly Instruction in Pre-exilic Israel," *VT* 23 (1973) 1-14, would classify this as "priestly proclamation."

[23]Exod. 23:14-18; 34:22-25; Lev. 23:4-44; Deut. 16:10-16. R. de Vaux, *Ancient Israel: 2. Religious Institutions* (New York: McGraw-Hill, 1961) 484-517, surveys these and some of the other festivals in Israel.

did celebrate. The "assemblies" may represent the climactic seventh day of the Feast of Unleavened Bread (Deut. 16:8) and the eighth day of the Feast of Booths (Lev. 23:36), but it probably has a more general reference to other festive days (Isa. 1:13-14) which became more like holidays than solemn assemblies.

2. God rejects their sacrifices (5:22)

The syntax of this verse, with its initial "even though," begins a conditional sentence.[24] It responds to the natural thought that God may desire more sacrifices at the festivals. Even though some might think that new or more sacrifices might make a difference, this is not so. Three terms for sacrifices are given: the burnt offering, the grain offering, and the peace offering. The burnt offering was totally given to God (Lev. 1:9, 13, 17). The grain offering could be a comprehensive term for any offering given as a gift to God, but the listing of several different specific types of sacrifices suggests that Amos had the "grain offering" in mind. It also was a "soothing aroma to the Lord" (Lev. 2:2, 9, 12). The third sacrifice is the peace offering, the only sacrifice which the worshipers themselves were able to eat (Lev. 3; 7:11-18; 22:29-30). Consequently the well-fed cattle were brought, for this sacrifice became a great feast of meat. It also was to be a pleasing aroma to the Lord (Lev. 3:5, 16).[25]

Amos categorically announces that these sacrifices will not have their intended result. They will not be accepted; God will not even look at them. This response would be expected only when a person did not follow the sacrificial procedure (Lev. 7:18; 19:7) or when the heart of the offerer was not right with God (Ps. 51:1-19; Isa. 59:1-3). The fact that God will hide his eyes (Isa. 1:15) and will not pay attention to any of their sacrifices is evidence of how totally useless their worship was. It had no value; in fact, earlier it was called a transgression (4:4-5).

3. God rejects their praise (5:23)

The singing and music that filled the air at times of festival and at the regular services in the temples are described as noise. First Chronicles 15:16-24 and 25:1-8 trace the use of music in worship back to the time of David, and numerous psalms begin with lines like, "Sing unto the Lord a new song"

---

[24]Wolff, *Amos* 258-59 connects this clause with what precedes and reads, "I will not savor your assemblies, unless you offer me burnt offerings." Although *kî 'im* can function in this way (GKC 163c), in this case the parallelism demonstrates that this line should be connected with what follows. Mays, *Amos* 105 and Hammershaimb, *Amos* 89 think a line is missing after the first line, while Cripps, *Amos* 196 wants to drop the first line, and Harper, *Amos* 135 thinks the last line is a gloss. The text does make good sense as it stands and does not require either an addition or the omission of a line.

[25]The use of the singular *šlm* "peace offering" is found only here. For the meaning of the sacrifices see H. H. Rowley, *Worship in Ancient Israel: Its Forms and Meaning* (London: SPCK, 1967) 111-43.

(Ps. 96:1; 98:1; 149:1) or have references in their titles to musical information.[26] It is assumed that some comparable use of music developed in the temples in Israel, but very little information is actually available. The type of music, the content of the songs, and the names of the God or gods praised are undefined. The music sung and melodies produced on the harp are particularly offensive, for in this verse God commands that they should be stopped. The imperative verb "remove" indicates some urgency and an active opposition to these hollow words of praise. To emphasize how useless this music is, God promises that he will not listen to any of it.

4. God accepts justice (5:24)

A sharp contrast is developed by changing the "I will not" to a positive encouragement, "let justice flow."[27] In the preceding verses God has rejected temple worship as a means of communicating with himself. Now God opens the door for true worship in his presence. The jussive form of the verb is an admonition to change the central focus of worship from the performance of the ritual to the establishment of justice and righteousness. This need not imply that the prophet rejects all types of worship as evil or unnecessary; it merely means that justice must have its central place in the lives of all those who wish to enter God's presence. God requires just and righteous living as a prerequisite of worship (Mic. 6:6-8; Isa. 1:10-17). If their social and legal relationships to each other, and especially to the poor and weak, are not consistent with the responsibilities outlined in the law of God, they can hardly expect God's approval.

The prophet draws upon imagery from his observation of the *wadi* (stream) in the countryside to depict the amount of justice God desires to see. After a sudden thunderstorm, a flood of water comes tumbling down the hillsides of Palestine and a *wadi* is created. The stream that Amos has in mind is not the temporary *wadi* which disappears almost as soon as the rain stops. God wants righteousness and justice to flow unabated and endlessly like a mighty river. A steady and continuous outpouring of justice is the product of lives that truly desire to please and worship God.

C. False worship will bring exile, not hope (5:25-27)

This section is brought to a conclusion with the announcement of judgment

---

[26]Rowley, *Worship in Israel* 203-11; C. H. Kraeling, "Music in the Bible," *Ancient and Oriental Music* I, ed. Egon Wellesz (Oxford: Oxford University, 1957) 283-312.

[27]The contrast could be interpreted as a statement of judgment, a prediction that justice and righteousness will be established (cf. Isa. 10:22). But Amos always relates justice to human actions (5:7, 14-15), and Isaiah's similar call for justice (Isa. 1:17) is clearly a demand placed on people. Würthwein, "Amos 5, 21-27," 148-52 and Weiser, *Zwolf Kleinen Propheten* I, 173, take the verse to be a statement of judgment, while J. P. Hyatt, "The Translation and Meaning of Amos 5, 23-24," *ZAW* 68 (1956) 17-24, believes Amos is referring to God's establishment of justice when he saves Israel.

and captivity in 5:27. The way in which verses 26-27 brings the audience
from God's rejection of sacrifices to the conclusion in 27 is problematic. The
interpretations of 25 and 26 are very diverse because they contain unique
ideas in Amos. Since the text, the syntax, the meaning of words, and the
overall intention are unclear, a conclusive explanation of the meaning of these
verses is probably impossible. Nevertheless, the general argument is apparent. The nation did not please God during the wilderness by just offering sacrifices (5:25), and Israel will not please God by their present worship which
includes the honoring of other gods beside Yahweh (5:26). Since their worship is unacceptable, God will send them off into exile beyond Damascus
(5:27).

1. The presence of true worship (5:25)

Amos begins this paragraph with a question which expects a negative answer.[28] The question inquires about the acceptability of the nation's worship
during their forty-year wilderness journey. The continuity with 21-24 is apparent, but the reason for illustrating from their wilderness behavior is uncertain. Some would find a prophetic tradition here which condemns the nation
for not sacrificing in the wilderness (cf. Jer. 7:21-23).[29] Could it be that God
did not give Israel the laws concerning sacrifices during the wilderness?
Since the Pentateuch contradicts the position that God did not give the laws
concerning sacrifice in the wilderness, some feel that the issue is that the people could not offer anything because they had no cattle with them and were
not able to raise crops for grain offerings.[30] On the other hand, if the idolatry
of 5:26 is placed during the wilderness period, then one could understand
5:25 as an accusation that the sacrifices were not brought to God, but to these
other gods. The future reference of 5:26 argues against this comparison.
Thus it may be that Amos' question asks if they only brought sacrifices. The
answer is no; they also walked in righteousness, gave God their obedience
(Jer. 7:22), and worshiped God out of a heart of faith and love.[31] Amos is calling the people to remember the past and follow the example of their fathers.

2. The presence of false worship (5:26)

The parallel verbs in 5:25 and 26 draw these two verses together. The
verb at the beginning of 26 could possibly introduce: (1) a conditional sentence; (2) a past tense in contrast to verse 25 (cf. Acts 7:43); (3) a future prediction connected to verse 27; or (4) a continuation of the question in verse
25.[32] Since the deities in this verse are Assyrian astral deities, this cannot be

---

[28]GKC 150d.

[29]Mays, *Amos* 111; Wolff, *Amos* 264-65 see Amos pointing to the wilderness time as a period
of faithfulness to God, without any necessity for offering sacrifices.

[30]Hammershaimb, *Amos* 92. Exod. 24; 32; 40:29; Lev. 8; 9; 10; Numb. 7; 8; and 9 describe
offerings during this period.

[31]Harper, *Amos* 136-37; Rowley, *Worship in Israel* 41.

[32]Harper, *Amos* 137, 139 surveys the various ways the *vav* has been understood.

an accusation of worshiping these deities in the past while Israel was in the wilderness. The verb refers to incomplete action in the present or future, but since 27 clearly begins the punishment and 26 is unlike any other statement of punishment in Amos, 26 should not be joined to 27 to form a judgment oracle.[33] The false worship in 26 must describe the present iniquity of Israel at the time of Amos.[34] Amos is contrasting the true religion of the nation in the wilderness with the false worship of his day. To heighten the relationship and contrast between 25 and 26, it seems best to translate 26 as a question: "And will you now lift up Sakkuth..."

The false worship described is complicated by variant readings in the Greek and Syriac translations (see the textual notes on 5:26). The reference to a star, which is their god, and their images are undisputed references to a false worship that had some astral characteristics.[35] Since Kaiwan is an excellent parallel to the Akkadian god *Kaywānu/Kaymānu,* the name for Saturn, and Sikkut is nearly identical to Akkadian *Sakkūt* (Ninurta or Ninib), which also refers to Saturn, it appears that Amos is describing only one particular kind of false worship in Israel.[36] Second Kings 17:30-31 refers to gods made by the Babylonians who later came to Israel as Succoth-benoth and Adrammelek. Based on this pattern Amos may be referring to Sakkuth-melek, but the pronominal suffix and the frequent reference to ancient Near Eastern gods as kings argues against this. A "to be" verb may be implied between each of the nouns (see the translation).[37]

Amos is accusing the Israelites of including the worship of false gods in their services (cf. 8:14). Instead of offering a loving heart of faithful obedience like their forefathers who sacrificed in the wilderness (5:25), the present generation's heart is so perverse that sacrifices are offered to other gods (see Hosea's frequent reference to such sins). Because of this, their worship of Yahweh is hated and unacceptable. Because of this, their great hopes and expectations will be dashed to pieces.

---

[33]This interpretation, which is very common today, takes verse 26 as an ironic statement that the Jews will have to carry into captivity the gods of those who will conquer them.

[34]Wolff, *Amos* 61; Mays, *Amos* 113; Cripps, *Amos* 201 and many others make 5:26 a later Deuteronomistic addition after the exile of Israel (2 Kings 17:29-31).

[35]S. Gevirtz, "A New Look at an Old Crux: Amos 5:26," *JBL* 87 (1968) 267-76, eliminates any reference to star worship by translating *kôkab* "host," based on Arabic and his interpretation of Numb. 24:17, but this seems unlikely.

[36]Gevirtz, "Old Crux: Amos 5:26," 271-72 thinks *kiyyun* should be translated "abode," and follows the Greek in translating Sakkut as "shrine, tent." Harper, *Amos* 137 prefers "shrine" instead of Sakkuth and treats the middle of the verse as a later gloss. W. W. Hallo, "New Moons and Sabbath: A Case-study in the Contrastive Approach," *HUCA* 48 (1977) 15, translates *sikkut* as "image" and *kiyyun* as "sacrificial cake." In support of the astral identification see S. Erlandsson, "Amos 5, 25-27," *SEA* 33 (1968) 76-82; E. A. Speiser, "Notes on Amos 5:26," *BASOR* 108 (1947) 5-6; Barstad, *Religious Polemics in Amos* 118-26. Prayers to Sakkuth are found in S. Langdon, *Babylonian Liturgies* (Paris: Geuthner, 1913) 124-30.

[37]This also improves the difficult relationship between "a star (to be) your god" which should not be formed into an adjectival, "your star-god," or construct relationship, "the star of your god."

3. The results will be exile (5:27).

The statement of punishment is announced in bold and forthright terms. "I will exile you beyond Damascus" leaves no doubt about what will happen, who will bring it about, or where the nation will be exiled.[38] No wonder the prophet lamented their future. The nation would not enjoy a great future day of light, but a dark day of military defeat (5:18-20). The conclusion to the next woe oracle in 6:14 also foreshadows a similar end for Israel (cf. 6:7; 7:17; 9:4). Later records verify that the Assyrians did exile Israel beyond Damascus (2 Kings 17:23-24).

After this brief but impressive conclusion, Amos affirms the validity of his prophecy with the oath-like confirmation formula, "Says Yahweh, the God of hosts is his name." (cf. 6:8).[39] It is not a gloss from a lost hymnic doxology (cf.4:13), but this closing refrain emphatically swears that the prophet's words and the punishment he described are certain.

Theological Development

The deceptive nature of religious tradition is lamentable. When a nation's dreams are inextricably intertwined with divine promises, expectations of hope can produce a deep and rewarding source of strength, as faith wells up in the heart of those who sense the presence of God. But even faith and great hope are no assurance that God will always bring salvation in a time of need. Divine wisdom can see purpose in what lies beyond the time and understanding of mortals. God's plans may run contrary to expectations, but when unfolded, they are good because God's sovereign will is accomplished (Eccl. 3:9-14). Such events may cause sorrow temporarily, yet the eye of faith is ever focused on yet greater and ultimate expectations. In spite of these truths, the longing for the fulfillment of human hopes can twist a divine promise into a false religious tradition. Even traditions which use all the right words and are based on the power and grace of Almighty God can be perverted. When the promise of God becomes more important than the presence of God, a deceptive hope is born.

Amos addresses Israel's fundamental hope in God's grace toward them on the Day of the Lord. God chose them to be his people from all the families on the earth (3:2). He delivered Israel from the bondage of Egypt (2:10; 3:1) and gave them the land of the Amorites (2:9-10). They worshiped God with sacrifices, sang his glory and knew that God was with them (5:14). The Day

---

[38]The Damascus Document from Qumran believes God intended to save his people in the land of Damascus, while Stephen's speech in Acts 7:42-43 replaces Damascus with Babylon. Stephen's speech is closer to the Greek text, but he and the Qumran evidence reinterpret the text different from Amos. For a complete comparison between the DSS, the Massoretic text, Acts 7, and the Greek translations see J. de Waard, *A Comparative Study of the Old Testament Text in the Dead Sea Scrolls and in the New Testament* (Grand Rapids: Eerdmans, 1966) 41-47.

[39]Crenshaw, *Hymnic Affirmation* 75-79.

of the Lord was a great tradition about how God would miraculously intervene on behalf of his people when he passed through their midst. Like God's
salvation of Israel from Egypt or the day of Midian's punishment (Isa. 9:4
[Heb. 9:3]), the history of the nation's past and future could be described as a
series of divine encounters where Israel saw the light of God's salvation.
Amos concludes that these expectations are filled with false hopes. The Day
of the Lord will not bring salvation but darkness. Israel has become the enemy of God, and it will suffer under his judgment in the near future. The
mourning of the prophet gives a new orientation to the events of that disastrous day. Although the people are not without hope (9:11-15), in this section
Amos sees only the dark cloud of God's judgment.

A related but distinctive basis for hope was the worship of the nation. The
national festivals celebrated God's great deeds for the nation. They reminded
the people of God's goodness and grace. The sacrifices symbolized the principles of salvation, dedication, and fellowship with God. Through confession
and forgiveness of sins, the people were able to come and worship at the holy
place where God dwelt. They would sing his praise and enjoy his blessings as
they humbly walked before God in righteousness.

The devastating attack on the nation's worship in Amos 5:21-27 appears at
first sight to be a total rejection of the whole sacrificial system. This was once
the common understanding of the prophets. The prophets were apparently
anti-sacrifice, anti-temple, and anti-priest.[40] It was thought that the prophets
rejected everything connected to temple worship and promoted a religion of
righteousness and justice. Isaiah (1:10-17), Jeremiah (6:20; 7:21-25), Micah
(6:6-8), Hosea (6:6), and Amos (4:4-5; 5:21-27) demonstrate that God despises sacrifices and desires loyalty, justice, and faithfulness to the covenant.
Although God did totally reject the worship associated with other gods, he
did not oppose worship that was an expression of true love to God. The problem was that the people's "hands were full of blood" (Isa. 1:15); they had not
"amended their ways" and turned to God (Jer. 7:1-5); their lives were full of
injustices which were contrary to the will of God.[41] They were not seeking
God (Amos 5:6) but seeking his approval. His promises and blessings were
more important than his presence in their daily lives and worship. Because
their worship included other gods (5:26) and did not follow the pattern established by their fathers in the wilderness, God hated what they paraded as religion and would not accept it. Ritual was designed to symbolize reality, but it
can just as easily cover up the attitude that is behind a mechanical performance of a duty. When this happens, one can only lament the deceptive expectations that false hopes engender and then declare the truth with honesty.

---

[40]J. A. Brewer, *The Literature of the Old Testament in its Historical Development* (New York:
Columbia University, 1924), 267.

[41]H. H. Rowley, "Ritual and the Hebrew Prophets," *From Moses to Qumran* (New York: Association Press, 1963) 116-18.

Woe Oracle Concerning False Security

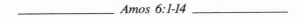

Introduction

After lamenting the death of Israel (5:1-17) and mourning the false hopes of the nation (5:18-27), Amos closes this major section of the book (3:1—6:14) with one final woe oracle. He has already condemned the people for not seeking God or justice (5:4-6, 14-15). The powerful mistreat the poor and pervert justice to establish themselves in wealthy homes (5:10-13). Nevertheless, their hopes for prosperity and power will soon be destroyed when God flashes forth in judgment against the strong (5:9). Death and destruction will be everywhere and everyone will be filled with mourning when God passes through their midst (5:16-17). In addition to the nation's death, Amos laments their false sense of hope in God's salvation on the Day of the Lord (5:18) and their sense of well-being because they have performed the required rituals within the cult (5:21-23). This mourning theme is continued in 6:1-14 where Amos laments the nation's false sense of security in their military power and wealth.

Thematic continuity within 3:1—6:14 is evident in the continued emphasis on judgment, destruction of the palace-fortresses and exile in 6:7-11, 14 (cf. 3:9-10, 14-15; 4:2-3; 5:5, 9, 11, 27), accusations against the powerful and wealthy in 6:1, 4-6 (cf. 3:15; 4:1; 5:11), and the perversion of justice in 6:12 (cf. 3:9-10; 5:7, 14-15, 24). The lament context and woe are continued in 6:1-14. This oracle is not identical to what precedes though, for there are no hopeful phrases like "seek me and live" (5:4-6, 14-15), no accusations concerning mistreatment of the poor (3:9; 4:1; 5:10-13), and no focus on worship (3:14; 4:4-5; 5:5, 21-26). Complacency and pride are the sins that have led the nation to its false sense of security. Even though the people feel that their present existence is bright and hopeful, God announces death, destruction and exile for Israel (6:7-14).

Background

Although the structure of 6:1-14 is quite different from the woe oracle in 5:18-27, both woe oracles have a background in lament.[42] A woe may mourn the death of a loved one, a city, or a nation. Amos senses the closeness of the day of calamity. Because he understands the inevitability and disastrous nature of the death (6:9-10) and destruction (6:3, 8, 11, 14) of that terrible

---

[42]For more information on the origin and setting of the woe oracle, see the Background for 5:18-27.

day, he mourns for the people he loves. The description of Israel's false security (6:1-6) has some of the characteristics of an accusation. Since 6:7 has "therefore" and an announcement of punishment, the whole section (6:1-7) mirrors the main characteristics of a prophetic judgment speech.

Within 6:4-7 the prophet describes the luxury of the wealthy who enjoy the rewards of affluence at a feast. The purpose of the feasting is not stated, but some find a religious background while others see a funeral setting for the *mirzah* "banquet" in 6:7. Once either setting is assumed, it significantly affects how one understands why Amos condemned what was happening at the banquet.

A religious or cultic setting is hinted at by the use of "large basins" (6:6), the kind that was used in sacrificial settings elsewhere (Exod. 27:3; 38:3; Numb. 4:14; 7:13; Zech. 14:20). Anointing with oil (6:6) also has Levitical connections (Exod. 30:22-33; Lev. 8:10-13). But the most important aspect is the *mirzah* "banquet." The word occurs in Elephantine, Phoenician, Nabatean, Palmyrean, Ugaritic, Rabbinic, and Greek texts as late as A.D. 400.[43] Some texts are so fragmentary that they reveal nothing, while others date much later than Amos. Thus, care must be taken in using sources from cultures and time periods very diverse from the setting of Amos. The Marseilles Tariff describes three groups which bring sacrifices: citizens, every family or clan, and every participant in a banquet (*mrzh*) for a god. A Nabatean text relating to the building of a dam mentions the "banquet of (*mrzh*) Dushara, the god of Galia."[44] Late inscriptions from Palmyra also confirm this association, while the Ugaritic texts from before the time of Amos describe both the banquet (*mrzh*) of the gods and the (*mrzh*) of men.[45] The *mrzh* had members, a leader, and a house of meeting, bu/t the bizarre sexual behavior that Pope connects to these feasts is not present in most references.[46] The practice of feasting is common throughout, and the high costs imply an upper-class setting. The *mirzah* is connected to funeral banquets in Jeremiah 16:5, which may have been the primary setting.[47] These

---

[43]See A. H. Sayce, "An Aramaic Ostracan from Elephantine," *Proceedings of the Society of Biblical Archaeology* 31 (1909) 154-55; The "Marseilles Tariff" *ANET* 502; J. Naveh, "Some Notes on Nabatean Inscriptions," *IEJ* 17 (1967) 187-89; H. Ingholt, "Un nouveau Thiase á Palmyre," *Syria* 7 (1926) 128-41; R. E. Friedman, "The *MRZH* Tablet from Ugarit," *MAARAV* 2 (1980) 187-206 and the survey of these in Barstad, *The Religious Polemics of Amos* 127-42; Rabbinic references include B. Mo'ed Qat. 28b; Ketub. 69a; Lev Rabbah, Par 5; Sifre Num. 131; Qohelet Rabbah to 7:1; Esther Rabbah to 1:2.

[44]A. Negev, "Nabatean Inscriptions," *IEJ* 13 (1963) 113-17.

[45]J. C. L. Gibson, *Canaanite Myths and Legends* (Edinburgh: T & T Clark, 1977) 39; P. D. Millar, "The *MRZH* Text," *The Claremont Ras Shamra Tablets* An Or (Rome: Pontifical Biblical Institute, 1971) 37-48.

[46]M. Pope, *Song of Songs*, AB 7 (Garden City: Doubleday, 1977) 210-29; See the criticism of Pope by J. M. Sasson, "M. H. Pope's *Song of Songs [AB. 7]*," *MAARAV* 1 (1979) 188-90.

[47]B. Porten, *Archives from Elephantine* (Berkeley: Univ. of California, 1968) 179-86; Pope, *Song of Songs* 210, 14, 19; B. Halpern, "A Landlord-Tenant Dispute at Ugarit," *MAARAV* 2 (1980) 125.

were similar to the *homotaphoi* in Greece and the *collegia funeraria* in Rome.[48] The purpose of the *mirzah* in Judah is explained in Jeremiah. He is forbidden to enter the "house of banqueting" to lament and to console those who mourn the dead because the people of his generation will die and will not be buried or lamented (Jer. 16:3-8). If a similar custom was observed in Israel, Amos is lamenting the death of the nation (Amos 6:3, 7-11, 14). In his lament he predicts an end to their "lamenting funeral banquets," which ironically do not "grieve over the ruin of Joseph" (6:6) but rejoice in their own wealth and security. The prophet's condemnation does not mention sexual perversions or the worship of other gods but focuses on the deceptive results of power and wealth.

In 6:8-14 the prophet uses an oath (6:8), some burial traditions (6:10), a proverbial saying about the absurd (6:12), and a current boast about one of Israel's recent military victories (6:13). The oath is of particular importance because it conveys to the listeners the finality of the judgment and the authority of the word of God. It expresses the assurance that God is speaking the truth. Although a curse and an oath overlap, the oath is a sworn promise usually sanctioned by God.[49] Oaths were taken very seriously and even rash statements carried obligations (Lev. 5:1-4; Judg. 11:29-39). Oaths confirmed covenants (Gen. 26:28-31), and Yahweh's fulfillment of his covenant with Israel is frequently described as the accomplishment of the oath that he swore to Abraham (Exod. 13:5; Numb. 14:16, 30; Deut. 1:8, 35). The full form of an oath may contain a conditional curse on the speaker if he does not do as he has sworn (Ruth 1:17; 1 Sam. 3:17; 2 Sam. 3:35).[50] To insure the validity of the oath, "as the Lord lives" was often added to sanction the promise. When God swears, his word is sanctioned by his own character or his own existence (Gen. 22:16; Ezek. 17:16; Amos 4:2; 6:8; 8:7). By communicating God's words of judgment in the form of an oath, Amos leaves no doubt about God's action, for his divinity and his very existence are behind what he says.

Structure and Unity

Structure

The syntactical structure of the text is displayed in the diagram of the text. The outline derived from this analysis is used to structure the exegesis of the text in the next section.

---

[48]Barstad, *Religious Polemics in Amos* 141 believes these banquets were condemned because of their connection to non-Yahwistic dieties. Gressmann's view that it was a cultic ritual to magically remove the threat of disaster runs contrary to the mood of self-confidence and security that existed in Israel.

[49]H. C. Brichto, *The Problem of "Curse" in the Hebrew Bible*, JBLMS (Philadelphia: JBL, 1963) 1-25, on the distinction between the oath and curse. Oaths in Egypt show a number of parallels in J. A. Wilson, "The Oath in Ancient Egypt," *JNES* 7 (1948) 129-56.

[50]S. H. Blank, "The Curse, the Blasphemy, the Spell, and the Oath," *HUCA* 23 (1950-51) 73-96; Crenshaw, *Hymnic Affirmation* 92-105; F. Horst, "Der Eid im Alten Testament," *EvT* 17 (1957) 370-73.

Woe Oracle Concerning False Security
Amos 6:1-14

		A. Woe, complacency brings disaster

Woe, those who are secure[a] in Zion,
    those who are carefree in Mount Samaria,
    those distinguished ones from the best of the nations,
        to whom the house of Israel comes.[b]
	6:1	1. Complacency in Samaria

Pass over to Calnah[c] and see! Go from there to Hamath the Great! Go down to Gath of the Philistines! [d]Are they better than those kingdoms, [e]or is their territory greater than your territory?	**6:2**	2. Samaria is no better than other cities
They are putting off[f] the day of disaster while you are bringing near the seat of violence.[g]	**6:3**	3. You bring disaster on yourself

		B. Woe, affluence will bring exile

(Woe) those who are lying[h] on couches of ivory,
    and those who are sprawling[i] on their beds;
    those who are eating lambs from the flock
        and calves[j] from the pen;
	6:4	1. Indulgences of the affluent

those who are singing wildly[k]
    to the sound of the lute.
They esteem themselves to be like David[l]
    on instruments of music;
	6:5	

those who are drinking from basins[m] of wine; they anoint themselves with the finest oils; but they do not grieve concerning the ruin of Joseph.	**6:6**	2. Indifference of the affluent
Therefore, they will now go into exile with the first exiles,[n] and the banquets of the sprawlers[o] will end.[p]	**6:7**	3. Exile will bring an end to affluence

		C. God's oath of destruction for pride

The Lord[q] Yahweh has sworn by himself,
    Yahweh, God of Hosts declares[r]
        [s]I abhor[t] the arrogance of Jacob,
        and I hate his fortresses;[u]
	6:8	1. Authority of the oath
		2. Oath of destruction for pride

Therefore I will deliver up the city and all its contents,
And it will be,[v]
    if ten men are left in one house,
        even they will die.
	6:9	3. An illustration of the oath's destruction

ᵛWhen their kinsman or cremator ̌ will lift them up,	6:10	
to remove the remains from the house,		
one will say to the other one		
who is in the backˣ part of the house:		
Is anyone still with you?		
And he shall answer:		
No one!		
Then he shall say:		
Silence, for it is no longer possible		
to call on the name of Yahweh.		
For truly, Yahweh is the one who commands.	6:11	4. Certainty of God's punishment
Indeed, he will smash the big house to pieces,		
and the little house to bits.		
		D. Absurd military pride will end
Do horses run on rocky cliffs?	6:12	1. Absurdities in nature, justice, and war
Or does one ploughʸ the sea with oxenᶻ?		
But you have changed justice into poison,		
the fruit of righteousness into bitterness.		
(You) are rejoicing over Lo-debar,ᵃᵃ	6:13	
(you) are saying:		
Surely, with our strength		
we have captured for ourselves Karnaim.ᵃᵃ		
For truly, I am raising up a nation against you,	6:14	2. The certainty of God's punishment
O house of Israel,		
declares Yahweh, God of Hosts,		
Indeed, they will oppress you		
from the entranceᵇᵇ of Hamath,		
unto the brook of the Arabah.		

6:1a. The Old Greek has "those who despise," which may be due to a confusion between *šnn* "secure" and *šnʾ* "hate, despise." Aq. has "those who live luxuriously" while Theod. translated this word "those who flourish," which is used to translate *šʾnn* in several other passages (Ps. 122:4; Isa. 32:9, 11; Prov. 1:32 in Sym. and Aq.).

6:1b. "The house of Israel" is made the subject of the verb in 6:2 in the Old Greek. W. Holladay, "Amos VI:1B*b*: A Suggested Solution," *VT* 22 (1972) 107-10 reads "harvest of bread" to get a parallel with "first" which he translates "firstfruits," but this is as unlikely as the emendation "and like gods they are in the house of Israel." See Wolff, *Amos* 270-71.

6:2c. Calnah is "all" in the Old Greek, a confusion of *klnh* "Calnah" and *kol* "all."

6:2d. The *h* interrogative at the beginning of the verse was understood as the article in the Old Greek.

6:2e. The last line begins with "if" in the Old Greek, but the Hebrew *ʾm* continues the question from the earlier line.

6:3f. Aq. translates the verb "those who are separating" while the Old Greek translators have "those who are approaching."

6:3g. "The seat of violence" is translated "false sabbaths" in the Old Greek because of a confusion between *šbt* "seat" and *šbt* "sabbath." To make sense out of the text they added an extra verb to give "and adopting false sabbaths."

6:4h. The Hebrew participle could refer to people lying or sleeping. The Old Greek translators chose the later.

6:4i. "Those sprawling" is "those who live luxuriously" in the Old Greek.

6:4j. The Greek translators have "sucking calves," a proper interpretation of the intent of the author, but it is not a literal translation.

6:5k. "Sing wildly" is difficult in Hebrew. The Greek translators rendered it "excel, have mastery" (some MSS) or "rattle, chatter."

6:5l. "Like David" is missing in the Old Greek, instead this line reads, "They reckon them [these pleasures] as permanent, not as fleeting." This last phrase is a confusion of "instruments of song." The confused state of the Greek text makes it impossible to use it to reconstruct the Hebrew or omit parts of it.

6:6m. The Old Greek has the people drinking "strained" wine instead of drinking from "basins, bowls" of wine.

6:7n. "With the first exiles" is translated "from the dominion of their leaders" in the Old Greek. "First" can refer to the head or leader but *gōlîm* "exiles" must have been read as *gedālîm* "great, powerful."

6:7o. The "banquets of the sprawlers" is translated the "neighing of the horses" in the Old Greek.

6:7p. At the end of the verse the Greek adds "from Ephraim," possibly to give a parallel to "of Joseph" in 6:6.

6:8q. The title "Lord" is missing from the Old Greek. The shorting of a double divine name is also found in Amos 1:8; 4:2; 5:16; 7:1, 4; 8:1, 3, 11, but it remains doubled in the Greek in 3:7, 8, 11, 13; 4:5, 13; 5:3; 8:9; 9:5, 8, 15.

6:8r. This whole line is omitted in the Old Greek, but the Vulgate and Origen include it. Wolff, *Amos* 273 moves it to the end of 6:7 to close off 6:1-7, but no textual support for this solution is available.

6:8s. The Old Greek precedes this line with "because" similar to 4:2.

6:8t. The Hebrew *mt'b* "desire" is a textual error for *mt'b* "abhor, detest." This fits the contest and matches the parallelism in 5:10. M. Dahood, "Amos 6:8: *meta'ab*," *Bib* 59 (1978): 256-66 divides the word into two words and translates, "truly, a foe" but this is an unlikely solution.

6:8u. "Fortresses" is "country, land" in the Old Greek as in 3:9, 10. See P. J. Heawood, "*'rmôn* and *'rm*," *JTS* 13 (1912): 66-73 for a full discussion of these terms.

6:10v. The Old Greek adds at the beginning of the verse, "a remnant will be left" or "their remains will be left." G. Box and W. Oesterley, "Amos 6:9 and 10," *ExpT* 12 (1900-01): 235-36 believe the Hebrew *hᵉśā'ô* was read *nš'r š'r* by the Greek translators. This phrase suggests that the bodies found in 6:10 were from the men in 6:9.

6:10w. "Corpse-burner, cremator" was translated as a verb "they shall endeavor" in the Old Greek. G. R. Driver, "Linguistic and Textual Problems: Minor Prophets II," *JTS* 39 (1938) 314-15; and most since take *s* in *msrp* as a variation of *ś*, thus giving *mśrp* "corpse-burner."

6:10x. "From the back, recesses" is made to refer to the person "put over" or in charge of the house in the Old Greek.

6:12y. For "plough" the Greek has "they will be silent." The two translations are taken from different roots of the same consonants *hrš*.

6:12z. To plough with oxen is not absurd. The cliffs could be implied from the first line, but a better solution would be to divide *babqārîm* "with oxen" into two words *bbqr ym* "with oxen the sea."

6:13aa. Lo-debar, the name of a city, means "nothing," but the Greek translates the term rather than transliterating the name of the city. The same is done with Karnaim. It is translated "horns" in the Old Greek.

6:14bb. "From the entrance" in the Old Greek is read "you shall not enter."

The structure of 6:1-14 is comparable to 5:18-27. Both begin with woe oracles (5:18-20; 6:1-7), refer to injustice (5:24; 6:12), and end with an announcement of punishment (5:27; 6:8-14).[51] Chapter 6 is divided into two

---

[51]van der Wal, "The Structure of Amos," 111 recognizes these elements but ends this section at 6:12, based on the repetition of the word "justice." This division is not convincing.

halves. The first section 6:1-7 has good parallelism, many plural participles (a characteristic of woe oracles), a consistent theme of complacency and affluence, and a concluding announcement of punishment which repeats vocabulary from 6:1, 6 (r'š "best, first, finest) and 6:4 srḥ "sprawl." This woe oracle has two paragraphs: 6:1-3 and 6:4-7.[52] The focus of the first is on complacency, while that of the second is on affluence. Each ends with a conclusion of punishment (6:3, 7) and has its own unique internal structure. Amos 6:2-3 is built around questions of comparison, while 6:4-7 contains a consistent series of plural participles.

The whole section of 6:1-14 is brought together by a common concern for the nation's false security, based on its complacency (6:1), its affluence (6:4-6), its arrogance (6:8), and its pride in military victories (6:13). In response to this false security is a consistent announcement that God will bring the nation to judgment (6:3, 7, 8-11, 14).

Unity

Although the structure of 6:1-14 presents a fairly unified whole, difficulties in understanding the historical setting and changes in literary style have raised serious questions concerning 6:2 and 6:9-10. In addition, some have objected to the references to Zion in 6:1, David in 6:5, or the placement of "Yahweh, God of host declares" in 6:8 and 6:14.[53]

Since Amos 6:1 and 4-6 contain numerous plural participles, the series of imperatives and comparative questions in 6:2 stand out as unusual in their context. This is particularily true if 6:3, which begins with a plural participle, is connected to the next paragraph. If it is concluded that Calnah, Hamath, and Gath were destroyed at this time, the date of 6:2 is later than the time of Amos and after the destruction of Hamath by Tiglath-pileser in 738 B.C.[54] Mays avoids the historical problem by taking this verse as the proud statement of the Israelite leaders (6:1) which Amos is quoting. Hammershaimb believes Amos is referring to the conquest of these cities well before the time of Amos.[55] The statement in 6:2 could also be comparing the prosperity of these cities. Once the historical problem is eased and 6:2-3 are connected, the unity of 6:1-3 becomes more apparent (see the exegesis of 6:2-3).

The secondary character of 6:9-10 is raised because these verses: (1) are prose rather than poetry; (2) interrupt the connection between verse 8 and 11; (3) are introduced by the weak connecting phrase "and it will be"; and (4) contain peculiar vocabulary and concepts not found elsewhere in Amos.[56]

---

[52]Cripps, *Amos* 205; Wolff, *Amos* 272, 275 put verses 3-7 together, but this is unacceptable.
[53]The issues related to the authenticity of individual words and phrases will be addressed in the exegesis of those verses. See Rudolph, *Amos* 214-26; Harper, *Amos* 141-52.
[54]Wolff, *Amos* 275; Harper, *Amos* 142.
[55]Mays, *Amos* 115; Hammershaimb, *Amos* 97-98.
[56]Harper, *Amos* 151; Rudolph, *Amos* 214 changes the order of the verses, giving 8, 11, 9-10.

The relationship of 6:9-10 is signaled by the "if " in 6:9. This narrative describes a hypothetical situation of the future disaster. The prophet illustrates the final disaster. Amos 6:11 is a conclusion; it returns to summarize the thoughts within 6:8. Although these verses are unique, there is nothing in the vocabulary or style which demands a later date.

Interpretation

A. Woe, complacency brings disaster (6:1-3)

1. Complacency in Samaria (6:1)

Amos begins this speech with another cry of woe. His initial outburst captures the attention of the audience and prepares them for the woe oracle that follows.[57] The disaster lamented in chapter 5 apparently had little effect on the people of Samaria. Instead of lamenting in sackcloth and ashes like the people of Nineveh (Jonah 3:5-9), instead of seeking God so that they might live (Amos 5:4-6, 14-15), the people ignored Amos because they believed that their nation was impregnable. Their optimism arose because Israel and Judah had defeated most of their enemies and were powerful nations. This led to complacency and a false sense of security in the affluent northern capital. Therefore, in this oracle Amos attempts to wake up the nation by lamenting its illusory world view.

Those who are secure and carefree include the residents of the capital city of Zion and Samaria.[58] They carelessly imagine that there are no military forces that can threaten them, no financial dangers that can deny them their affluent life, and no political enemies that can undermine their powerful political status. Since Assyria and Syria were weak, these attitudes were somewhat justified. Although the size of the northern army of Jeroboam II is unknown, it must have been somewhat comparable to the southern army of Judah which had 307,500 men (2 Chron. 26:9-16). With an army so large it is not surprising that a certain sense of power and safety developed in both Samaria and Jerusalem (Isa. 32:9-11).

The reference to Zion in this oracle against Samaria seems unusual. Some commentators emend the text to remove the reference to Zion, while others see Zion as a later addition designed to make the message of Amos applicable in Jerusalem. These objections are only necessary if Amos could not (nor ever did) refer to the southern nation during his ministry in Samaria.[59] Since

---

[57]See the introduction to the woe oracle in the section on Background for 5:18-27.

[58]The semantic field of $\check{s}$ 'nn and its root $\check{s}$ 'n (used only fifteen times) extend from the concept of being at ease because there is no danger (Job 3:18; Isa. 32:18; 33:20; Jer. 30:10; 46:27), to the idea of foolish feelings of security when there are dangers (Isa. 32:9, 11; Amos 6:1), and even to the idea of pride or arrogance (2 Kings 19:26; Isa. 37:29; Ps. 123:4). Deut. 28:52 warns against trusting in one's cities.

[59]Rudolph, Amos 214-15 reads "in the fortress" for in Zion; Wolff, Amos 270 sees this word as a later deuteronomistic addition to the text; G. Fohrer, "Zion-Jerusalem in the Old Testament,"

Amos knew the situation in Jerusalem, elsewhere condemns Judah (2:4-5), and creates a perfect poetic parallel by using Zion, the reference to Zion should not be removed too quickly.[60]

The prophet's main attack is marshaled against those "notable or distinguished ones" from the "best of the nations." They are the prominent persons in society who have achieved notoriety and status in government.[61] Their security is enhanced by the fact that they are leaders in Israel, one of the best or foremost nations of that day.[62] Their feelings of superiority were heightened because the people of Israel depended on them. The text is silent on the nature of this reliance; it does not state why the people come to them.[63] The people's action furthered the leader's perception of their importance and perverted their understanding of the real danger that awaited this nation because its confidence was not in God. Amos' description carries an ironic undercurrent, for these influential, international leaders were ignorant of the precariousness of their situation.

2. Samaria is no better than other cities (6:2)

The interpretation of this verse is complex because of textual, grammatical, structural, and historical ambiguities. The understanding of the verse depends on: (1) the pronominal suffixes used in the last line; (2) whether the h in 6:2b is an article or an interrogative particle; (3) the structural relationship between 6:2-3; and (4) the historical situation in the cities described in 6:2. The textual and grammatical problems relate to the interpretation of the last two lines in the verse. The initial h was understood to be an article rather than a question marker by the Syriac and Greek translators, but the traditional pointing of the text and the context argue for a question at the end of 6:2. Because "these kingdoms" could refer to either Zion and Samaria (6:1) or Calnah, Hamath, and Gath (6:2) and because the subject is undefined, it is possible to translate the second half of 6:2: "Are you (implied) better than these kingdoms (Calnah, etc.)," or "Are they (implied) better than these kingdoms (Zion and Samaria)." If the first option is chosen, it is necessary to switch the pronominal suffixes in the last line. Since the second option fits

---

TDNT 7, 295, believes that Samaria was the Zion of the north. This is an intriguing idea that Amos was capable of conceiving, but there is no way to support this interpretation, since it would be unique in Amos and the prophets.

[60]May, *Amos* 113-14; Harper, *Amos* 143; R. Gordis, "Composition and Structure of Amos," *HTR* 33 (1940) 244, and others keep Zion in 6:1. Jeremiah many years later condemned Jerusalem for its trust in the presence of the temple (Jeremiah 7). The plural reference to "these kingdoms" in 6:2 requires a reference to more than one nation in 6:1.

[61]*nqb* is used parallel to "chosen" (1 Chron. 16:41) and designates an individual with specific duties (Numb. 1:17; 1 Chron. 12:32), but it is not clear if they are elected or appointed officials, or how they achieved their high status.

[62]"Best, foremost" $r\ddot{e}\ddot{s}it$ functions as a superlative in this context: GKC 133g.

[63]Wolff, *Amos* 275 thinks that the people come "to them," that is the nations, not the leaders of Israel. This cannot be the intention of Amos here. Some suggest that the people came to settle court cases, to honor the wealthy, or to learn foreign customs from these influential leaders.

the order of the pronominal suffixes now in the text, this translation is preferable if it can make sense in the context.[64]

Three distinct settings are proposed for 6:2. First, Mays and Maag think 6:2 is Amos' quotations of the proud leaders of Samaria. They boastfully challenge anyone to compare their power with that of any other nation. The quotation proves Amos' point that the leaders in 6:1 are complacent and overconfident.[65] A second interpretation sees 6:2 as a warning by Amos. He challenges his audience to notice that greater nations than Samaria and Judah have been destroyed, thus their sense of security is inappropriate. This view involves switching the pronouns in the last line and dating the whole of 6:2 sometime after the destruction of Calnah by Tiglath-pileser in 738 or possibly even after Sargon II subjugated Gath and Hamath in 720 and Calnah in 711 B.C. (*ANET* 283-84).[66] A third approach takes 6:2 as an encouragement intended to raise the confidence of Israel and Judah and an exhortation for them to thank God for his grace (2:9-11; 9:7). Since Amos is condemning pride and self-confidence in 6:1, 8, this later opinion seems impossible. It is possible to interpret the verse as a quotation of the secure leaders in 6:1, even though no introduction is given, but it does not seem necessary to attribute the verse to a later disciple who added the verse after 738 or 711 B.C. A fresh look at the historical setting of these three towns suggests that Amos chose them not because they were prosperous or destroyed but because they were not secure and self-confident like Samaria.

Calnah is probably identical to Calno in Isaiah 10:9 and the Assyrian town of Kullani. It was north of Aleppo and not far from Arpad.[67] Hamath the Great was located on the river Orontes in northern Lebanon. It was on the northern border of Palestine in the time of Joshua (Numb. 13:21; 34:8), David (2 Sam. 8:9-12), Solomon (1 Kings 8:65), Jeroboam II (Amos 6:14; 2 Kings 14:25), and the ideal nation of the future (Ezek. 47:20; 48:1). The historical setting around 760 B.C. provides a clue to their use as illustrations in Amos.

The struggle for power in the ancient Near East included the major powers of Assyria, Egypt, Babylon and the Hittites as well as smaller local city-states. Assyria, Syria, Urartu, Judah, and Israel fought for control over the

---

[64]Mays, *Amos* 113 and Wolff, *Amos* 270-01 keep the Hebrew text without emendation rather than adopting the form in Nah. 3:8.

[65]Elsewhere Amos quotes his enemies in 4:1; 5:14; 6:13; 7:10, 11, 12, 14; 8:5; 9:10, but he always introduces these quotations. Mays, *Amos* 115.

[66]Wolff, *Amos* 274-75 also objects to the authenticity of 6:2 on the literary grounds that the imperatives interrupt the plural participles which are characteristic of this and other woe oracles; Hammershaimb, *Amos* 99 accepts the view that these cities are destroyed; but he places their destruction before 800 B.C. It is unlikely that any remains of these defeats would still be visible; thus this suggestion is unlikely.

[67]W. Albright, "The End of 'Kalnah in Shinar'," *JNES* 3 (1944) 254-55, distinguished the Calnah in Amos from the one in Gen. 10:10. *ANET* 282 gives a record of Tiglath-pileser's campaign against the city in 738 B.C.

Hamath area just before the time of Amos. The Assyrian king Adad-nirari III (811-783) defeated Damascus just before 800 B.C. and thus weakened Syrian power in Lebanon. Joash (2 Kings 13:22-5) and Jeroboam II were thus able to expand the borders of Israel to Hamath (2 Kings 14:25). These victories probably did not come until after 773, when pressure from Urartu required most of the Assyrian king's time (Assur-dan: 773-755). Since his reign was relatively weak and his army stayed home in 768, 764, 757, 756 B.C., Israel and Judah had an opportunity to expand. Campaigns against Hadrach in 765, 755, 754 and Arphad in 754 are recorded, but from 765 to 756 there is a lull.[68] These factors suggest that Hamath and Calnah lived in a no-man's land, not far from Arphad. These cities were within reach of Assyria, Urartu, Israel, and Syria. They were extremely insecure; they could not be careless about their defenses, for war from one of their enemies was possible at almost any time. This may be the lesson that Amos wants the leaders to learn.

Gath of the Philistines which was omitted in 1:6-8 is quite distant from Hamath and Calnah.[69] Second Kings 12:17 indicates that Gath was defeated by Hazael of Syria around 815 B.C., and 2 Chron. 26:6 records Uzziah's destruction of part of the walls of Gath during the lifetime of Amos. Unfortunately, it is impossible to date this event in relationship to Amos 6. Since Amos grouped the three towns together, one would expect the situation in Gath to be similar to the other two cities. None of them were secure and complacent, for all were vulnerable to attack and destruction.

The comparative questions at the end of 6:2 ask whether Hamath, Calnah, and Gath are better than "these kingdoms" of Judah and Israel. The obvious answer to this rhetorical question would be no. The Israelites would claim that they are better, stronger militarily, more affluent, and the leaders of nations. The parallel question compares the size of the nations. Again the Israelites would have claimed that the size of their territory was much greater than Calnah, Hamath or Gath. Their attitudes confirm that the people have become confident and lulled to sleep by their leaders.

3. You bring disaster upon yourself (6:3)

The participle at the beginning of 6:3 creates tension with the second person plural verb in the second half of the verse. Some imply a "you" subject before the initial participle to make the two lines parallel. This solution creates a paradox by having the same group of people "putting off" and "drawing near" to the day of disaster.[70] To solve this problem, it is suggested

---

[68]Helpful summaries are found in W. W. Hallo, *The Ancient Near East: A History* (New York: Harcourt, Brace, Jovanovich, 1971) 129-33; M. Haran, "The Rise and Decline of the Empire of Jeroboam Ben Joash," *VT* 16 (1966) 278-84; H. H. Hallo, "From Qarqar to Carchemish: Assyria and Israel in the Light of New Discoveries," *BAR* 2, (Garden City: Doubleday, 1964) 166-68.
[69]Rudolph, *Amos* 216 omits this line for metrical reasons, because Gath is not in 1:6-8, and because the situation in Gath is different than the other two cities. For the location of Gath see H. E. Kassis, "Gath and the Structure of 'Philistine' Society," *JBL* 84 (1965) 259-71.
[70]The *l* before day introduces the accusative: GKC 117n.

that the people *think* they are putting off the day of disaster, but really they are bringing it near. Others refer "the day of disaster" to the Assyrian threat of destruction, and the "seat of violence" to injustices the leaders of Israel carry out against the poor. On the other hand, if the contrast between Israel and the nations in 6:2 is continued in 6:3, the subject of the participle "the ones putting off" would be Calnah, Hamath, and Gath. They are putting off the day of disaster because they are not living with some false sense of security. They know they are not well off or one of the major powers; therefore they cannot afford complacency. The contrast in the second half of the verse describes the opposite tendency in Israel. By its complacency, the nation Israel is bringing near the day of violence. In response to the question in 6:2, the Israelites claimed that they were better and bigger. This comparison shows the opposite is true. Amos announces their judgment.

The "day of disaster" is probably a synonym for the Day of Yahweh (5:18-20).[71] It announces God's judgment on Samaria in a form consistent with earlier (2:13-16; 3:2, 11-15; 4:2-3; 5:2-3, 9, 11, 27) and later oracles (6:7, 8-14). The "seat of violence" is not a reference to the judgment seat in the court but a metaphor of the throne of a king who rules with violence.[72] On this interpretation, the punishment in 6:3 in some ways matches 6:7. Amos 6:2 and 3 are closely tied together, and 6:3 is not part of the next paragraph 6:4-7.[73] The topic of luxury and affluence in 6:4-7 is absent from verse 3.

B. Woe, affluence will bring exile (6:4-7)

1. Indulgences of the affluent (6:4-6b)

The picture painted in the following verses is that of a feast or banquet. Extra-biblical references and Jeremiah 16:4-9 suggest that the setting of the *mrzḥ* banquet came from funeral ceremonies where the dead were mourned and the survivors comforted. This text indicates that the callous upper-class in Samaria have turned these banquets into a sham and have ignored the death of the nation (6:6).[74] The opulence of the rich upper-class is one more reason for the nation's careless ease and false sense of security.

The people eat at their banquets while lounging on couches and beds of ivory (Ezek. 23:41; Esther 1:6). The normal practice was for people (Gen. 27:19; Judg. 19:6; Ruth 2:14; 1 Kings 13:20) as well as kings (Gen. 43:33; 1

---

[71]Mays, *Amos* 116.

[72]Cf. Ps. 74:20-21; 99:1; 122:5; Isa. 10:13. The Assyrians were well known for their inhuman violence. Ashur-nasir-apli II (883-859 B.C.) writes (*ANET*, 276): "I caught the survivors and impaled (them) on stakes in front of their towns" or Shalmaneser III (858-824): "smashed all his enemies as if (they be) earthenware . . . who shows no mercy." Wolff, *Amos* 275; Harper, *Amos* 146 believe the violence is injustice in Israel.

[73]Rudolph, *Amos* 218 follows this structure, but Wolff, *Amos* 275 makes 6:3-7 a unit.

[74]See the section on Background where the *marzah* banquet is discussed. One wonders if woe oracles were part of the original ceremony at these banquets.

Sam. 20:5, 24; Ezek. 44:3) to sit to eat. The practice of lying on couches was followed in the Persian court (Esther 1:3-8; 7:8) and has negative connotations in Ezekiel 23:40-42. Although this custom was not uncommon in New Testament times (Matt. 9:10; 26:7), in the Old Testament it was probably borrowed by the upper-class from foreign practices. The negative tone in Amos is heightened by the presence of ivory inlays in the frames of these couches.[75] This expensive commodity was a barometer of wealth and prestige, a result of conquests and abusive treatment of the poor, and one of the signs of security.

The behavior of the participants who reclined to dine appears to be somewhat immodest. Their "sprawling" is suggestive of rather undisciplined relaxation which may be a combination of immodesty, extravagance, and intoxication (6:6). This rather provocative display conveyed the attitude that they did not have a care in the world or any inhibition in their lifestyle.

The last two parallel lines in 6:4 describe the sumptuous menu at these banquets. Fresh tender beef and lamb were the diet of the rich. The young lambs were carefully selected from the flock on the basis of fatness and age.[76] The calves were pen-fattened animals (cf. 1 Sam. 28:24; Jer. 46:20-21), not the old tough bony carcasses which had to make do with minimal amounts of grass. The philosophy of eat, drink, and be merry was practiced to the point of hedonism. In the eyes of a shepherd, this kind of waste was shocking and inexcusable.

Amos 6:5 describes the music provided at these banquets. The meaning of the roots *prṭ*, sometimes translated "improvise," and *ḥšb*, which some translate "invent," obscure the understanding of the text. Solutions to these problems are available from comparative Semitic lexicography, textual emendation, or a meaning extrapolated from Leviticus 19:10.[77] Since David is not known as an inventor of musical instruments, *ḥšb* must mean "to think, esteem, reckon" instead of "invent, plan." The last line describes how some "esteem themselves to be like David on instruments of music."[78] In this

---

[75]See the picture of King Ashurbanipal banqueting on his royal couch with ivory inlays in *TANE* fig. 122. Various annals refer to beds of ivory: Ashurbanipal II lists tribute from a Hittite king, "beds of boxwood, astic-chairs, tables of boxwood, (all) inlaid with ivory" (*ANET* 288). The banquet of Ashur-nasir-apli II (883-59 B.C.) describes the elaborate palace, splendid furniture, large amount of meat and wine and lists a total of 69,574 guests who came and were bathed with oil (*ANET* 558-60). The gods at Ugarit also enjoyed gorgeous couches, furniture, music, enormous amounts of wine, and the fattest small cattle (*ANET* 132, 136).

[76]Lamb *kr* is used nine times, and in four of these it is associated with ideas of fatness (Deut. 32:14; 1 Sam. 15:9; Isa. 34:6; Ezek. 39:18).

[77]Driver, *Amos* 241, uses the Arabic root "to exceed the bounds, act extravagantly, be immoderate, improvise." A textual emendation, changing *prṭ* to *ptr* "to set free, to let loose," could be explained as a scribal error of metathesis. Rashi and Ibn Ezra use Lev. 19:10 and conclude that this root describes how a singer divides his words in unusual ways to fit the music. S. Daiches, "Amos VI:5," *ExpT* (1914-15) 521-22; J. A. Montgomery, "Notes from the Samaritan," *JBL* 25 (1906) 49-54, found *prṭ* as a synonym for "sing" in a Samaritan hymn.

[78]Similar usages are found in Job 18:3, "Why are we esteemed as beasts?" or 41:29 [Heb. 41:21], "Clubs are thought of as stubble."

regard they reveal their pride, for David had great musical abilities (1 Sam. 16:16, 23).[79] The comparison is to David's ability, not the type of music he played. Irony is evident because David was a godly man whose musical ability was used to glorify God; these feasts glorified mortal achievements. The root *prt* must describe some type of "wild singing" to the sound of the lute.[80]

In 6:6 the final evidence of affluence at these banquets is their drinking, and use of expensive oils. The use of wine is not unusual, but the large basins used for the wine points toward excessive intemperance. The *mzrq* "bowl, basin" was a large wide-mouthed container, similar to those used in the temple (1 Kings 7:40; Exod. 24:6, 8; 38:3), rather than a dainty goblet. The more the behavior of the wealthy on their couches became extreme, the more they filled themselves with wine.

It was not uncommon for people to rub oil into their skin after bathing (Ruth 3:3). Olive oil was used for this purpose and to give a pleasant fragrance (Deut. 28:40; Song of Sol. 1:3; 4:10). The oil used at these banquets was the finest and most expensive oil one could buy. It is another example of their self-centered philosophy of pleasure at any cost.

2. Indifference of the affluent (6:6b)

At the end of this long description of the banquet of the wealthy, Amos defines what they do not do. This line serves as a transition to the announcement of judgment in 6:7. Since the leaders were not worried about the security of the nation, they did not grieve at their funeral banquets. They were not upset or sick about the destruction of their people. They had no pain because they enjoyed the best that life could offer. With money and power they had everything they wanted and did not care about others or the future. In contrast to their complacency is the true status of the house of Joseph. It is sick, wounded, and soon to be ruined. The nation is not as powerful and impregnable as the upper-class supposes. The "ruin" does not refer to the social and religious depravity that is rampant within Israel (2:6-8; 3:9-10; 4:1; 5:10-13, 21-27) but to the imminent destruction which threatens Samaria.[81]

3. Exile will bring an end to affluence (6:7)

The announcement of punishment is short and interrelated to the vocabulary of 1-3 and 4-6. The author's rhetorical skill is demonstrated by the repetition of the root "best, finest, first" from 6:1, 6, and *srh* "sprawl" from 6:4. The sarcastic twists of words and use of alliteration (the *sr* sounds) function

---

[79]Several believe "like David" is a post-exilic addition, or due to a corrupt text. See Rudolph, *Amos* 217.
[80]Wolff, *Amos* 276 translates the root "howl," an appropriate description of their wild singing.
[81]Wolff, *Amos* 277 believes this line was added by a disciple after the nation was ruined by the Assyrians during the Syro-Ephramite war 734-33 B.C. Mays, *Amos* 117 points to the violent oppression of the poor, while Hammershaimb, *Amos* 101-02 regards the division of the kingdom after the death of Solomon as the national catastrophe that the prophet is describing.

to drive the point home. The first people will be the first exiles; the sprawlers will spend their days in captivity. The place of exile is not defined, but 5:27 points beyond Damascus. The leaders will receive royal treatment as they march in shame at the head of the line of exiles. When the Babylonians conquered Jerusalem many years later (2 Kings 24:14-16), they too were particularly concerned with exiling the leading officials and skilled craftsmen.

The party is over for the wealthy upper class. The luxury of the leaders who over-indulged will end. Their perverted funeral banquets will be a thing of the past. No one will mourn their death, for they did not mourn the death of their nation. The funeral banquet (*mirzaḥ:* see the section on Background) did not remind those feasting that their days were numbered or that a house of mourning sometimes brings more wisdom than a house of feasting (Eccl. 7:2-4). The prosperity, power, and security of the leaders of Israel filled the palace-fortresses with revelry, but this deceptive façade will be unmasked when the ruin of Joseph brings these banquets to an end.

C. God's oath of destruction for pride (6:8-11)

1. Authority of the oath (6:8a)

Amos begins this paragraph by announcing an oath and the authority behind the oath. The oath is similar to God's irrevocable decision in the oracles against the foreign nations and the sworn oath of punishment in 4:2. An oath confirms that a final decision has been made and a total commitment to a course of action is being undertaken. A sworn promise sanctioned by God binds his action to the terms of the agreement. Faithfulness to the oath is required. By using this device, God binds himself in the most solemn way possible. He must now act in accordance with the content of the decree. In past times God swore he would give a blessing. Now God turns the warning of exile in 6:7 into an unalterable statement of fact. This oath reveals the tragedy of receiving the wrath of God.

The source of the oath is God himself and he is the authority behind the oath. The oath is based "on his life, on himself " for there is no higher power; there is no other power to assure the oath is carried out. His divinity, his life, his character are staked on his solemn decision to accomplish his will. The dual reference to Yahweh as the source of the oath strengthens the rhetorical force of the statement; there is no need to remove one as a redundant addition.[82] The second reference to God introduces the speaker as in messenger speeches.[83] The title, "Yahweh, God of hosts" emphasizes the power of the divine warrior to bring this judgment upon the nation.[84]

---

[82]See the textual note. Rudolph, *Amos* 215 puts the second line at the end of 6:7, following J. Weingreen, "Rabbinic-type Glosses in the Old Testament," *JSS* 2 (1957) 162.

[83]In Jacob's instruction to his servants he uses the messenger formula: He also commanded them saying, "Thus you shall say to Esau, 'Thus says your servant Jacob' " (Gen. 32:4).

[84]This title in various forms is found nine times in Amos (3:13; 4:13; 5:14, 15, 16, 27; 6:8,

2. The oath of destruction for pride (6:8b)

The enemies of God receive this oath because of their sinful arrogance. The strong palace-fortresses are the concrete symbols of the status and life-style of the powerful and wealthy.[85] The nation's pride in the majesty of God (8:7) has been replaced by a complacent arrogance based on security and riches. Although the location of the fortresses is left unnamed, the city of Samaria is probably intended (6:1).

God's response to their pride is stated in strong terms filled with the agony of pathos. God loathes, detests, abhors, and hates this kind of attitude. To loathe or abhor expresses a deep repulsion felt toward something that is abominable.[86] The worship of other gods is an abomination (Deut. 7:25-26), and pride is equally abhorrent. God detests the palace-fortresses because the people trust in them and center their life around the luxury and violence within them (Amos 2:6-8; 3:9-10; 4:1; 5:10-13; 6:1-7). God is no longer the sovereign power that controls their personal or national life. The mighty fortress is their god. Its security and power make God's protection and blessing irrelevant crutches in the real world of economic and political influence.

The result of this oath involves the removal of the objects God abhors. Their cities and all the proud people within them will be "delivered up" to the enemy (cf. 3:11-12; 5:27; 6:14; 7:17).[87] Their riches, beds of ivory, lavish parties, secure palaces, and the people themselves will bear the brunt of the destructive power of God.

3. An illustration of the oath's destruction (6:9-10)

These verses are set off as an illustration by the hypothetical (marked by "if") nature of the situation. The clauses and more prose-like structure are distinct when compared to the first person oath in 6:8.[88] These differences are literary clues which signal the presence of the illustration, but their theology and themes of death and destruction fit the context of 6:8 and 11.

The illustration is a bird's-eye view of the extent of destruction brought about by God's oath. The introductory "and it will be" orients the reader to a future scene of disaster. The setting seems to be built on the assumed destruc-

---

14; 9:5). Wolff, *Amos* 287-88 believes the title is secondary since it is not used frequently until the book of Jeremiah. The connection of "Yahweh of hosts" with the ark traditions (1 Sam. 1:3, 11; 4:4; 15:2; 17:45; 2 Sam. 6:2, 18; 7:8, 26, 27) and holy war before the time of Amos provides a possible source for the traditions that Amos used. The temptation to harmonize or constrain prophetic individuality by attributing unique characteristics to later redactors must be avoided. If this was a redactional addition, greater regularity in the formulation of the title might be expected.

[85]The prophets condemned people for having pride in secular power, wealth, armies, and buildings: Isa. 2:7-11; 13:11; 16:6; Nah. 2:3; Jer. 13:9; Ezek. 16:49, 56; 32:12.

[86]See the textual notes.

[87]*sgr* means "to shut up, enclose, imprison." The causative stem can mean "to deliver" (Deut. 23:15 [Heb 23:16]; 1 Sam. 23:11).

[88]See the section on Unity. Some see 6:9-10 as a later addition to the text of Amos.

tion of "the city and all it contains" in 6:8. The date is unknown, and the cause is left unspecified. God is the ultimate cause, but military defeat (2:13-16; 3:11-15; 4:2-3; 6:7) and a plague may be the means God uses. The conditional sentence is capable of fulfillment in the present or future.[89] If perchance men should be left after the war and if there were as many as ten left in one house, they would all die. The example is unusual because it would be unlikely that ten would be left in a house, if several others had died. It is possible that Amos had in mind a large palatial home where an extended family lived. The wealthy may have used their wealth and influence to keep their sons out of battle in order to avert the tragedies of war. All such efforts are put into the perspective of God's uncompromising statement of judgment: "even they will die." To clarify this illustration the Greek translation adds between verses 9 and 10, "and their remains will be left"; these are the remains found in 6:10 (see the textual note).

The graphic scene in 6:10 describes what will be found when relatives come to see if anyone has survived God's judgment. Although the initial verb "lift up" is singular, it appears that two people, rather than one, come to the house to find out if there are any survivors.[90] These individuals are a kinsman or uncle of the dead men and a corpse-burner.[91] Since Israelites did not usually burn their dead (except criminals: Lev. 20:14; 21:9; Josh. 7:15, 25), some have suggested that this person was responsible for burning spices at the grave (Jer. 34:5; 2 Chron. 16:14). Driver connects the word with "anointing" for purposes of embalming, but it appears that the plague was so severe that the normal method of burial was impossible, and cremation was required.[92]

Upon coming to the house, the immediate reaction of the kinsman is to remove the dead bodies and see if anyone is still alive. Each room, from front to back, is searched. During this investigation the two men who have come to care for the dead inquire of one another concerning any survivors.[93] The question, "Is anyone still with you?" is a circumlocution for, "Is anyone alive?" and it is met with the simple and solemn response, "No one." The tragedy is too great for words to describe; the sense of shock and disbelief are rhetorically communicated by the terseness of the conversation. The call for

---

[89]GKC 112ff, 159b, s describe the nature of this conditional sentence.

[90]GKC 146f indicates that the verb may agree in gender and number with the nearest subject in sentences that have compound subjects.

[91]The pronominal suffix on these two nouns is singular, since the ten who have died are treated as one unit: GKC 145m. See the textual note on "cremator."

[92]G. R. Driver, "A Hebrew Burial Custom," *ZAW* 66 (1954) 314-15. G. W. Alstrom, "King Josiash and the *DWD* of Amos vi.10," *JSS* 26 (1981) 7-9, believes it is not a kinsman *dôr* who will bring out the bones but a Davidite *dwd*, Josiah. The ten men in 6:9 represent the ten tribes, and Josiah uncovered their bones and burned them in 2 Kings 23:15-20 about one hundred years after Amos. This interpretation is less convincing than the traditional view.

[93]In light of verse 9 it is improper to hypothesize that a survivor is speaking in 6:10. See Harper, *Amos* 154.

silence at the end of the verse is explained in the subordinate clause that follows. Some translate the verb modally and make the explanation a warning: "One must not mention the name of Yahweh."[94] Wolff sees undertones of a magical fear that speaking of the name of Yahweh may cause the curse of death to return.[95] A better setting is the silence that accompanies the grief of removing the many corpses, as in Amos 8:3. If the modal sense is that of possibility, silence would be appropriate because "it is no longer possible to call on the name of Yahweh" to save the lives of anyone.[96] When one says to the other that it is no longer possible to pray, he means that all are dead, and it will no longer do any good to invoke God for mercy and deliverance. Similarly, David ceased weeping and praying after the death of his son, because at that point there was no hope that God would save the boy (2 Sam. 12:16-23).

4. The certainty of God's punishment (6:11)

The initial *kî hinnēh* "For behold, For truly" connects the illustration in 6:9-10 with the authority that will carry out the judgment; it focuses attention on the certainty of God's command. Wolff appropriately translates the phrase "Indeed (it shall be) so," for this concluding statement confirms that it is the power of God that will bring destruction.[97] This introductory phrase in 11 and 14 sets the verses apart as concluding statements which emphasize the certainty of God's action and his oath (in 6:8).

The subject of the verb "smite, smash in pieces" and its connection to what precedes is unclear. If "the houses" are the subject, and the verb has a logical connection to what precedes, the translation might be: "the houses will be smashed to pieces."[98] But in this case it seems best to make the verb parallel to the first clause and have God as the subject: "Indeed, he will smash to pieces."[99] This translation focuses attention on the action of God in short, pointed, declarative statements.

The action of God will fulfill the oath of 6:8. He will destroy the city and all it contains by reducing to one large pile of rubble the great palace-fortresses (3:15) as well as the small homes of the poor. The totality of the effect might suggest a strong earthquake (8:8; 9:1), but the method God will use is not stated. The result of God's oath and command will destroy the pride of Samaria (6:8) and reveal the powerful wrath of God.

---

[94]Mays, *Amos* 118-20; Wolff, *Amos* 280, 283.

[95]Wolff, *Amos* 283. In other contexts silence is the human response to a theophany of God (Zeph. 1:7; Hab. 2:20).

[96]The use of the infinitive construct in the sense of obligation, permission, prohibition, or possibility is discussed in GKC 114*l*. Compare Josh. 17:12, "It was not possible for the sons of Manasseh to take possession of these cities." See also Judg. 1:19; Ps. 40:5 [Heb 40:6]; Eccl. 3:14; 1 Chron. 15:2; 2 Chron. 26:18.

[97]Wolff, *Amos* 280.

[98]GKC 112m, x, aa. See also 1 Sam. 2:31, "Behold the days are coming *that* I will cut off."

[99]May, *Amos* 119.

D. Absurd military pride will end (6:12-14)

1. Absurdities in nature, justice, and war (6:12-13)

The final paragraph continues the prophet's discussion of Samaria's pride and God's coming judgment. The paragraph is complex, with rhetorical questions similar to Amos 3:3-8 (6:12a), an accusation (6:12b), a quotation of the foolish pride of Samaria (6:13), and a concluding prediction of exile (6:14). Three absurdities are described in 12-13 to demonstrate the foolishness of Samaria's injustice and pride. Although the participles in 6:13 are without a subject, it may be supplied from the second person verb in 6:12.[100]

The two rhetorical questions from the agricultural world set the stage for the accusations in 12b and 13. Even a fool knows that you do not run a horse on cliffs or rocky ground, for the horse's ability to run would be minimal, and the chances of a broken leg would be nearly certain. Such action would be absurd and unthinkable. By asking an obvious question, the prophet gets the listener to label certain acts absurd; thus it will be more difficult for the audience to ignore the absurdity of its own action. The second question is equally absurd. Only a lunatic would plow the sea with oxen (see the textual notes).[101] The salt would prohibit the growth of crops and the action of the waves would soon erase the effects of the plow. A farmer who tried this would be laughed to shame and called insane. Surely a smile must have passed over the face of the listeners as they thought of how stupid these ideas were. These illustrations of absurdities set the stage for even greater absurdities sanctioned by the people of Samaria.

The second half of 6:12 accuses the Israelites of an absurd response to justice. By changing justice into poison and by transforming the pure fruit of righteousness into something vile or bitter, the people have behaved as strangely as the farmer who plows in the sea. The type of injustice is not identified, but elsewhere Amos uses these terms in reference to social and legal mistreatment of the poor (5:10-15) and in the context of worship at the temple (5:21-24). The concepts should be understood broadly as applying to all areas of life. The people are not doing the will of God, living according to the standards of the law, or demonstrating actions consistent with a pure life with God. What should epitomize the life of a faithful man of God has turned into poison, the root of death.[102] This insanity is absurd.

The final absurdity revolves around the nation's pride in its military accomplishments (6:13). Although the grammatical and thematic connections be-

---

[100]A "woe" should not be inserted at the beginning of 6:13 as Rudolph, *Amos* 225.

[101]Szabo, "Textual Problems in Amos and Hosea," 506-07, hypothesizes an error of metathesis and reads, "Does one plough among tombs." See also M. Dahood, "Can One Plough Without Oxen? (Amos 6:12). A Study of *ba-* and *'al*," *The Bible World: Essays in Honour of C. H. Gordon*, ed. G. Rendsburg, *et al.* (New York: KTAV, 1980) 13-23.

[102]*r'š*, "poison" may be a conscious play on *r'š* in 6:1, 6, 7. Isa. 5:20 describes similar perversion in Judah.

tween 12 and 13 are not very apparent, the two indefinite plural participles in 6:13 ("rejoicing, saying") can be tied to 6:12 by deriving their subjects from the second person verb in the preceding clause. On this understanding, 6:13 continues the accusation of absurdity from 6:12. The reason why their military pride is so ridiculous is hidden in the names of the cities they have defeated. The people boast and rejoice over the army's victory at Lo-debar, but if Lo-debar is translated, the name of the town means "no-thing." A second pun is made of the name of the city Karnaim. It means "horn, might"; thus Amos is quoting them to say: "Surely, with our own strength we have captured might (Karnaim) for ourselves." By their singing and arrogant boasting they are making fools of themselves, for it is really "no-thing" at all. Although the army of Jeroboam II may have conquered these cities, Amos understands these victories at war as insignificant. Some suggest that these victories were mostly propaganda to encourage the people, for 1:3 and 4:10 indicate some setbacks in the nation's war efforts.[103] There may be some truth to this suggestion, but the condemnation of Amos is not merely a stab at overzealous nationalism. Lo-debar was a city in the Transjordan area near Mahanaim (Josh. 13:26) just north of the Jabbok River, and Karnaim was also in the Transjordan near the Yarmuk River (1 Macc. 5:26; Gen. 14:5).[104]

These victories imply a situation after Amos 1:3-5 when God's judgment against the territory of Syria was partially fulfilled. With Syria weak, Assyria occupied heavily with Urartu to the north, Jeroboam II was able to gain a position of dominance. Amos' sarcasm transforms these victories into absurd boasts. Israel does nothing in its own strength. Yahweh, the God of hosts, the divine warrior is in charge of all battles. No one prevails in battle unless God gives their enemies into their hands. The Israelites are claiming for themselves the power of God. No wonder God detests their arrogance; no wonder their boasting is absurd.

2. The certainty of God's punishment (6:14)

This final statement of punishment begins like 6:11, for both emphasize the certainty of God's action. The trustworthiness of the prediction is enhanced by the claim to divine authority. No hope is present. God has already chosen another nation and he will bless them with victories over Israel. The nation is not named, but the reference to "beyond Damascus" in 5:27 provides a hint. The nation that comes is not one which raises itself to strength but one which God purposely raises to power.[105]

---

[103]S. Cohen, "The Political Background of the Words of Amos," *HUCA* 36 (1965) 153-60 and A Soggin, "Amos 6:13-14 and 1:3 auf dem Hintergrund der Beziehungen Zwichen Israel und Damascus in 9, und 8. Jahrehundret," *Near Eastern Studies in Honor of W. F. Albright*, ed. H. Goedicke (Baltimore: Johns Hopkins, 1971) 433-41.

[104]Although Karnaim could refer to the Assyrian province of Qarnini, it seems to be a city here.

[105]The participle *mēqîm* "am raising up" represents uninterrupted activity of God in present time. GKC 116a, n.

The oath in 6:8 relates punishment to a city and its contents, but this statement of punishment extends the judgment to include all cities, all houses, and all people in the nation. With the reference to the northern tip (Hamath) and the southern tip (the brook of the Arabah), the oppression is broadened to cover the whole territory controlled by Jeroboam II. The exact limits of the holdings of Israel are not known since the name of the brook in the Arabah is not given. It probably refers to some brook at the north end of the Dead Sea, which functioned as a border between Israel and Judah. The great boasts, the security, and the wealth of Samaria will soon be removed when God afflicts the whole land and humbles the nation with defeat; what God had promised through Jonah (2 Kings 14:25) is now taken away because the Israelites did not recognize God as their source or security and the author of their victories.

Theological Development

The deception outlined in this woe is not based on religious traditions which Israel perverted (cf. 5:18-27). In this lament Amos describes false hopes based on the nation's estimation of their own political security and status, their affluence, their pride, and their military victories. Success in each of these areas produced a false sense of security based on human accomplishments. The promises of God and the protection of God were no longer necessary, because the people saw that they were bigger and better than any other nation around them. As long as they had the money to maintain their lifestyle, they could be happy. As long as they could live peacefully and at ease in their secure palace-fortresses, they were sufficiently insulated from the world of reality around them. They believed they were the leaders of the most powerful nation in the world and had a strong army to protect them. This humanistic tendency to idealize one's ability to determine the future purely through the manipulation of human forces within the economic and political structures of society is an illusion which Amos laments. Samaria's trust *bṭḥ* (6:1) was not in God; thus it was a careless and empty security that they enjoyed.

The traditions on which Amos depends are paralleled elsewhere in Scripture. Deuteronomy 28:52 warns against trusting in the security of the walls of a city. The Psalms call upon the king and the nation to trust in God rather than the horse and bow (Ps. 20:7; 33:16-17; 44:6 [Heb 44:7]) or wealth (Ps. 49:6 [Heb. 49:7]; 52:7 [52:9]). From the exodus experience (Exod. 3:8; 6:6; 14:13-14), the conquest (Deut. 7:1-2; Josh. 3:10), Gideon's defeat of the Midianites with three hundred men (Judg. 7:22), and David's defeat of Goliath (1 Sam. 17:45), God taught that victory in war and security in the land were gifts of God not dependent on the strength of men. Later Jeremiah warns Judah not to boast in wealth, might or wisdom, but to boast in their knowledge of God (Jer. 9:23-24; 17:5-8). Pride and boasting are the reasons why God judged Babylon (Isa. 13:11; 14:4-21), Moab (Isa. 16:6), Tyre (Isa. 23:8-9), Assyria (Isa. 10:4-16), and the daughters of Jerusalem (Isa. 3:16-4:1). Pride is repeatedly condemned in Daniel (5:29-37; 5:17-24), Obadiah (verse 3), Zephaniah (2:8-10), and Jeremiah (48:29-30). Abundant food, affluence, and careless ease brought condemnation on Sodom, but Samaria and Judah followed in their ways (Ezek. 16:47-51). Ezekiel seems to relate these values to learning the ways of the Assyrians (23:5, 9, 12, 23) and the Babylonians (23:14-17, 23), who loved feasts on couches with plenty of wine and oil. The high fashion in Jerusalem (Isa. 3:16-24) and their security and ease (32:9-13) are a further testimony of the influence of other cultures on God's people. They too desired to determine their own future with their own power. Amos laments the human tendency of people in all cultures to usurp God's control of history. He hates those who take the benefits of power from others to further the personal affluence and ease of their own situation.

This trend is also lamentable because it ignores the plight of the weak and poor. God will surely bring ruin upon a people preoccupied with self and a life of ease. Amos mourns over their careless security because they are bringing near their own judgment (6:3). Their affluence causes them to forget about judgment; thus exile will be all the more tragic (6:4-7). Pride and trust in their palace-fortresses will result in an unbelievable plague of death and the destruction in the nation's proud cities and homes (6:8-11). Boasts of great military victories will seem empty and meaningless when God brings a strong nation against his people to remove their military strength (6:12-14). The reality of the future punishment makes the pride and security of Israel absurd. Israel's action is absurd because it has left God out of its life and ignored his demands for justice and righteousness.

PART THREE
VISIONS AND EXHORTATIONS OF THE END

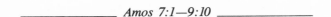

Amos 7:1—9:10

A new direction is signaled by the introductory clause, "Thus the Lord Yahweh showed me" (7:1). It is also repeated at the beginning of the second, third, and fourth visions (7:4, 7; 8:1). The final vision in 9:1 uses the same root verb *r'h* "to see, show," but the formula is altered. The first person dialogue sets the visions apart from what precedes. This section could include all of chapter 9 if the final paragraph of the book is understood to be a bright vision of the future. But the last few verses in chapter 9 are not introduced by the vision formula, run contrary to the judgment themes in the visions, are not a dialogue, and give no symbolic revelation. Although some make a break just after the hymn of praise in 9:5-6, a more natural division between the visions and the final section of the book comes after 9:10.[1] The hymn in 9:5-6 does not mark the thematic movement from the visionary messages of total judgment to the final emphasis on the eventual restoration of the Davidic kingdom (9:11-15). The hymn is in the center of 9:1-10, much like the hymn in 5:8-9 is in the center of 5:1-17.

The unity within 7:1—9:10 is strengthened by the regular structure of the five visions, the use of "my people" only after 7:1, the first-person accounts (even 7:10-17) that record Amos' experiences, and the common themes of desolation, exile, and the end of the land, its priest, its king, and its wealthy inhabitants. This unity is complicated by the historical non-visionary materials in 7:10-17 and 8:4-14 and by critical attempts to correlate the visions in 7:1—9:10 with the historical circumstances of Amos' ministry. Since the two non-visionary paragraphs are thematically related to their surroundings, a historical or editorial connection may be hypothesized.[2] Since the visions are not dated or interrelated to other experiences in the life of the prophet, it is precarious to identify these events with the prophet's call. A distinction

---

[1]Cripps, *Amos* 217 makes a break after 9:10; Harper, *Amos* cxxxii divides these sections at 9:8*b*; Fosbroke, *Amos* 849 puts all of 9:8-15 in the epilogue; C. Coulot, "Propositions pour une structuration du livre d'Amos au niveau rédationnel," *RSR* 51 (1977) 169-86 ends the visions at 9:10; Koch, *Amos* 2, 107-12 sees the doxologies as conclusions to sections; Hammershaimb, *Amos* links 9:8-15 together while de Waard and Smalley, *Amos* have 9:7-15 as the epilogue.

[2]Rudolph, *Amos* 249-271 treats the non-visionary material separately after all the visions, thus disconnecting them from the editorial location given in the canonical text. Harper, *Amos* 169, 174 sees a close connection between the visions and the non-visionary material.

should also be made between the experience of having the visions and the public use of them in the ministry of Amos.[3]

The structure of the sub-units within 7:1—9:10 are rhetorically marked by the introductions to new visions. The first unit is made up of visions (7:1-3, 4-6) paired by means of similar words of intercession by the prophet (7:2, 5) and identical responses of mercy by God.[4] The third and fourth visions (7:7-9; 8:1-3) are also paired by means of God's response, "I will spare them no longer." Because the third and fourth visions are expanded by exhortations (7:10-17; 8:4-14), each vision with its exhortation (7:7-17 and 8:1-14) forms a somewhat independent unit by itself. The final section (9:1-10) is made up of a final vision (9:1-4), a hymn (9:5-6), and a dispute (9:7-10) somewhat similar to 7:7-17. The two short visions at the beginning are balanced by the short vision and the dispute at the end. The lengthy expansion of the paired visions in the middle creates a rhetorical symmetry within the whole.

The reference to the sanctuaries of Israel (7:9), the king's sanctuary at Bethel (7:13), and the altar (9:1) suggests that Amos gave these reports of his visions at or near Bethel. The attempt to exclude Amos from the northern sanctuary (7:10-17) does not require one to hypothesize that Amos spoke the remaining visions while he was in Judah. Amaziah belittles the prophet and tries to remove him from the temple, but Amos holds his ground and delivers the word of the Lord (7:14-17). The text never reports the results of this encounter, but 8:1-14 and 9:1-4 are evidence that Amos did not change his message.[5] The common view that Amos was immediately forced from Israel is open to question.[6]

---

[3]May, *Amos* 126 believes Amos received all the visions before beginning his ministry in Israel; Würthwein, "Amos-Studien," 10-15, thinks Amos initially was a prophet of salvation for Israel, as the first two visions (7:1-3, 4-6) and the oracles against the foreign nations indicate (1:3—2:3). Later he received new visions and became a prophet of doom. Cripps, *Amos* 217, 310-11 holds that the visions are out of chronological order in the book. Gordis, "The Composition and Structure of Amos" 247 divides the book into two collections: 1—7:9 before his rejection at Bethel, 8-9 after this event. It should not be assumed that Amos never spoke another word of prophecy in Israel after 7:10-17. Weiser, *Amos* 249-71 sees the "Book of Visions" as a separate book, later added to the "Book of Words."

[4]The oracles against the foreign nations (1:3—2:16) and the chastenings in 4:6-11 appear in paired groups.

[5]Hammershaimb, *Amos* 113 puts 7:10-17 at the end of the visions because he does not believe Amos spoke again in Israel after this incident; Gordis, "The Composition and Structure of Amos" 240 indicates that Marti and Sellins also place 7:10-17 after 9:6; Wolff, *Amos* 311 properly sees Amaziah attempting to supervise the prophet out of the temple to avoid problems, since Amaziah did not have the power to expell Amos without the king's word.

[6]Watts, *Amos* 33-35, 49 places the visions at critical turning points in the prophet's ministry, not at the time of his calling. He thinks Amos gave the visions after 7:10-17 at some Judean sanctuary on the first and second anniversary of his rejection from the New Year's festival at Bethel.

Compassion Within Visions of Judgment

_____ *Amos 7:1-6* _____

Introduction

In the first two visions (7:1-3, 4-6) God reveals that he intends to bring a disastrous plague of locust and a consuming fire on the nation's crops. Each vision pictures the prophet in the role of an intercessor who pleads for pardon and mercy. Amos is deeply moved with pathos for Israel and speaks out on behalf of those who will be punished. His first-hand encounter brings a new depth to the word of God and to his potential function in relationship to God's plan for Israel. At this point no accusation is made (it is assumed from 1:3—6:14), and the nation involved is perceived only from the prayer of the prophet. The Lord's mercy and compassion are abundant and quick to remove the threat envisaged. The repetition of a second similar vision, and later a third, fourth, and fifth vision suggests that a delaying of judgment is possible, but ultimately there will be a time when God will no longer withhold his judgment.

These visions need not be chronologically connected to the spring coming of locust, the fires of the summer dry season, or the fall picking of fruit (8:1-3).[7] There is no sign that they were received before the "words of God" in 1:3—2:16 or 3:1—6:14. If the visions portray the execution of God's previous words of warning, their placement here in the middle of the book makes sense. Now God intends to act, to fulfill his oath, to pass through their midst. The prophet's perception moves from a clear understanding of God's word about that disastrous day (3:1—6:14) to a full experience of the immediate presence of God's power (7:1—9:10). A new reality of God appears in a new mode, and it brings new perspectives and new authority to the prophetic message.

Background

The study of visions can be approached from several angles: (1) psychological experience, (2) structure, and (3) setting.

(1) Lindblom attempts to show that ecstatic experiences were common in many countries over many centuries. He groups these experiences into visions (revelations that are visual in nature) and auditions (revelations that

---

[7]Hammershaimb, *Amos* 107-08 connects each vision to events in a different season over about half a year; Wolff, *Amos* 296 has a similar interpretation.

contain a word which is heard). The visions themselves are further divided into pictorial and dramatic visions. Although he classifies most of the visions in Amos as pictorial visions, 8:1-2 is called a "symbolic perception" based on everyday facts in the real world. Lindblom derives the stylistic form of the vision reports from the didactic methods of the wisdom schools.[8]

(2) M. Sister, who makes a close connection between dreams and visions, divides visions into groups on the basis of: (a) the presence of God; (b) the presence of self-explanatory images; and (c) the presence of images that need interpretation.[9] The work of Horst uses some of these same categories in his division of visions into: (a) presence visions; (b) word-symbol visions, including word plays (Amos 7:7-9; 8:1-2); and (c) event visions.[10] He pays very little attention to the setting of the visions, but Reventlow's study of Amos sees a connection between the visions and the cult.[11] Long refuses to connect visions to any societal, institutional, or cultural setting but does see a connection with acts of divination by the prophets. His three categories of visions are the: (a) oracle-visions (Amos 7:7-8; 8:1-2) which focus on a proclamation and not the visionary image; (b) dramatic word visions (7:1-6) that include a complex and broad group of categories; and (c) revelatory-mystery visions that reveal divine secrets with rather bizarre images (Zechariah 1-5).[12] Each of these approaches recognizes significant differences between various visions, but they are generally descriptive of several structures and give limited information about setting.

(3) Visions are found earlier in the Old Testament and also in the ancient Near Eastern world. Abraham had a vision of covenant making which included symbolic action as well as an interpretation (Gen. 15:1-21). Jacob had a dream at Bethel (Gen. 28:12-22) and a vision just before he went to Egypt (Gen. 46:2). The Pharaoh, Joseph, and others had symbolic dreams (Genesis 35-41) and Micaiah ben Imlah received a vision of the divine council (1 Kings 22). Many of the prophets after the time of Amos receive communications from God through visions (cf. Zechariah 1-6; Daniel).

The interpretation of dreams and visions was also important in Egypt and Mesopotamia. This is known from the Joseph-Pharaoh and Daniel-Nebuchadnezzar stories as well as in extra-biblical literature. Dreams or visions are recorded in the Gilgamesh Epic (*ANET* 76), the Vision of the Nether World (*ANET* 109-10), the Prophecies from Mari (*ANET* 624-31) and other

---

[8]Lindblom, *Prophecy in Ancient Israel* 122-39. Lindblom also has a fourth category of literary visions.

[9]M. Sister, "Die Typen der prophetischen Visionen in der Bibel," *Monatsschrift für Geschichte und Wissenschaft des Judentums* 78 (1934) 399-430.

[10]F. Horst, "Die Visionsschilderungen der alttestamentlichen Propheten," *EvT* 20 (1960) 193-205.

[11]Reventlow, *Amos* 42-43.

[12]B. O. Long, "Reports of Visions among the Prophets," *JBL* 95 (1976) 353-65.

documents (*ANET* 451, 560-63).[13] Although the setting, topics, and structure of these revelations vary considerably from the visions in Amos, these examples demonstrate that visions were considered authoritative messages from the gods/God. Since the individual settings are so diverse, it must be concluded that the setting is significant only to the extent it enables one to understand the message.

If it is proper to distinguish between the original setting and the way this material was used by Amos after it was received, two rather different backgrounds are possible. Because the date for the original reception of these visions by Amos is unknown, the setting is somewhat hypothetical. None of the visions contain the call of Amos. The visions assume that Amos knows who was being punished and why they were being punished. Amos already has assumed the prophetic role of an intercessor; the visions likely came while the prophet was ministering in Israel and not at the beginning of his ministry. The social setting is directly related to the function of the prophet whose role was to receive and declare words and visions from God (1 Kings 22:19-23). The experience of seeing and hearing divine communications was fundamental to prophetic life and essential to authoritative functioning as messengers of divine revelation. The different types of visions are all characteristic of prophetic revelation, and each functions to provide a distinctive emphasis. Since the visions contain proclamations of the word of God, a strong distinction between the vision and the word would exaggerate the essential unity within these methods of revelation.

The setting for the proclamation of these visions is suggested by the literary connection between the third vision (7:7-9) and the narrative dialogue between Amaziah and Amos at the temple in Bethel (7:10-17). The references to "turning your festivals into mourning" (8:10) and the destruction of an altar (9:1) also fit a setting in the temple. But it should not be assumed that all discussion of the temple took place at the temple or during a festival.[14] The fact that Amaziah accuses Amos of conspiring against Jeroboam II "in the midst of the house of Israel" (7:10) instead of "in the midst of the temple of Israel" may indicate activity outside as well as inside the temple (7:13). Amaziah's statement that the land cannot endure all his words (7:11) shows that Amos spoke a number of times in the Bethel area.

Structure and Unity

Structure

The syntactical structures are highlighted in the diagram of the text. The outline derived from this analysis is used in the exegesis of the text.

---

[13]S. Niditch, *The Symbolic Vision in Biblical Tradition* (Chico: Scholars Press, 1983) 30-33.
[14]Watts, *Amos* 35-50 carries the festival context far beyond what the text implies.

Compassion Within Visions of Judgment
Amos 7:1-6

A. Compassion instead of a locust plague

1. Vision of locusts

Thus the Lord[a] Yahweh showed me;   **7:1**
  Behold, he was forming[b] a locust-swarm,
    when late crops began to sprout,[c]
  (And behold, it was the late crop after the king's harvest).[d]

And it happened,[e]   **7:2**
    when he determined to destroy the vegetation of the land,
  then I said:

2. Prophetic intercession for mercy

    Lord Yahweh, please forgive![f]
    How can Jacob survive?[g]
    Indeed, it is so small.

Then Yahweh had compassion[h] concerning this.   **7:3**
  It shall not happen,
  said Yahweh.

3. God's compassion stops the locusts

B. Compassion instead of fire

1. Vision of fire

Thus the Lord Yahweh[i] showed me,   **7:4**
  Behold, the Lord Yahweh was calling forth
    a rain[j] of fire.
  When it had consumed the great deep,
    and it was about to consume the fields,[k]
  then I said: **7:5**

2. Prophetic intercession for mercy

    Lord Yahweh,[l] please cease!
    How can Jacob survive?[m]
    Indeed, it is so small

Then Yahweh had compassion[n] concerning this.   **7:6**
  This also shall not happen,
  said Yahweh.

3. God's compassion stops the fire

7:1a. "Lord" is missing from some Greek MSS (this also happens in 7:4, 6).

7:1b. The Syriac and Old Greek vocalized the participle from *ysr* "forming" as a noun which gave the sense of "offspring." The participles in 7:4, 7 support the Hebrew MT.

7:1c. The Old Greek specifies that these locusts are "coming from the east" instead of "when the late crop began to sprout."

7:1d. The Old Greek permits an apocalyptic interpretation of the locust and reads, "and behold one catapillar was Gog the king" which represents a confusion between *lqš* "late crop" with *ylq* "locust," *'hr* "after" with *'hd* "one," and *gog* "Gog" with *gzê* "mowing." Theod. and Sym. are closer to the Hebrew giving, "late after the cutting of the king."

7:2e. The Hebrew and Old Greek appear to have "and it will be," but this translation of the Hebrew does not fit. J. Huesman, "The Infinitive Absolute and the Waw + Perfect Problem," *Bib* 37 (1956): 410-34 thinks the form should be vocalized as an infinitive absolute. GKC 112uu lists it as an error for *vav* plus imperfect (many commentaries follow this reading).

7:2f. The Targum paraphrastically calls on God to leave behind a remnant of the house of Jacob.

7:2g. The Old Greek translates *mî* "who," which is its usual meaning (cf. 5:2), rather than "how," which is an infrequent adverbial usage. Thus it reads "who will raise up Jacob," which is quite reasonable.

7:3h. The quotation of the prophet continues into verse three in the Old Greek. The verb is an imperative requesting that God have mercy and change. Aq. and Sym. have a passive verb from, "call, invoke."

7:4i. Only one divine name appears in the Old Greek.

7:4j. *lrb* "to contend" is "for judgment" in the Old Greek. D. Hillars, "Amos 7:4 and Ancient Parallels," *CBQ* 26 (1964): 221-25 derives the word from *rbb* "rain" while Rudolph, *Amos* 232-33 follows Elhorst's emendation of *hbt* "flame."

7:4k. The Old Greek adds Lord giving "the Lord's field."

7:5l. The Old Greek omits one divine name.

7:5m. See note *g* in 7:2.

7:5n. See note *h* in 7:3.

The structure of this section is simplified by the large amount of repeated vocabulary and an identical step-by-step structure. Each vision contains: (1) an introductory formula; (2) a transitional particle, "behold"; (3) a description of the vision in which God is acting (using participles); (4) a progression or development of the main idea; (5) intercession by the prophet; and (6) God's decision. The exactness of the parallelism between the visions emphasizes the unity of this pair of visions. Almost identical words of intercession by the prophet and words of compassion by God strengthen the thematic emphasis between the pair.[15]

Unity

Because of the overwhelming structural similarity between the two visions, few have questioned their unity. Rudolph and Harper consider the explanatory clause at the end of 7:1 to be a gloss, while others question the authenticity of some of the double divine names (cf. 7:4) which are not found in the Old Greek.[16] Neither issue creates a problem in the text. Each in its own way adds emphasis or clarity to the vision and matches similar structural patterns in the other vision (see the exegesis below).

Interpretation

A. Compassion instead of a locust plague (7:1-3)

1. Vision of locusts (7:1-2a)

The introductory formula records the prophet's reception of a revelation from the Lord Yahweh. Divine authority stands behind the meaning derived from this new message. A new divine initiative, not the prophet's own desires are responsible for what the prophet saw. The means of revelation was a vision that contained both images and words. There is no indication that this was a dream or some ecstatic experience. Amos understood what he saw and reacted compassionately in ways consistent with his prophetic role. The

---

[15]Watts, *Amos* 28-31.

[16]Rudolph, *Amos* 229; Harper, *Amos* 161; Wolff, *Amos* 297; Cripps, *Amos* 218.

calmness and somewhat normal reactions should not be used to deny the visionary character of the experience.

Within the vision Amos saw God involved in the process of "forming, creating" locusts (cf. 4:13 where God forms the mountains).[17] Locusts were also employed as a punishment when God chastened Israel because they did not return to God (4:9). In both cases the swarms of locusts were intent on devouring every living green plant. The timing of this plague is particularly significant because the late spring pastures and grain fields (probably during April) have just begun to grow.[18] If the locust appeared earlier, the crops would not be up, and if later, the crops would only be set back, not destroyed. Power believes this timing also affected the earlier crops that were in the heading stages just before harvest.[19] Thus a whole year's crops were in danger.

The final parenthetical clause is difficult to understand because the meaning of gzi "mowing, harvesting, sheep shearing" is problematic. Some assume that a portion of the grass was cut for horses in the king's army (1 Kings 18:5), but this custom is not known as a regular levy on the people. First Kings 4:26-28 (Heb. 5:6-8) does record the normal procedure of supplying barley and straw. The significance of this timing is not totally clear.[20] The text surprisingly suggests that the king and his army are well supplied, but the common farmer has nothing. This situation may have heightened the prophet's sense of compassion, for the small farmers and peasants were left in a hopeless situation.

The description of the vision in 7:1 sets the plot, but so far no destructive action has taken place. The threat of a massive invasion of locusts on every living green plant is envisaged in 7:2a. The introductory phrase is grammatically difficult if the Hebrew text is followed (see the textual notes). Many emend the text (changing the usual "and it will happen" to "and it happened"), but similar anomalous forms are found in the Old Testament with a past meaning.[21] A second difficulty arises because the usual translation, "when it had finished eating the vegetation" seems to place the prophet's intercession after the locusts have destroyed the crops. Some change the perfect verb into a participle "was about to finish," but klh can also mean "to determine, decide, complete a plan" (1 Sam. 20:7, 9, 33; Esther 7:7; Prov.

---

[17]The participle is used to describe the continual uninterrupted exercise of an activity: GKC 116a. "Locust" gbi is only used elsewhere in Nah. 3:17. See Driver, *Amos* 82-91 and Wolff, *Amos* 27-8 for further information on the various words for locusts (esp. in Joel) and biological information on their behavior.

[18]*ANET* 320 uses $lqš$ "late planting" in the agricultural calendar from Gezer.

[19]E. Power, "Note to Amos 7:1," *Bib* 8 (1927) 87-92.

[20]Keil, *Commentary on the Old Testament: X Minor Prophets,* 306-08 interprets the section spiritually, concluding that God is the king, and the mowing of grass is the partial judgment already executed against Israel.

[21]S. R. Driver, *A Treatise on the Use of the Tenses in Hebrew* (Clarendon: Oxford, 1892) 158-62; Power, "Note to Amos 7:1," 87-92; GKC 112uu emends *whyh* to *wyhî.*

16:30).[22] With this translation the intercession of Amos comes when he realizes that God has determined to release the locust on the vegetation of the land. At that point he sees the danger for Israel and cries out for mercy.

2. Prophet's intercession for mercy (7:2b)

Amos cries out to the Lord Yahweh, the originator of the locusts and the one who has determined to use the locust to destroy Israel's crops. He, and only he, has the authority and sovereign power to avert this disaster. Since God has proven himself to be a God of mercy who is longsuffering and forgiving in the past, Amos prays for compassion (see Exod. 20:6; 34:6-7; Numb. 14:18; Deut. 5:10; 7:9; Ps. 103:8; 145:8; Jonah 4:2). This is not so much an argument for action based on the covenant or Israel's rights but on groaning for mercy, which the Lord can hear.[23] The prophet's prayer is a lament and petition for grace. Lamentations sometimes ask, "how long, why"; questions which reveal the intense pain of suffering (Ps. 13:1-2; 42:5, 11[Heb 42:6, 12]; 79:5; 94:16)[24] Each question exposes the depth of pathos and identification with those in misery. Although some have forcefully interceded on the basis of evidence (Exod. 32:11-14; Numb. 14:11-19), most Psalms of lament and prophetic prayers of intercession simply rely on the mercy and forgiveness of God (Ps. 25:11; Dan. 9:19). Forgiveness is normally associated with a previous response of repentance (1 Kings 8:30-39, 48-50; 2 Chron. 7:14; Isa. 55:6-7). It results in a pardoning from the punishment which was required for some sinful act. In this case the sins of Amos 1-6 are assumed to be the cause of the locust plague. Since no repentance on the part of Israel is recorded elsewhere in Amos, it is impossible to assume that Israel has repented or will repent. Thus Amos is calling on God to forgive and bear the sins of Israel without repentance. This would be pure grace.

The lament carries a reason why Amos desires God's special intervention. Jacob cannot survive; Israel is too small! Amos repeats no covenant promises and appeals to no national or religious tradition, unless it is God's past record of blessing the insignificant and "little" people (Gen. 27:15; 32:10 [Heb. 32:11]; 48:19; Deut. 7:7; 1 Sam. 9:21; 15:17; 16:11; 1 Kings 3:7). The orphan, widow, and poor were insignificant, but they received God's special care (Exod. 22:22; Deut. 10:18; 24:17-22; 26:12; Ps. 146:9; Isa. 1:17; Jer. 7:6; Zech. 7:10). In this context, the nation of Israel is not little nor the army of Jeroboam II weak. Amos refers to the common farmers who will have no harvest after the locusts. They will be helpless, insignificant, and of little importance to the rich in Samaria (6:1-7). Without God's help they will have no

---

[22]C. C. Torrey, "On the Text of Amos 5:25; 6:1; 7:2," *JBL* 13 (1894) 63; Harper, *Amos* 162; Hammershaimb, *Amos* 109; Mays, *Amos* 127—all change the perfect verb to a participle.

[23]W. Brueggemann, "Amos' Intercessory Formula," *VT* 19 (1969) 385-99, places these formulas within the legal language of the covenant. He sees Amos as a covenant mediator trying to renew the covenant between God and Israel.

[24]*mî* "who" is translated "how": GKC 118m, ff.

means of survival. Death awaits them if no one comes to raise them up (cf. 5:2) and if God does not have mercy.

3. God's compassion stops the locusts (7:3)

The response of God is that of compassion (*nḥm*). This act of mercy, sometimes translated by the anthropomorphic "God repented, God changed his mind," expresses the personal interaction and sensitivity of God to the people's plight and the prophet's prayer. A positive compassionate act of grace is not inconsistent with God's character. But the depth of the act is only understood when it is measured against the sinfulness of the recipients. But since God is not a theological abstract or a mindless absolute force that mechanically rules without sensitivity and care, he can respond even to the sinner. Because Amos prayed, God's wrath is stayed and a new decree is given. "It shall not be," reverses the locust threat. There is no indication that Israel's sins are forgiven or that the people have turned from their sins. The removal of the locusts postpones the wrath of God to another day.

B. Compassion instead of fire (7:4-6)

1. Vision of fire (7:4)

The second vision follows the same structure. This vision pictures God calling forth a great fire to destroy the earth. The fire is traditionally related to God's desire "to contend" (*rîb*), but it is hardly a legal contest if God is sending fire to devastate the world. Some emend the text to read "flames of fire" instead of "contend by fire," but Hillars redivides the consonants to give "rain of fire" (*rbb 'š* for *rb b'š*) which makes more sense (see the textual notes).[25] The fire is not from burning grass and trees ignited by the heat of the summer sun. This fire is so powerful and ferocious that the "great deep" (Gen. 1:2) is consumed. The subterranean waters (not the ocean) which supply the springs and rivers (Gen. 7:11; 49:25) were considered so vast that nothing could begin to dry them up. This only emphasizes the enormous destructive power of the fire. As the prophet watches, the fire begins to consume the farm land. Although the territory is not specified, Amos' intercessory prayer for Jacob implies that God was about to destroy the field of Israel, the land he gave to his people.[26]

---

[25]D. R. Hillars, "Amos 7:4 and Ancient Parallels," *CBQ* 26 (1964) 222-23 finds this root six times in the Old Testament, in the Ugaritic epics and in Akkadian literature. The expression is very similar to the phrase found in Gen. 19:24 and Ezek. 38:22. Hillars' connection of the fire with ancient mythology is unnecessary since fire plays an important role in God's punishment in Amos 1-2. P. D. Millar, "Fire in the Mythology of Canaan and Israel," *CBQ* 27 (1965) 256-61 surveys numerous passages where fire is the means God uses to judge (i.e., Isa. 66:15-16). Rudolph, *Amos* 232-3 and Fosbroke, *Amos* 832 prefer "flames of fire."

[26]The purpose of the visions is circumvented by attempts to identify the locust or the fire with the military defeat of Israel by Ben Hadad (2 Kings 13:3), or the later defeat by the Assyrian king Tiglath-pileser III (2 Kings 15:19-29), or the final judgment of the heathen nations (Isa. 66:15-16), or the final destruction of people and the earth (2 Pet. 3:7-13).

2. Prophet's intercession for mercy (7:5)

Again Amos cries out to God for mercy. Since God sent the fire, he has the power and authority to remove it. This prayer is almost identical to the intercessory prayer in the first vision. Amos laments Israel's fate and calls out for Yahweh to cease, to stop the fire. There is no request for forgiveness, only compassion and an end to the fire before Israel is consumed. The groanings of the lament focus on the smallness of Israel and her inability to survive the onslaught of God's wrath. The rhetorical connection between the two visions is strengthened by the repetition of the same prayer and God's identical response.

3. God's compassion stops the fire (7:6)

Once again God decrees that the judgment will not take place. Truly he is longsuffering and his compassion is eternal. The mercy previously granted does not extend God's intervention beyond the limits of his grace. The message is simply that God has been gracious again and again. Indeed, God is willing to patiently wait, but these two visions are a sign of God's intention in Israel, if his grace is ignored.

Theological Development

In these two visions two themes stand together in tension: God's judgment and his compassion. The tension is more pronounced because God is the source of both judgment and compassion and because both are given to the same nation. The antithesis between them is real and strengthened by the fact that Israel never repents. Yet God is compassionate enough to change his plans, to be inconsistent for the sake of mercy. His sovereign purposes are sometimes conditional, based on human response to God (cf. Jer. 18:1-8). At other times his compassion may be revealed through his patient and longsuffering approach to sinful people (Gen. 15:16), his concern to sanctify and magnify his name in the sight of nations (Ezek. 38:16, 23; 39:7, 25, 27), or through the intercession of a godly person.

Abram interceded with God for Sodom and Gomorrah (Gen. 18:22-33) on the basis of the justice of God toward the righteous who lived among the wicked. Moses interceded for Israel after the worship of the golden calf (Exod. 32:11-14) on the basis of his oath to Abraham, God's reputation in the eyes of the nations, and the mighty acts of grace shown to his people in the past. But at other times God seems merciless and unwilling to change (1 Sam. 15:29). Although Jeremiah confessed the nation's sins and pleaded for God to remember his covenant and not reject Judah (Jer. 14:19-22), God's answer was that if even Moses and Samuel interceded, he would not have mercy on his people. Compassion is not balanced with justice, but it is a factor which conditions the timing of judgment. In the two visions of Amos, judgment is not totally removed, but it is delayed through the intercession of Amos (cf. 7:7-9; 8:1-3).

The vision of Amos is a challenge to the prophet's compassion and a testimony of his prophetic role. The visions are a dramatic portrayal of God's intentions for his people. Words of judgment have been given, but now their fulfillment is re-enacted and accomplished before the prophet. At this crucial juncture Amos may take God's point of view and declare to Israel his vision of God's just judgment of the nation, or he may stand as an intermediary between God's plan and the people. Amos knows the nation has not repented to deserve God's compassion, he knows God's oath that Israel will be destroyed, and he himself has identified with God's decision to destroy Israel (3:1-6:14). Yet a petition of compassion, a lament for mercy immediately springs forth from the prophet's mouth. Amos identifies with his audience and appeals for mercy. The compassion of God toward this sinful people graphically reveals the extent to which God himself identifies with his own people. In the midst of wrath a thread of mercy shines forth with stark beauty (cf. Hab. 3:2). God's ways are mysterious and beyond reason, full of compassion and responsive to the person who prays.

Destruction, Not Forgiveness, for King and Temple

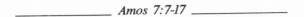

Introduction

The second pair of visions (7:7-9; 8:1-3) is drawn together by the divine response, "I will no longer forgive them" and a similar structure of dialogue within both visions. Because each vision is expanded by a paragraph related to the message of the vision (7:10-17; 8:4-14), each vision with its amplification forms a unit. Although the visions are closely related, each has a distinctive character. The third vision focuses more on why the nation is judged (they are not plumb), while the fourth assumes this and sees the nation as ripe for judgment. The implications of the third vision bring destruction to the king and the temple (7:9, 11, 13, 17), but these are not mentioned in the fourth vision. On the other hand, the fourth vision emphasizes the judgment and wailing of the nation (8:3, 8-10) for all their social evils (8:4-7). The third describes the rejection of God's word (7:10-13), while the fourth predicts a day in which the nation will seek the word of God and not find it (8:11-14).

In the third vision the plumb line of Yahweh will measure Israel and will bring judgment. Destruction instead of compassion will be forthcoming. God will no longer forgive them; he will no longer pass over their sins without doing something about them. This vision specifically predicts the destruction of the temple at Bethel and the king, Jeroboam II. In the expansion of the vision, the prophet's words against the king (7:11) and the temple (7:12) are rejected. In spite of this opposition, Amos confirms his calling to prophesy in Israel (7:14-15) and announces God's rejection of those who reject God's word (7:16-17).

Background

The vision in 7:7-9 has a number of peculiarities when compared to the earlier pair of visions in 7:1-3, 4-6. The vision itself has no dramatic action in it but depends on word plays, includes a dialogue with the prophet (7:8), has an oracle after the explanation of the vision (7:9), and contains no prophetic intercession. Although many classify 7:7-9 and 8:1-3 in a different category than 7:1-6, the same general background can be implied for all the visions.[27]

_____

[27]See the section on Background for 7:1-6.

Niditch finds in Amos 7:7-9 and 8:1-2 a paradigmatic structure of: (1) seeing a vision, (2) description of the vision, (3) questioning of the prophet, (4)
prophetic response, and (5) interpretation by God. A key term is repeated and
nuanced in the interpretation to give the whole meaning. A terse rhythmic
style predominates the framework of dialogue in these visions. Niditch places
these visions in the broader background of early visions in the Pentateuch,
the early prophets like Micaiah, and early divination practices (urim and
thummin) that request help or information from God.[28] This type of vision report is found later in Jeremiah (1:11-12, 13-16; 24:1-3) and in a more developed form in Zechariah. The prophetic vision report continued to be an
important means for God to communicate his message in a dramatic and omi-
nous way throughout the prophetic period.

The dialogue between Amos and Amaziah (7:10-17) is often defined as a
biographical insertion into the series of visions.[29] However, recent studies
have consistently rejected the biographical approach from two perspectives.
(1) Some believe the story is about Amaziah, not Amos, and classify the form
as an apothegm. It explains the setting of a prophetic oracle in order to make
its message understandable.[30] (2) Others reject the biographical narrative
description of 7:10-17 and call it a "story of prophetic conflict," a dispute in
dialogue form that ends with a prophecy of judgment (7:17). The biographical data is indirectly presented, and prophetic authority is the point of controversy.[31] This section can be compared with other controversy passages (1
Kings 13; 2 Kings 9-15; 2 Chron. 24-25) and labeled as one of several judgment narratives on the Northern Kingdom.[32] In the first interpretation, Amaziah found himself caught between the authority of the king and the prophet;
thus he counseled Amos to leave Israel but was not critical of his viewpoint.
In its present context, the editor used these issues to assert the sovereignty of
God over all human authorities and "sacred" institutions (royal and cultic).[33]
In the second interpretation 7:10-17 reflects a controversy among later read-
ers over the authority and validity of Amos' message.[34] Both perspectives
show that 7:10-17 is more than a biographical insertion or a narrative describing Amos' calling. The thematic connections between 7:9 and 10-17 focus the
dispute on the judgment Amos declared against the king and the temple. To
remove this threat, Amaziah commands Amos to leave and return to Judah

---

[28]Niditch, *The Symbolic Vision in Biblical Tradition* 9-15.

[29]Mays, *Amos* 134; Watts, *Amos* 31.

[30]Wolff, *Amos* 308.

[31]G. Tucker, "Prophetic Authority. A Form Critical study of Amos 7:10-17," *Int* 27 (1973)
423-34, compares this passage to a similar controversy in Jeremiah 26 and 28.

[32]P. Ackroyd, "A Judgment Narrative between Kings and Chronicles? An Approach to Amos
7:9-17," *Canon and Authority,* ed. G. W. Coats and B. O. Long (Philadelphia: Fortress Press,
1977) 71-87.

[33]Wolff, *Amos* 308-16 finds an accusation, disputation, and a judgment speech in 7:10-17.

[34]Overholt, "Commanding the Prophets," 524-25.

(7:12). Amos' response indicates that God sent him to Israel to preach against Israel (7:15-16).

In this dispute three terms for prophet are used: *hōzeh* "seer," *nābî'* "prophet" and *ben nābî'* "son of a prophet." The *hōzeh* "seer" refers to singers in the temple (1 Chron. 25:5; 2 Chron. 29:30), royal court seers of kings (1 Chron. 21:9; 2 Chron. 9:29; 19:2; 33:18-19), and to persons parallel to prophets (Mic. 3:6-7; Isa. 29:10). There is some evidence to support Petersen's contention that "seer" *hōzeh* was a title given to any prophet from Judah who worked for the king. Others have associated the seer with Israel's nomadic traditions.[35] Most see the terms as fairly synonymous, but Amaziah probably used the term negatively to degrade the prophet's reputation and more forcefully argue against his right to participate in activities at the Bethel temple. His use of traditional terms may include a caricature of what a seer is or does, and this consideration must enter the discussion of 7:12.

Amos denies any association with the sons of prophets. The "son of a prophet" was a disciple who followed or studied under another prophet (1 Kings 20:35). These were well known in Israel from the traditions about Elisha (2 Kings 2-9). Amos also dissociates himself from the *nābî'* "prophet." This term is used very broadly of a person who speaks for a god/God. Even the false worshipers of Baal are called prophets (1 Kings 18:29). Although some have classified the prophet as an ecstatic, others argue that the *nābî'* was an Israelite prophet or a professional cultic prophet.[36] The interpretation of the conversation between Amaziah and Amos (7:12-15) is thoroughly dependant on these traditions, and exegetical conclusions vary dramatically because of our incomplete understanding of the complex prophetic movement as well as the ambiguous grammar in 7:14. Amos could be arguing that he is not a certain type of prophet, or he could merely be stating that he was not a prophet when the Lord sent him to announce a negative message against Israel. Since we have little information on how these terms were understood by Amaziah before the time of Amos, every interpretation is beset with a certain number of unproven assumptions (see further p. 237).

Structure and Unity

Structure

The diagram reproduces the flow of the message. The English outline will be used in the exegesis of the text.

---

[35]D. L. Petersen, *The Roles of Israel's Prophets* (Sheffield: JSOT, 1981) 51-58; Petersen's definition of role differences between the prophet and the seer seems to make too much of the distinctions between Israel and Judah. See S. V. Smith, "Prophet, Prophecy," *ISBE* (Grand Rapids: Eerdmans, 1986) III, 986-1004.

[36]Petersen, *Roles of Israel's Prophets* 58-63; R. R. Wilson, *Prophecy and Society in Ancient Israel* 136-41, 254-56; H. H. Rowley, "The Nature of Old Testament Prophecy in the Light of Recent Study," *The Servant of the Lord* (Oxford: Blackwell, 1965) 97-108.

Destruction, Not Forgiveness, for King and Temple
Amos 7:7-17

A. No forgiveness in a vision of the plumb line

Thus he[a] showed me: **7:7**   1. Vision of the plumb line
  Behold, the Lord[a] was standing by a plumb[b] wall,
    with a plumb line[b] in his hand.
And Yahweh said unto me: **7:8**
  What do you see Amos?
And I said:
  A plumb line![c]
Then Yahweh said: 2. Plumb line results in no forgiveness
  Behold, I am putting a plumb line[c]
    in the midst of my people Israel.
  I will no longer forgive them.
  Then the high places of Isaac[d] will be destroyed,   **7:9**   3. Plumb line brings destruction to temple and king
    the sanctuaries[e] of Israel will be desolate.
  I will rise up against the house of Jeroboam
    with the sword.

B. Destruction of temple and king rejected, then confirmed

Then Amaziah, the priest of Bethel sent unto Jeroboam,   **7:10**   1. Rejection of Amos' destructive words concerning the king
  king of Israel,
    saying:
      Amos has conspired against you,
      in the midst of the house of Israel.
      The country is not able to bear all his words.
        For this is what Amos says,   **7:11**
        Jeroboam will die by the sword,
          and Israel will surely go into exile
          away from its land.

Then Amaziah said to Amos: **7:12**   2. Rejection of Amos' destructive words concerning the sanctuary
  Seer, go, flee to the land of Judah,
    eat bread[f] there,
    prophesy there.

  Do not prophesy again at Bethel,   **7:13**
    for it is a sanctuary of the king,
    it is a state temple.
Then Amos answered and said to Amaziah: **7:14**   3. Confirmation of Amos' call to prophesy to Israel
  I am[g] not a prophet,
  and I am not the son of a prophet,
  but I am a herdsman,
    a grower[h] of sycamores.
  But Yahweh took me from the flock   **7:15**
  and Yahweh said to me:
    Go, prophesy to my people Israel.

And now hear the word of Yahweh:	**7:16**	4. Confirmation of
You are saying:		Amos' words of
You shall not prophesy against Israel!		destruction
You shall not preach[i] against the house of Isaac.[j]		
Therefore, thus says Yahweh:	**7:17**	
Your wife will be a harlot in the city,		
Your sons and daughters will fall by the sword,		
Your land will be parceled with a line,		
You yourself will die on unclean land.		
Indeed, Israel will surely go into exile from its land.		

7:7a. The Old Greek has a divine name similar to 7:1, 4 but does not have a divine name in the second line. In the second line some Greek MSS have "man."

7:7b. The unusual *'nk* "plumb, plumb line" is "hard, adamant" in the Old Greek, "shining" in Aq., and "molten" in Theod. Some change *'nk* to *'bn* "stone," but many believe it is a dittography from the next line.

7:8c. See note 7:7*b*.

7:9d. Isaac which means "laughter" is translated "joyful, laughter" in the Old Greek. Sym. has Jacob. Isaac is spelled with a *ś* instead of *ṣ* here and in 7:16.

7:9e. Instead of sanctuaries the Old Greek refers to the "rites, festival" that go on in these sanctuaries.

7:12f. Eat bread is translated much more generally in the Old Greek as "pass life."

7:14g. The Hebrew has no verb, but the Old Greek has a past tense verb.

7:14h. For this rare word the Old Greek has "scratch, nip," Theod. "mark," Aq. "search, examine," and Sym. "own."

7:16i. The Old Greek has "to disturb a mob, cause a tumult," while Aq. has "drip," a literal translation of the Hebrew.

7:16j. "Jacob" replaces Isaac in the Old Greek (cf. 7:9).

The structural continuity between the visions in 7:7-9 and 8:1-3 sets 7:10-17 off as a different paragraph. The structure of the dialogue between God and Amos in the vision (7:7-9) is not at all like the structure of the dialogue between Amaziah and Amos (7:10-17). The first paragraph introduces God's oracle of judgment (7:9), and in the second Amaziah rejects this word from God.

The vision in 7:7-9 (cf. 8:1-3) includes: (1) an introductory formula; (2) a transitional particle "behold"; (3) a description of the vision; (4) a dialogue between God and the prophet; (5) an explanation of the vision; and (6) an interpretation of the significance of the explanation. A rhetorical play on *'nk* "lead, plumb line" draws the vision together. The absence of verbal connections between 7:7-8 and 7:9 weakens its connection to the vision. In the preceding visions (7:1-3, 4-6) there was no need for additional explanations after God stopped the fire and the locust. In the second pair of visions the final oracle of judgment after the vision (7:9; 8:3) reveals the significance of God's destruction in some specific way.

Amaziah's exhortation to Amos and the prophet's countering exhortation are structured into a dispute over God's word of destruction for the king and the temple (7:9, 11, 13, 17). The paragraph could be divided into two halves:

(7:10-13) Amaziah's speeches against Amos and his prophecy; (7:14-17) Amos' speeches against Amaziah.[37] The first part contains a quotation of Amos by Amaziah (7:11), while the second part has a quotation of Amaziah by Amos (7:15). Each part can be further divided into two parts: (7:10-11) Amaziah rejects Amos and his words against the king; (7:12-13) Amaziah rejects Amos and his words against the temple; (7:14-15) Amos confirms that his words are for Israel; (7:16-17) Amos confirms his words of destruction. In each case prophetic freedom and the validity of God's message of judgment for his people are the central issues.

Thematic repetition creates a rhetorical unity between the vision (7:7-9) and the dispute (7:10-17).[38] These interconnections demonstrate that 7:10-17 is not an unrelated historical parenthesis thrown into the midst of the visions by a manipulative editor. These repetitions reveal Amos' persuasive efforts to convince his audience to believe God's word. The format builds tension between the accepted positions of the royal and cultic institutions and the prophetic word of God. The absence of a conclusion in the structure, suggests that this tension was not resolved in this encounter.

Unity

Although many think *'nk* "plumb" in the phrase "a plumb wall" (7:7) is a dittography and should be dropped or emended to *'bn* "stone," the two main problems relating to the unity of 7:7-17 are: (1) the relationship of 7:9 to the rest of the vision and (2) the location of the narrative (7:10-17) between the parallel visions in 7:7-9 and 8:1-3.

Wolff attributes 7:9 and 7:10-17 to the Amos school of disciples (735 B.C.) rather than the prophet. The style of 7:9 is more poetic, its content is not directly connected to the imagery of the vision, and there is no parallel to it in the first pair of visions.[39] In spite of these apparent differences, the structure of 7:7-9 does match 8:1-3 and the typology of other similar visions.[40] The content of 7:9 applies the interpretation of the vision to the future history of Israel, making clear to the audience the significance of a plumb line in their

---

[37]Tucker, "Prophetic Authenticity" 425-28, considers 7:10-11 as background to the dispute between Amos and Amaziah in 7:12-17; Mays, *Amos* 134 divides the paragraph into three parts: 7:10-11, 12-13, 14-17.

[38]Repeated words include: "Jeroboam" in 7:9 and 7:10, 11; "in the midst of my people Israel" in 7:8 and "in the midst of the house of Israel" in 7:10; "Israel will surely go from its land into exile" in 7:11 and 17; "my people" in 7:8 and 7:15; "the sword" in 7:9 and 7:11, 17; "Isaac" in 7:9 and 7:16; "the sanctuary" in 7:9 and 7:13; and the "plumb line" (7:7-8) and the "line" (7:17) are associated as synonyms elsewhere (2 Kings 21:13; Isa. 28:17; 34:11).

[39]Wolff, *Amos* 295; Watts, *Amos* 41; Ackroyd, "A Judgment Narrative," 72-73 connects 7:9 with 7:10-17 rather than 7:7-8; A. J. Bjorndalen, "Erwägungen zur Zukunft des Amazja und Israels nach der Überlieferung Amos 7, 10-17," *Werden und Wirken des Alten Testament* (Göttingen: Vanderhoeck and Ruprecht, 1980) 237 n 3.

[40]Niditch, *The Symbolic Vision in Biblical Tradition* 21-34, finds a symbol, an interpretation, and a future orientation as common elements in dreams and visions.

midst. It explains 7:7-8 and creates a link with the dispute in 7:10-17. The role of 7:9 in the unit is essential, its absence would destroy the unity of 7:7-17.[41]

The nonvisionary character of 7:10-17 in many ways is an intrusion into the visionary context. Some believe 7:10-17 should be placed: (a) before the visions begin; (b) after the final vision in 9:1-4 which completes the ministry of Amos in Israel; or (c) after chapter 3.[42] The second option is most popular, but it is based on the assumption that Amos was forced to leave Israel after the dispute with Amaziah in 7:10-17. Since the text is silent on that issue, and the historical order of events in the life of Amos is unknown, the most profitable approach to 7:10-17 queries the literary not the historical placement of the paragraph. In light of the fact that the structure of the second pair of visions is identical and each vision is followed by an interrelated paragraph which amplifies the themes introduced in the vision, 7:10-17 is required to balance 8:4-14. Some themes in 8:4-14 are picked up from 7:10-17; therefore, its proper location must be prior to the fourth vision. The theological hardening of those who reject God's word (7:10-17) is important to the visions because it explains why God will no longer forgive (7:8, 8:2). The rejection of God's word of death and exile may explain why the prophet no longer interceded for the nation. The expansion of the themes of the visions in 7:10-17 and 8:4-14 permits the development of those themes in powerful dimensions far beyond the emphasis gained from the brief capsulization of the visions in one verse.

Interpretation

A. No forgiveness in a vision of the plumb line (7:7-9)

1. Vision of the plumb line (7:7-8a).

The introductory formula is slightly altered (cf. 7:1, 4), but it functions the same as in the earlier introductions. It reveals the source of the prophet's knowledge; God made the future known to Amos in a vision. Amos saw Yahweh standing beside a wall holding something. The key term *'nk,* is used four times in this vision but nowhere else in Scripture. Traditionally, this root has been identified as an Akkadian loan word for "lead" and connected to a "plumb line" used to measure the straightness of a wall. More recent studies have translated *'nk* as "weapon, tin, crowbar," but the ancient translations have "molten, shining and hard" (see the textual notes).[43] The crowbar is an

---

[41]Rudolph, *Amos* 236-37; Mays, *Amos* 124.

[42]Gordis, "The Composition and Structure of Amos," 239-40 and Watts, *Amos* 31-33 review several options taken in the past. Cripps, *Amos* 310-11 sees a connection between the destruction of Bethel in 3:15 and 7:10, 11, 17.

[43]B. Landsberger, "Tin and Lead: The Adventures of Two Vocables," *JNES* 24 (1965) 285-96 and W. L. Holladay, "Once More, *'*NAK = 'TIN,' Amos 7:7-8," *VT* 20 (1970) 292-94,

iron instrument which symbolizes the destruction of a wall, while tin was a metal alloyed with copper to make weapons of bronze.[44] But if iron or bronze were intended, the regular Hebrew words could have been used. Since tin is a soft metal, it is not an effective ore to use in making weapons. Others emend the text by dropping the first 'nk (in a construct relationship to "wall") or by changing 'nk to 'bn giving "stone wall."[45] The present Hebrew "wall of a plumb line" refers to a "plumb wall" or a wall built with the use of a plumb line. This wall is not identified as the wall of Bethel, Samaria, the temple, or any other wall. The other uses of 'nk are not joined to nouns and probably refer to a plumb line. The regular Hebrew word for plumb line $m\check{s}qlt$ is found parallel to qw "line" (2 Kings 21:13; Isa. 28:17; 34:11; cf. Lam. 2:8), and these occur both in construction as well as destruction contexts. In all these cases the instruments are used to test or measure the the quality of something. The reason for using an Akkadian loan word instead of the usual Hebrew word is not apparent.

In the second pair of visions (7:7-9; 8:1-3) a dialogue between God and Amos is developed. No dramatic action is portrayed, but the prophet is asked to identify the object in the vision. Amos recognizes the main object, but the significance of the symbolism remains obscure. The structure of question-and-answer demonstrates a stylistic flexability in the form of the visions and removes Amos from the passivity of the side lines into an active participating role. This is not a mechanism of magic or divination in which the prophet puts questions to the deity.[46]

2. Plumb line results in no forgiveness (7:8b)

The explanation of the vision uses the key word "plumb line" to unfold God's plan for Israel. He will test Israel by placing his plumb line in their midst. The use of the same word in the explanation is unexpected since a play on words is found in similar visions (8:1-3; Jer. 1:11-12). The word 'nk could be changed to 'anōkî "I," yielding "I will set myself in your midst," or two words could be joined to give $\check{s}im'anka$ "I am setting you," but neither change is really satisfactory.[47] God's plumb line exposes the true state of his

---

strongly support the translation tin on the basis of Akkadian texts. G. Brunet, "La Vision de l'étain: réinterprétation d'Amos 7:7-9," VT 16 (1966) 387-95, also prefers "tin," but Rudolph, Amos 234-85 has "crowbar," and A. Condamin, "Le prétendu fils a plomb de la vision d'Amos," RB 9 (1900) 584-94, translates the word "weapon, war hammer,"

[44]R. J. Forbes, Studies in Ancient Technology, IX (Leiden: Brill, 1964) 124-70, locates the tin-producing areas of the ancient world and describes its use in making bronze. The only tin in Palestine was a small deposit near Byblos and Aleppo, so the ore must have been imported to Israel. He also believes AN.NA = 'nk was "tin" but thinks it was sometimes confused with lead.

[45]Rudolph, Amos 234 has "stone wall." F. Horst, "Die visions schilderungen der alttestamentlichen Propheten," EvT 20 (1960) 201-02 emends 'nk to 'nhh "wailing."

[46]Niditch, The Symbolic Vision 33-34.

[47]Petersen, Role of Israel's Prophets 77-78, follows the suggestion of S. McBride and finds in this vision the commissioning of Amos to go to Israel: "I am setting you in the midst of my people Israel."

people. It tests their plumbness to see if it is time to tear down the wall. Although the vision remains undeveloped, the context implies that God is testing the moral character and faithfulness of his people. In the earlier visions (7:1-3, 4-6) guilt is implied but forgiveness is granted after the prophet intercedes. This vision explains why God's judgment will come. Having seen this information, Amos does not intercede for mercy, for the level shows that Israel is not upright.

The plumb line is set among "my people Israel" (7:8b). The personal pronoun and the term 'm "people" describe the personal covenant relationship between God and Israel (Exod. 3:10; 6:4-7; Deut. 4:20; 7:6-10). The basis for God's accusations and the measure of his testing is covenantally based on the failure of the nation to be the people of God (Amos 3:1-2). The expression "my people" draws a close connection between God and the nation; thus the announcement of punishment with no forgiveness is a judgment on something that belongs to God. The results have a personal effect on God's people, the ones he loves and for whom he cares. There is an agony in announcing the measurement of his own people.

The final declaration, "I will no longer forgive," points to the end of the longsuffering patience of God and the nearness of the day of accountability, and is derived from the expression "not pass over" (cf. Prov. 19:11; Mic. 7:18). In the first pair of visions God intervened and stopped the fire and locust (7:1-3, 4-6). Amos requested pardon, and God in compassion said, "it shall not happen." In this vision God will not pass over, he will pass through their midst (cf. 5:17) and bring forth his judgment. The effect will be desolation, destruction, and death from the sword. The verbs of destruction graphically portray the disastrous effects of military defeat and the utter ruin of everything that the nation prized so highly.

3. Plumb line brings destruction to temple and king (7:9)

The significance of the plumb line is hinted at in 7:8, but the specific application to Israel is undefined. The role of 7:9 is to clarify the implications of the vision by describing the form of punishment God intends to bring on Israel. Two areas of national significance are marked for destruction: the royal and cultic powers and institutions. These two institutions provide cohesion, purpose, and security to the people. Their destruction portends the end of the nation; God rejects the political and religious institutions that influence the nation's relationship to God. The religious places of worship are described as the "high places" and "sanctuaries, holy places."[48] Since this is the only time "high places" bāmah is used in Amos, it is possible to refer the term to sanctuaries on the tops of hills all over Israel or to the major sanctu-

---

[48]W. F. Albright, "The High Place in Ancient Palestine," *VTS* 4 (1957) 242-58; C. C. McCowan, "Hebrew High Places and Cult Remains," *JBL* 69 (1950) 205-19; P. H. Vaughan, *The Meaning of 'bama' in the Old Testament* (Cambridge: Cambridge Univ., 1974).

aries at Bethel, Dan, Gilgal, and Beersheba. Other prophets condemn the Baal cult high places which were open-air sanctuaries with carved pillars and wooden poles, but Amos does not focus on the Canaanite cult. Thus the high places may be identical to the official sanctuaries. The reason for their destruction is assumed from Amos 3:14; 4:4-5; 5:5-7, 21-24. The reference to Isaac (cf. 7:16) should not limit the destruction to high places only in the Transjordan area of Israel near Penuel and Mehanaim or merely to Beersheba where Isaac worshiped (Gen. 26:25).[49]

In addition to the total destruction of places of worship, God will bring a sword against the king of Israel, Jeroboam II. The assassination of Jeroboam's son Zechariah by Shallum in 2 Kings 15:10 records the destruction of the "house" or dynasty of Jeroboam. Yahweh himself is the primary power that will determine the future of king and nation. To destroy the sanctuaries and the nation as a whole, God later sent a military force from beyond Damascus (Amos 2:13-16; 3:11-12; 4:2-3; 5:27; 6:8-14; 2 Kings 17:1-6).

B. Destruction of temple and king rejected, then confirmed (7:10-17)

1. Rejection of Amos' destructive words concerning the king (7:10-11)

This dialogue between Amaziah and Amos is closely tied into the themes of the vision in 7:7-9 and is much more than a biographical intrusion into a series of visions (see the section on Structure and on Background). The report of Amaziah assumes that Amos is well known and has spoken for some time in Israel, but no exact date during the reign of Jeroboam II can be identified. The events took place at the temple that Jeroboam I built after the division of the kingdoms (1 Kings 12). Jeroboam I erected a golden calf, installed non-Levitical priests, and set new festival dates. These innovations were intended to drive a wedge between Israel and Judah; they provide a distinctive Israelite expression of nationalism and worship.

Amaziah is described as a priest at Bethel, though his position of authority suggests that he was the high priest. If so, he was an important government official with considerable power to supervise, regulate, and protect the sanctity of the nation's religion. The attack on the sanctuary and the king himself (7:9) was a threat that Amaziah took seriously and reported to the king. His report includes an accusation against Amos (7:10b) and the evidence for his accusation in the form of a quotation of Amos (7:11). This initial response by Amaziah is a rejection of Amos' words against the king while the following verses (7:12-13) respond to the prophet's words against the Bethel sanctuary.

---

[49]Wolff, *Amos* 302 points to Beersheba while A. van Selms, "Isaac in Amos," *Studies on the Book of Hosea and Amos* OTWSA 7-8 (Potchefstroom: Rege-Pers Beperk, 1965) 157-65, thinks Amos is using Genesis 31-33 and the "Fear of Isaac" (Gen. 31:53) tradition from a Transjordan area. As van Selms indicates, the spelling of Isaac is unusual. *yshq* is found 107 times while *yśhq* is used only four times (Ps. 105:9; Jer. 33:26; Amos 7:9, 16).

Amaziah charges Amos with a conspiracy (*qšr*), an act of treason. The charge is not unreasonable for Amaziah probably knew of traditions about how Samuel the prophet anointed another king while Saul was still king (1 Sam. 16:1-13), how Ahijah the prophet predicted the division of the kingdom (1 Sam. 16:1-13), or how Elisha conspired with Jehu to overthrow Joram (2 Kings 9:1-28; 10:9). Although Amos was not part of a personal conspiracy to depose the king, Amaziah was unaware of his connections or intentions; thus an announcement of death to Jeroboam II is dealt with seriously. If Amos would continue to make such radical statements, surely some dissidents who disliked the king's policies would sooner or later join forces with Amos to enact the sentiments of the prophet. The attack on Amos was probably in some sense a tactic of fear to quiet the king's opposition. It misrepresents Amos' words that "Yahweh will rise up" against Jeroboam II and imputes negative motives and personal plans to Amos himself. Because Amos speaks these words in Israel where Jeroboam II rules, and because Amos spoke against the temple, Amaziah concludes that their country is not able to bear or endure (*kul*) such attacks.[50] This implies that Amaziah is aware of many other negative words by Amos.

The reason for Amaziah's attack and the proof of his accusation is given in 7:11. The quotation is not an exact representation of any words of Amos, although the substance conforms to what Amos says in 7:9; 5:5, 27; and 6:7. Amaziah perverts the words of Amos by failing to recognize these as the words of Yahweh. His words and visions are not the imaginations of his heart. Amaziah avoids the theological core of the words of Amos and deals with them as political propaganda. This paragraph demonstrates that Amaziah rejects Amos; but more importantly, he rejects God's words of judgment on the king.

2. Rejection of Amos' destructive words concerning the temple (7:12-13).

The verbal attack on Amos is not the result of a royal decree from King Jeroboam II. If the priest had received a royal pronouncement, the prohibition would have a proper introductory clause. The command by Amaziah is based on his own authority to regulate events within the temple compound at Bethel.[51] Amaziah tells Amos what he is to do (7:12) and what he is not to do (7:13). He rejects the prophet and particularly his words against the sanctuary of the king at Bethel. Amos is prohibited from prophesying at Bethel and commanded to return to Judah.

The command to Amos is intrinsically related to the answer of Amos in 7:14-15. The most controversial part of Amaziah's command is his use of the word "seer" *hozeh*. Many commentaries have assumed that *hozeh* and *nābî'*

---

[50]The word is sometimes used for the amount of a substance something is able to contain. Jer. 10:10 uses the word in a way similar to that found here in Amos.

[51]Hammershaimb, *Amos* 115 believes Amaziah acted with the king's authority behind him.

"prophet" in 7:14 are synonymous, that neither is a derogatory term, and that the key to understanding this dialogue has nothing to do with the use of two different words by Amaziah and Amos.[52] Some believe *hozeh* is used in a negative sense of a prophet who tells the future for money, while a third group suggests that it is a technical term for a southern prophet who works for the king of Judah.[53] The first two interpretations focus on the way the prophet makes his living (7:12), while the latter view emphasizes that Bethel was the Israelite king's temple (7:13). The response of Amos in 7:14-15 will help to determine the better approach to this problem.

The command to Amos was more than advice or counsel to avoid conflict; it was a rejection of Amos' prophetic role at Bethel and his message against the sanctuary of the king.[54] The charge of treason against Jeroboam implies a significant attempt to get rid of the influence of Amos. The command to "flee" *brh* carries a threat of violence or persecution. Judah, the prophet's homeland, is ruled by another king; therefore it is a haven of safety for Amos. Although it is unclear whether "seer, visionary" is spoken with a negative intonation, the final clause in 7:12 imputes negative motivations to Amos' prophetic ministry.[55] Amaziah classifies Amos as a professional prophet who prophesies for pay; he tells Amos that he will make more money in Judah than in Israel.

Whether Amos takes Amaziah's advice or not, one thing is clear, he will not prophesy again at the Bethel temple (7:13). This emphatic prohibition excludes Amos from declaring other prophecies in the temple itself but does not profess to regulate his activity outside the temple. Amaziah does not exceed the bounds of his authority, for expulsion from the country would have required a royal decree. He pushes Amos to go to Judah, to live there, to prophesy there, but he forbids further activity only in the temple. The basis for this limitation was bound up in the character of the Bethel sanctuary. It was a "sanctuary of the king, a state temple." His words against the king and against the king's temple were radical treason. The reference is not to a royal "house or residence" at Bethel, but to a "temple" owned and operated by the state.[56] The rejection of Amos and his destructive words are a rejection of Yahweh's announcement of death and desolation for the king and his temple.

---

[52]Mays, *Amos* 136; Wolff, *Amos* 310-11.

[53]H. H. Rowley, "The Nature of Old Testament Prophecy in the Light of Recent Study," *The Servant of the Lord* (Oxford: Blackwell, 1965) 120-01; Harper, *Amos* 170-01; Hammershaimb, *Amos* 116 believe the two words are synonymous but that Amaziah uses "seer" in a disparaging sense, suggesting that Amos was a professional fortune teller who worked only for the money he could collect. But Petersen, *Roles of Israel's Prophets* 56-57; Z. Zevit, "A Misunderstanding at Bethel: Amos VII:12-17," *VT* 25 (1975) 784-90, consider a *hzh* to be a Judean court prophet.

[54]Wolff, *Amos* 311 views Amaziah as a neutral figure giving helpful advise to Amos lest Jeroboam II expel him from Israel. This is essentially the view of Würthwein, "Amos Studien," 19-20.

[55]Although Samuel may have received some pay (1 Sam. 9:7, 8), Micah (3:11), and later Ezekiel (13:17-23) strongly oppose these professional prophets.

[56]House refers to a temple in 1 Kings 6:2-3; 7:50; 2 Chron. 29:3.

3. Confirmation of Amos' call to prophesy to Israel (7:14-15)

The enormous controversy over the interpretation of Amos' defense in 7:14 has overshadowed the very significant quotation of Yahweh's words to Amos concerning prophesying in Israel in 7:15.[57] The purpose of 7:14 is not to give a biographical account of Amos; its purpose is to explain the basis for the authoritative message that Yahweh commanded Amos to deliver to "my people Israel" (cf. 7:8). Amos' response to Amaziah confirms that God is behind his freedom to prophesy in Israel; the king and the priest do not determine God's message or the place where God sends his prophets. Amos is counteracting Amaziah's demand that he not prophesy at Bethel (7:12-13) by showing that this is a denial of the command of God. In Amos' eyes, Amaziah has no authority over God.

To support his claim to divine authority to prophesy in Israel, Amos briefly declares what he is not (7:14*a*) and what he is (7:14*b*-15*a*). Because Amos' response to Amaziah has no verbs, the tense and mood of the verbs must be supplied. The syntactical use of the negative *l'* and the meaning of the word "prophet" are also problematic. Two rather antithetical approaches are proposed: (1) Amos denies he is a professional prophet or seer who prophesies for pay; instead he bases his activity on the call of God; (2) Amos rejects Amaziah's conclusion that he is a "seer" and claims to be a "prophet" by using *l'* "no" as an absolute denial ("No, I am a prophet") or by taking the negative as an interrogative particle ("Am I not a prophet?").[58] Numerous variations of these basic proposals exist. Those who follow the first solution are divided into two groups on the basis of the tense of the verb they supply in 7:14. One group interprets Amos to say, "I am not a professional prophet" using the present tense. Another group uses a past tense based on 7:15 and the fact that Amos was a prophet; therefore, they translate the verse "I was not a prophet...when Yahweh took me."[59]

Although Amos earlier identifies with the prophetic task (2:11; 3:7-8), and both Amaziah and Amos use the verb "prophesying" in this context, the solution which has Amos saying, "No I am a prophet," or "Am I not a

---

[57]Tucker, "Prophetic Authenticity," 428, 433, believes 7:15 is the key verse in the paragraph; Mays, *Amos* 138 agrees.

[58]Representatives of the first position are: Mays *Amos* 136-38; Cripps, *Amos* 232-33; Wolff, *Amos* 311-13; Rowley, "Old Testament Prophecy in Recent Study" 120-01. The second position is supported by S. Cohen, "Amos Was a Navi," *HUCA* 32 (1961) 175-78; Zevit, "A Misunderstanding at Bethel," 783-90, has a similar position, but thinks Amos rejects the title "seer" because Amaziah thinks he is a royal court seer from Judah; S. R. Driver, "Amos 7:14," *ExpT* 67 (1955-56) 91-92; Watts, *Amos* 11; and P. R. Ackroyd, "Amos 7:14," *ExpT* 68 (1956-57) 94 make this difficult clause a question.

[59]Those supporting the present tense include Hammershaimb, *Amos* 117; Cripps, *Amos* 233; Wolff, *Amos* 306, 312-13; Harper, *Amos* 171; Fosbroke, *Amos* 835; Rudolph, *Amos* 249-50, and all those who claim that Amos is saying "No, I am a prophet," but H. H. Rowley, "Was Amos a Nabi?" *Festschrift Otto Eissfeldt*, ed. J. Fück (Halle: Niemeyer, 1947) 191-98; A. H. J. Gunneweg, "Erwägungen zu Amos 7, 14," *ZTK* 57 (1960) 1-16; Reventlow, *Amos* 16-20; Clements, *Prophecy and Covenant*, 36-39; and Mays, *Amos* 136-38 support a past tense verb.

prophet?'' has difficulty explaining how Amos in the next breath could identify himself as the "disciple, son of a prophet." Although Ackroyd sees no
problem with maintaining that Amos was a member of a prophetic guild, others attempt to avoid this conclusion by taking the first clause positively, the
second negatively.[60] These solutions are less satisfactory than the more
common view that Amos is denying that he is a professional prophet.

Significant grammatical or contextual reasons can be given in support of a
present or past tense verb in 7:14. The present tense verb seems preferable if
Amos wants to deny that he is a prophet who works for money (7:12) by arguing that he is making a living by working with sheep and sycamore trees
(7:14). For this response to hold weight, Amos must maintain that he is, not
was, supporting himself by other employment.[61] If a present tense is required
in 7:14b, then it is best to supply present tense verbs throughout. Thus Amos
is rejecting Amaziah's insinuation that he is a common professional prophet
in the business for the money.

The prophet describes his income-producing employment using two rare
roots: bqr and bls (7:14b). The first is a participle from bqr "cattle," and it
identifies Amos as one who works with flocks of sheep and goats (7:15). This
is in agreement with 1:1 where Amos is called a nqd, a "shepherd" of some
stature and probably a manager of other shepherds.[62] In addition to this
source of income, Amos also worked with sycamore or mulberry trees.
These trees grew near the Mediterranean Sea and in the Jordan Valley (1
Kings 10:27; 1 Chron. 27:28; Luke 19:1, 4), but the exact nature of Amos'
work with these trees is unclear. The root bls is found only here, but in Arabic the root means "fig." It is commonly thought that the word means "to
slit" and describes the practice of making an incision in the figs so that the
fruit will have a sweet instead of a bitter taste.[63] Recent studies indicate that
Palestinian figs do not need to be incised before they ripen as the Egyptian
figs; thus Wright suggests that bls may refer to the "mixing" (from Mishnaic
Hebrew) of fig leaves or fruit with barley to feed the sheep.[64] Although none
of these alternate translations are overly convincing, the main point is clearly

---

[60]Richardson, "A Critical Note on Amos 7:14," *JBL* 85 (1966) 89; Cohen, "Amos was a
Navi," 175-78; and Zevit, "A Misunderstanding at Bethel," 783-90 lack consistency and produce
a very awkward shift from a positive to a negative idea. At least P. R. Ackroyd, "A Judgment
Narrative," 83, is consistent in taking both clauses positively.

[61]Rudolph, *Amos* 256 argues this point. See A. S. van der Woude, "Three Classical Prophets:
Amos, Hosea, Micah," *Israel's Prophetic Tradition: Essays in Honor of P. R. Ackroyd*, ed. R.
Coggins, *et al.* (Cambridge; Cambridge Univ., 1982) 36, agrees with Rudolph.

[62]Hammershaimb, *Amos* 117; Cripps, *Amos* 234; Morgenstern, "Amos Studies," I, 35 and
others believe the b and n, and the d and r were confused in 7:14.

[63]J. J. Glück, "Three Notes on the Book of Amos," *Studies on the Book of Hosea and Amos*
OTWSA 7-8 (Potchefstroom: Rege-Pers Beperk, 1965) 119, emends blš to bls "to search,"
which results in the rather strange view that Amos sustained himself on sycamore figs, a peasant's diet.

[64]T. J. Wright, "Amos and the Sycamore Fig," *VT* 26 (1976) 362-68.

understood. Amos is presently involved with two lines of work; he does not make a living off his prophesying like other professional prophets.

Amos came to declare God's words to Israel under quite exceptional circumstances. He was working with the sheep one day when "Yahweh took" him and sent him in a different direction (7:15). Yahweh was the initiator of this change, and he was responsible for the new direction. When Amos was taken by God, he became God's servant and was sent to do God's work.[65] This new service caused a radical change in Amos' life because God said, "Go prophesy to my people Israel" (7:15b). This phrase confirms the prophet's call to do what Amaziah has said he cannot do. Amaziah is rejecting and opposing a power much greater than Amos, he is conspiring against the will of God. Amos obeyed God's command (cf. 3:7-8), for the authority of God's word is irresistible. This word from God which Amos delivers to God's people is Amos' only basis for his right to prophetic freedom in Israel. He is not a royal or cultic prophet subordinate to the king or the priest; he is subordinate only to God and his command to go and speak.

4. Confirmation of Amos' words of destruction (7:16-17)

With boldness which is almost frightening, Amos pronounces a judgment speech against the priest himself. It begins with a call to hear and an accusation that quotes Amaziah's treasonous words (7:16); and it concludes with a messenger formula and an announcement of punishment (7:17). The contrast between what "Yahweh said" (7:15), what "you are saying" (7:16), and what "Yahweh says" (7:17) is highlighted by the juxtaposition of one text next to the other. Amaziah's statement, "prophesy not in Israel" (7:16), is directly contradictory to Yahweh's "prophesy to my people Israel" (7:15). The quotation proves the guilt of Amaziah and justifies Yahweh's punishment. Amaziah tries to expel Amos from Israel, but now God will expel Amaziah from Israel (7:17). In spite of Amaziah's attempt to quiet the prophet, Amos continues to declare the word of God with power and freedom.

The quotation of Amaziah is not a direct repetition of words recorded earlier in the dialogue but a restatement of 7:13. Some small linguistic adjustments suggest a one-sided understanding of Amos' role. Yahweh sent Amos to prophesy (nb') to ('l) my people Israel (7:15), but Amaziah describes his task as prophesying (nb', ntp) against ('l) Israel and the house of Isaac (7:10). Although Amaziah does treat Amos with respect, these changes suggest a negative characterization of the prophet's ministry.[66] The prophet's love for God's people, his call for them to "seek God and live," and his prayers of in-

[65]Compare the Levites in Numb. 8:6-19.

[66]Overholt, "Commanding the Prophets" 525-26 thinks ntp "drip, prophesy" was understood as the positive announcements of prophecy, which support the established religious and political institutions by repeating the positive guarantees of the covenant promises. Since Amos did not function in this officially acceptable way, his words were rejected.

tercession are colored by the constant flow of hostile words of death and destruction.

Amos confirms God's words of destruction (7:9) by announcing a severe individual punishment on Amaziah (7:17) who is preventing Amos from proclaiming God's word. The future of Amaziah and his family is described with horrible detail. This curse-like announcement will affect his wife, his sons, his daughters, his property, Amaziah himself, and his country. His "wife will become a harlot" is stronger than the statement that the defeated nation's women will be ravished (Isa. 13:16; Zech. 14:2; Deut. 28:30).[67] Her behavior is shameful because it is a voluntary act publicly pursued in the city. The city is not identified. Amaziah's children will be slain, his sizable priestly holdings in land will be parceled out to others with a measuring line (2 Kings 17:24; Jer. 6:12).[68] Amaziah's death on unclean soil may refer to his death in a foreign land (Hos. 9:3; Ezek. 4:13), or it could describe his death on the polluted soil of Israel. The final line repeats 7:11b and confirms that Amaziah's nation will be exiled as Amos has said. Its repetition in a personal oracle against Amaziah is a bit unexpected. Its placement here in the writing of Amos' oracle creates a rhetorical emphasis on this theme, an ironic reversal of what Amaziah rejected.[69]

Theological Developments

The theological dispute over the word of God in the third vision is based on an end to the compassion of God for Israel (cf. 7:1-3, 4-6). Although God earlier stopped his judgment of locust and fire, the key response of God in the third and fourth vision is, "I will no longer forgive them" (7:8; 8:2). In God's forbearance and patience he enslaved the descendants of Abram for four hundred years until the iniquity of the Amorites was full (Gen. 15:16), saved the nation of Israel from immediate destruction (Numb. 14:1-19), and had compassion on the people of Nineveh (Jonah 3:5—4:2). But eventually the Amorites were destroyed for defiling the land (Lev. 18:24-30; Deut. 9:1-4), the generation of Israelites who refused to enter Canaan died in the wilderness (Numb. 14:28-35), and Nineveh was destroyed (Nahum). The traditions of earlier and later years indicate that God's mercy on sinful people will not last forever. Eventually the day of intercession and compassion will pass, and the freedom of God to judge the guilty will happen (Jer. 14:19—15:2).

The withdrawal of God's compassion (of passing over sin) may involve the destruction of sacred institutions. Amos announces the end of the covenant

---

[67]D. Hillars, *Treaty-Curses and the Old Testament Prophets* (Rome: Pontifical Biblical Institute, 1964), 58-59 finds similar curses in ancient Near Eastern texts.

[68]The measuring line is parallel to a plumb line in 2 Kings 21:13; Isa. 28:17; 34:11.

[69]Björndalen, "Erwägungen zur Zukunft des Amazja und Israels nach der Überlieferung Amos 7, 10-17," discusses the relationship of 7:11b to 7:17b.

nation "my people" (7:8, 11, 17), the royal dynasty in power, and the "holy places of Israel" (7:9-13). These words were considered treason, political conspiracy, and theological nonsense. They violated God's promises of blessing to Isaac (Gen. 26:3-4, 24) and Jacob (Gen. 28:3-4, 13-17) that they would have many descendants and possess the land. How could God allow destruction for their sacred temples? How could he destroy the kingdom he established according to the prophecy of Ahijah (1 Kings 11:29-39)? How could God go back on his promise to establish an "enduring house... built for David" (1 Kings 11:38)? Some of the same theological impossibilities that faced Judah later (Jeremiah 7) faced many Israelites who were deceived by believing the false prophets and priests (Hos. 4:1-10) in Bethel and Samaria. Amos' prophecies are truly revolutionary because they require a radical rejection of nationalistic and religious traditions of hope. Amos is labeled a false prophet, and his words from God are rejected. Amos is not the only prophet who faced this kind of official opposition; in fact, almost every true prophet was sooner or later brought into conflict with the royal or cultic institutions. This confrontation with earthly power-figures severely tested Amos' prophetic call to prophesy in Israel (7:10-12), tempted him to run for the safety and security of Judah, and tried his commitment to his own message. His prophetic role was nearly destroyed.

Amos' authority and prophetic consciousness were firmly established in the memory of his call (7:15). His function was that of a messenger who delivered the words of Yahweh to a specific audience. He distinguished himself from other "prophetic types" who made a living by prophesying. His motives for service were independent of financial considerations and uninhibited by the professional, social, or religious rank or class of his audience. Communication of the message, inspite of controversy or rejection, was his highest priority. He argues not for his own authority but for the authority of the words of Yahweh. At times he may intercede to delay the work of God's judgment (7:1-6); at other times he must faithfully deliver the terrible implications of God's judgment (7:17). At this point God has called Amos to announce the new message to Israel. The end of the nation Israel is at hand!

Wailing, Not Forgiveness in the End

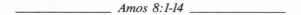

Amos 8:1-14

Introduction

This unit completes the central portion of the vision sequence in 7:1—9:10. The fourth vision (8:1-3) matches the third vision in the divine response, "I will no longer forgive them" (7:7-9). The fourth vision assumes the earlier visions and announces the end of Israel. The judgment speech in 8:4-14 expands the message of the vision. But the expansion of the vision is not built around a dispute as in 7:10-17, nor is it centered around the destruction of the temple and the king. This vision and exhortation stress the mourning of the nation (8:3, 8-10) due to God's judgment for social and economic abuse of the poor (8:4-6). On that day the people will not reject the word of God (cf. 7:10-13) but seek for it and not find it (8:11-14).

Background

The vision in 8:1-3 has the same characteristics and structure as the vision in 7:7-9 (see the section on Background for 7:7-17). The responsibility of the prophet was to declare the revelation of God received in visions and words. The experience of seeing and hearing a divine communication was fundamental to the prophet's ability to function as a messenger of God. The close connection between the vision and the words of exhortation in the judgment speech point to the continuity between various methods of revelation. This vision should not be connected to the autumn season when the summer fruit ripens.[70] Its function as a pair with 7:7-9 demands a relatively short time span between these visions.[71] The first vision of the pair announced that there was no longer any forgiveness. This vision repeats the message and has the rhetorical effect of confirming or sealing the matter in the mind of the prophet and his listeners. The basic message of "no forgiveness" in 7:7-17 included only a brief symbolic justification for this conclusion and limited the judgment to the king and the temple. The second vision in the pair connects this decision to the end, while the judgment speech develops a rationale for this conclusion (8:4-6).

---

[70]Wolff, *Amos* 318; Cripps, *Amos* 99; and Hammershaimb, *Amos* 107-08 needlessly try to associate the visions with different seasons.

[71]This vision was probably not given in the Bethel temple but nearby in Israel. There is no decree from the king that Amos must leave Israel in the book of Amos. Watts, *Amos* 34 puts the fourth vision at a New Year's festival at some Judean sanctuary a year after Amos was ejected from Bethel, but there is no evidence for this background to 8:1-3.

Within the judgment speech the prophet draws on several traditions used earlier in the book.[72] The accusations concerning the abuse of the poor in 8:4-6 are closely related to other accusations (2:6-8; 3:9-10; 4:1; 5:10-13). Amos 8:4 is nearly identical to 2:7a, and 8:6a to 2:6b, but 8:5-6 introduces new ideas that explain how the merchant class cheats the poor and ignores sacred traditions. Traditional values are fading as the nation increasingly abandons the ancient religious ordinances of observing the holy days of God. The merchants and traders operate out of greed for wealth, and these economic policies have resulted in a sociological reorganization of the people into non-Yahwistic patterns. Amos does not suggest social revolution to gain liberation or demand a new social system, but he states the basis for God's judgment of the nation.[73] A second theme is the death, lamentation, and mourning idea in 8:3, 8, 11, 14. Amos 8:3 is closely related to 6:9-10, 8:14 repeats a line from 5:2, and 8:8 and 11 draw on the idea of lamentation similar to 5:16-17 (see the section on Background for each of the references). These themes describe the results of God's judgment.[74] A third theme picked up from 5:18-20 is the Day of Yahweh. The "day" which is coming (8:11) marks the bitter end (8:10) and came to be known by the circumlocution "that day" (8:3, 9, 13). It is not a day of light but a day of darkness for Israel (5:18, 20; 8:9). God's judgment will fall with previously unknown severity. In addition, Amos uses an oath in 8:7, 14 (cf. 4:2; 6:8), imagery of a famine in 8:11-12 (cf. 4:6-8) and parts of a hymn in 8:8-9 (cf. 4:13; 5:8; 9:5-6).

The individual settings for these various themes are made subordinate to the intergrating role that each plays in the overall unity of Amos' theology. The creative process of restructuring, developing, and repeating images and forms of speech already familiar to the orator or writer is expected when the same basic message is repeated in a new situation. Speeches vary according to the audience, the setting and the events that have transpired since the last time the same themes were employed. Unfortunately, in 8:1-14 the new setting is not clearly defined. If Amos 1-6 was spoken at Samaria and 7-9 at Bethel, then many of those in the audience at Bethel did not know of Amos' condemnation of the nation's abuse of the poor (2:6-8) or his prediction of the coming Day of Yahweh with its mourning (5:18-20). Their understanding of the basis for God's judgment in the visions would be incomplete and the implications of his wrath only faintly imagined. The integration of these themes with the visions gives a brief overview of God's earlier words. The way in which the themes are reused gives insight into the redactional process at work to meet the needs of a new setting. The references to the temple songs (8:3), the sabbath and new moon (8:5), festivals (8:10), seeking the word of

---

[72]See the section on Background for 2:6-8.

[73]H. B. Huffmon, "The Social Role of Amos' Message," *The Quest for the Kingdom of God: Studies in Honor of G. E. Mendenhall* (Winona Lake: Eisenbrauns, 1983) 109-16.

[74]See the section on Background for 5:1-17, where the theme of mourning is dealt with.

Yahweh (8:12), and swearing by a god at various temple locations (8:14) reveal a shift of these themes toward a temple audience, probably in the Bethel area. Together they emphasize that the end is here, that God's day of forgiveness is past, that his coming day will be filled with mourning and bitterness because of their iniquity.

Structure and Unity

Structure

The outline of the text reproduces something of the parallelism between the words and the flow of thought within each paragraph. The English outline will be used to structure the exegesis of the text.

Wailing, Not Forgiveness in the End
Amos 8:1-14

		A. No forgiveness in a vision of summer fruit
Thus the Lord[a] Yahweh showed me:	**8:1**	1. Vision of summer fruit
Behold, a basket of summer fruit.[b]		
And he said to me:	**8:2**	
What do you see Amos?		
And I said:		
A basket of summer fruit![c]		
Then Yahweh said to me:		2. Summer fruit means the end, no forgiveness
The end has come for my people Israel!		
I will no longer forgive them!		
The songs[d] of the temple will be wailing,	**8:3**	3. The end will bring wailing and death
in that day, there will be many corpses,		
declares the Lord Yahweh,		
in every place, they will throw them.		
Hush![e]		
		B. The end will bring wailing but no word from God
		1. Abusive economic actions bring an end to the poor
Hear this, you who are trampling[f] the needy,	**8:4**	a. Accusations of abuse
to bring an end[g] to the poor of the land,		

8:1a. Some Greek MSS omit Lord. Vaticanus and other texts include it (cf. 7:1, 4, 7).

8:1b. The Old Greek has "fowler's pouch," but the other versions have "basket of summer fruit." In Jer. 5:27 this root refers to a bird cage.

saying:
  When will the new moon[h] end,
    that we may sell grain;[i]
  the sabbath
    that we may open wheat sales,[j]
      reducing a bushel's size,
      enlarging a shekel's weight,
      defrauding by deceitful scales
	8:5	b. Methods of
		   economic
		   abuse

to buy the poor for silver,
          the needy for a pair of sandals,
  and that we may sell the refuse[k] of the wheat?
	8:6	

		2. These actions
		   will bring God's
		   mournful day in
		   the end

Yahweh has sworn by the majestic one of Jacob:
  Indeed, I will never[l] forget[m] their actions.
	8:7	a. God's oath
		   because of sin

Will not the land quake because of this,
  and everyone in it mourn?
Indeed, all of it[n] will rise like the Nile,[o]
  it will be tossed about,[p]
  and will sink[q] like the river of Egypt.
	8:8	b. Signs of
		   God's oath in
		   nature

And it will come about on that day,
declares the Lord Yahweh,
    that I[r] will make the sun set at noon,
    and I will bring darkness to the earth in daylight.
	8:9	

Then I will turn your festivals to mourning,
  and all your songs to lamenting;
and I will bring sackcloth on all loins,
  and baldness on every head;
and I will make it like mourning for an only son,
  and the end of it[s] like a bitter day.
	8:10	c. The end will
		   be mourning

		3. There will be no
		   new word from
		   God, only death

Behold the days are coming,
declares the Lord Yahweh,
    when I will send a famine in the land,
      not a famine for bread,
      and not a thirst for water,
      but[t] for hearing the words of Yahweh.
	8:11	a. The absence
		   of the word
		   of God

They[u] will stagger from sea to sea,
they will wander from north to east,
    to seek the word of Yahweh,
    but they will not find it.
	8:12	

In that day the beautiful virgins,
  and the young men will faint from thirst,
	8:13	b. The absence of
		   help from the
		   gods/God of Israel

those who swear by the guilt[v] of Samaria,
      and say:
        As your god lives, O Dan!
      and:
        As the power[w] of Beersheba lives!
        they will fall and never rise again.
	8:14	

8:2c. See note 8:1*b*.

8:3d. The Old Greek may have had *šôrôt* instead of *šîrôt* in its Hebrew original; thus it has the "ceiling" of the temple. Many commentators emend "songs" to "singing women." Aq. has "sockets," Sym. "ode," and Theod. "the former ones."

8:3e. The Hebrew "Hush, Silence" is rather abrupt. The Old Greek connects the last two words "I will bring silence" because they did not understand the hush as an interjection.

8:4f. The root *ša'ap* "to yearn, desire" is, confused with *šûp* "to oppress, crush, trample" which fits the context here. The same problem is found in Amos 2:7. The Old Greek recognized this confusion and properly translated the text, "to oppress, rub out, grind down." It adds "in the morning" after this participle, but there is nothing in the MT to suggest this.

8:4g. *lašbît* (see GKC 53q) an infinitive construct is the participle "overpower" in the Old Greek, but Theod. has *luo* which usually is translated "loose, set free"; in some cases it can mean to "break down, lay low, demolish."

8:5h. The Old Greek has "month," a good translation of *hdš*, but in the context of the sabbath this must refer to the "new moon" festival.

8:5i. "Grain" is omitted in the Old Greek translation. The word may have been treated as a dittography of the verb by the translators or by a Hebrew scribe.

8:5j. The Old Greek and Syriac have "treasure, store house for treasure" which is an adequate translation.

8:6k. "Refuse" *mpl* was read as *mkl* "from all" by the Greek translators.

8:7l. "Ever, forever" was misunderstood as "for victory," as in Amos 1:11.

8:7m. The verb is a first person singular with "I," Yahweh as the subject in Hebrew, but the Old Greek makes "their deeds" the subject and gives it a passive sense.

8:8n. "All of it" *klh* is understood as the noun *klh* "destruction" in the Old Greek.

8:8o. The Hebrew *k'r* "as light" is a misreading of *ky'ôr* "as the Nile" as in Amos 9:5.

8:8p. This whole line is omitted in the Old Greek and in Amos 9:5.

8:8q. The Hebrew reading *nšqh* "to give to drink" is written in the text, but the Qere properly adjusts the reading to *nsq'* "to sink," as in Amos 9:5.

8:8r. The sun is the subject of the verb in the Old Greek, but "I" (meaning Yahweh) is the subject in Hebrew.

8:10s. The Old Greek has "those with them," while Sym. and Theod. have "the end of the earth."

8:11t. After the conjunction, the Old Greek supplies the implied "famine."

8:12u. The waters are the subject of the verb in the Old Greek, not the people as in the Hebrew.

8:14v. "The guilt" is translated "propitiation" in the Old Greek, depending on the root *'šm* not *'šmh*.

8:14w. The Old Greek omits "the way" *drk* and has "your god" which may point to the Ugaritic *drkt* "power, dominion."

The structure of 8:1-3 includes: (1) an introductory formula, (2) a transitional particle "behold," (3) a description of the vision, (4) a dialogue between God and Amos, (5) an explanation of the vision, and (6) an interpretation of the significance of the vision. A rhetorical play on *qāyiṣ* "summer fruit" (8:1-2) and *qēṣ* "end" (8:2) draws the vision together, but the absence of a verbal connection with 8:3 weakens its connection with the vision. The general concept of the end of Israel in 8:2 is consistent with the picture of corpses and wailing in 8:3, and both themes are united in 8:10. This vision is parallel in structure to 7:7-9, and both emphasize the end of God's forgiveness of Israel.

The judgment speech (8:4-14) attached to the fourth vision matches the paragraph (7:10-17) connected to the third vision.[75] These two non-visionary

---

[75]See the Introduction to 7:7-17, where these connections are described.

sections are not parallel in structure, but a thematic relationship is apparent. The fourth vision and its exhortations assume the previous material and describes the broader effects of God's judgment on the people, not just the king and the temple as 7:10-17. The rejection of God's word in 7:10-17 develops into a thirst for God's word in 8:11-14.

The paragraphs within 8:4-14 include accusations and statements of punishment. The first section (8:4-6) is an accusation. It is unified by its reference to the "needy" *'ebyôn* (8:4,6), "selling" *šbr* (8:5-6), infinitives and first person plural verbs (8:5-6), and topics concerned with economic abuses in selling grain. The first paragragh could be extended through 8:8—thus the next paragraph would start with the introductory "and it will come about in that day" (8:9, cf. 8:11)—but 8:7-8 have thematic continuity with the verses that follow.[76] The second paragraph (8:7-10) is a punishment statement closely connected to 8:4-6 by the reference to "their actions" (8:7) and "because of this" (8:8). The paragraph describes the effects of God's judgment on the land (8:8), the sun (8:9), and the people (8:10). Mourning and lamentation (8:8, 10) will characterize that day when the normal order of things will be turned upside down (8:8-10). Ideas of mourning and death, songs and festivals, and the events of "that day" unite the vision in 8:1-3 with the fuller explanation in 8:7-10. The final paragraph (8:11-14) is divided into two sections by references to the "day" (8:11, 13), but the two are brought together by the common theme of thirst (8:11, 13) and the absence of a positive word from God (8:11-12) or any other gods (8:14). The end has come (8:2), the days are coming (8:11), and the end of it will be a bitter day (8:10) because Israel will fall and not rise again (8:14; cf. 8:3). These diverse emphases, drawn from earlier oracles, integrate this vision into the broader message of Amos to persuade this new audience that the end has come for Israel (8:3, 10, 14).

Unity

The complex arrangement of several diverse themes weakens the unity of the whole. Discussion of the unity of chapter 8 focuses on: (1) the broad question of the redactional nature of 8:4-14; (2) the relationship of 8:3 to the vision; (3) the deuteronomic character of 8:11-12; and (4) the date of the idolatry described in 8:14. Numerous commentators identify short redactional alterations in the text, but there is little agreement on these details.[77]

Wolff attributes 8:3, 4-10, 13-14 (and 7:9-17) to the disciples of Amos somewhere around 733 B.C. He uses the peculiarities of style, the repetition

---

[76]Mays, *Amos* 142 and Rudolph, *Amos* 261 put 8:4-8 together.

[77]Harper, *Amos* 174 omits 8:2a; Wolff, *Amos* 143; Rudolph, *Amos* 238; and Niditch, *Symbolic Visions in Biblical Traditions* 36, omit "declares Yahweh" in 8:3; Harper, *Amos* 175 omits 8:6 because it repeats 2:6; Wolff, *Amos* 322; Mays, *Amos* 142 and Rudolph, *Amos* 261 omit "and it will be tossed about" in 8:8; and Harper, *Amos* 175 omits the stereotyped phrase, "Behold the days are coming, declared the Lord Yahweh" in 8:11.

of earlier themes from Amos, and the proximity of ideas in Hosea to 8:14 to support this position.[78] If Amos was facing a new audience at Bethel, it would be natural for him to support his vision reports with a summary of his earlier prophetic oracles. Amos repeatedly returns to older themes throughout the book (i.e., social injustice in 2:6-8; 3:9-10; 4:1; 5:10-13; 6:4-7; 8:4-6), so the only thing unusual is the exactitude of the references.

Harper relocates 8:3 after 8:9, Robinson puts it after 8:14, while Duhm places it after 6:8-11.[79] Although 8:3 is topically similar to 8:9 and 6:8-11, the structural parallelism in the paired visions (7:7-9; 8:1-3) and the need for an explanation of the significance of the vision weighs in favor of the authenticity of 8:3. The supposed conflict between a literal and figurative thirst in 8:11-12 is illusory, as is the thought that "in that day" is the sole property of the deuteronomic school.[80] The non-eschatological use of "in that day" should not be denied to Amos (cf. 5:18-20) since he (cf. 2:16; 3:14; 4:2; 6:3) and other pre-exilic prophets (Isaiah, Micah, Hosea) use the clause that way. The reference to temples and gods at both Samaria and Dan strongly weakens the claim that 8:14 describes the idolatry of Israel after 621 B.C.[81] Each of these challenges limits the literary and prophetic freedom to restate known themes in new and fresh ways. Since repetition is such an integral part of Amos' style throughout the book, the appearance of older issues, combined in a unique complex of messages, is not surprising.

Interpretation

A. *No forgiveness in a vision of summer fruit (8:1-3).*

1. Vision of summer fruit (8:1-2a)
    The fourth vision begins with the regular introductory formula (cf. 7:1, 4, 7) to acknowledge the source of this new revelation. Amos did not just happen to see a basket sitting in the market or next to someone's house and imagine that it could serve as a clever word-play illustration for his next sermon—this vision had a divine origin. The object that God showed Amos was a basket-like container used in the transportation of fruit during harvest time.[82] The basket of fruit is a sign or symbol of the message; there is no dramatic activity involving the basket. Instead a dialogue, identical to 7:8, records Amos' identification of the object he sees (8:2a). The root *qyṣ* does not refer simply to "summer" but the goods that summer produces. There is no

---

[78]Wolff, *Amos* 295-96, 318, 325-26.

[79]Harper, *Amos* 174; Cripps, *Amos* 241-42.

[80]Cripps, *Amos* 250, 252; Wolff, *Amos* 326.

[81]Mays, *Amos* 148.

[82]*Kᵉlūb* "basket" is used only here and in Jer. 5:27. In Jeremiah it holds birds, so the word must be a general term for a woven container to carry things. There is no indication that this basket carried fruit for the autumn festival. Mays, *Amos* 141 and Watts, *Amos* 38 argue the opposite.

way of knowing whether the basket had grapes, olives, figs, or some other agricultural product in it. Since the crop has been picked, the idea of harvesting at the end of the summer season is associated with these images.

2. Summer fruit means the end, no forgiveness (8:2*b*)

The explanation of the vision is based on a word-play between "summer fruit" *qyṣ* and the "end" *qṣ*. The absence of the middle letter *y* in the Gezer Calendar (a ninth-century B.C. agricultural calendar) suggests the possibility of an identical spelling at the time of Amos and also a similar word-play between the month of "summer fruit" and the "end" month.[83] The divine interpretation that "the end has come for my people Israel" encapsulates the heart of Amos' message throughout the book.[84] The end carries a finality that marks the completion of an era. However, it marks a break in a connection that goes deeper than a temporal change, for God is announcing the end of a nation, his own people Israel. Such a drastic step implies death and destruction for cities, armies, men, women, and children. The loss of life and land, the blessings of God, is the result of the end of God's covenant relationship with his people. In Amos this separation is not a temporary divorce (cf. Hosea) but the end. The absoluteness of the end of the nation must be integrated with earlier messages of hope for the remnant (5:14-15), the existence of many people in exile (4:2-3; 5:27; 6:7; 7:11, 17), and specific references to God's plans to fulfill his promises and re-establish his people (9:11-15). But these themes should in no way weaken the force or reality of this disastrous announcement. The end has come for Israel.[85] The prophecy is unqualified and without hope of change, for God will not pass over their sins anymore, his forgiveness is no longer available. Their destruction is guaranteed, for the compassion of God has ended.

The "end" in later books marks the destruction of Judah (Lam. 4:18; Ezek. 7:2, 3, 6), some other nation (Jer. 51:13), or the eschatological end of time (Dan. 8:17, 19; 9:26; 12:4, 6, 9, 13). In this case the end refers specifically to the nation Israel. The clause "in that day" (8:3) describes this time of death and destruction in Israel. An eschatological reference to "in that day" (8:3, 9, 11, 13) seems out of place in this context. The Day of Yahweh (5:18-20) will bring great darkness on Israel.

3. The end will bring wailing and death (8:3)

The interpretation of the significance of the vision amplifies what will

---

[83]B. D. Rahtjen, "A Critical Note on Amos 8:1-2," *JBL* 83 (1964) 416-17; R. Coote, "Ripe Words for Preaching: Connotative Diction in Amos," *Pacific Theological Review* 8 (1976) 13-19, goes beyond the text in suggesting an additional play between *'osip* "pass over" and *'asip* "harvest" since the later term does not occur here. For the text of the Gezer Calendar see *ANET* 320.

[84]Rudolph, *Amos* 239.

[85]An earlier prophet gave God's word concerning the end of a king's rule (1 Kings 14:10; 16:2-3; 21:20-22), but Amos' prophecy has a finality that is of a totally different character, for the Abrahamic, Mosaic, and Davidic promises are threatened with eternal non-fulfillment.

happen in the end. The oracle in 8:3 clarifies what is implied by the vision. The strong and wealthy nation of Israel will undergo a phenomenal change. Military power, economic wealth, international prestige, and religious security will vanish when the end comes. In the context of the optimism at the Bethel temple, Amos pays particular attention to the overwhelming change from life and joy to death and wailing. The joyful songs which filled the air at the temple will soon be songs of lamentation and mourning.[86] Their rejoicing at harvest time will turn into a disastrous tragedy of wailing when God makes an end of the people and the temple (7:9). With gruesome detail, Amos depicts the scene of death. Bodies will lie everywhere, unburied in open shame (cf. 6:10). The casting out of the dead to the wild animals is one of the most severe curses that could fall on a person (Josh. 8:29; 10:27; 1 Kings 14:11; 2 Kings 9:25-26; Jer. 22:19). The picture is so tragic, so far beyond belief and emotional response, that silence is the only thing appropriate.[87]

B. The end will bring wailing, but no word from God (8:4-14)

1. Abusive economic action brings an end to the poor (8:4-6)

Those who misuse the poor here are not identified as the "cows of Bashan" in Samaria (4:1) or those who live in palace fortresses (3:9-10; 5:9-13; 6:4-8). Nevertheless, the continuity between the accusations in 8:4-6 and earlier references to the unjust treatment of the weak (cf. 2:6-8) suggests that Amos may be condemning the same group. Both trample the needy and buy the poor for small amounts of money. In spite of these similiarities, those who find a homogeneous class of urban elite persecuting the poor probably have oversimplified a much more complex social setting.[88] Huffmon believes these oppressors in 8:4-6 are middle class merchants who sold or loaned wheat to the poor for planting in times of famine, while Lang derives these abuses from a rent capitalism system.[89] Rather than limiting the activity in 8:4-6 to one class or basing it on one particular economic system, it is likely that several groups and methods were employed to take advantage of the situation of the poor. Amos is not condemning an economic system or a class of people; it is rather the abuse of workable economic arrangements by persons having significant economic control to manipulate things to their advantage. These new ways of doing business ignore the religious and ethical standards within the traditions of Yahweh.

---

[86]*hêkāl* probably refers to the temple, not the palace as Wolff, *Amos* 320 and Rudolph, *Amos* 238 maintain.

[87]The rather magical interpretation of "hush, silence" is to be rejected. Niditch, *Symbolic Vision in Biblical Tradition*, 40 and Wolff, *Amos* 320 accept it.

[88]M. Fendler, "Zur Socialkritik des Amos," *Ev T* 33 (1973) 32-53 opposes the homogeneous oversimplification represented in the study of H. Donner, "Die soziale Botschaft der Propheten im Liche der Gesellschaftordnung in Israel," *Or Ant* 2 (1963) 229-45.

[89]Huffmon, "The Social Role of Amos' Message," 109-10; Lang, "The Social Organization of Peasant Poverty in Biblical Israel," 58-59.

a. Accusations of abuse (8:4) begin with a summons to attention similar to 3:1, 9, 13; 4:1; 5:1. The summons is followed by a general description of oppression of the weak using words nearly identical to 2:7a (see the exegesis of 2:7). The results, not the method of oppression, are described in 8:4. The weak and poor citizens are trampled (see the textual note) and crushed (cf. 4:1; Isa. 3:15) in direct opposition to the admonitions to aviod taking advantage of the poor who are protected by God (Ps. 72:12-13; 83:3-4 [Heb 83:4-5]). Israel's legal traditions (Exod. 22:20-23; Deut. 16:11, 14; 24:19-21) require sharing openly with the poor, and the early prophets opposed those who took advantage of the weak (Isa. 1:17; Micah 3:1-12). The general accusation is not limited to a court setting, it was only one of many settings where ruthless actions were taken against the defenseless. The effect of these policies was to "exterminate, bring to an end" the lower class by robbing them of what little life and freedom they had left. The infinitive construct "in order to put an end to" interprets the motives of the oppressors.[90] Their goals were directly contrary to Yahweh's purpose of protecting the poor. In an ironic twist, Amos announces their end (8:2) because they are trying to bring about the end of the poor (8:4).

b. Methods of economic abuse (8:5-6) are spelled out in specific terms applicable to the audience at Bethel. The validity of the charge is heightened by introducing a quotation, a favorite tactic of Amos (cf. 2:12; 4:1; 5:14; 6:13; 7:10, 14; 8:10, 14, 16; 9:10). Amos has either heard people say similar things or puts words in their mouth on the basis of the behavior he has observed. The primary theme is deceit in the business of trading grain. The perversity of these traders is illustrated in several ways. Their greed for economic grain far outweighs their concern for the worship of God on the sabbath or the new moon. They impatiently wait for the end of the religious festivals of joy, rest, and praise to God. The sabbath was to be a holy day (Exod. 20:8-11; Deut 5:12-15) with no work or selling (Jer. 17:21-27; Neh. 13:15-22). The new moon celebration at the beginning of each month (Lev. 23:23-25; Numb. 10:10; 28:11-15; 1 Sam. 20:5; Isa. 1:13-14; Hos. 2:11 [Heb. 2:13]; 5:7) and the sabbath restricted the merchants' exploitation of the people who were liberated by the sabbath. In other societies, a seventh day restriction on work enhanced rather than restricted market place activities, but Israel maintained some semblance of orthodoxy at least in the outward observation of these days.[91] Such "orthodoxy" was not without its critics from the profit minded traders who were hoping to gouge another victim. Their formal piety is betrayed by their true feelings about God's holy day.

Their desire was to sell grain, to open the wheat market for sales. The ac-

---

[90] GKC 114f; not as a continuation of the participle as Harper, *Amos* 185, who follows Driver, *Tenses* 206.

[91] N. Andreasen, *The Old Testament Sabbath: A Tradition-Historical Investigation* (Missoula: SBL, 1972) 1-15.

cusation goes beyond their improper zeal to include the way they do their
business. By falsifying weights and measures the commercial transactions
could result in a substantial gain for the seller. If the ephah (the unit for measuring grain) was slightly less than a standard ephah, the poor purchaser
would pay the regular price per unit but not get the standard amount of
grain.[92] If the shekel (the weight used on a scale) was made heavier, the poor
seller would have to supply more grain to receive the standard price per
shekel. A third method of deception was to tamper with the balance scale
itself, so that it would always give a fraudulent reading. Finally, Amos
mentions (8:6b) the practice of adding chaff, dirt, and other useless fillers in
the bottom of a sack of grain. These business principles brought handsome
incomes to the merchants, but they ran contrary to the Mosaic and wisdom
traditions. Yahweh required just weights and measures (Lev. 19:35-36;
Deut. 25:13-15; Prov. 20:10; Mic. 6:10-11) and despised false or deceptive
scales (Prov. 11:1; 16:11; 20:23) because their employemnt resulted in stealing what belonged to another person.[93]

The final part of the quotation (8:6a) repeats 2:6 to demonstrate that one
of the purposes for this total disregard for justice in trade relationships is the
potential of eventually owning everything the poor had, including their
flesh. As debts mounted, a man and his family would sell themselves into
slavery to cover some indebtedness. Such greed for money had no boundaries. Because God cares for the poor and the weak, because God had
redeemed his people from such slavery, and because this action is contrary
to the law of God, the nation is ripe for judgment. Its end is near.

2. These actions will bring God's mournful day in the end (8:7-10)

a. God's oath because of sin (8:7) is a direct response to the accusations
in 8:4-6. God swears and binds himself to judgment because "of their
action." God will not pass over or forgive their sins any longer (8:2); he will
never ever forget how they have brutally mistreated the poor. His earlier oaths
were based on his holiness (4:2) or on himself (6:8), but here he swears on
the "pride, majestic one" of Jacob. The phrase is unusual and open to different interpretations. The pride of Jacob was the reason for the oath in 6:8, but
elsewhere this phrase refers to the land of Israel (Ps. 47:4[Heb. 47:5]; Isa.
58:14).[94] Since pride is not the topic of 8:4-6, it is better to take ge'ôn "pride,
excellence, majesty, glory" as an ironic name for Yahweh. Israel did not treat
God as majestic—their action demonstrated that they were not particularly
proud of Yahweh—but God swears on the basis of his glorious and majestic
name (Micah 5:4 [Heb. 5:3]; Jer. 2:11; 1 Sam 15:29) to regain his glory and

---

[92]The ephah was about forty liters or eight gallons. See R. B. Y. Scott, "Weights and Measures
of the Bible," BAR 3, ed. E. F. Campbell and D. N. Freedman (Garden City: Doubleday, 1970)
345-58; Hammerschaimb, Amos 123-24.

[93]Egyptian standards of justice condemn these practices also, ANET 388.

[94]Cripps, Amos 245; Wolff, Amos 328 and the Old Greek make pride the reason for the oath.

defend his majesty (Ezek. 38:16, 23; 39:7, 21, 25). The actions which follow are what God swears he will do.[95]

b. Signs of God's oath in nature (8:8-9) include effects on the earth and the sun. On account of Israel's evil deeds God will bring what appears to be an earthquake and an eclipse. The land will tremble and quake (2:13; 9:1) when God in theophanic power curses it.[96] Using images of darkness and a bitter day (8:9-10) from the Day of Yahweh, Amos describes the horror of God's wrath and the mourning that will overtake Israel. To develop the picture, imagery from the hymn in 9:5 is employed to compare the movement of the land with the rising of the Nile in Egypt. Obviously, the speed with which the Nile rises and falls is not the point of comparison. The movement of solid land is terrifying, and any shifting that "tosses about" the land represents a major collision of the earth's surface plates. The later report of an earthquake about two years after the preaching of Amos (1:1) may well be the fulfillment of this prophecy. The cursing of the land due to the sins of the people in it is a common theme throughout Scripture (Gen. 3:17-19; Isa. 24:1-6).

The setting of the sun at noon and the resulting darkness (8:9) is another sign of God's miraculous intervention into the affairs of nature. The Day of Yahweh will not be a day of light but of darkness (5:18, 20). The events of "that day" of judgment for Israel are the actions of God; humans are nothing in the presence of Almighty God. The prophet is not forseeing the final eschatological end of the world. The imagery of the end of the nation Israel was elsewhere expanded in the development of worldwide eschatological themes of God's final judgment.[97] An eclipse in 763 B.C. may have been a powerful sign which confirmed these words of Yahweh.

c. The end will bring mourning (8:10). The Bethel temple festivals and joyous songs (cf. 8:3) will be transformed into wailing and lamenting when God judges Israel in that day (cf. 5:16-17). The temple itself will be destroyed (7:9). The customary signs of mourning will be everywhere as people put on sackcloth and shave or pull out their hair (2 Sam. 3:31; Isa. 15:2; 22:12; Jer. 48:37; Ezek. 7:18; 27:31). The sorrow and mourning will be especially great because of the death that will accompany God's wrath (8:3). People will grieve deeply like someone weeping over the death of an only son (Jer. 6:26). This is the end of "my people Israel" (8:3), and the end of this time of judgment will not bring joy or victory but unusual bitterness and distress. The sorrow of the nation will not only be due to the loss of life but the loss of hope, for it is "I" Yahweh who will bring an end to Israel on this mournful day.

3. There will be no new word from God, only death (8:11-14)

---

[95]The *'m* is sometimes translated "if," but in the shortened form of a curse or oath it came to mean "verily, not." GKC 149b.

[96]Crenshaw, "Amos and the Theophanic Traditions," 210.

[97]Isa. 24:1-6, 19-20; Joel 2:10; 3:14-16 [Heb. 4:15-16]; Matt. 24:29.

a. The absence of the word of God (8:11-12) will make these mournful days even more intolerable. When the day of judgment comes (4:2; 8:2, 9, 13) on Israel, the people in their mourning and weeping will remember God and seek a new word of hope or direction concerning the future of Israel. This absence of God's longsuffering compassion and protection will create a new thirst for a prophetic word. This is not a hunger for food or a thirst for water (cf. 4:6-8), but the vocabulary and themes are similar. Earlier they had God's word and were warned, but they refuse to return to God. They told the prophets not to speak (2:11-12) and rejected Amos and his message when he brought God's word (7:9-17). Now in the deepest moment of need they finally seek a response from God. The oaths to other gods in 8:14 suggest that they really are not committed to God; their real interest is in a promise of salvation from any god who would listen. They do not come with hearts of true repentance before God. God's abandonment of his people (cf. Ezek. 9:9; 11:22-23), his refusal to answer their prayers with a prophetic word (Lam. 2:9; Ezek. 7:26), means that the time for repentance is past (Ps. 32:6; Isa. 55:6). They must now suffer alone without God.[98] The repetition of famine, thirst, and the word of God (8:11-12) focuses attention on this deep desire which is unfulfilled. Seeking for the word of God was encouraged by Amos (5:4-6, 14-15), but now it is impossible to find it. This divine search is described as a staggering, misdirected, and futile roaming that is essentially ignorant of how to find Yahweh. The nation has lost contact with God so long as they do not know how to inquire of him. They frantically rush about like headless chickens, staggering aimlessly, blindly groping for some relief from their sorrow. But no answer comes, for the end of Israel has come (8:2).

b. The absence of help from oaths to the gods of Israel (8:13-14) continues the description of the hopelessness of the nation "in that day." The severity of famine and thirst in 8:13 is emphasized by describing the weakness or fainting of the strongest members of society. The healthy young men and women will be overcome (cf. 5:2-3) by this day of destruction and mourning, and they too will give up on their own strength. They will have to admit that they need a word from God.[99]

In this state of dire need, the people in confusion will turn to their places of worship in Samaria, Dan, and Beersheba to take oaths of loyalty to the deity worshipped there (8:14). Swearing an oath by the name of Yahweh or some other god was an act of worship and an affirmation of belief in the power and authority of the deity named. Deuteronomy calls upon the Israelites to fear, serve, cling, and swear by Yahweh (Deut. 6:13; 10:20), and elsewhere the na-

---

[98]In the "Lamentation over the Destruction of Ur," (*ANET* 455-63) the gods abandoned Ur; thus the people take up a bitter lament because the city was destroyed. M. Greenberg, *Ezekiel 1-20* AB (Garden City: Doubleday, 1983) 200-201, discusses other texts where the gods abandon their temples before they are destroyed.

[99]Verse 13 does not refer to a natural thirst for water as claimed by Hammershaimb, *Amos* 128 ad Cripps, *Amos* 252.

tion is warned against swearing by the name of other gods (Josh. 23:7-8; Jer. 12:16; Zeph. 1:4-5).[100] The oath formula "as Yahweh lives; by the life of Yahweh" may be appended to a vow or statement to declare its truthfulness (1 Sam. 14:39, 45; 19:6; 20:3; 28:10). The oaths in 8:14 accompanied statements of loyalty and devotion to bind the speaker to his words. This form of speech was intended to impress the deity with the seriousness of the worshiper's commitment to the promises he had sworn.

The three oaths are slightly different in wording, but the intention is the same. The oaths are connected to a deity and a place. The clearest oath is, "as your god lives, O Dan." The city of Dan was on the northern border of Palestine (Josh. 19:47) and was the site where Jeroboam I placed one of the golden calves (1 Kings 12:29). Amos does not say who this god is, but the negative context and parallelism supports the view that it was not Yahweh.[101] In light of Hosea, and the Baalistic tendencies introduced by Ahab and Jezebel (1 Kings 16:29-33), it is unlikely that a pure cult of Yahweh continued in Dan. Archaeological excavations have uncovered what may be the site of the high place and a horned altar, but these imply very little about the worship there.[102] At best, it was a syncretistic place of worship where Yahweh and other gods were worshiped.

The worship of Samaria (8:14a) is more difficult because it is unclear whether this refers to the nation or city of Samaria, and because 'šmt is sometimes translated "guilt" or taken to be a reference to the goddess Ashima or Asherah. Some believe Samaria refers to the national shrine at Bethel, but elsewhere in Amos (3:9, 12; 4:1; 6:1) Samaria always describes the city, not the nation.[103] It is peculiar that Bethel is omitted, but Amos is at Bethel and is describing people going elsewhere to find divine words of comfort. First Kings 16:32 reports the construction of a Baal temple in Samaria which Amos probably had in mind. The swearing at Samaria is described as the "guilt of Samaria." The Hebrew text need not be emended, for circumlocutions like the "sins of Baasha, sin or way of Jeroboam" (1 Kings 15:26, 30, 34; 16:2, 13, 19, 26; 2 Kings 10:29, 31) are common ways of making a judgmental statement rather than a factual statement about false worship at a par-

---

[100]Swearing by the name of a personal god was common in the ancient Near Eastern world. See J. Pedersen, *Der Eid bei den Semiten* (Strassburg, 1914); F. Horst, "Der Eid im Alten Testament," *EvT* 17 (1957) 366-84; M. R. Lehmann, "Biblical Oaths," *ZAW* 81 (1969) 74-92; M. Greenberg, "The Hebrew Oath Particle *HAY/HE*," *JBL* 76 (1957) 34-39.

[101]S. B. Gurewicz, "When Did the Cult Associated with the 'Golden Calves' Fully Develop in the Northern Kingdom?" *ABR* 2 (1952) 41-44.

[102]A. Biram, "Tel Dan" *BA* 37 (1974) 26-51 and "An Israelite Horned Altar at Dan," *BA* 37 (1974) 106-07.

[103]Harper, *Amos* 184 and Hammershaimb, *Amos* 128 believe Amos is talking about the calf at Bethel, which is parallel to the calf at Dan in the next line. Several commentaries follow Wellhausen and emend the text to read Bethel instead of Samaria, but this is pure conjecture. Rudolph, *Amos* 268 and Kapelrud, *Amos* 49 prefer "guilt" but do not indicate that Amos is speaking about the calf at Bethel.

ticular shrine. It is not always easy to determine what a circumlocution stands for. Without changing the text, it is possible to hold that Amos purposely chose 'šmt because it was a play on the name of the goddess of Ashima who was worshiped in Samaria. Second Kings 17:30 indicates that Ashima was worshiped by the people who were settled in Israel after the Israelites were taken into captivity in 722/1 B.C. Since the borders of Israel stretched to the gates of Hamath (6:14), it would not be surprising to find the worship of Ashima during Amos' time. Some believe Ashim-Bethel was the name of a female deity worshiped by Jews in southern Egypt at Elephantine two or three centuries after the time of Amos, but others translate the word "the name of Bethel" or "Isum," a Babylonian god.[104] This possible play on words suggests a syncretistic worship at Samaria of both Yahweh and Ashima.

The third oath is related to worship at Beersheba. The oath refers to the *derek* "customs, way" of Beersheba (cf. the ways of Jeroboam). In this translation, Amos pictures the people swearing by the pilgrimage to or sins of Beersheba, but many commentators find this translation odd and prefer to emend the text. Neuberg suggests that *dr* means "assembly" from Ugaritic, and on the basis of the parallelism with the preceding line he reads "as the assembly (of your gods) live, O Beersheba," while Dahood takes Ugaritic *drkt* "dominion, power, throne" as an appellative for a god equivalent to Hebrew *drk*.[105] Many emend *drk* to *ddk* "your patron diety" or hypothesize a connection between *drk* and the fish god Derketo of Ashkelon.[106] The Ugaritic evidence of Dahood yields an acceptable meaning, but many prefer to maintain the traditional "way, pilgrimage."[107] Since oaths are sworn to gods or people, and that is the reference in the parallel examples, a reference to a deity must be assumed. They call to a power that has no power, a god who is absent and does not exist.

Those who swear by these gods, whether they be foreign gods (cf. 5:27) or perversions of Yahweh through syncretism, will not receive a word of salvation, protection, or comfort from the death and sorrow that Yahweh will send. There will be no help from God or the gods. Instead Israel will fall and not rise again (cf. 5:3).[108] Death will bring an end to the people of Israel (8:2).

---

[104]A. Cowley, *Aramaic Papyri of the Fifth Century B.C.* (Oxford: Oxford Univ., 1923) 123-25 gives the text. See Barstad, *The Religious Polemics of Amos* 167-78, who gives a complete discussion and bibliography on this matter.

[105]F. J. Neuberg, "An Unrecognized Meaning of Hebrew DÔR," *JNES* 9 (1950) 215-17; P. R. Ackroyd, "The Meaning of Hebrew *dwr* Reconsidered," *JSS* 13 (1968) 4; M. Dahood, "Ugaritic *drkt* and Biblical *drk*," *TS* 15 (1954) 627-31.

[106]Maag, *Amos* 56; Hammershaimb, *Amos* 129-30, and others prefer "your patron diety," while Barstad, *The Religious Polemics of Amos* 196-97 describes the god of Ashkelon. Wolff, *Amos* 323-33 surveys several of these options.

[107]Rudolph, *Amos* 268; Wolff, *Amos* 323.

[108]Rudolph, *Amos* 268 puts this line at the beginning of 8:14, but this is unnecessary.

Theological Development

The theological emphasis that God will "no longer forgive" is identical to the third vision (see 7:7-9). In the third vision this concept is applied to the destruction of the sacred royal and cultic institutions, but in the fourth vision (8:1-3) the death or end of the people of Israel in that day of judgment is more central. These concepts are further developed particularly in the clauses of punishment (8:7-14).

The expectations of the nation at this time were high for practical and theological reasons. Prosperity abounded, political influence was high, and the military power of the army of Jeroboam II was great. The nation was God's (8:2; cf. 3:1-2). They were redeemed from Egypt and given the land of Palestine (2:9-10). They were the inheritors of the promise of Abram, David, and Jeroboam I. They had experienced the compassion and forgiveness of God. Death and the end of Israel as the covenant people of God was contrary to what they had been taught and what they saw all around them. Amos was not announcing the end of the rule of a wicked king but the end of God's mercy, the end of life, and the end of a nation. The end will be bitter (8:10), a time of corpses everywhere (8:3), of mourning and lamenting (8:8, 10), of no joy or song (5:17-18). Everything will be turned upside-down and destroyed when God judges his people. His coming will be a time of darkness (8:9; 5:18-20) not light, because that day will bring the power of God himself against the land. In that day of judgment nothing will resist his might; even the earth will quake like water tossed about (8:8). Men will stand in awe and silence before the terrible outpouring of God's wrath (8:3) when he fulfills his decree of judgment.

The reason for the end of Israel is directly related to the attempt by many in the nation to bring the weak and poor to an end. Through dishonesty, cheating, and oppressive economic practices, the livelihood and life was being stolen from the lower class. Business practices were unmerciful, and greed was the primary motivating force. Because God cares for the poor, the widow, and the orphan, God opposes those who destroy them (Ps. 82:3; Isa. 1:17; Jer. 22:3). God hates inhumanity (1:3-2:16) and he hears the prayers and groanings of the oppressed of his people when they are in bondage (Exod. 2:23-24; 3:7; 6:5).

But he does not hear the prayers of those who reject his word. He rejects them, and his words of comfort and salvation are absent. Although they seek, they will not find a word from God to remove his curse. The point at which God abandons a people is the time of their demise. Though they swear allegiance to Yahweh or some other religious cause or duty, when the final decree is given, the absence of God and his word leaves a void which cannot be filled. In the end without God, they will never rise again (8:14).

No Sinners Can Escape God's Judgment

——————————— *Amos 9:1-10* ———————————

Introduction

The vision cycle is closed by the fifth vision (9:1-4), a hymn (9:5-6), and a dispute over the vision (9:7-10). The first pair of visions demonstrated God's mercy and longsuffering attitude toward his people and the deep concern that Amos had for Israel (7:1-3, 4-6). The next pair of visions (7:7-9; 8:1-3) revealed that God would no longer act in compassion and forgive his people but would destroy the northern sanctuaries, Israel's king (7:9), and many of God's people (8:2-3). Each vision in the second pair (7:7-9; 8:1-3) is complemented by an extended discussion of the implication of the visions to confirm their validity. The fifth vision has no visionary pair but is structured with a hymn-like verse in the middle of the explanation of the vision.[109] Amos 9:7-10 closes this paragraph with a dispute similar to the dispute that arose because of the third vision (7:10-17). A number of similar features connect the vision cycle (7:1—9:10) with the cycle of oracles against the nations (1:3—2:16). Both contain pairs, predict an earthquake (2:13; 9:1), have climactic final oracles that use similar vocabulary (2:13-16; 9:1-4), use the messenger speech formula "says Yahweh," and announce God's determination not to revoke his words of judgment.[110] These observations indicate a connection between the sections and suggest a common authorship behind these rhetorical patterns.

The final vision (9:1-4) describes the enactment of the predictions in the third and fourth vision. The earlier visions announced the destruction of the temple and the end of Israel, but the final vision describes the events when God shatters the temple and destroys the sinful nation (but not every person). In 9:1-4 God stresses human inability to escape from the hand of God's judgment. To emphasize this, the hymn (9:5-6) describes the power and judgment of Yahweh who made and controls the heavens and the earth. It is Yahweh, the God of Israel, who will set himself against Israel to bring her to an end. In the final paragraph, Amos disputes with objectors (cf. 7:10-17) who believe they are protected by God. Then Amos announces that no sinner will escape (9:7-10).

Background

The vision was a special gift (see Background to 7:1-6) and an impor-

---

[109]The visions in 7:1—9:10, the threats in 4:6-11, and the conditional clauses in 9:2-4 are structured in a fivefold pattern.
[110]Wolff, *Amos* 151.

tant means of communication between God and the people. The experience of seeing and hearing God's word was fundamental to Amos' ability to function as an authoritative messenger of God. The vision in 9:1-4 is unique when compared to the earlier pairs. It has no word-play or dialogue, and it omits several of the small parts of the pattern in the other visions. It has a unique imperative command to some unidentified character and an extended development (9:2-4) of one theme in the vision. It is a divine symbolic action-vision, not a commissioning of the prophet as Reventlow maintains.[111]

Terrien and Crenshaw find several thematic connections between the vision and wisdom or theophany traditions. God's power over Sheol and the inability of anyone to flee from the presence of Yahweh are primarily discussed in wisdom texts (Prov. 15:11; Job 26:6; Ps. 139:8). Job 5:8-18 and 9:2-12 also contain striking similarities to the hymns in Amos and include allusions to images elsewhere associated with theophanies. These figures are joined with descriptions of God as a holy warrior bringing judgment (cf. 4:12-13; 5:8-9).[112] Watts believes the setting and background for this vision is the second anniversary of the New Year's festival after Amos was excluded from Bethel (7:7-17). He places the vision at some Judean sanctuary around 750 B.C., but his cultic interpretation goes far beyond the evidence. Some believe the temple in 9:1 is the Jerusalem temple, yet the content of 9:1-4 and its relationship to 2:13-16 suggest that Amos gave this and all the other visions in the vicinity of the Bethel temple, though the last two were not in it.[113]

The hymn has close relationship to the earlier hymns in 4:13 and 5:8-9. The hymns were borrowed from traditional hymns which glorified the power of God in a theophany. In their present context, Amos transforms the good news of God's power into a warning of destruction, because God will declare war against Israel rather than its enemies. The hymn reminds the nation that Yahweh is creator and destroyer, the sovereign power that controls the earth. The references to mourning and pouring out a flood of water over the face of the earth are clear reminders of his destructive force.

The dispute in 9:7-10 begins with two rhetorical questions designed to refute an implied objection by the audience. They claim that Israel's earlier deliverance from Egypt demonstrates God's protection of them from destruction (9:7, 10). The opponents reject the strong statements of destruction in 9:1-4. A similar dispute arose after the third vision (7:10-17), but the form of dispute used here has more similarities with the dispute in 3:1-8. Amos 2:13-16 announced no escape from destruction, so the people objected.

---

[111]Reventlow, *Amos* 49 sees God commanding Amos to smite the temple, but this is an act of God or his agents quite different from Ezekiel's call and symbolic act in 3:22-27.

[112]Terrien, "Amos and Wisdom," 110-11; Crenshaw, "Amos and Theophanic Traditions," 210 or *Hymnic Affirmation* 132-35.

[113]A. Weiser, *Das Buch der zwölf kleinen Propheten*, ATD (Göttingen: Vandenhoeck and Ruprecht, 1949) 188.

Amos responded by reversing common exodus traditions (3:1-2) and asked a series of rhetorical questions (3:3-6). This dispute is also preceded by an announcement of no escape (9:1-4), contains a reversal of Israel's exodus tradition (9:7), rhetorical questions (9:7), and a quotation of the position of his opponents (9:10; cf. 4:1; 5:14; 6:13; 7:13; 8:5-6).[114] Both disputes use illustrations from experiences of rural living (9:9; cf. 3:3-5). The purpose of both disputes is to persuade the audience of the truth of some new revelation which runs contrary to their traditional formulation of Israel's dogma. Amos claims that God will declare war on his sinful people. Redemption, election, and the promises of God will not protect Israel in that day. Although this sinful nation will be destroyed, not every individual in the nation will die, for God is primarily against the sinners (9:10).

Structure and Unity

Structure

The syntactical diagram reproduces something of the parallelism of this paragraph. The English outline will be used to structure the exegesis of the text.

No Sinners Can Escape God's Judgment
Amos 9:1-10

		A. No escape in a vision of the temple
I saw the Lord,	**9:1**	1. The vision of the temple destroyed
standing beside the altar;		
And he said:		
Shatter the heads of the columns[a]		
so that the thresholds shake;[b]		
Smash them on all their heads!		
Then I will slay their remnant with the sword;		2. The destruction of all who remain
their refugees will not flee,		
their fugitives will not escape.		
Though they break into Sheol,	**9:2**	3. None can hide from God
from there my hand will take them;		
though they climb into heaven,		
from there I will bring them down;		
though they hide themselves on top of Carmel,	**9:3**	
from there I will search and take them;		
though they hide themselves from my sight		
in the bottom of the sea,		
from there I will command a serpent[c]		
and it will bite them;		

---

[114]Rudolph, *Amos* 273; Mays, *Amos* 156; and Wolff, *Amos* 345 grant the disputation genre.

though they go into exile before their enemies,
    from there I will command the sword,
        and it will slay them.
    I will watch over them for evil,
        not for good.
	9:4	

		B. Reminder of God's power to bring judgment

The Lord, Yahweh[d] of Hosts,
    who touches the land and it totters
        and all who dwell in it mourn;
        all of it[e] will rise up like the Nile,
            and will sink like the river of Egypt;
	9:5	

who builds in the heavens his upper chambers,
    and establishes over the earth his vault;[f]
who calls for the waters of the sea,
    and pours them on the face of the earth;
Yahweh[g] is his name.
	9:6	

		C. Destruction for the sinful nation

Are you not like the sons of Cush to me,
    O sons of Israel?
	9:7	1. Israel's previous
		   deliverance is
		   not a lasting

declares Yahweh.		protection

Did I not bring up Israel from the land of Egypt,
    and the Philistines from Caphtor,[h]
    and the Syrians from Kir?		

Behold the eyes of the Lord Yahweh
    are against the sinful kingdom,
	9:8	2. Israel will be de-
		   stroyed, but not

So I will destroy it from the face of the land. Yet I will not completely destroy the house of Jacob,		totally
declares Yahweh.		

For truly I am commanding,
    I will shake the house of Israel among all nations,
        as one shakes with a sieve,
            and a stone[i] will not fall to the ground.
	9:9	

All the sinners of my people will die by the sword,
    those who say:
        Disaster will not touch
            nor overtake us.
	9:10	3. Disaster will
		   overtake the
		   sinner

9:1a Through a confusion of metathesis, *hkptōr* "capital" was read *hkprôt* "mercy seat" in the Old Greek. Aq. has "the building," while Sym. and Theod. have "cup."

9:1b The Old Greek has a passive verb and "porch" instead of "threshhold."

9:3c For "serpent" the Old Greek has "dragon" the great sea serpent, probably referring to Rahab (Ps. 89:10 [Heb 89:11]) or Leviathan (Ps. 74:14).

9:5d The Old Greek adds "God."

9:5e Hebrew *klh* "all of it" was interpreted as a verb *klh* "destroy" in the Old Greek and Syriac.

9:6f "His vault" is "his promise" in the Old Greek.

9:6g The Old Greek has "Lord God Almighty" like the Hebrew in 4:13. The Greek also makes 5:8c consistent with the Hebrew in 4:13.

9:7h The Old Greek, Sym., Syriac, and Targum have Cappadocia as in Deut. 2:24, while Aq. and Theod merely transliterate the word. G. A. Wainwright, "Caphtor-Cappadocia," *VT* 6 (1956): 199-210 suggests that Caphtor was Cappadocia, not Crete.

9:7i Sym. has "Cyrene," Aq. and Sym. transliterate *qîr*; Theod. has "wall," and the Old Greek "deep" a confusion of *qôr* and *qîr*.

9:9j The Old Greek has a "stumbling block," Aq. "pebble," and Targum "stone."

The structure of 9:1-10 is divided into three paragraphs: Amos 9:1-4 is a vision with its interpretation; 9:5-6 is a hymn; and 9:7-10 is a dispute over the message of the vision. The vision contains: (1) a shortened variation of the introduction formula (cf. 7:1, 4, 7; 8:1); (2) a description of the vision with symbolic action; (3) a development of the main idea; and (4) an application of the vision to the people. A regular five-fold pattern of *'m* "though" plus *mšm* "from there" unifies 9:2-4.[115] The rhetorical effect is a persuasive case against anyone who might think that they can escape from the effects of God's judgment. Hope of survival is removed; hope to avoid the problem is destroyed. The third masculine plural "they" is effectively contrasted with the first person "I" of God's response. The extremes of Sheol and heaven, the top of Carmel and the bottom of the sea, emphasize the extent of God's control and his unlimited knowledge. Together, they convince the listener that there is no way to circumvent the plan of God. This expansion (9:2-4) is connected to the vision (9:1*a*) and its explanation (9:1*b*) by the references to the sword and escaping. Amos 9:1*b* summarizes what they will not do; 9:2-4 describes why they will not do this. Although the destruction of the temple is the main part of the vision, the destruction of the people is central to the rest of the paragraph.

The hymn in 9:5-6 describes Yahweh as the builder of the heavens and the regulator of the waters of the sea. The hymn is tied to 9:1-4 in that it gives proof that you cannot hide from God in the heavens (9:2) or in the bottom of the sea (9:3). Since God has power over the earth and can make it totter and rise up and down like the Nile (9:5), he can shake the thresholds of the temple with an earthquake (9:1). Because of his judgment, the nation will mourn (9:5), for God will destroy them (9:1).

The hymn itself is characterized by an initial and final reference to the name of Yahweh, four participles, and a style and theme comparable to 4:13 or 5:9. References to God's power in the creation and the destruction of nature is prominent. It praises the power of Yahweh but in the process creates a fearful image in the mind of the audience who will experience his wrath. The hymn has a central pivotal role just like the hymn in 5:8-9.

The final paragraph (9:7-10) is unique in that it has two messenger speeches, an illustration (9:9), a quotation (9:10), a reversal of Israel's redemption tradition (9:7), and two rhetorical questions (9:7). These are characteristics of a disputation speech. Verbal connections with the preceding paragraphs are evident from the repetition of "the eyes of the Lord" in 9:3-4

---

[115]Story, "Amos—Prophet of Praise," 75, sees a close connection between the structure of chapter 4 and 9:1-6.

and 9:8; "I will destroy them" in 9:8 is a common thought throughout 9:1-4; "from the face of the earth" is in 9:6 and 9:8; divine orders are found in 9:3-4 and 9:9; and the shaking in 9:9 is reminiscent of the shaking of the temple (9:1) and God's shaking of the earth (9:5). Both sections refer to the use of the sword (9:1, 10), and "evil, calamity" (9:4, 10) is what God will bring on those who think they are protected from catastrophe. These repetitions demonstrate the close connection between the dispute in 9:7-10 and the vision in 9:1-4.

Unity

The authenticity of the hymnic fragment in 9:5-6 is questioned (cf. 4:13; 5:8-9) because: (1) it interrupts the context; (2) has a unique hymnic style; (3) has an elevated theological perspective; and (4) uses titles for God characteristic of later periods.[116] Each of these issues was discussed in conjunction with 4:13 and 5:8-9, and similar results apply to 9:5-6. Amos 9:5-6 is integrated into the context of 9:1-10 (see the section on Structure above) and is located at the center of the section similar to the placement of 5:8-9. The hymnic style is unique and was probably borrowed from a hymn familiar to the audience. Since creation theology was common in Egyptian, Ugaritic, and Mesopotamian literature well before the time of Amos, it can no longer be supposed that it appeared in Israelite thinking in the exilic period (see the section on Unity for 4:6-13). The names of God are not foreign to Amos or his time; thus there seems to be little evidence to demonstrate that a redactor added this hymn at a later date.[117]

The disputation style in 9:7-10, the reversal of exodus traditions, and the practice of quoting an opponent's opinion are found elsewhere in Amos (cf. 3:1-8; 7:10-17). Some commentators think the statement that the house of Jacob will not be totally destroyed (9:8b) is contrary to the unqualified denial of any escape in 9:1-4, 8a and the rest of the book.[118] Two reasons support the authenticity of 9:8b. First, the presence of 9:9-10 seems to be directly dependent on 9:8b. If all will die, then the sifting illustration (9:9) is out of place and the specific reference to sinners (9:10) is unnecessary. Their presence demands a clause like 9:8b. Secondly, the idea of a remnant is fully in line with what Amos has said earlier in 3:12, 5:2-3, and particularly in 5:14-15. If individuals will seek God, forsake sin, and establish justice in the gate, God may be gracious to the remnant of Jacob. These messages of a small remnant

---

[116]Crenshaw, *Hymnic Affirmation* 5-24; Wolff, *Amos* 215-16; Mays, *Amos* 83-84, 155; Cripps, *Amos* 246, 261.

[117]Story, "Amos—Prophet of Praise," 67-80; Hammershaimb, *Amos* 133; Rudolph, *Amos* 241, 246, 249.

[118]Harper, *Amos* 187, 193; Mays, *Amos* 160 believes the redactor was a Judean editor who saw that Judah survived her captivity, while Wolff, *Amos* 346, 348 finds unusual vocabulary, a strange style, and a message which points to a time after the death of Jeroboam II. Many also assign 9:9 to a later Judean editor.

were not great messages of hope, for all are found in the midst of severe judgment oracles. On the other hand, it cannot be maintained that Amos saw absolutely no hope. There was indeed no hope for the nation, but the sinners rather than the remnant in the nation were the main target for God's wrath.

Interpretation

A. No escape in a vision of the temple (9:1-4)

1. Vision of the temple destroyed (9:1a)

The introductory formula is altered from the previous clauses, "Thus the Lord Yahweh showed me" (7:2, 4, 7; 8:1) to the brief "I saw." The authority of the vision is not limited by this abbreviated form, because the method is still visionary and the message communicated is a word from the Lord. The appearance of Yahweh himself, exercising destructive power over temple and people, was an awesome sight, as the hymn in 9:5-6 declares. The Lord is standing by an altar in a temple, the place where the glory of God traditionally dwelt. The vision describes no sacrifice or worship within the temple, but these could be assumed. The temple itself is not identified, but the context of the Bethel temple in the other visions strongly argues in favor of that location. Although Yahweh is associated with the Jerusalem temple in Judean theology, the northern tribes probably had similar theological beliefs about God's presence in their temple. This place of protection, blessing, and joyous fellowship with God is transformed into a place of judgment by the command of the Lord that follows.

The word of God in the vision is not preceded by a question (7:8; 8:2) but begins with an imperative order to destroy the temple and kill the worshipers with the falling debris. The person commanded to destroy the temple is unidentified. Driver and Harper believe an angel is addressed, but others emend the verb to a thrid person "he (God) smote" and put "and he said" later in the verse.[119] Some believe Amos symbolically smites the temple with his hand, but Yahweh rather than Amos is the main power. To emphasize this, Rudolph adds a first person verb to the text.[120] Since the text omits any reference to an agent and focuses on the power of God, the imperative must be a rhetorical device to emphasize the certainty of the destruction of the temple.[121]

The two commands give instructions for the destruction of the temple and the worshipers in it. The columns that hold the roof are struck by a mighty

---

[119]Driver, *Amos* 202; Harper, *Amos* 188; Wolff, *Amos* 334-35 follow several others who emend the text.

[120]Reventlow, *Amos* 48 points to Amos, while Rudolph, *Amos* 241 follows Sellin and Duhm.

[121]Mays, *Amos* 153.

force which shakes the very foundation of the temple. An earthquake is envisaged (cf. 9:5).[122] Its power is tremendous, for the whole building falls on the people who have come to the temple. The columns and the roof will be smashed to pieces when they land on the heads of the worshipers at Bethel. The vision does not describe God trying to break into the temple to destroy the people who have sought to escape the wrath of God.[123] The Israelites believe that "God is with them" (5:14), that no calamity will overtake them (9:10).

2. Destruction of all who remain (9:1b)

The focus of the vision turns from the destruction of the temple to the death of the people. Yahweh will pursue those who remain, with the relentless purpose of destroying them (cf. 4:2).[124] The sword implies military defeat (cf. 2:14-16; 3:11-12; 4:2-3; 5:2-3, 27; 6:7-11, 14; 7:17), but primary attention falls on the inability of the people to flee or escape from God (cf. 2:14-16). The final two lines are constructed parallel to one another. Those who flee will not be able to flee, those who escape will not be able to escape. Flight is hopeless, hiding is useless, security from Yahweh is illusory.

3. None can hide from God (9:2-4)

The message of total annihilation was no doubt rejected by many in the audience because Israel was a secure, powerful nation with a strong army (cf. 6:1). To convince the audience of the magnitude of God's strength and the determination of his will, a series of five parallel conditional clauses are given.[125] Each couplet shows that attempts to escape his sovereign "hands" or "eyes" are futile, for they have no limits or constraints. If they would try to hide somewhere, God will find and destroy them. The origin of this style of poetry is uncertain, but its similarity to the themes and styles of some Psalms (27:3) suggests that Amos may have transformed some hymnic material of hope into a hopeless satire.

The unlimited sphere of God's rule is poetically expressed by presenting extremes. If the people break into Sheol, an almost inaccessible place of the dead, or make the impossible climb up into heaven, God will find them and remove them from their place of desired escape. No matter how extreme the distance, the hand of God is present (cf. Ps. 139:7-9). This concept is not in

---

[122]Rudolph, *Amos* 241-42 emends the second imperative to a passive participle and *br'š* "on their head" to *br'š* "with an earthquake." These alterations make good sense but change an acceptable text. Maag, *Amos* 45 changes the second imperative into a first person verb to match the next line.

[123]J. Ouellette, "The Shaking of the Thresholds in Amos 9:1," *HUCA* 43 (1972) 23-27 takes this interpretation and finds several ancient Near Eastern parallels where a god tries to break into a temple.

[124]Gese, "Kleine Beiträge zum Verständnis des Amosbuches," 436-37, discusses the use of "rest, remnant, end" in 9:1, 8:10; 4:2 and 1:7, and calls it "die irreale synchorese."

[125]GKC 159b, l, n, q describes conditional clauses with the imperfect to express a condition or consequence that is capable of fulfillment.

tension with the laments that decry the distance between God and the person
who enters Sheol (Psalm 88; Isa. 38:18). If neither heights nor depths can
separate people from the love of God (cf. Rom. 8:38-39), they are also unable to hide them from the wrath of God. The second set of conditional
clauses contrasts the top of Mt. Carmel with the bottom of the sea (9:3). Carmel was known for its thick forests and over a thousand limestone caves
(Judg. 6:2; 1 Sam. 13:6; 1 Kings 18:4). The bottom of the sea was a deep,
dark, uninhabitable area where the foundations of the earth were laid (Jonah
2:3-6). God will find them or send a sea serpent to bite them. The serpent
and the sea are not mythological deified powers, for the serpent obeys the
command of God (cf. Job 41). In the fifth conditional clause (9:4a), the emphasis changes from hiding to escaping into captivity alive (cf. 4:2-3; 5:27;
6:7; 7:17). Even this avenue of escape will be guarded by the sword of Yahweh (cf. 9:1). He will not be satisfied with the shame of exile but will exact
life from them.

The vision ends (9:4b) with a summary similar to "it shall not be" (7:3, 6)
or "I will spare them no longer" (7:8; 8:2). The statement, "I will watch
over them" describes the positive act of God setting his eyes on those he loves
(Jer. 24:6; 29:10-11) or the negative act of God against those he hates. The
contrast, "for evil, not for good," stresses the tragedy of Israel's situation. In
the past God has poured out his grace, protected his people from their enemies, and blessed them abundantly with power and prosperity, but the future
will bring about a radical shift in the way God looks at Israel (Jer. 21:10;
Ezek. 15:7). Yahweh, the mighty warrior, will bring a curse instead of a
blessing upon his people.

B. Reminder of God's power to bring judgment (9:5-6)

These verses stand out from their context because of their style and theological emphasis. Although some maintain that the discontinuity demonstrates this hymn was added by a later redactor, it is just as reasonable to
conclude that Amos himself quoted a hymn, possibly one that his audience
knew.[126] The hymn celebrated the power of God described in the vision (9:1-
4) and supports the prophet's contention that Israel could not escape God's
judgment. Amos transforms the good news of God's glorious power into a
fearful warning of judgment.

The hymn begins and ends with a declaration of the name of Yahweh and
contains several unique forms. Reconstructions of the hymn are abundant,
but few agree with one another.[127] The "Lord, Yahweh of hosts" is the Yahweh of the vision (9:1-4) who functions as a mighty warrior. Crenshaw traces

---

[126]See the section on Unity as well as the discussion of the other hymns in 4:13 and 5:8-9.

[127]Watts, *Amos* 57-60; Crenshaw, *Hymnic Affirmation* 47-74 give a fairly complete summary of
these emendations.

this title and the naming of Yahweh at the end of the hymn (9:6; cf. Exod. 15:3) back to contexts where creation, judgment, idolatry, and swearing are prominent.[128] The first part deals with God's judgment of the earth (9:5), the second section touches on creation (9:6a) and the third returns to judgment (9:6b). When God passes through their midst (5:17) he will touch the land, it will rise and fall, it will totter (cf. 8:8) and shake the temple (9:1).[129] The results will be disastrous for the inhabitants because of terror and grief. Nothing can stand before the theophany (cf. 9:1). The judgment is similar to what will happen on the Day of Yahweh, but there is no reference to that day in this hymn or in 9:1-6. Mays goes beyond the evidence when he suggests that the Day of Yahweh is raised to universal proportions in the hymn.[130] The song is a hymn of praise to honor God's present power rather than an eschatological prophecy. It supports the vision and unveils the almighty sovereignty of Yahweh who will act according to the prophetic vision.

God's creation of the heavens and the earth (9:6a) makes it ridiculous to escape to some remote part of Sheol, the heavens, the sea or Carmel (9:2-3). His sovereign knowledge of and control over each is assured because it is all the result of his craftsmanship.[131] The unlimited vault of the heavens which is founded on the earth is his magnificent design. He also controls the sea and can use it to destroy the face of the earth. The hymn of praise, which is a hymn of judgment to Israel, does not even mention God's destruction of people or the captivity of the nation. The focus is Yahweh; he is in complete control of the world.

C. Destruction for the sinful nation (9:7-10)

1. Israel's previous deliverance is not a lasting protection (9:7)

The dispute begins with a refutation of an implied objection by the audience. They claimed that they were protected from danger (9:10) when delivered from Egypt. God will not destroy Israel and fight against her; he fights for his people as the experience of the exodus demonstrates.

Amos compares God's deliverance of Israel from Egypt with his acts on behalf of other nations. Using the question, Amos draws the listener into the process of argumentation by inviting them to think about the implications of what God has done. This more indirect method of debate is often more effective than a direct statement of fact. The more direct approach may automatically receive a negative response just because of who says it or the way it is

---

[128]Crenshaw, *Hymnic Affirmation* 75-114.

[129]A similar response of God's power is found in Ps. 46:6 [Heb. 46:7]; Mic. 1:3-4; Neh. 1:5; Hab. 3:6, 10. The idea is that of "trembling, quaking, tottering" rather than "melting, dissolving." Story, "Amos—Prophet of Praise," 76-77.

[130]Mays, *Amos* 154.

[131]*m'lôtô* "ascent, staircase" may be a variant of *'lîtô*, or the initial *m* may be present due to dittography from the preceding word.

said. The two questions raise issues related to the uniqueness of God's relationship to Israel. The prophet does not deny Israel's tradition (3:1-2) or reject the doctrine of election but raises questions about the false sense of inviolability present in Israel based on God's one great act of grace on their behalf.

Three nations are compared to Israel: Cush, Philistia, and Syria. Cush is the name given to the southern part of the Nile valley known as Nubia and often equated with Ethiopia. The choice of comparison is not due to the sudden rise to power of the Ethiopian King Piankhi (725-09 B.C.), for this happened well after the time of Amos.[132] The reason for choosing the sons of Cush is unclear; perhaps they were despised by some (Numb. 12:1), or maybe they were simply representatives of peoples far away who live in the God-forsaken fringes of the civilized world. If the Israelites are no different than the Cushites, Israel has no special position of privilege or status before God. Their security (6:1, 13) is illusory if this is true; their sense of pride is shaken. Amos expresses God's sovereign control and involvement with other nations in a radical way to force the Israelites to reconsider the real basis for God's special favor.

The second question compares God's mighty deliverance of Israel from Egypt with his bringing of the Philistines from Caphtor and the Syrians from Kir. This question puts Israel on the same level as two of Israel's bitter enemies. Certainly the Israelites do not believe that God's acts of mercy for these two nations is an eternal protection that guarantees their security from destruction in the future. The comparison highlights the difference as well as the similarities between Israel and these nations. The audience cannot argue that God is not sovereignly in control of history. They cannot deny God's grace and deliverance in all these cases. But they can point to a special relationship with Yahweh based on faith, trust, and obedience. Since this relationship does not presently exist in Israel (9:8), the basis for God's future deliverance of Israel is in question. Past acts of holy war against Israel's enemies do not determine God's future acts, if the commitment of Israel changes. Election (3:1-2) and deliverance from Egypt (2:9-10) do not rule out the possibility of his destruction of the nation (cf. Exod. 32:10; Numb. 14:11-12). David had defeated the Philistines through God's power (1 Sam. 17:46-54; 18:7; 2 Sam. 5:17-26; 8:1), and Joash and Jeroboam II had recently defeated the Syrians (2 Kings 13:22-25; 14:25-28) in spite of God's earlier acts of grace on behalf of these two nations. Thus God's deliverance in the past is not the sole basis for determining God's treatment of Israel or any other nation in the future. If anything, God's acts of grace put a nation under greater obligation, for greater privilege carries greater responsibility.

Amos had a wealth of knowledge concerning world history (cf. 1:3-2:3). The original home of the Philistines is traced back to Caphtor. Amos may

---

[132]Harper, *Amos* 191.

have drawn this information from early Israelite traditions (Deut. 2:23) or his own dealings with people from these countries. Caphtor is often associated with the island of Crete, but the Old Greek and recent studies by Wainwright suggest a location in Southern Asia Minor or possibly both locations (cf. Jer. 47:4; Ezek. 25:16; Zeph. 2:5).[133] Their movement was part of the migration of the peoples of the sea known from Egyptian history. The original home of the Syrians was Kir, and Amos predicts they would return to this place (1:5; 2 Kings 16:9).

This broadening of Israel's perspective on the work of God is not a denial of Israel's history or its rich theological tradition but a reversal of the implication drawn from this tradition. God's holy war on behalf of his nation at one point does not limit his freedom to sovereignly deal with his people in a different way in the future.

2. Israel will be destroyed, but not totally (9:8-9)

Having questioned Israel's false sense of security, Amos returns to the announcement of judgment in the vision (9:1-4) and explains who will be judged. The eyes of Yahweh (9:3-4) are specifically against the sinful kingdom. The kingdom could refer to any kingdom or this sinful kingdom of Israel.[134] In the context of several nations in 9:7, Amos announces the principle that each kingdom is dealt with according to its sin. Past deliverances (9:7) of the Philistines, Syrians, and Israelites are not the key to God's sovereign control of their history. Particularly in Amos 1:3—2:16 God has demonstrated how the transgressions and sins of each nation determine its destiny. The application of this principle to Israel is obvious, for Amos has already described her destruction in 9:1-4.

But this principle is not a blanket condemnation of every person, for God is also concerned about the heart of the one who has not sinned. If sin is the criteria, then those who seek God and seek justice in the gate can expect to become the remnant of God (5:14-15). The exceptive clause "nevertheless" expresses in very emphatic language the assurance that there is hope for those who are not sinners.[135] "I will not totally destroy" is God's solemn promise that sin makes the difference in determining both who will be destroyed, as well as who will not be destroyed. This clause is a clarification of the message of no escape in 9:1-4, but it is not a contradiction added by some later hand, for the identification of sin as the basis of judgment requires a differentiation of the two groups and the two destinies.[136]

---

[133]G. A. Wainwright, "Caphtor-Cappadocia," *VT* 6 (1956) 199-210, or "Early Philistine History," *VT* 9 (1969) 73-84.

[134]Mays, *Amos* 159; Cripps, *Amos* 264; and Driver, *Amos* 220 believe the article designates a class (see GKC 126l-m), while others believe the kingdom (8*a*) is Judah and the house of Jacob (8*b*) is Israel (see Wolff, *Amos* 348).

[135]GKC 113n. The infinitive absolute before the finite verb strengthens the verbal idea to emphasize the certainty or completeness of the occurrence.

[136]To attribute this to a later editor who contradicts the message of Amos does not make any

The illustration in 9:9 describes the process of judging the house of Israel, which distinguishes between the sinners and the remnant (cf. 9:10). The nations are the instrument of God who will bring destruction and captivity to Israel (3:11-12; 4:2-3; 5:27; 6:7, 14; 7:17; 9:4).[137] The process of distinguishing the good from the bad is likened to the process of cleaning grain with a sieve. The meaning of the illustration is made difficult by the use of the rare word *ṣeror*, which may refer to a "pebble" that is taken out of the good grain, or to the firm or solid "kernels" of good grain. The metaphor of shaking Israel like shaking grain may describe a large mesh sieve which separates straw and other larger stones from the grain which falls through, or it may refer to a fine mesh sieve which separates the good grain from the fine dust and chaff which falls through. If "falling" to the ground is negative, then the good grain must be the *ṣeror* which stays in the sieve. However, if it is a neutral clause describing the process of separating the grain from useless trash, then either interpretation is possible. The main focus is the separation of the good from the bad. Since the next verse relates to the punishment of the sinners, the process of shaking separates the sinners so that they can be destroyed. Although a small ray of hope is present in this verse, judgment is the overwhelming thrust of the punishment in 9:8-10 (cf. 5:3).

3. Disaster will overtake the sinner (9:10)

The prophet closes the dispute with a final clarifying statement which applies the metaphor of 9:9. "All the sinners within my people will die by the sword" (cf. 9:1, 4) pinpoints only certain individuals who are characterized by sin, and it excludes the remnant. This group is specifically identified by the quote in 9:10b. Those who trust in God's protection, regardless of their character will be overtaken by a great disaster or evil (cf. 9:4). Those who think that God's past redemption assures them of eternal blessing will be surprised when the sword of the Lord comes against them. Those who ignore Amos' message and his warning of disaster will one day be confronted with the stark reality that Amos' words were true. On the Day of Yahweh, God's wrath will destroy them.

Theological Developement

God's power and rule of the world is described with great vividness in the vision and hymn. His universal control is not limited by Sheol, the sea, or the furthest reaches of the heavens. Since he designed and built the magnificent heavens, there is nothing beyond his reach. The eyes and hands of the Lord are able to see and determine the people's future. Hiding or escaping from God's presence is impossible. He can shake the foundations of the earth or

---

sense, for he would essentially be declaring that Amos was a false prophet.

[137]Rudolph, *Amos* 272; Wolff, *Amos* 344 and others take "among the nations" as a later gloss, but Hos. 9:17 and Isa. 11:11-12 contain similar phrases.

pour out the waters of the sea on the earth to shape the destiny of those who dwell in it. The sword and the serpent obey his command. There is no enemy nation or any other place where the Israelites can go to avoid God's judgment. He will even use his power to destroy temples, the dwelling place of a god/ God. When Yahweh purposes to judge there is no escape.

The depth and breadth of God's power is consistent with the picture in the oracles against the foreign nations (1:3—2:6) and the other hymnic fragments (4:13; 5:8-9; 8:8). Amos is not propounding a new universalism different from what he has already stated. The new theological emphasis is on human inability to escape from God's punishment. Although previously Amos announced the end of the temple and the nation (7:7-9; 8:1-3), the people knew that they could run to Tyre, Edom, or into the hills to escape the threat of enemy invasion. Even captivity was a bittersweet escape or a temporal delay of the more ultimate punishment of death. These and any other hopes of survival are devastated by this message. Individual hopes for those remaining after God's initial judgment are reduced to zero because of God's sovereign rule.

The judgment of God is not an irrational force which destroys without reason or goal. God stands boldly against sin and the sinful nation that presumes on the grace of God. A past relationship with God is not a license for sin or a promise of continual protection from judgment. God acts with abundant grace toward people and nations around the world, but each is held accountable for its behavior. God sees and tests the hearts of people; he knows the sins that hide so deep within their hearts. His sovereign control of history is guided by his goal to judge the sinner and separate out a remnant that is faithful to himself.

An Epilogue:
The Restoration After Judgment

Introduction

This paragraph does not claim to be a vision, and it does not begin with the introductory clause, "thus the Lord Yahweh showed me" (7:1, 4, 7; 8:1; 9:1). Some of the topics arise out of the issues in the visions and have similarities with positive promises in other prophetic books. These new themes have led to many questions about the authorship and date of this prophecy.

The fulfillment of the judgment on Israel is assumed. Because of this, concepts of hope based on the presence of God with them (5:14), his protection (9:10), and the bright future of the Day of the Lord (5:18-20) are addressed with positive rather than negative responses. The events of "that day" (3:14; 4:2; 6:3; 8:3, 9, 11, 13) are full of promise instead of death and destruction. The contrast between these words and most of the rest of the book is striking, but the fulfillment is directed toward those "who call on the name of the Lord" (9:12) and not the sinful nation of Israel. This promise is fitting for the remnant of Jacob who seeks the Lord (5:14-15).

The date and setting for this paragraph is a matter of much debate. Some believe the references to rebuilding the fallen Davidic "booth" and the restoration of the fortunes of his people (9:11, 14) imply a Judean setting in exilic or post-exilic times. Others attribute these words to Amos, since the united Davidic empire was divided long before the time of Amos. Prophecies of hope and salvation are characteristic of all the early prophets (see the section on Unity below).

Background

This final salvation oracle is concerned with God's restoration of his people "in that day" when God fulfills his promises. The background of these theological traditions have some contact with the Day of Yahweh ideas (cf. 5:18-20).[1] Mowinckel, Watts, and others have traced the celebration of the Day of the Lord back to a worship setting at the autumn New Year's festival. This ceremony recognized God as king, renewed the covenant, recited the saving deeds of God on behalf of his people, and looked forward to the establish-

---

[1]See the Background for the Day of Yahweh in 5:18-20.

ment of God's future kingdom. Since God's promises were never completely realized in Israel's historical experience, they were idealized into a future time when God would bring great blessing and rule in power.[2] This cultic background is a hypothetical syncretistic joining of a pagan festival with Yahwistic theology. Although syncretism was rampant in Israel, there is little evidence that this kind of festival was ever celebrated at Bethel and little indication of a cultic background in 9:11-15. Reventlow also derives this salvation oracle from a cultic context, but bases the "Blessing Ritual" (9:13-15) and the "Cursing Ritual" (4:6-11) on the role of Amos as a covenant mediator.[3] Although his understanding of the role of Amos is in doubt, covenantal connections are behind the promises in 9:11-15. References to the continuation of Davidic rule, prosperity, and dwelling in the land given to God's people are derived from the covenants and promises of God found in earlier traditions.

Although some make Amos out to be a Judean nationalist who is against the Bethel temple and king—because only the Jerusalem temple and Davidic rule are legitimate—it is important to remember that Amos was in Israel and could draw on the rich heritage of that nation. The promises to David (2 Samuel 7) and the theology of many Psalms witness to the strength of the nation's early hopes and the extent to which the promises, blessings, and covenants were a part of the nation's religious tradition.[5] These promises of blessing were basic to the early covenants and did not first appear in the exilic period. Amos, in his "Day of Yahweh" address (5:18-20), confronted a very live understanding of this bright day when God would pour out his blessings on his people. Thus critical problems with the positive statements in 9:11-15 are due not to the lack of traditions about these positive promises but to how these positive promises fit into the ministry of Amos in Israel.

Structure and Unity

Structure

The structural relationships between the parts of this section are reproduced in the diagram of the text. The outline of the text describes the flow of thought and will be used later in the exegesis.

---

[2]Watts, *Amos* 68-84; S. Mowinckel, *He That Cometh* 81-102.

[3]Reventlow, *Amos* 75-92.

[4]H. J. Krause, "Der Gerichtsprophet Amos, ein Vorläufer des Deuteronomisten," *ZAW* 50 (1932) 221-39, may go too far in his emphasis on the Judean nationalism of Amos; H. Gottlieb, "Amos und Jerusalem," *VT* 17 (1967) 454-62.

[5]Psalms 2, 18, 20, 21, 45, 72, 89, 110, 132, 144.

The Restoration After Judgment
Amos 9:11-15

		A. Restoration of the kingdom
In that day	**9:11**	1. The kingdom of David will be raised
I will raise up the fallen booth[a] of David,		
and I will repair its[b] breaches;		
I will raise up its[b] ruins,		
and I will build it as in the days of old,		
that they may possess[c]	**9:12**	2. Other kingdoms will be included
the remnant of Edom,[d]		
and all the nations		
which are called by my name,		
declares Yahweh who will do it.		
		B. Restoration of the land
Behold the days are coming,	**9:13**	1. It will be productive
declares Yahweh,		
when the one who ploughs[e]		
will overtake the one who reaps,		
and the one who treads[f] grapes,		
the one who sows seed;		
then the mountain will drip with new wine		
and all the hills will flow[g] with it.		
When I restore the fortunes of my people Israel,	**9:14**	2. It will be inhabited by my people
then they will rebuild the ruined cities and inhabit them,		
plant vineyards and drink their wine,		
make gardens and eat their fruit.		
When I plant them in their land,	**9:15**	3. It will have peace
then they will never again be uprooted from their land		
which I have given them,		
says Yahweh your God.[h]		

9:11a. Booth is "tabernacle, tent" in the Old Greek, which may refer to the temple.

9:11b. The pronominal suffixes are feminine singular in the Old Greek, agreeing with tent. Syriac has third masculine plural suffixes while the Hebrew has third feminine plural, third masculine singular and then a third feminine singular.

9:12c. The Old Greek has "they will seek" and makes the remnant the subject rather than the object of the verb. Acts 15:17 follows the Greek; see J. de Waard, *A Comparative Study of the O.T. Text in the Dead Sea Scrolls* (Leiden: Brill, 1965) 26.

9:12d. Edom *'edôm* was understood as "man", *'ādām* in the Old Greek.

9:12e. The Old Greek reads "the harvest will overtake the vintage harvest."

9:13f. The Old Greek refers to the "ripened" grapes rather than "treading" the grapes, but the same time period is assumed in both texts.

9:13g. All the hills are "planted" according to the Old Greek.

9:15h. The name of God in the Greek is "Lord God Almighty."

The structure of 9:11-15 can be divided into two interrelated oracles introduced by "in that day" or "behold the days are coming" (9:11, 13). The first section is divided into a series of first person statements (9:11) and a result clause (9:12). The theme of restoring the ruined is predominant, but the restoration includes both Jews and Gentiles who are called by God's name. The second paragraph contrasts three temporal clauses describing God's acts, with the result which his people will enjoy. The focus is on the land and its productivity. The positive message of hope unites the whole. "Building" (9:12, 14) of the "ruins" (9:11, 14) and "planting, possessing inhabiting" (9:11, 14, 15) the "land" are key terms in the reversal of the destruction predicted earlier in the book.

The structural connections between this paragraph and the preceding paragraph are important. "In that day" is repeated in the fourth vision (8:3, 9, 11, 13) but not in the vision in chapter 9.[6] If one hypothesizes a purposeful contrast between 9:11-15 and 9:1-10, the false hope in the protection of God in 9:10 is reversed in 9:15. The destruction of the sinful nation (9:8) is contrasted to the restoration of the fortunes of God's people (9:14). The exile from and destruction of the land (9:8) will change to dwelling in and planting of fertile land (9:13-15). The nations will shake Israel (9:9) but later Israel will possess the remnant of the nations (9:12). At first disaster will "overtake" them (9:10), but later God's blessing will "overtake" them (9:13). The contrast is striking because the recipients of God's acts are different. The sinners will be destroyed (9:10), but those called by God's name will be blessed (9:12). Since most of the oracles of Amos speak to the first group, some find it difficult to understand how this final short promise of blessing relates to the overall ministry of Amos.

Unity

Commentators are evenly divided between those who believe 9:11-15 is an integral part of the message of Amos and those who attribute this section to some later redactor. Those who reject 9:11-15 as an original part of Amos' preaching do so because: (1) the picture of restoration is inconsistent with the threats of destruction throughout the rest of the book; (2) the positive attitude toward Judah and the Davidic kingdom is not appropriate for an Israelite audience; (3) the emphasis on material blessing without ethical demands is contrary to Amos' preaching elsewhere; (4) several linguistic terms have greater affinity with other post-exilic books than pre-exilic books; and (5) the historical background presupposes the ruin of Jerusalem, captivity, and emnity between Judah and Edom.[7] Although Kellermann assigns these verses to a Deuteronomistic editor, most prefer a post-exilic date because of signs of the

---

[6]Watts, *Amos* 48 sees a parallelism between the end of chapters 8 and 9.

[7]Most commentaries give a fairly similar list of reasons. See Harper, *Amos* 195-96; Driver, *Amos* 119-24; Cripps, *Amos* 67-77.

fall of Jerusalem.[8] Some include 9:8-15 within this late section, others believe only 9:11-15 are late, while a few find evidence of a later hand only in 9:12.[9]

Several of the arguments brought against these verses have a limited influence on deciding this issue. The sudden change from "total destruction" to positive promises of restoration is abrupt, but the change to a more positive word is not inherently contradictory to Amos or his book. The early prophets included both judgment and salvation oracles (Hosea 1-3; 11:8-11; 14:2-9; Mic. 2:12-13; 4:1-8; 5:1-9; 7:7-20) and later prophets followed a similar pattern (Jeremiah 30-33; Ezek. 33:21-37:28). In fact, the prophets seldom predict simply destruction, rather they speak of the destruction of nations, or individuals who are sinners. Prophetic judgments also contain the implied or stated condition, if you do not repent, you will be destroyed (Jonah, Jeremiah 18). Amos saw hope for the remnant of Jacob (5:14-15) and realized God's judgment was specifically aimed at the sinner (9:10). It is also falacious to suppose that Amos is offering hope in 9:11-15 to the Israel of his day. Amos did not neutralize his message of destruction by reminding the nation that "those who are called by God's name," the true people of God, will enjoy the great blessings of God which the present nation will miss.

Those who reject 9:11-15 because it promises material blessings without any ethical demands are able to come to this conclusion only by (1) depriving 9:11-15 of its contextual location after 9:7-10, (2) ignoring what Amos has said earlier about the remnant of Jacob in 5:14-15, (3) rejecting the traditional ethical formulations of earlier promises and covenants which informed Amos' understanding of who would receive God's blessing, and (4) interpreting "all who are called by my name" (9:12) in a strict political sense of ownership without any moral or religious commitment to Yahweh on the part of the people.[10] The renewed granting of the land (9:14) and the prosperity of the land (9:13) are covenantally available only to those who "walk in my statutes" (Lev. 26:1-6). Even the Davidic covenant envisaged chastening in the midst of eventual blessing, if his son would forsake God (2 Sam 7:15; Ps. 89:30-37).

The linguistic terms in 9:11-15 do have a great deal in common with later prophetic books, but the dating of terms is notoriously difficult. Of much greater significance is the historical background presupposed in the passage. The Davidic kingdom is in ruins (9:11), the people will return to the land once more, rebuild its cities (9:14), and not be rooted out again (9:15). Two different settings have been proposed for this paragraph: (1) a period some time after the fall of Jerusalem (587/6 B.C.), after Judah has been destroyed,

---

[8] U. Kellermann, "Der Amosschluss als Stimme deuteronomistischer Heilshoffnung," *EvT* 29 (1969) 169-83.

[9] Kapelrud, *Amos* 53-59 believes 9:8-10 are genuine, while Maag, *Amos* 6-62, 246-51 finds exilic signs only in 9:12.

[10] Hasel, *Remnant* 173-207 discusses the remnant concept in passages before 9:11-15.

Edom has taken advantage of the Jews, and the people are in exile;[11] or (2) sometime after the division of David's kingdom into two nations in 930 B.C.[12] Often the major argument has pivoted on the interpretation of the participle *nplt* (9:11) as "falling, about to fall" or "fallen." Since either is possible, other factors must decide the issue.[13] If Amos saw the division of the kingdom as a major problem, then he, like Isaiah (7:17), could have referred to that here. But this issue is not brought up elsewhere in Amos' preaching to Israel. In addition, the description of ruins (9:11), rebuilding ruined cities (9:12), planting vineyards (9:14), planting them in the land, and not rooting them out of the land again (9:15) cannot be twisted into metaphorical pictures of the division of the kingdom. Amos repeatedly predicted exile from the land and the destruction of Israel's cities (3:11-15; 4:2-3; 5:1-3, 9-13, 27; 6:7-11, 14; 7:9-17; 8:1-3; 9:1-4). Amos 9:11-15 refers to what will happen after that destruction. This does not require that the exile is now history, for Amos through the gift of prophecy places himself in 5:1-17 after the fall of the nation to see the mourning in Israel. Although Amos is aware of the future fall of Judah (2:4-5), he refers not to Jerusalem or Judah in 9:11-15 but to the captivity of "my people Israel" as a major fracturing of the Davidic kingdom. Thus it is not the division of the kingdom but the destruction of part of the kingdom that Amos has in mind here and throughout the book. The promises of blessing are a reversal of earlier curses of destruction (cf. 5:11). Although many commentators apply these promises only to Judah, Amos boldly proclaims God's matchless grace to Israel and Gentiles who profess the name of Yahweh and submit to his rule.

Finally, there is the objection that the prophet's positive attitude toward Judah and the Davidic kingdom is inappropriate for Israelite audiences. Since Judah and Jerusalem are not mentioned, only the reference to the Davidic kingdom needs explanation.[14] Is the Davidic tradition the sole property of Judah? Is this a bit of Amos' Judean heritage shining through, or was David important in Israel too? The only other direct reference to David in Amos is the comparison with David's playing and singing in 6:5. However, David's revenge of the death of Saul (2 Sam. 1:11-16), lament for Saul and Jonathan (2 Sam. 1:17-27), lament for Abner (2 Sam. 3:20-39), revenge of Ishbosheth (2 Sam. 4:1-12), covenant with the northern nation of Israel (2 Sam. 4:1-3), and kindness to Mephibosheth, the son of Jonathan (2 Samuel 9) strengthened

---

[11]Harper, *Amos* 195-96; Kapelrud, *Amos* 56-58; Driver, *Amos* 122-23; Mays, *Amos* 164-67; Kellermann, "Der Amosschuss als Stimme deuteronomistischer Heilshoffnung," 169-83; Cripps, *Amos* 67-77.

[12]Hammershaimb, *Amos* 135-38; Reventlow, *Amos* 92; Gottlieb, "Amos und Jerusalem," 456-57; Rudolph, *Amos* 281; Hasel, *Remnant* 210-11; Clements, *Prophecy and Covenant* 111-12.

[13]GKC 116a, c, d.

[14]Hammershaimb, *Amos* 138 suggests that Amos possibly spoke this oracle after he returned to Judah. This view is attractive, but there is no indication of a new setting. If it were added during the writing process, a connection to what precedes is supposed, since no introductory information warns the reader of a new situation.

David's relationship with Israel. The men of Israel even believed they had more claim on David than the men of Judah (2 Sam. 19:43). Ahijah promised that God would build an enduring house in Israel like the house of David, if Jeroboam I would follow God (1 Kings 11:30-38). Hosea foresaw the regathering of Judah and Israel, under one leader (Hos. 1:11 [Heb. 2:2]) in the tradition of David, (3:5) as a significant promise to an Israelite audience.[15] Although the "house of David" in Isaiah (7:2, 13), 1 Kings (12:16-26; 13:2; 14:8), 2 Kings (17:21), and 2 Chronicles (10:16-19) refers to the government of Judah, it seems that Amos and the Israelites considered themselves as partial inheritors of the Davidic promises (1 Kings 11:38; Hos. 3:5); thus Amos is reminding them of their rich heritage and its blessings which some will miss and others enjoy.

The new revelation that Amos brings is the radical announcement of the end of Israel (8:1-3). The light and joy of divine blessings are limited to the remnant who seek Yahweh (5:14-15). Amos maintained continuity with the traditional interpretation of the blessings of the covenant, but he interposed an intermediate step of God's judgment on sinners before that day of blessing. The blessings and curses of the covenant allow for both perspectives, based on faithfulness or disobedience. Amos' eschatology was not a narrow, exclusivistic, Judean, sectarian type. He saw the doors of the kingdom spread wide open to include not just Judeans but Israelites and peoples from all the nations.

Interpretation

A. Restoration of the Kingdom (9:11-12)

1. Kingdom of David will be raised (9:11)

"In that day" immediately moves the historical reference to a future time when God will miraculously intervene in the affairs of the world. It is associated with the "end" of Israel (8:3, 9, 11, 13), but here Amos moves beyond the judgment to the promise of blessing which will come after that judgment. When there is ruin, then mercy and God's power will bring the people back to the land again (9:14). The force behind this new day is set forth in the four first person singular verbs. God himself is the active agent performing these deeds. His activity involves rebuilding, raising up, and a restoration of a destroyed or damaged object to its former glory. Although walls and ruins are described, no city is mentioned, for the reference is to the Davidic kingdom and to the several breaches of its united status. The "booth of David" is prob-

---

[15]F. I. Andersen and D. N. Freedman, *Hosea* AB 21 (Garden City: Doubleday, 1980) 307; A. Gelston, "Kingship in the Book of Hosea," *OTS* 19 (1974) 76-80; Jeremiah who has strong connections to Israel is also well aware of the Davidic traditions (Jer. 30:9; 33:15, 21).

ably a substitute for the pre-Solomonic term "house of David" (2 Sam. 7:11, 13, 16), an expression that stands for the kingdom of David. The booth was a small shelter of branches piled on a simple frame. It was a temporary, make-shift protection for troops in the field (2 Sam. 11:11), watchmen in a vineyard (Isa. 1:8), or someone needing protection from the sun (Jonah 4:5). Booths were constructed on the Feast of Booths (Lev. 23:40, 42; Deut. 16:13) to remind the Israelites of their days of wandering in the wilderness. This structure which is fallen is a prophetic metaphor of the future state of the Davidic kingdom. Instead of a powerful and secure kingdom, as in the time of David's united monarchy, it will be more like a dilapidated little hut. But God will rebuild and restore it to its former glory.

The choice of David need not refer to the government of Judah, for David and his promises relate to the entire nation of chosen people, not one part of it. The destruction and ruin that Amos describes is not the fall of Jerusalem but the demise of the Davidic kingdom through the destruction of the sinful northern kingdom (9:8).[16] The suffixes, "breaches of *them,* ruins of *it,*" and "rebuild *it*" are all different. There is no problem with the singular suffix, but the plural is unusual. It may refer to the breaching of the two kingdoms, initially after the death of Solomon (930 B.C.) and finally with the fall of the nation of Israel (721 B.C.).[17] These kingdoms will be reunited and strong under Davidic rule, as in the nostalgic days of old (Ezek. 37:15-28), but no mention is made of the Davidic Messiah.

2. Other kingdoms will be included (9:12)

The restoration of the kingdom will result in the inclusion of other nations in the kingdom. The specific reference to Edom has led some to conclude that a later editor singled out Edom because of its mistreatment of the Jews in Jerusalem after it was defeated by the Babylonians in 587/6 B.C. (Obad. 10-21; Lam. 4:21-22; Ps. 137:7; Ezek. 25:12-14; 35:1-36:15).[18] The history of Edom's relationship with the Davidic kingdom is full of incidents of revenge and hatred before the time of Amos (Numb. 20:14-21; 1 Sam. 14:47; 2 Sam. 8:13-14; 2 Kings 8:20-22; 14:7, 22; 2 Chronicles 20; Amos 1:11-12), so a late date is not required. But why is Edom rather than Syria mentioned? The parallelism of Edom with the nations here and in Isaiah 63:1-6; 34:1-8; Obadiah 15-21 suggests that Edom may have functioned as a representative of the human race (*'dm*) as the Old Greek and the New Testament translate it.[19] Thus there is no historical reason but a literary reason for

---

[16]Most commentators believe that the prophetic books were edited in Judah. This section supports an Israelite inclusion in the promises, the covenant, and the eschatological blessings (which often focus upon Judah and Jerusalem). The prophets consistently refer to the regathering of Judah and Israel. Israelite theology could be Davidic without being Judean. Mays, *Amos* 165 believes that Amos was untouched by "Jerusalemite Davidic theology."

[17]Keil, *Minor Prophets* 330.

[18]Mays, *Amos* 164; Cripps, *Amos* 273.

[19]G. V. Smith, "Alienation and Restoration: A Jacob-Esau Typology," *Israel's Apostasy and Res-*

the choice of Edom. Possession of the remnant of Edom (or humankind) and the nations pictures the revival of power and authority for the Davidic empire far beyond the old Davidic kingdom. Amos is not announcing the doom of Edom as much as a positive promise of blessing on Edom and all the nations (Gen. 12:3; 28:14) owned and committed to Yahweh (cf. Deut. 28:9-10; Jer. 14:9). They will enjoy the blessings of this restored kingdom just like the remnant of Israel. In rather hymnic fashion Amos declares, it is Yahweh who will do this great thing.[20]

B. Restoration of the land (9:13-15).

1. It will be productive (9:13)

The concluding paragraph promises rich blessings from the land's fertility. These blessings reverse the curse (5:11) into a tremendous benefit (Gen. 49:10-12; Lev. 26:5). The "good land" will exceed "the land flowing with milk and honey" at this time. Crops will produce so much that the one ploughing will overtake the reaper who is still attempting to harvest all of last year's crops. Usually ploughing is done in October and the barley harvest in May, but when the next October comes the harvesters will still not be finished with the May harvest. Similarly, grapes harvested in August/September will still not be completely processed by December when it is time to plant barley. The grapes will be so lush that wine is pictured as flowing down the hills like a river from the excess of the grapes. It is as if the Garden of Eden were reborn when Yahweh causes the land to produce his blessings for his remnant who are called by his name (cf. Joel 3:18 [Heb. 4:18]).

2. It will be inhabited by my people (9:14)

A reversal of the fortunes indicates a change of circumstances from experiencing God's wrath to enjoying his blessing.[21] The remnant is affectionately and proudly called "my people Israel" (contrast 9:10), and their return to inhabit and populate the land is celebrated. The reconstruction of cities, vineyards, and gardens will turn the desolation of Israel into a place of life and vitality (cf. 5:11). The land promised to Abram, Isaac, Jacob, and the children of Israel will once again be the place where God's people will live and make their living.

---

toration in Prophetic Thought: Essays in Honor of R. K. Harrison, ed. A. Gileadi (Nashville: Thomas Nelson, (1987) 171-180; M. W. Woodstra, "Edom and Israel in Ezekiel," *CTJ* 3 (1968) 21-35. The New Testament use of this verse is discussed by W. Kaiser, "The Davidic Promise and the Inclusion of the Gentiles," *JETS* 20 (1977) 97-111 and M. A. Braun, "James' Use of Amos at the Jerusalem Council: Steps toward a Possible Solution of the Textual and Theological Problems," *JETS* 20 (1977) 113-21.

[20]B. Childs, *Introduction to the Old Testament as Scripture* (Philadelphia: Fortress, 1979) 407, has recognized the hymn-like character of this line; Hasel, *Remnant* 214 has emphasized the positive blessing that this promise will bring on Edom and the nations.

[21]The text could be translated "restore the fortunes" or "restore the captivity." A similar expression is found in the Sifire stele from the eighth century B.C.; see Wolff, *Amos* 76 n. 19.

3. It will have peace (9:15)

The planting of the people is compared to the planting of the gardens. The idea of being firmly established as a permanent part of the landscape comes with the metaphor. They will possess the land and not be rooted out of the land (cf. 2:9) which God gave them. This expression promises peace without enemies and an eternal dwelling place. This is the fulfillment of what God promised to give their fathers and their seed. God will do as he has said; he will keep his promise and pour out his covenant blessings, for to these people he is "your God." Although these blessings are totally due to the mercy and power of God, they are present at this time because of the new relationship between God and his people.

Theological Development

The final salvation oracle brings several theological streams together as part of the future hope of Israel. Unfortunately, there is limited information about the structure and connection between these themes before the time of Amos. The prophets Hosea, Micah, Isaiah, Jeremiah, and Ezekiel discuss the Davidic Messiah, but Amos omits any specific reference to the Messiah or the nature of his rule. He is content to focus on God's role in restoring the Davidic kingdom. A Davidic king is implied but left undeveloped. This does not mean that Amos knew nothing about the Davidic covenant (2 Sam. 7:1-16; Psalm 89) or the Messiah. This factor makes it impossible to describe fully Amos' eschatological hope. The task must be limited to the brief summary of his beliefs in 9:11-15. This summary should be interpreted not as a Judean theological statement but should be read through Israelite eyes. Although the two approaches had much in common, Amos was not offering a false hope to Israelites, which was really intended only for the people of Judah. The later reappearance of many of these themes in a fuller form in Hosea (1:10—2:1 [Heb. 2:1-3]; 2:18-23 [Heb. 2:20-25]; 3:5; 14:4-8) testifies to their importance to Israelite thinking.

The nation's hope was an outworking of the promises and covenants which God had given earlier to the patriarch (Gen. 12:1-3; 17:1-8; 26:1-3; 28:14), to the nation in the wilderness (Leviticus 26; Deuteronomy 27-28), and to David (2 Samuel 7; Psalm 89). Behind each fulfillment of God's promises of blessing is the "I will" of God's sovereign rule of history. The enormity of the acts of salvation and blessing must never be more exalted than the God who graciously bestows them. The marvelous description of restoration and prosperity are not hymns to success but assurances that God will be faithful, "Yahweh will do it" (9:12). The restoration is a study in the contrast between the grace of God (9:11-15) and the wrath of God (9:1-10). Both reveal what God is really like, but the pictures are very different.

This future kingdom is marked by its contrast with the present. It will be a future work of God that brings life rather than death (9:1-10), prosperity and peace in the land rather than disaster and captivity (9:4, 10). God's acts in 9:1-10 relate to the sinner and the sinful kingdom, while 9:11-15 concern those who submit to God. This later group will never be rooted out of the land (9:15) and will dwell in the land in peace forever. Somewhat unexpectedly though, Amos indicates that the kingdom will be made up of non-Israelites (9:12) as well as "my people Israel" (9:14).[22] The presence of many foreigners in Israel may have encouraged the inclusion of this point.

The idea of the kingdom is present in the early promises. Genesis 12:1-3 looks forward to: (1) a great land and nation; (2) blessings from God; (3) a blessing on all the families of the earth; and (4) protection from the curse of others. The relationship of Abram and the nations is central to his intercession for Sodom (Gen. 18:17-25) and remains a significant part of the promise to Abraham (Gen. 22:18), Isaac (Gen. 26:4), and Jacob (Gen. 28:14). God's blessing on Jacob brought blessing to Laban (Gen. 30:27), and Joseph brought blessing to Potiphar (Gen. 39:5). The blessing of Jacob on Judah looks forward to a ruler, the subordination of the nations, and prosperity (Gen. 49:8-12). The plagues on Egypt are carried out so that "they will know that I am Yahweh" (Exod. 7:5, 17; 8:10, 22; 9:14, 29). Consequently a mixed multitude went up with Israel out of Egypt (Exod. 12:38). Deuteronomy pictures Israel as lending the fruit of God's blessing to other nations and ruling over them (Deut. 15:6; 28:12). The Psalms particularly emphasize God's rule over all the nations (Ps. 22:28; 47:2, 8), with their eventual worship of Yahweh (Ps. 22:27; 86:9; 96:3). The early prophets Mic. and Isaiah (Mic. 4:1-3; Isa. 2:2-4) see the nations gathered together at the mountain of God, including Egypt and Assyria (Isa. 19:18-25). Isaiah, Jeremiah, and many of the other prophets expand this theme.[23] God's restoration will bring a revival of all peoples and all the earth. His kingdom will have no limits and no opposition. For them "Yahweh will be king over the whole earth, in that day." Yahweh will be the only one, and his name will be the only one" (Zech. 14:9). "All flesh shall come to worship" (Isa. 66:23), "all peoples, nations and languages shall serve him. His dominion is an everlasting dominion, which shall not pass away" (Dan. 7:14).

---

[22]The development and use of the remnant idea in Israelite and non-Israelite texts before and after the time of Amos are fully dealt with by Hasel, *Remnant*.

[23]D. H. Odendaal, *The Eschatological Expectations of Isaiah 40-66 with Special Reference to Israel and the Nations* (Philadelphia: Presbyterian and Reformed Publ., 1970) 171-85.

Bibliography

1. Commentaries on Amos

Cripps, Richard S. *A Critical and Exegetical Commentary on the Book of Amos*. London: SPCK, 1969.

Driver, Samuel Rolles. *The Books of Joel and Amos*. The Cambridge Bible for Schools and Colleges. Cambridge: Cambridge University, 1915.

Edghill, Ernest Arthur, and G. A. Cooke. *The Book of Amos*, Westminster Commentaries. London: Methuen, 1914.

Fosbroke, Hughell E. W. "The Book of Amos: Introduction and Exegesis." In *IB* 6, 761-853. Nashville: Abingdon, 1956.

Frey, Hellmuth. *Das Buch des Ringens Gottes um seine Kirche: Der Prophet Amos*. Stuttgart: Calwer, 1958.

Hammershaimb, Erling. *The Book of Amos: A Commentary*, translated by John Sturdy. Oxford: Blackwell, 1970.

Harper, William Rainey. *A Critical and Exegetical Commentary on Amos and Hosea*. ICC. Edinburgh: T. & T. Clark, 1905.

Hyatt, J. Philip. "Amos." *The Jerome Biblical Commentary*, edited by Matthew Black and H. H. Rowley, 617-25. London: Thomas Nelson, 1963.

McKeating, Henry. *The Books of Amos, Hosea and Micah*, The Cambridge Bible Commentary on the New English Bible. Cambridge: University Press, 1971.

Marti, Karl. *Das Dodekapropheton erklärt*. Kurzer Hand-Kommentar zum Alten Testament 13. Tübingen: J. C. B. Mohr, 1904.

Mays, James Luther. *Amos: a Commentary*. OTL. Philadelphia: Westminter, 1969.

Rudolph, Wilhelm. *Joel-Amos-Obadja-Jona*. KAT 13/2. Gütersloh: Gütersloher Verlagshaus (Gerd Mohn), 1971.

Snaith, Norman H. *The Book of Amos*. 2 vols. London: Epworth, 1945-46.

Wolff, H. W. *Joel and Amos*. Hermeneia. Philadelphia: Fortress, 1977.

2. Select Monographs and Articles on Amos

a. General Studies on Amos

Barstad, Hans M. *The Religious Polemics of Amos*. SVT. Leiden: Brill, 1984.

Budde, Karl. "Zu Text und Auslegung des Buches Amos." *JBL* 43 (1924):46-131, (1925): 62-122.

Coote, Robert B. *Amos Among the Prophets: Composition and Theology*. Philadelphia: Fortress Press, 1981.

Driver, Godfrey Rolles. "Difficult Words in the Hebrew Prophets." In *Studies in Old Testament Prophecy Presented to Professor Theodore H. Robinson*, edited by H. H. Rowley, 52-72. Edinburgh: T. & T. Clark, 1950.

Eissfeldt, O. "Amos und Jona in volkstumlicher Überlieferung." *Kleine Schriften* 4 (1968): 137-42.

Eybers, I. H., et al. *Studies in the Books of Hosea and Amos*. OTWSA. Potchefstroom: Rege-Pers Beperk, 1965.

Gese, Hartmut. "Kleine Beiträge zum Verständnis des Amosbuches." *VT* 12 (1962): 417-38.

Glück, J. J. "Three Notes on the Book of Amos." *Studies on the Book of Hosea and Amos*. OTWSA 7-8, 115-21. Potchefstroom: Rege-Pers Beperk, 1965.

Hunter, A. V. *Seek the Lord! A Study of the Meaning and Function of the Exhortations in Amos, Hosea, Micah, and Zephaniah*. Baltimore: St. Mary's Seminary, 1982.

Johnson, Aubrey R. "Amos—The Prophet of Re-Union." *ExpT* 92 (1981): 196-200.

Kapelrud, Arvid S. *Central Ideas in Amos*. Oslo: Aschehoug, 1956.

Koch, K., et al. *Amos, untersucht mit den Methoden einer strukturalen Formgeschichte* 1-2. Neukirchen-Vluyn: Neukirchener Verlag, 1967.

Krause, Hans Helmut. "Die Gerichtsprophet Amos, ein Vorläufer des Deuteronomisten." *ZAW* 50 (1932):221-39.

Maag, Victor. *Text, Wortschatz und Begriffswelt des Buches Amos*. Leiden: Brill, 1951.

McCullough, W. S. "Some Suggestions About Amos." *JBL* 72 (1953): 247-54.

Mitchell, H. G. *Amos: An Essay in Exegesis*. Boston, 1900.

Montgomery, James A. "Notes on Amos." *JBL* 23 (1904): 94-96.

Morgenstern, Julian. "Amos Studies I." *HUCA* 11 (1936): 19-140.

_____ . "Amos Studies II." *HUCA* 12-13 (1937-38): 1-53.

_____ . "Amos Studies III." *HUCA* 15 (1940): 59-304.

_____ . "Amos Studies IV." *HUCA* 32 (1961): 295-350.

Neher, André. *Amos. Contribution à l'étude du prophétisme*. Paris: J. Vrin, 1950.

Ward, James M. *Amos and Isaiah: Prophets of the Word of God*. Nashville: Abingdon, 1969.

Watts, John D. W. *Vision and Prophecy in Amos*. Grand Rapids: Eerdmans, 1958.

Weiser, Artur. *Die Profetie des Amos*. BZAW 53. Giessen: Töpelmann, 1929.

Wolfe, Rolland Emerson. *Meet Amos and Hosea, the Prophets of Israel*. New York: Harper, 1945.

Würthwein, Ernst. "Amos-Studien." *ZAW* 62 (1950): 10-52.

b. The Text of the Book of Amos

Arieti, James A. "The Vocabulary of Septuagint Amos." *JBL* 93 (1974): 338-47.

Howard, George. "Some Notes on the Septuagint of Amos." *VT* 20 (1970): 108-12.

Johnson, S. E. *The Septuagint of Amos.* Chicago: Univ. of Chicago, 1936.

Muraoka, Takamitsu. "Is the Septuagint Amos 8:12—9:10 a Separate Unit?" *VT* 20 (1970): 496-500.

Oesterley, W. O. E. *Studies in the Greek and Latin Versions of the Book of Amos.* Cambridge: University Press, 1902.

Snaith, Norman Henry. *Notes on the Hebrew Text of Amos.* London: Epworth, 1945-46.

Szabo, A. "Textual Problems in Amos and Hosea." *VT* 25 (1975): 500-24.

Waard, J. de. "Translation Techniques Used by the Greek Translators of Amos." *Bib* 59 (1978): 339-50.

c. The Role of the Prophet Amos

Ackroyd, Peter R. "Amos 7:14." *ExpT* 68 (1956-57): 94.

Bič, Miloš. "Der Prophet Amos–ein Haepatoskopos." *VT* 1 (1951): 293-96.

Cohen, Simon. "Amos Was a Navi." *HUCA* 32 (1961): 175-78.

Craigie, P. C. "Amos the *NOQED* in Light of Ugaritic." *Studies in Religion* 11 (1982): 29-33.

Danell, Gustaf Adolf. "Var Amos verkligen en nabi?" *SEÅ* 16 (1951): 7-20.

Driver, Godfrey Rolles. "Amos 7:14." *ExpT* 67 (1955-56): 91-92.

Glück, J. J. "Nagid-Shepherd." *VT* 13 (1963): 144-50.

Gunneweg, Antonius H. J. "Erwägungen zu Amos 7:14." *ZTK* 57 (1960): 1-16.

Lehming, Sigo. "Erwägungen zu Amos." *ZTK* 55 (1958): 145-69.

MacCormack, J. "Amos 7:14." *ExpT* 67 (1955-56): 318.

Murtonen, A. E. "The Prophet Amos–a Hepatoscoper?" *VT* 2 (1952): 170-71.

Reventlow, Henning Graf. *Das Amt des Propheten bei Amos.* FRLANT 80. Göttingen: Vandenhoeck und Reprecht, 1962.

Richardson, H. Neil. "A Critical Note on Amos 7:14." *JBL* 85 (1966): 89.

Rothstein, Gustav. "Amos und seine Stellung innerhalb des Prophetismus." *Theologische Studien und Kritiken* 78 (1905): 323-58.

Rowley, Harold Henry. "Was Amos a Nabi?" In *Festschrift Otto Eissfeldt*, edited by Johann Fück, 191-98. Halle: Max Niemeyer, 1947.

Smend, Rudolf. "Das Nein des Amos." *EvT* 23 (1963): 404-23.

Stamm, J. J. "Der Name des Propheten Amos und sein sprachlicher Hintergrund." In *Prophecy: Essays Presented to G. Fohrer on His Sixty-fifth
Birthday*, edited by J. A. Emerton, 137-42. Berlin: Walter de Gruyter,
1980.

Vogt, Ernest. "Waw-explicative in Amos 7:14." *ExpT* 68 (1956-57): 301-02.

Watts, John D. W. "Amos, The Man." *RevExp* 63 (1966): 387-92.

d. The Structure and Unity of the Book of Amos

Balla, Emil. *Die Droh–und Scheltworte des Amos*. Leipzig, 1926.

Botterweck, G. Johannes. "Zur Authentizität des Buches Amos." *BZ* N. F. 2
(1958): 176-89.

Coulot, C. "Propositions pour une structuration du livre d'Amos au niveau
rédactionnel." *RSR* 51 (1977): 169-86.

Crüsemann, Frank. "Kritik an Amos im deuteronomistischen Geschich-
tswerk." In *Probleme biblischer Theologie (Gerhard von Rad zum 70.
Geburtstag)*, edited by Hans Walter Wolff, 57-63. München: Chr.
Kaiser, 1971.

Fuhs, H. F. "Amos 1:1. Erwägungen zur Tradition and Redaktion des Amosbuches." *Bausteine biblischer Theologie: Festschrift G. J. Botterweck*. BBB 50 (1977): 271-89.

Gordis, Robert. "The Composition and Structure of Amos." *HTR* 33 (1940):
239-51.

Hobbs, T. R. "Amos 3:1*b* and 2:10." *ZAW* 81 (1969): 384-87.

Hoffmann, Hans Werner. "Zur Echtheitsfrage von Amos 9:9f." *ZAW* 82
(1970): 121-22.

Jozaki, Susumu. "The Secondary Passages of the Book of Amos." *Kwansei
Gakuin University Annual Studies* 4 (1956): 25-100.

Kellermann, Ulrich. "Der Amosschluss als Stimme deuteronomistischer
Heilshoffnung." *EvT* 29 (1969): 169-83.

Koch, Klaus. "Die Rolle der hymnischen Abschnitte in der Komposition des
Amos-Buches." *ZAW* 86 (1976): 504-37.

Lust, J. "Remarks on the Redaction of Amos 5:4-6, 14-15." *OTS* 21 (1981):
129-54.

Melugin, R. F. "The Formation of Amos: An Analysis of Exegetical
Method." In *SBL 1978 Seminar Papers*, 369-91. Missoula: Scholars
Press, 1978.

Schmidt, Werner H. "Die deuteronomistische Redaktion des Amosbuches.
Zu den theologischen Unterschienden zwischen dem Prophetenwort
und seinem Sammler." *ZAW* 77 (1965): 168-93.

Smalley, W. A. "Recursion Patterns and the Sectioning of Amos." *BT* 30
(1979): 118-127.

Staples, W. E. "Epic Motifs in Amos." *JNES* 25 (1966): 106-12.

Tucker, G. M. "Prophetic Superscriptions and the Growth of a canon." In *Canon and Authority*, ed. G. W. Coats and B. O. Long, 56-70. Philadelphia: Fortress Press, 1977.

Waard, J. de. "The Chiastic Structure of Amos 5:1-17." *VT* 27 (1977): 170-07.

Watts, John D. W. "The Origin of the Book of Amos." *ExpT* 66 (1954-55): 109-12.

Wer, A. van der. "The Structure of Amos." *JSOT* 26 (1983): 107-113.

e. The Historical and Cultural Background of Amos

Beek, M. A. "The Religious Background of Amos 2:6-8." *OTS* 5 (1948): 132-41.

Bentzen, Aage. "The Ritual Background of Amos 1:2—2:16." *OTS* 8 (1950): 85-99.

Berg, Werner. *Die sogennante Hymnenfragmente im Amosbuch*. Frankfurt: Peter Lang, 1974.

Botterweck, Johannes. " 'Sie verkaufen den Unschuldigen um Geld.' Zur sozialen Kritik des Propheten Amos." *Bibel und Leben* 12 (1971): 215-31.

Brueggemann, Walter. "Amos 4:4-13 and Israel's Covenant Worship." *VT* 15 (1965): 1-15.

Cohen, Simon. "The Political Background of the Words of Amos." *HUCA* 36 (1965): 153-60.

Collins, John J. "History and Tradition in the Prophet Amos." *ITQ* 41 (1974): 120-33.

Crenshaw, James L. "Amos and the Theophanic Tradition." *ZAW* 80 (1968): 203-15.

———. *Hymnic Affirmation of Divine Justice: The Doxologies of Amos and Related Texts in the Old Testament*. Society of Biblical Literature Dissertation Series 24. Missoula, Montana: Scholars Press, 1975.

———. "The Influence of the Wise on Amos." *ZAW* 79 (1967): 42-51.

Donner, H. "Die soziale Botschaft der Propheten in Lichte der Gesellschaftordnung in Israel." *Or An* 2 (1963): 230-45.

Dürr, L. "Altorientalische Recht bei dem Propheten Amos und Hosea." *BZ* 23 (1935/36): 150-57.

Farr, Georges. "The Language of Amos, Popular or Cultic?" *VT* 16 (1966): 312-24.

Fendler, Marlene. "Zur Sozialkritik des Amos. Versuch einer wirtschafts- und sozialgeschichtlichen Interpretation alttestamentlicher Texte." *EvT* 33 (1973): 32-53.

Fensham, F. Charles. "Common Trends in Curses of the Near Eastern Treaties and *kudurru*-Inscriptions compared with Maledictions of Amos and Isaiah." *ZAW* 75 (1963): 155-75.

———. "Widow, Orphan and the Poor in Ancient Near Eastern Legal and Wisdom Literature." *JNES* 21 (1962): 129-39.

Gaster, Theodore H. "An Ancient Hymn in the Prophecies of Amos." *Journal of the Manchester Egyptian and Oriental Society* 19 (1935): 23-26.

Gottlieb, Hans. "Amos und Jerusalem." *VT* 17 (1967): 430-63.

Hallo, W. W. "From Qarqar to Carchemish: Assyria and Israel in the Light of New Discoveries." *BAR* 2 (Garden City: Doubleday, 1964): 152-90.

Haran, Menahem. "Observations on the Historical Background of Amos 1:2—2:6." *IEJ 18* (1968): 201-12.

———. "The Rise and Decline of the Empire of Jeroboam ben Joash." *VT* 17 (1967): 266-97.

Heicksen, H. "Tekoa: Historical and Cultural Profile." *JETS* 13 (1970): 81-89.

Horst, Friedrich. "Die doxologien im Amosbuch." *ZAW* 47 (1929): 45-54.

Janzen, Waldemar. *Mourning Cry and Woe Oracle*. BZAW 125. Berlin: Walter de Gruyter, 1972.

Lang, B. "The Social Organization of Peasant Poverty in Biblical Israel." *JSOT* 24 (1982): 47-63.

Peiser, Felix Ernst. "Šenātayim lipnē hārā'aš. Eine philologische Studie." *ZAW* 36 (1916): 218-24.

Smith, G. V. "The Concept of God/the gods as King in the Ancient Near East and the Bible." *Trinity Journal* 3 (1982): 18-38.

Soggin, J. Alberto. "Amos 6:13-14 and 1:3 auf dem Hintergrund der Beziehungen zwischen Israel und Damaskus im 9. und 8. Jahrhundert." In *Near Eastern Studies in Honor of William Foxwell Albright*, edited by Hans Goedicke, 433-41. Baltimore: Johns Hopkins, 1971.

———. "Das Erdbeben von Amos 1:1 und die Chronologie der Könige Ussia und Jotham von Juda." *ZAW* 82 (1970): 117-21.

Speiser, E. A. "Of Shoes and Shekels." In *Oriental and Biblical Studies*, edited by J. J. Finkelstein and M. Greenberg, 151-59. Philadelphia: Univ. of Pennsylvania, 1967.

Stuhlmueller, Carroll. "Amos, Desert–Trained Prophet." *TBT* 1 (1962-63): 224-30.

Terrien, Samuel. "Amos and Wisdom." In *Israel's Prophetic Heritage: Essays in Honor of James Muilenburg*, edited by Bernhard W. Anderson and Walter Harrelson, 108-15. New York: Harper & Brothers, 1962.

Wagner, S. "Uberlegungen zur Frage nach der Beziehungen des Propheten Amos zum Südreich." *TLZ* 96/9 (1971): 653-70.

Watts, John D. W. "An Old Hymn Preserved in the Book of Amos." *JNES* 15 (1956): 33-39.

Wolff, Hans Walter. *Amos the Prophet: The Man and His Background*. Trans. by Foster R. McCurley. Philadelphia: Fortress, 1973.

f. The Theology of Amos

Barackman, Paul F. "Preaching from Amos." *Int* 13 (1959): 296-315.

Benson, Alphonsus. "'From the Mouth of the Lion.' The Messianism of Amos." *CBQ* 19 (1957): 199-212.

Fensham, F. C. "A Possible Origin of the Concept of the Day of the Lord." *OTWSA* 7-8 (1966): 90-97.

Gray, J. "The Day of Yahweh." *SEÅ* 39 (1974): 5-37.

Hoffman, Y. "The Day of the Lord as a Concept and a Term in the Prophetic Literature." *ZAW* 93 (1981): 37-50.

Hogg, Hope W. "The Starting-Point of the Religious Message of Amos." In *Transactions of the Third International Congress for the History of Religions*, vol. 1, 325-27. Oxford, 1908.

Howie, Carl G. "Expressly for Our Time: The Theology of Amos." *Int* 13 (1959): 273-85.

Huffmon, H. B. "The Social Role of Amos' Message." In *The Quest for the Kingdom of God: Studies in Honor of G. E. Mendenhall*, 109-116. Winona Lake: Eisenbrauns, 1983.

Hyatt, J. Philip. "The Book of Amos." *Int* 3 (1949): 338-48.

Irwin, W. A. "The Thinking of Amos." *AJSL* 49 (1932-33): 102-14.

Kapelrud, Arvid S. "God as Destroyer in the Preaching of Amos and in the Ancient Near East." *JBL* 71 (1985): 33-38.

———. "New Ideas in Amos." *Volume du congrès, Genève, 1965.* SVT 15, 193-206. Leiden: E. J. Brill, 1966.

Klein, R. W. "The Day of the Lord." *CTM* 39 (1968): 517-25.

Labuschagne, C. J. "Amos' Conception of God and The Popular Theology of his Time." *Studies of the Book of Hosea and Amos.* OTWSA 7-8, 122-33. Potchefstroom: Rege-Pers Beperk, 1965.

Leahy, Michael. "The Popular Idea of God in Amos." *ITQ* 22 (1955): 68-73.

Leeuwen, C. van. "The Prophecy of the YOM YHWH in Amos 5:18-20." *OTS* 19 (1974): 113-34.

Morgenstern, Julian. "The Universalism of Amos." In *Essays Presented to Leo Baeck on the Occasion of His Eightieth Birthday*, 106-26. London: East & West Library, 1954.

Paton, Lewis Bayles. "Did Amos Approve the Calf-Worship at Bethel?" *JBL* 13 (1894): 80-91.

Rad, G. von. "The Origin of the Concept of the Day of Yahweh." *JSS* 4 (1959): 97-108.

Seilhamer, Frank H. "The Role of Covenant in the Mission and Message of Amos." In *A Light unto My path: Old Testament Studies in Honor of Jacob M. Myers*, edited by Howard N. Bream, *et al.*, 435-51. Philadelphia: Temple University, 1974.

Snyder, G. "The Law and Covenant in Amos." *Restoration Quarterly* 25 (1982): 158-66.

Weiss, M. "The Origin of the Day of Yahweh Reconsidered." *HUCA* 37 (1966): 29-72.

Williams, Donald L. "The Theology of Amos." *RevExp* 63 (1966): 393-403.

Wolff, Hans Walter. *Die Stunde des Amos. Prophetie und Protest.* München: Chr. Kaiser, 1969.

g. Specialized Studies in Amos

Ackroyd, P. "A Judgment Narrative between Kings and Chronicles? An Approach to Amos 7:9-17." In *Canon and Authority*, edited by G. W. Coats and B. O. Long, 71-87. Philadelphia: Fortress Press, 1977.

Barré, Michael L. "Amos 1:11 Reconsidered." *CBQ* 47 (1985): 420-27.

Barstad, Hans M. "Die Basankühe in Amos 4:1." *VT* 25 (1975): 286-97.

Barton, J. *Amos's Oracles against the Nations.* Cambridge: Cambridge University, 1980.

Baumgartner, Walter. "Amos 3:3-8." *ZAW* 33 (1913): 78-80.

Berridge, J. M. "Zur Intention der Botschaft des Amos. Exegetische Überlegungen zu Am. 5." *TZ* 32 (1976): 321-340.

Bewer, Julius A. "Critical Notes on Amos 2:7 and 8:4." *AJSL* 19 (1903): 116-17.

Björndalen, A. J. "Erwägungen zur Zukunft des Amazja und Israels nach der Uberlieferung Amos 7, 10-17." In *Werden und Wirken des Alten Testament,* 236-251. Göttingen: Vandenhoeck und Ruprecht, 1980.

Boyle, Marjorie O'Rourke. "The Covenant Lawsuit of the Prophet Amos 3:1—4:13." *VT* 21 (1971): 338-62.

Braun, M. A. "James' Use of Amos at the Jerusalem Council: Steps toward a Possible Solution of the Textual and Theological Problems." *JETS* 20 (1977): 113-21.

Brueggemann, Walter. "Amos' Intercessory Formula." *VT* 19 (1969): 385-99.

Brunet, Gilbert. "La vision de l'étain: réinterprétation d'Amos 7:7-9." *VT* 16 (1966): 387-95.

Budde, Karl. "Amos 1:2." *ZAW* 30 (1910): 37-41.

Christensen, D. L. *Transformations of the War Oracle in the Old Testament.* Missoula: Scholars Press, 1975.

_____ . "The Prosodic Structure of Amos 1-2." *HTR* 67 (1974): 432-34.

Condamin, Albert. "Le prétendu 'fil à plomb' de la vision d'Amos." *RB* 9 (1900): 586-94.

Coote, Robert B. "Amos 1:11: *RHMYW*." *JBL* 90 (1971): 206-08.

_____ . "Ripe Words for Preaching: Connotative Diction in Amos." *Pacific Theological Review* 8 (1976): 13-19.

Crenshaw, J. L. "A Liturgy of Wasted Opportunity." *Semitics* 1 (1970): 27-36.

Dahood, Mitchell J., "Can One Plough Without Oxen? (Amos 6:12). A Study of *Ba-* and '*al.*" In *The Bible World: Essays in Honor of C. H. Gordon,* edited by G. Rendsburg, et al., 13-23. New York: KTAV, 1980.

_____ . "To pawn one's cloak." *Bib* 42 (1961): 359-66.

Daiches, S. "Amos III: 3-8." *ExpT* 6 (1914-15): 237.

_____ . "Amos VI:5." *ExpT* (1914-15): 521-22.

Dobbie, Robert. "Amos 5:25." *Transactions of the Glasgow University Oriental Society* 17 (1959): 62-64.

Driver, Godfrey Rolles. "A Hebrew Burial Custom." *ZAW* 66 (1966): 314-15.

_____ . "Two Astronomical Passages in the Old Testament." *JTS* N. S. 4 (1953): 208-12.

Fensham, F. C. "The Treaty Between the Israelites and the Tyrians." *SVT* 17 (1968): 71-87.

Fishbane, Michael. "Additional Remarks on *RHMYW* (Amos 1:11)." *JBL* 91 (1972): 391-93.

_____ . "The Treaty Background of Amos 1:11 and Related Matters." *JBL* 89 (1970): 313-18.

Freedman, David Noel, and Francis I. Andersen. "Harmon in Amos 4:3." *BASOR* 198 (1970): 41.

Frost, S. B. "Asservations by Thanksgiving." *VT* 8 (1958): 380-90.

Gevirtz, S. "A New Look at an Old Crux: Amos 5:26." *JBL* 87 (1968): 267-76.

Gitay, Y. "A Study of Amos's Art of Speech: A Rhetorical Analysis of Amos 3:1-15." *CBQ* (1980): 293-309.

Glanzman, George S. "Two Notes: Am 3:15 and Os 11:8-9." *CBQ* 23 (1961): 227-33.

Hesse, Franz. "Amos 5:4-6:14f." *ZAW* 68 (1956): 1-17.

Hillers, Delbert R. "Amos 7:14 and Ancient Parallels." *CBQ* 26 (1964): 221-25.

Hoffmann, G. "Versuche zu Amos." *ZAW* 3 (1883): 110-11.

Holladay, William L. "Amos 6:1b: A Suggested Solution." *VT* 22 (1972): 107-10.

_____ . "Once More, *'nak* = *'tin,*' Amos 7:7-8." *VT* 20 (1970): 492-94.

Hyatt, J. Philip. "The Translation and Meaning of Am 5:23-24." *ZAW* 68 (1956): 17-24.

_____ . "The Deity Bethel and the Old Testament." *JAOS* 59 (1939): 81-98.

Jacobs, Paul F. " 'Cows of Bashan'—A Note on the Interpretation of Amos 4:1." *JBL* 104 (1985): 109-110.

Junker, Hubert. "Text und Bedeutung der Vision Amos 7:7-9." *Bib* 17 (1936): 359-64.

Kaiser, W. "The Davidic Promise and the Inclusion of the Gentiles." *JETS* 20 (1977): 97-111.

Knierim, R. P. " 'I will not cause it to return' in Amos 1 and 2." In *Canon and Authority*, edited by G. W. Coats and B. O. Long, 163-75. Philadelphia: Fortress, 1977.

Leeuwen, C. van. "The Prophecy of the *Yom YHWH* in Amos 5:18-20." In *Language and Meaning: Studies in Hebrew Language and Biblical Exegesis*, 113-34. *OTS* 19. Leiden: E. J. Brill, 1974.

Limburg, James. "Amos 7:4: A Judgment with Fire?" *CBQ* 35 (1973): 346-49.

Loretz, Oswald. "Vergelich und Kommentar in Amos 3:12." *BZ* N. F. 20 (1976): 122-25.

Mackenzie, H. S. "The Plumb-Line (Amos 7:8)." *ExpT* 60 (1948-49): 159.

Malamat, Abraham. "Amos 1:5 in the Light of the Til Barsip Inscriptions." *BASOR* 129 (1953): 25-26.

Mauchline, J. "Implicit Signs of a Persistent Belief in the Davidic Empire." *VT* 20 (1970): 287-303.

Mittmann, S. "Amos 3:12-15 und das Bett der Samarier." *ZDPV* 92 (1976): 149-67.

Moeller, Henry R. "Ambiguity at Amos 3:12." *BT* 15 (1964): 31-34.

Neubauer, Karl Wilhelm. "Erwägungen zu Amos 5:4-15." *ZAW* 78 (1966): 292-316.

Neuberg, Frank J. "An Unrecognized Meaning of Hebrew *DÔR*." *JNES* 9 (1950): 215-17.

Ouellette, Jean. "The Shaking of the Thresholds in Amos 9:1." *HUCA* 43 (1972): 23-27.

Overholt, T. W. "Commanding the Prophets: Amos and the Problem of Prophetic Authority." *CBQ* 41 (1979): 517-32.

Paul, Shalom M. "Amos 1:3—2:3: A Concatenous Literary Pattern." *JBL* 90 (1971): 397-403.

_____ . "Amos III: 15—Winter and Summer Mansions." *VT* 28 (1978): 358-60.

_____ . "Fishing Imagery in Amos 4:2." *JBL* 97 (1978): 183-190.

Pfeifer, G. "Denkformenanalyse als exegetische Methode, erläutert an Amos 1,2-2,16." *ZAW* 88 (1976): 56-71.

_____ . "Unausweichliche Konsequenzen. Denkformenanalyse von Amos iii: 3-8." *VT* 33 (1983): 341-47.

Power, E. "Note to Amos 7:1." *Bib* 8 (1927): 87-92.

Preuss, H. D. " '... ich will mit dir sein'." *ZAW* 80 (1968): 139-73.

Priest, J. "The Covenant of Brothers." *JBL* 84 (1965): 400-06.

Rabinowitz, Isaac. "The Crux at Amos 3:12." *VT* 11 (1961): 228-31.

Rahtjen, B. D. "A Critical Note on Amos 8:1-2." *JBL* 83 (1964): 416-17.

Raitt, T. M. "The Prophetic Summons to Repentance." *ZAW* 83 (1971): 30-49.

Ramsey, George W. "Amos 4:12—A New Perspective." *JBL* 89 (1970): 187-91.

Rector, L. "Israel's Rejected Worship: An Exegesis of Amos 5." *Restoration Quarterly* 21 (1978): 161-75.

Reider, Joseph. "*dmšq* in Amos 3:12." *JBL* 67 (1948): 245-48.

Rendtorff, Rolf. "Zu Amos 2:14-16." *ZAW* 85 (1973): 226-27.

Richardson, H. N. "Amos 2:13-16: It's Structure and Function." In *SBL 1978 Seminar Papers*, 361-67. Missoula: Scholars Press, 1978.

Roth, W. M. W. "The Numerical Sequence x/x + 1 in the Old Testament." *VT* 12 (1962): 300-11.

Rudolph, Wilhelm. "Amos 4:6-13." In *Wort—Gebot—Glaube. Beiträge zur Theologie des Alten Testaments (Walther Eichrodt zum 80. Geburtstag)*, edited by Hans Joachim Stoebe, 27-38. Zürich: Zwingli, 1970.

_____. "Die angefochtenen Völkersprüche in Amos 1 und 2." In *Schalom. Studien zu Glaube und Geschichte Israels (Alfred Jepsen zum 70. Geburtstag)*, edited by Karl-Heinz Bernhardt, 45-49. Stuttgart: Calwer, 1971.

Schmidt, Nathaniel. "On the Text and Interpretation of Am 5:25-27." *JBL* 13 (1894): 1-15.

Schmidt, W. H. "suchet den Herrn, so werdet ihr Leben." In *Ex Orbe Religionum I: Festschrift für Widengren*, edited by J. Bergman, et al., 127-40. Leiden: Brill, 1972.

Schoville, Keith N. "A Note on the Oracles of Amos Against Gaza, Tyre, and Edom." In *Studies on Prophecy*, 55-63. SVT 26. Leiden: E. J. Brill, 1974.

Schwantes, S. "Notes on Amos 4:2*b*." *ZAW* 79 (1967): 82-83.

Sinclair, L. A. "The Courtroom Motif in the Book of Amos." *JBL* 85 (1966): 351-3.

Soper, B. Kingston. "For Three Transgressions and for Four. A New Interpretation of Amos 1:3, etc." *ExpT* 71 (1959-60): 86-87.

Speier, Salomon. "Bemerkungen zu Amos." *VT* 3 (1953): 305-10.

Speiser, Ephraim Avigdor. "Note on Amos 5:26." *BASOR* 108 (1947): 5-6.

Story, C. "Amos - Prophet of Praise." *VT* 30 (1980): 67-80.

Talmon, Shemaryahu. "The Gezer Calendar and the Seasonal Cycle of Ancient Canaan." *JAOS* 83 (1963): 177-87.

Thomas, David Winton. "Note on *nō'ādu* in Amos 3:3." *JTS* N. S. 7 (1956): 69-70.

Torrey, Charles Cutler. "On the Text of Am 5:25; 6:1, 2; 7:2." *JBL* 13 (1894): 63.

Tromp, N. J. "Amos 5:1-17: Toward a Stylistic and Rhetorical Analysis." *OTS* 23 (1984): 56-84.

Tucker, Gene M. "Prophetic Authenticity: A Form-Critical Study of Amos 7:10-17." *Int* 27 (1973): 423-34.

Vriezen, Theodorus C. "Erwägungen zu Amos 3:2." In *Archäologie und Altes Testament. Festschrift für Kurt Galling*, edited by Arnulf Kuschke and Ernst Kutsch, 255-58. Tübingen: J. C. B. Mohr, 1970.

———— . "Note on the Text of Amos 5:7." *VT* 4 (1954): 215-16.

Watts, J. "A Critical Analysis of Amos 4:1ff." In *SBL 1972 Seminar Papers*, II, 489-500. Cambridge: Society of Biblical Lit., 1972.

Weiser, Artur. "Zu Amos 4:6-13." *ZAW* 46 (1928): 49-59.

Weiss, M. "Methodologisches über die Behandlung der Metaphor dargelegt an Amos 1, 2." *TZ* 23 (1967): 1-25.

———— . "The Pattern of Numerical Sequence in Amos 1-2: A Re-examination." *JBL* 86 (1967): 416-23.

Whitford, John B. "The Vision of Amos." *BibSac* 70 (1913): 109-22.

Williams, A. J. "A Further Suggestion about Amos IV:1-3." *VT* 29 (1979): 206-11.

Wright, T. J. "Amos and the Sycamore Fig." *VT* 26 (1976): 362-68.

Würthwein, Ernst. "Amos 5:21-27." *TLZ* 72 (1947): 143-52.

Youngblood, Ronald. *"lqr't* in Amos 4:12." *JBL* 90 (1971): 98.

Zevit, Ziony. "A Misunderstanding at Bethel, Amos 7:12-17." *VT* 25 (1975): 783-90.

Zolli, Eugenio. "Amos 4:2b." *Antonianum* 30 (1955): 188-89.

h. Literature on Amos

Craghan, John F. "The Prophet Amos in Recent Literature." *BTB* 2 (1972): 242-61.

Kelley, Page H. "Contemporary Study of Amos and Prophetism." *RevExp* 63 (1966): 375-85.

Mays, James Luther. "Words about the Words of Amos. Recent Study of the Book of Amos." *Int* 13 (1959): 259-72.

Subject Index

Author Index

(Frequently cited commentaries listed on pages xii–xiii are not included)

Scripture Index

(Except Amos)